D1590177

MAGNA

MUSE & MENTOR

CARTA

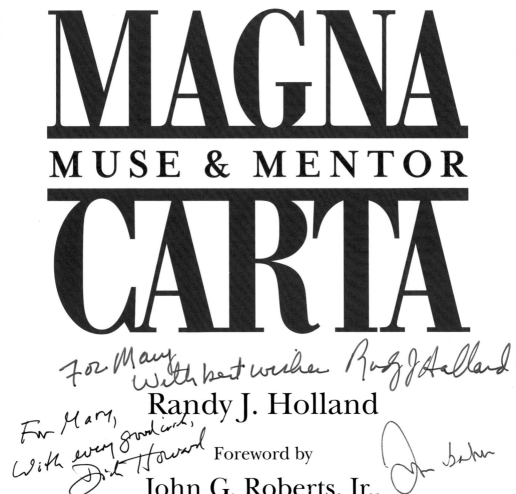

Randy J. Holland

Foreword by

John G. Roberts, Jr.,

Chief Justice of the United States

THOMSON REUTERS

LIBRARY OF
CONGRESS

Published by Thomson Reuters, in association with the Library of Congress

legalsolutions.thomsonreuters.com

www.loc.gov

Mat. # 41692317

© 2014 Thomson Reuters

Dust jacket image credits:

King John of England (r.1199–1216). 1215 Exemplar of Magna Carta. Great Charter of Liberties. Manuscript on parchment, June 1215. Courtesy of Lincoln Cathedral, England (front cover)

The signing of Magna Carta illustrated in Cassell's History of England, Volume 1. London: Cassell, 1903. General Collections, Library of Congress (back cover)

England's Lord Chief Justice Edward Coke bars King James I from the "King's Court" making the court, by law, independent of the executive branch of government. Bronze doors of Supreme Court, Washington, D.C. Collection of the Supreme Court of the United States (inside front flap)

Table of Contents

MAGNA CARTA AND CULTURE

Magna Carta Regis Johannis XV. die Junii anno regni XVII A.D. MCCXV. London, 1816--1818.
Law Library, Library of Congress

ABOUT THE EDITOR

RANDY J. HOLLAND is the youngest person to serve on the Delaware Supreme Court, having been recommended to the Governor by a bipartisan merit selection committee. Prior to his appointment and confirmation in 1986, Justice Holland was in private practice. In 2011, he was reappointed by the Governor and unanimously confirmed by the Senate for an unprecedented third twelve-year term. Justice Holland is the past national President of the American Inns of Court Foundation. Justice Holland has received numerous awards, including the 2014 AIC Justice Lewis Powell, Jr. national award for Professionalism and Ethics. In 2011, he received the AJS Dwight Opperman national award for Judicial Excellence. He is an honorary Master of the Bench of Lincoln's Inn in London. Justice Holland has written, co-authored, or edited eight books.

ABOUT THE AUTHORS

LADY JUSTICE MARY ARDEN was called to the Bar of England and Wales in 1971, and became a Queen's Counsel in 1986. She is a graduate of Cambridge and Harvard, and holds several honorary degrees. She was appointed a Justice of the High Court of Justice of England and Wales in 1993, being the first woman judge to be assigned to the Chancery Division. From 1996 to 1999 she was the chair of the Law Commission of England and Wales. In 2000 she acted as an ad hoc judge of the European Court of Human Rights in Strasbourg. In 2000 she was appointed a Lady Justice of Appeal. She has sat on cases on a wide range of subjects, including human rights, constitutional law, asylum, Community law, housing, VAT, tax, and directors' duties. From 2004 to 2006, Lady Justice Arden was chair of the Judges' Council Working Party on Constitutional Reform, which was heavily involved in the draft legislation which became the Constitutional Reform Act 2005 and the Judicial Discipline (Prescribed Procedures) Regulations 2006. In April 2005 Lady Justice Arden was appointed Judge in Charge, now Head, of International Judicial Relations for England and Wales, a post she continues to hold. She has traveled extensively to help promote the rule of law and to further her personal interest in meeting judges in other jurisdictions and in comparative human rights and constitutional law. Lady Justice Arden has given numerous lectures and written articles and books (or contributions to books) on human rights, company law, terrorism, and other subjects.

***

SIR JOHN BAKER QC, LLD, FBA, an honorary bencher of the Inner Temple and Gray's Inn, was Downing Professor of the Laws of England at Cambridge from 1998 to 2011 and Literary Director of the Selden Society for over thirty years. He was educated at University College London and called to the bar by the Inner Temple. Since 1971 he has been a Fellow of St. Catharine's College, Cambridge. He has taught briefly at Harvard and Yale, and for twenty years he was a visiting professor at New York University School of Law. In 2003 he was knighted for services to English legal history, and he holds an honorary doctorate from the University of Chicago. Among his publications are *An Introduction to English Legal History* (4th ed. 2002), volume VI of the *Oxford History of the Laws of England* (2003), covering the period 1483–1558, and *Collected Papers on English Legal History* (Cambridge, 2013) in three volumes.

***

JANE FRECKNALL-HUGHES is currently professor of accounting and taxation at the University of Hull in the UK. After graduating from the University of Oxford, she became a chartered accountant and chartered tax consultant with KPMG. In 1992 she joined the University of Leeds, gaining postgraduate teaching qualifications and a PhD (in revenue law and tax practice) and was awarded a master's degree (with distinction) in commercial law from the University of Northumbria in 2007. She is a fellow of the Higher Education Academy. After moving to the University of Sheffield in 2005, she then joined The Open University in 2008 as professor of accounting, later holding the posts of professor of law, head of the Open University Law School, and then professor of revenue law.

Her research focuses on taxation from an interdisciplinary perspective, which is reflected in her publication record in this area. In addition to undertaking research within the area of tax law, she has been instrumental in leading tax research forward into the areas of history (including legal history), strategic management (with particular reference to multinational enterprises and tax planning), international business, finance, ethics, e-commerce and corporate governance. This has involved successful co-operation with scholars in those fields and is on-going. She has taught a wide range of subjects in the accounting and business law area, including taxation, and her textbook, entitled *The Theory, Principles and Management of Taxation: An Introduction*, is due to be published by Routledge in October 2014.

***

BRYAN A. GARNER, president of LawProse Inc. in Dallas, Texas, has been the editor in chief of *Black's Law Dictionary* since the mid-1990s and has been responsible for each of the four unabridged editions to have appeared since then. He is the author of more than twenty books on legal writing, advocacy, jurisprudence, and English grammar and usage, as well as a translation into plain English of *The Rules of Golf.* He serves as Distinguished Research Professor of Law at Southern Methodist University.

***

ROBIN GRIFFITH-JONES, DLitt, is the Reverend and Valiant Master of the Temple at the Temple Church, London, and senior lecturer in theology at King's College, London University. He has worked extensively on law and religion. The Temple Church is the collegiate church of the two legal colleges or Inns of Court, Inner and Middle Temple; it is famous as 'the mother-church of the Common Law.' Griffith-Jones arranged and curated an exhibit in the Church on German-Jewish lawyers persecuted under the Third Reich. He ran the public discussions on Islam and English Law, which began with the then archbishop of Canterbury's famous lecture on sharia law in the UK, and edited the consequent book.

The Temple played a central role in the gestation of Magna Carta, and in the spread of the Charter's principles to America and throughout the world. In the Temple Church itself, in use by 1162, are the effigies of William Marshal, 1st Earl of Pembroke and hero of Runnymede, and of his son the 2nd Earl, one of the Charter's Surety Barons. Griffith-Jones is active in the UK's preparations for the celebration of Magna Carta; his booklet *Magna Carta, 1215–2015: London's Temple and the Road to the Rule of Law* has been widely read. He ran the international conference on Magna Carta, Religion and the Rule of Law at the Temple in June 2014, and is co-editing the book. In November 2014 he took the Temple Church Choir to Washington, DC, for the opening and the gala of the Library of Congress Magna Carta Exhibit.

***

CAROLYN HARRIS is a historian based in Toronto, Ontario, Canada. She currently teaches history at the University of Toronto, School of Continuing Studies. Harris completed her PhD in history at Queen's University at Kingston, Canada, in 2012. She contributes articles on King John and Magna Carta to the Magna Carta 2015 Canada website. Harris is an expert in the history of European monarchy and has been interviewed by numerous media outlets, including the CTV News Channel, CNN, BBC Radio 5, CBC syndicated radio, Radio Canada International, TVO's "The Agenda," *The Toronto Star*, the *National Post*, and the *Globe and Mail.* Her writing concerning the historical context for issues facing the British monarchy today has appeared in the *BBC News Magazine, Smithsonian*

Magazine, Military History Monthly, Globe and Mail, Ottawa Citizen, Bloomberg News, *Toronto Sun* and *Kingston Whig-Standard.*

***

A. E. DICK HOWARD is the White Burkett Miller Professor of Law and Public Affairs at the University of Virginia. A Rhodes Scholar at Oxford University, he served as a law clerk to Mr. Justice Hugo L. Black of the Supreme Court of the United States. He was the chief architect of Virginia's present constitution and directed the successful referendum for its ratification. Often consulted by constitutional draftsmen in other states and abroad, he has compared notes with revisors at work on new constitutions in such places as Brazil, Hong Kong, the Philippines, Hungary, Czechoslovakia, Poland, Romania, Malawi, South Africa, and Zimbabwe. In 1996, the Union of Czech Lawyers awarded him their Randa Medal—the first time this honor had been conferred upon anyone but a Czech citizen. An authority on constitutional law, Professor Howard is the author of a number of books and articles, including *The Road from Runnymede: Magna Carta and Constitutionalism in America* and *Magna Carta: Text and Commentary.* Wake Forest University, the College of William and Mary, James Madison University, the University of Richmond, and Campbell University have conferred upon him the honorary degree of Doctor of Laws. In 2007, the Library of Virginia and the *Richmond Times Dispatch* included Professor Howard on their list of the "greatest Virginians" of the twentieth century. In 2013, the University of Virginia recognized Professor Howard with its Thomas Jefferson Award—the highest honor given to faculty members. The award commended him "for advancing through his character, work, and personal example the ideals and objectives for which Jefferson founded the University."

***

RT. HON. THE LORD IGOR JUDGE was born on May 19, 1941, in Malta, where he was educated until 1954. Thereafter he attended the Oratory School, Woodcote, until 1959, where he was captain of the school and captain of cricket, which continues to be a source of constant interest. Lord Judge was awarded an Exhibition to Magdalene College Cambridge in 1959, where he read history and law. While at Cambridge he entered the Honourable Society of the Middle Temple and was subsequently called to the Bar in 1963. Appointed a Recorder of the Crown Court in 1976, Lord Judge was appointed Queen's Counsel (QC) in 1979. He served on the Professional Conduct Committee of the Bar between 1980 and 1986 and the Judicial Studies Board from 1984 to 1988. In 1987 he was elected Leader of the Midland and Oxford Circuit and a Bencher of the

Middle Temple. In 1988 Lord Judge was appointed a High Court Judge, Queen's Bench Division, and knighted. From 1990 until 1993, and again between 1996 and 1998, he was chairman of the Criminal Committee of the Judicial Studies Board. Between 1993 and 1996 he was Presiding Judge of the Midland and Oxford Circuit. In 1996 he was appointed Lord Justice of Appeal and sworn in as a Privy Councillor.

From 1998 until 2003 Lord Judge was Senior Presiding Judge for England and Wales, and from 2003 to 2005, Deputy Chief Justice. In 2005 he was appointed as the first President of the Queen's Bench Division. In October 2008 Lord Judge was appointed Lord Chief Justice of England and Wales and Head of the Judiciary of England and Wales. Shortly afterwards he was created a life peer. He retired as Lord Chief Justice in September 2013. Lord Judge has been President of the Selden Society since 2006. He has been awarded honorary degrees by several universities. These include an honorary Doctorate of Law from Cambridge University, where he is an Honorary Fellow of Magdalene College. He is also an honorary Doctor of Laws at Kings College London, where, since 2013, he has been Dickson Poon Distinguished Fellow and Visiting Professor. Lord Judge is Treasurer of the Middle Temple in 2014.

**

WILLIAM C. KOCH JR. is currently the dean of the Nashville School of Law. Before his appointment, Dean Koch served as a justice of the Tennessee Supreme Court from 2007 to 2014. He earned his undergraduate degree from Trinity College in Hartford, Connecticut, in 1969, his JD from Vanderbilt University School of Law in 1972, and his LL.M. in judicial process from the University of Virginia Law School in 1996. Prior to serving on the Tennessee Supreme Court, he served for twenty-three years on the Tennessee Court of Appeals, where he was the presiding judge of the Middle Section of the Court from 2003 to 2007. He was named Tennessee Appellate Judge of the Year in 2002 and was recognized as one of the 500 Leading Judges in America in 2006. Before his appointment to the appellate court in 1984, Dean Koch served as counsel to Governor Lamar Alexander and as Governor Alexander's commissioner of personnel. In addition, he served as deputy attorney general for the state of Tennessee. Dean Koch has taught constitutional law at the Nashville School of Law since 1997. He has also received appointments as an adjunct professor at Vanderbilt University School of Law and Belmont University College of Law. He is a founding member and current president of the Harry Phillips American Inn of Court and a founding member and current vice president of the Belmont College of Law American Inn of Court. He currently serves as the vice president of the American Inns of

Court Foundation. He has also served on the board of trustees of the Foundation and as the chair of the Foundation's Leadership Council.

***

DAVID S. MAO is the 23rd Law Librarian of Congress. He manages the operation and policy administration of the Law Library of Congress, which contains the world's largest collection of legal materials and serves as the leading research center for foreign, comparative, and international law. Mr. Mao describes the position as part law librarian to Congress, part steward for the law collections, and part ambassador to the word's legal and library communities.

Prior to becoming the Law Librarian of Congress, Mr. Mao served as the first Deputy Law Librarian of Congress. In that position, he served as a key member of the Law Library's leadership team and managed the Law Library's global legal research portfolio, including the Global Legal Research Center and the Global Legal Information Network. Prior to his appointment as Deputy Law Librarian, Mr. Mao was a section head at Congressional Research Service (CRS), Library of Congress.

Mr. Mao is a graduate of The George Washington University, where he majored in international affairs with a minor in Chinese language and literature. After earning his law degree from the Georgetown University Law Center, Mr. Mao was in private practice for several years before returning to graduate school to pursue a master's degree in library science at The Catholic University of America. Before arriving at CRS he held positions at the Georgetown University Law Library and within the research library of the international law firm of Covington and Burling LLP. He also was an adjunct professor at the University of Maryland College of Information Studies.

Mr. Mao served a three-year term as the treasurer of the American Association of Law Libraries and was a member of its executive board. He currently serves on the executive board of directors of the Chinese and American Forum on Legal Information and Law Libraries, and on the advisory council of the University of Texas at Austin School of Information. A member of the American Bar Association, he is admitted to the bars in the District of Columbia and Pennsylvania.

***

THOMAS J. McSWEENEY is an assistant professor at William and Mary Law School. His research focuses on the first century and a half of the common law, the period between the establishment of the writ system in the 1160s and the end of the thirteenth century. He is particularly interested in the ways the early justices of the royal courts began to define themselves as England's first legal professionals through their writing, which incorporated elements of Roman and canon law. His published articles have explored the Roman and canon law origins of English case law, the problems of trying to overlay English land customs with the Roman law of property, and the connections between Magna Carta and canon law. He is currently working on a book tentatively titled *Priests of the Law: Roman Law and the Making of England's First Legal Professionals*, on the justices who wrote the *Bracton* treatise in the thirteenth century.

***

JUSTICE SANDRA DAY O'CONNOR (RETIRED) was the first woman to serve on the Supreme Court of the United States of America. She received her BA and LL.B. from Stanford University. She served as deputy county attorney of San Mateo County, California, from 1952 to 1953 and as a civilian attorney for Quartermaster Market Center, Frankfurt, Germany, from 1954 to 1957. From 1958 to 1960, she practiced law in Maryvale, Arizona, and served as assistant attorney general of Arizona from 1965 to 1969. She was appointed to the Arizona State Senate in 1969 and was subsequently re-elected to two two-year terms. In 1975 she was elected judge of the Maricopa County Superior Court and served until 1979, when she was appointed to the Arizona Court of Appeals. President Reagan nominated her as an associate justice of the Supreme Court of the United States of America, and she took her seat September 25, 1981. Justice O'Connor retired from the Supreme Court on January 31, 2006.

***

SUSAN REYBURN is a writer-editor in the Library of Congress Publishing Office. She is the author of *Football Nation: Four Hundred Years of America's Game* (Abrams, 2013); *Women Who Dare: Amelia Earhart* (Pomegranate, 2006); and *Landscapes and Gardens of the National Trust* (NTHP, 1999); and a co-author of *Baseball America: Treasures from the Library of Congress* (HarperCollins, 2009); *The Library of Congress World War II Companion* (Simon & Schuster, 2007); and *The Library of Congress Civil War Desk Reference* (Simon & Schuster, 2002). She has also written for a wide variety of Library of Congress publications on classic American film, theater, art, and architecture, and numerous works for the National Trust for Historic Preservation. Reyburn has appeared as guest on more than thirty radio programs discussing Library of Congress collections and sports history. She also appeared as a commentator in the documentary film *Game On: The Story of Electric Football* (2015). She holds an MLS, specializing in cultural heritage information management, from Catholic University, and a BA in history from the University of California, Los Angeles.

***

G. ALAN TARR is director of the Center for State Constitutional Studies and Board of Governors professor of political science at Rutgers University–Camden. He serves as editor of Commentaries on the State Constitutions of the United States, a 50-volume reference series (Oxford University Press). He is co-editor of *Constitutional Dynamics in Federal Systems: Sub-national Perspectives* (McGill-Queens University Press), *State Constitutions for the Twenty-first Century* (State University of New York Press), *Constitutional Origins, Structure, and Change in Federal Countries* (McGill-Queen's University Press), and *Federalism, Subnational Constitutions, and Minority Rights* (Praeger). He is the author of *Without Fear or Favor: Judicial Independence and Judicial Accountability in the States* (Stanford University Press), *Understanding State Constitutions* (Princeton University Press), and *Judicial Process and Judicial Policymaking* (Wadsworth), and co-author of *State Supreme Courts in State and Nation* (Yale University Press) and *American Constitutional Law* (Westview Press). Three times the recipient of fellowships from the National Endowment for the Humanities, he has more recently been a Fulbright fellow in Ottawa, Canada, and a James Madison fellow at Princeton University. He has lectured on state constitutionalism throughout the United States and on subnational constitutionalism and federalism in Africa, Asia, Europe, and South America.

***

JUSTIN WERT is the Associates Second Century Presidential Professor and associate professor of political science at the University of Oklahoma. He completed his BA at Colorado State University (1996) and his MA (2001) and PhD (2005) at the University of Pennsylvania. He is the author of *Habeas Corpus in America: The Politics of Individual Rights* (Kansas) and *The Rise and Fall of the Voting Rights Act*. He has published articles in the *Stanford Law & Policy Review*, the *Cornell Journal of Law and Public Policy*, *American Review of Politics*, *PS: Political Science and Politics*, *Faulkner University Law Review*, and several book reviews and chapters in edited volumes.

To

His Royal Highness

The Prince Regent

This

SPECIMEN of ART,

is by Permission

Dedicated

By his most devoted obedient

and humble Servant,

John Whittaker.

Principality of Wales

Dukedom of Cornwall.

Earldom of Chester

Principality of Brunswic

Dukedom of Rothsay.

The Earldom of Carrick

Barony of Renfrew

The Lordship of the Isles

Magna Carta Regis Johannis XV. die Junii anno regni XVII A.D. MCCXV. London, 1816–1818.
Law Library, Library of Congress

FOREWORD

The north wall of the Courtroom at the Supreme Court of the United States features a frieze of "Great Lawgivers" in an historic procession. In the center stands King John holding Magna Carta. The king, forced to cede some of his power and submit to the rule of law, appears forlorn. But those who cherish freedom have cause for celebration.

Whether King John and the barons knew it or not, the events at Runnymede 800 years ago marked the commencement of a social transformation. Magna Carta laid a foundation for the ascent of liberty and the rule of law. True, the barons sought to advance their own narrow interests, and some of their concerns have neither force nor relevance today. But they bolstered their case with statements of principle that spoke to broader issues of governance, including due process, separation of powers, freedom from arbitrary action, and the elements of a fair trial. The Magna Carta of 1215 contains only the seeds of what we now regard as essential liberties. But those seeds have taken root. Great lawyers, judges, and legal theorists have recognized the enduring principles embedded in Magna Carta, adapted them to new circumstances, and extended their reach to distant shores. We celebrate Magna Carta not only for what it was, but for what it became in the hands of those committed to the cause of freedom and justice.

I am pleased to invite you to explore the Great Charter through *Magna Carta: Muse and Mentor.* The distinguished contributors have drawn upon diverse sources of scholarship to offer new insights into Magna Carta's origins, historical legacy, and current relevance. They confirm that, although Magna Carta is now 800 years old, it still beckons new learning. *Magna Carta: Muse and Mentor* is an engaging work of scholarship that celebrates eight centuries of struggle and progress in advancing the rule of law. Studying that history can help spark a renewed commitment to take on the unfinished challenge of securing liberty for all.

John G. Roberts, Jr.
Chief Justice of the United States

Frieze from the wall of the courtroom of the U.S. Supreme Court.
Collection of the Supreme Court of the United States

INTRODUCTION

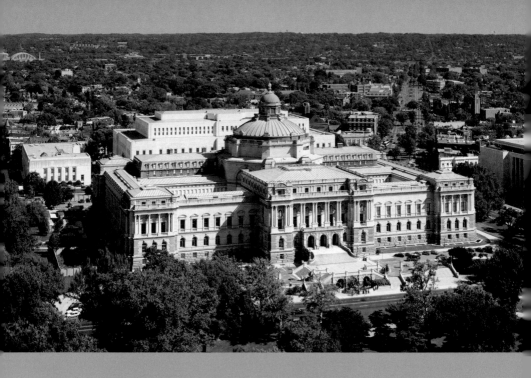

MAGNA CARTA: MUSE AND MENTOR

Nearly eight hundred years ago, on June 15, 1215, a group of barons compelled King John of England to commit to a set of liberties that subjugated royal power to the rule of law. That pledge was the genesis of Magna Carta, a document that has over time gained an unmatched reputation as a major milestone on the road to modern constitutional government. For Americans, its stature is similar to the Declaration of Independence, the United States Constitution, and the Bill of Rights. No list of the great documents of liberty is complete without it. It is remarkable, however, that in the twenty-first century people continue to admire a medieval charter that is not law in any world jurisdiction, and that contains provisions relating generally to customs and institutions that have not existed anywhere for hundreds of years. The range of topics Magna Carta covers and many of the specific interests it protects are unquestionably out of date. Yet despite the document's archaic applications, and its uncertain relationship to contemporary civil liberties, Magna Carta's reputation endures.

When beginning preparations for an exhibition to commemorate Magna Carta's eight centuries, the Library of Congress decided that the exhibition had to address the question of how a document that on close inspection appears so foreign to contemporary laws and society could have become so central to the political identity of the United States. This question is not the same as asking why Magna Carta is still relevant. The question of Magna Carta's relevance relates to how Magna Carta continues to impact lives today, which indeed it does. Instead, the Library's exhibition illustrates and explains the broader tradition of Magna Carta's long life in American memory—not only what it is to people today, but also what it has been to the nation throughout American history. Magna Carta's reputation endures to this day in part because generations of Americans have continued to honor it. The Library hopes that its exhibition will explain this long-lasting American fascination with a feudal charter granted by a foreign king, in a distant country eight hundred years ago.

The Jefferson Building (1897) of the Library of Congress, Washington, D.C. Carol M. Highsmith, Prints and Photographs Division, Library of Congress (LC-DIG-highsm-12559)

Perhaps the reasons Americans revere Magna Carta today are not necessarily the same reasons why they commemorated the document even a hundred years ago. The understanding of medieval England has changed over time, enriching the contemporary view of what Magna Carta meant in its original context and consequently changing the way people evaluate its virtues and vices. Likewise, changing political and intellectual fashions over the past century have provided different perspectives about the rise of constitutional government in early modern Europe compared to those perspectives prevalent in 1915. As a result, scholars have reevaluated Magna Carta's impact on that story as well.

Looking across the span of historical writings on Magna Carta, the Library discovered that for centuries the meaning people have attributed to the Great Charter in politics and law has depended most of all on what their contemporary historians said it meant. As a result, Magna Carta has presented several very different faces over the centuries, influencing events sometimes as a treaty, sometimes as legislation, sometimes as constitutional law, and sometimes only as a piece of political symbolism. While historical knowledge always informed the use and interpretation of Magna Carta, the most influential writers on the topic sometimes have written the history that the times required. Magna Carta's story cannot be told without recognizing that the story one tells about the past may have been far more important than what really existed.

Among the variety of historical opinions that the Library encountered in Magna Carta literature, this last insight stood out as a constant. What people have thought about Magna Carta over the centuries since its creation—what they have imagined it to be—has often been more influential than what Magna Carta really was for its creators on that day in June of 1215. This idea became the starting point for the Library of Congress's exhibition. Rather than trying to say what Magna Carta means to people today, the Library envisioned an exhibition that would illustrate the document's importance by showing what it has meant to people, especially Americans, in those times and places when Magna Carta's memory guided and inspired some of the most significant legal, constitutional, and political changes that have shaped the world.

The Library of Congress exhibition *Magna Carta: Muse & Mentor* tells the story of Magna Carta from its creation until its recognition as one of the sources of fundamental law in England. It then changes direction and traces the history of Magna Carta's incorporation into law in British America and its continuing legacy in the constitutional law of the United States. The exhibition's narrative thread follows several important instances during the last eight centuries in which innovative uses

The Great Hall in the Jefferson Building (1897), the Library of Congress, Washington, D.C. Carol M. Highsmith, Prints and Photographs Division, Library of Congress (LC-DIG-highsm-03185)

or interpretations of Magna Carta directly contributed to major legal and political developments. The exhibition gives special attention to those historical moments in which the memory of Magna Carta helped to shape American constitutionalism.

The exhibition draws items from collections across the Library of Congress, including those from the Law Library, the Prints and Photographs Division, the Rare Book and Special Collections Division, the Manuscript Division, and the Music Division. In all, the exhibition brings together seventy-seven items to tell the story of how people have understood and appealed to Magna Carta over the centuries to influence the events of their day. From the rise of modern civil liberties in England to the founding of the United States, the exhibition traces Magna Carta's enduring legacy into contemporary times. The Lincoln Cathedral's 1215 Magna Carta is the centerpiece of the exhibition, serving as an august reminder of the bedrock upon which the United States was founded.

The exhibition's first two sections provide visitors with a historical overview of the events that led to Magna Carta's creation. One section discusses King

John—both in the context of the political issues of his time, and in the way generations of writers and historians have portrayed him since then. Another section discusses the reasons for the barons' revolt and the background of the reforms they demanded.

The next four sections of the exhibition represent documented instances in which changing historical understandings of Magna Carta made it possible for people to appeal to King John's battlefield treaty to advance a variety of legal and political causes. The section "Confirmations by Kings and Parliament" describes the way that King John's successors, and later, Parliament, used Magna Carta as a pledge to uphold the rule of law. "Interpreting the Rule of Law" documents the influence of common law historiography on Magna Carta and Magna Carta's use as constitutional law in Parliament's conflict with Charles I. "Rights of Englishmen in British America" explores the liberties granted to English colonists through the various charters that established and governed their settlements in the Americas. Finally, "No Taxation without Representation" recounts the use of Magna Carta in the development of the independence movement in colonial America.

A single section entitled "Magna Carta and the United States Constitution" chronicles the creation of the constitutions of the several United States as well as the federal Constitution and Bill of Rights and their debt to Magna Carta.

The next four sections of the exhibition single out some of the most significant constitutional principles that emerged from Magna Carta, and trace their historical arc from the middle ages to present day American jurisprudence. These significant principles, which resonate with all Americans today, include due process of law and the right to a trial by jury; the writ of habeas corpus and freedom from unlawful imprisonment; and constitutional checks on executive power. For each of these principles, collection items from the Middle Ages and the early modern period appear side by side with contemporary artifacts to show both change and continuity in the understanding and application of those principles.

The exhibition finishes on a light note with a section that relates some of the ways Magna Carta has been celebrated in English and American culture, from satire and music to public commemorations and Magna Carta-themed genealogical associations. All of these examples demonstrate that Magna Carta, a source of American constitutional principle, has also become an enduring symbol of national identity.

This book is a companion volume to the Library of Congress exhibition. Justice Holland has brought together an impressive international array of distinguished jurists and scholars. Their engaging and enlightening Magna Carta articles correspond with each section of the exhibition and are illustrated with exhibition images. The work represents a rich intellectual vein that legal scholars and historians can mine two-hundred years from now, when the world celebrates the millennial anniversary of Magna Carta. The Library of Congress anticipates that at that time, the principles of Magna Carta will still be alive in this country and around the world.

David S. Mao
Law Librarian of Congress

MAGNA CARTA

AND THE

UNITED STATES CONSTITUTION

MAGNA CARTA AND THE RULE OF LAW
Justice Sandra Day O'Connor

The greatest contribution from the legal systems of Great Britain and the United States toward peace in the world has been the principle that all nations should live under the Rule of Law. The concept of the Rule of Law—that laws should be enacted by democratically elected legislative bodies and should be enforced by independent judiciaries—is fundamental to a free society. The knowledge that there are certain basic rights of the individual that are enforceable even against the state has been the hallmark of our system of governance.

The significance to our constitutional heritage of Magna Carta, the document signed by King John of England in 1215 limiting his own monarchical powers as a settlement with his own warring barons, is acknowledged in the Supreme Court building itself. On the two bronze doors through which most people enter the Court is a scene depicting King John sealing the Magna Carta. In the courtroom itself, where I sat on the bench, I could see a marble frieze portraying the great lawgivers of history. There, among Chief Justice John Marshall, Napoleon, and Justinian, stands King John—clothed in chain-mail armor and clutching a copy of Magna Carta.

We might wonder that a treaty extracted "at the point of the sword" from a feudal king would have such a powerful and enduring influence on constitutional development in England, the United States, and other nations. Magna Carta, however, expresses an idea that retains vitality today, 800 years after King John met the barons at Runnymede. That idea, as described by Sir Winston Churchill, is the "sovereignty of the law" as protection against attempts by governments "to ride roughshod over the rights or liberties" of the governed.[1]

The origins of Magna Carta gave little hint of its subsequent importance. King John acceded to the demands of the barons in an unsuccessful effort to ward off a civil war. Some of the specific clauses of Magna Carta, it is fair to say, reflected a self-interested effort by rebellious barons to restore feudal custom and to protect themselves from

Bronze doors of the U.S. Supreme Court, Washington, D.C. The panels depict major events related to the Rule of Law. In the second row, on the right, are Edward Coke and King James I. On the bottom right, King John is attaching his seal to Magna Carta. Courtesy of U.S. Supreme Court

1

U.S. Supreme Court courtroom, Washington, D.C. Courtesy of U.S. Supreme Court

the king. The charter was annulled only two months after King John affixed his seal. In the next two centuries, Magna Carta was repeatedly issued, withdrawn, reissued, and confirmed. The 1297 confirmation provided that the king's "Justices, Sheriffs, Mayors, and other Ministers shall allow ... the Great Charter as the Common Law" and "[t]hat if any Judgment be given from henceforth contrary to ... the Charter ... shall be undone, and holden for nought."[2] Magna Carta was of great political importance in England in the struggles between Crown and Parliament. It was cited as embodying the fundamental law of the realm, binding on all persons—including the king.

The first colonists brought with them to America the perception of Magna Carta as the written embodiment of fundamental law protecting the rights and liberties of all Englishmen everywhere. This view was expressed in various colonial charters, including the Virginia charter of 1606 written in part by Sir Edward Coke, one of the greatest exponents of Magna Carta. The Massachusetts General Court resolved in 1635 that "some men should be appointed to frame a body of grounds of laws, in resemblance to a Magna Carta, which ... should be received for fundamental laws."[3]

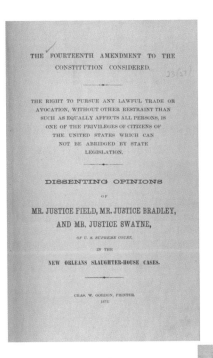

THE FOURTEENTH AMENDMENT TO THE
CONSTITUTION CONSIDERED.

THE RIGHT TO PURSUE ANY LAWFUL TRADE OR
AVOCATION, WITHOUT OTHER RESTRAINT THAN
SUCH AS EQUALLY AFFECTS ALL PERSONS, IS
ONE OF THE PRIVILEGES OF CITIZENS OF
THE UNITED STATES WHICH CAN
NOT BE ABRIDGED BY STATE
LEGISLATION.

DISSENTING OPINIONS

OF

MR. JUSTICE FIELD, MR. JUSTICE BRADLEY,
AND MR. JUSTICE SWAYNE,

OF U. S. SUPREME COURT,

IN THE

NEW ORLEANS SLAUGHTER-HOUSE CASES.

CHAS. W. GORDON, PRINTER.
1873.

Stephen J. Field. *The Fourteenth Amendment to the Constitution Considered: The Right to Pursue Any Lawful Trade or Avocation, Without Other Restraint....: Dissenting Opinions ... of U.S. Supreme Court, in the New Orleans Slaughter-House Cases.* [Washington, D.C.]: Chas. W. Gordon, 1873. Daniel A. P. Murray Pamphlet Collection, Rare Book and Special Collections Division, Library of Congress

Draft United States Constitution: Report of the Committee of Style, September 8–12, 1787. Printed document with annotations by George Washington and Convention Secretary William Jackson. George Washington Papers, Manuscript Division, Library of Congress

3

Portrait of John Bingham (1815–1900), between 1860 and 1875. Prints and Photographs Division, Library of Congress. (LC-DIG-cwpbh-00568)   John Armor Bingham One Country, One Constitution, and One People [speech of Hon. John A. Bingham, of Ohio, in the House of Representatives]. Washington, D.C.: Congressional Globe Office, 1866. Rare Book and Special Collections Division, Library of Congress

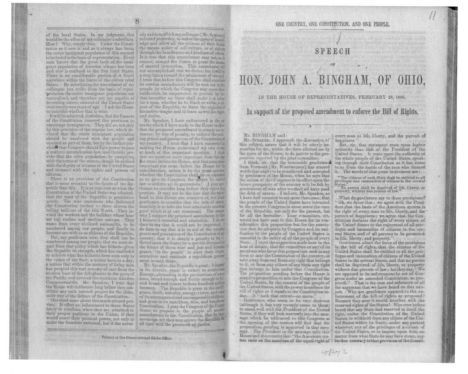

During the American Revolution, Magna Carta again served as a rallying point for those seeking protection against arbitrary government. As John Adams observed in 1778: "Where the public interest governs, it is a government of laws and not of men…. If, in England, there has ever been such a thing as a government of laws, was it not Magna Carta?"[4]

When it came time to draft our own Constitution and Bill of Rights, the Founders adopted both certain concepts found in Magna Carta and the more general notion of a written statement of fundamental law binding upon the sovereign state. Examples of important provisions of our Constitution that draw from Magna Carta are the requirement of legislative approval of taxation,[5] the guarantee of freedom of religion,[6] the requirement of speedy trials in criminal cases,[7] and the establishment of an independent judiciary.[8] Especially significant, of course, is the Due Process Clause of the Fifth Amendment.

To appreciate the relation between Magna Carta and our constitutional right to due process, we need only recall the language of Chapter 39 of Magna Carta:

"No free man shall be taken or imprisoned or disseized or outlawed or exiled or in any way ruined nor will we

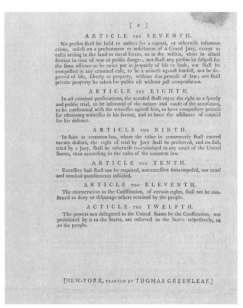

Proposed Articles of Amendment to the Federal Constitution [Bill of Rights], September 14, 1789. [James Madison's personal copy of printed broadside]. New York: Thomas Greenleaf. Rare Book and Special Collections Division, Library of Congress

5

go and send against him, except by the lawful judgment of his peers or by the law of the land."[9]

This language was echoed in our own Constitution nearly six centuries later in the Fifth Amendment to the Constitution, which declares:

"No person shall be held to answer for a capital, or otherwise infamous crime, unless on a presentment or indictment by a Grand Jury … ; nor shall any person … be deprived of life, liberty, or property, without due process of law …"[10]

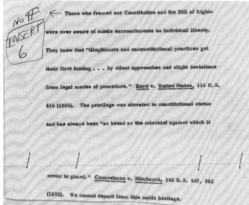

Earl Warren (1891–1974). Notes concerning the Miranda Decision. *Miranda v. Arizona.* 1966. Typescript pages with handwritten notes. Earl Warren Papers, Manuscript Division, Library of Congress

The impact of Magna Carta on our constitutional development is not merely an historical one. The Supreme Court continues to refer to Magna Carta for inspiration and guidance in identifying those rights that are fundamental. Indeed, in the last fifty years the Court has cited Magna Carta in more than eighty written opinions. These references, moreover, are not merely the sentimental acknowledgment of a fondly, but dimly, remembered ancestor. Instead, our Court has looked to concepts embodied in Magna Carta in important decisions that concern, for example, the Eighth Amendment prohibition of cruel and unusual punishment,[11] the requirement that trial by jury be afforded in state criminal prosecutions,[12] and the access of indigents to review of criminal convictions.[13]

Magna Carta relied on "the law of the land" to secure the citizen against the arbitrary action of the Crown.[14] The underlying idea of written fundamental law that protects the people from excesses by their government profoundly influenced, and still continues to guide, our constitutional development.

U.S. Supreme Court building, Washington, D.C. Courtesy of U.S. Supreme Court

LINCOLN CATHEDRAL
MAGNA CARTA

MAGNA CARTA IN AMERICA

FROM WORLD'S FAIR TO WORLD WAR

Susan Reyburn
Publishing Office, The Library of Congress

Shortly after participating in the dramatic events at Runnymede in 1215, the bishop Hugh of Wells returned to Lincoln Cathedral with his diocese's copy of Magna Carta, the medieval document that restricted the English king's power and brought about a temporary peace with his rebellious barons. For the next seven centuries, the charter remained behind the cathedral's towering stone edifice[1]—in a muniment room over the Galilee Porch, where it once shared quarters with a vicar's pigeons,[2] in a "common chamber" atop the vestry, and later in Christopher Wren's neoclassical library above the arcaded gothic cloister. It survived the English Civil War, "the ruthless hand of the unlettered spoiler," persistent dampness, and a dreadful era in which collectors, for a few shillings, were allowed to snip out a decorative capital letter or two from illuminated manuscripts shelved nearby.[3]

From at least the late nineteenth century on, though, Lincoln's Magna Carta, addressed to *Lincolnia* on the back and one of only four surviving original copies,[4] was displayed in the cathedral library.[5] Then, after centuries of a sedentary existence, in April 1939 the wisp of vellum, measuring 17⅛ by 17½ inches, was placed in a customized "waterproof, burglar proof, fireproof, and bullet proof"[6] case of wood, bronze, and glass held together by invisible screws.[7] The priceless document—insured, nonetheless, for £100,000—quietly departed Britain aboard the *Queen Mary*[8] and began a nearly seven-year odyssey, encountering some 15 million people who could rightly claim to have benefited from its legacy.

Magna Carta's destination was the New York World's Fair, a gleaming Art Deco extravaganza that heralded an optimistic "World of Tomorrow" and rose up on 1,200 acres of a former ash dump in Queens. The fair was also intended

King John of England (reigned 1199–1216). 1215 Exemplar of *Magna Carta*. Great Charter of Liberties. Manuscript on parchment, June 1215. Courtesy of Lincoln Cathedral, England.

to mark the 150th anniversary of President George Washington's inauguration. Such divergent themes—neither of which was likely to bring Magna Carta immediately to mind—made the fair a seemingly odd choice for the document's first major appearance in more than 700 years. Yet there were considered reasons for the charter's inclusion at the fair, a celebration of science, industry, culture, and a hopeful future, all within view of Frank "Bring 'em Back Alive" Buck's Jungle Land, the Flying Turns bobsled run, and a 74-foot-tall revolving cash register.

As Nazi Germany made its own world of tomorrow a worsening prospect for its anxious neighbors, Britain hoped to strengthen ties with its former American colonies. Part of this effort included dispatching King George and Queen Elizabeth to the United States on a goodwill tour that dovetailed neatly with a stop at the fair. In hosting one of the fair's largest foreign pavilions, with Magna Carta Hall as its centerpiece, His Majesty's government was hopeful that the Great Charter would convey the depth of British and American kinship, both philosophical and genealogical. "It is felt that Magna Carta symbolizes more than any other document the common origins of British and American democracies," explained R. A. Mitchell, the dean of Lincoln Cathedral. In a deft touch, the British delegation placed alongside Magna Carta *The Pedigree of George Washington,* which depicted the president's descent from King John and nine of the barons that were party to the charter.[9] On

Magna Carta Hall in the British Pavilion, New York World's Fair, 1939-1940. The Great Charter is shown at the far end of the hall under the canopy. As one of the most popular attractions in the fair's foreign pavilions, Magna Carta drew millions of visitors. Robert E. Coates, Prints & Photographs Division, Library of Congress (LC-DIG-ds-02061)

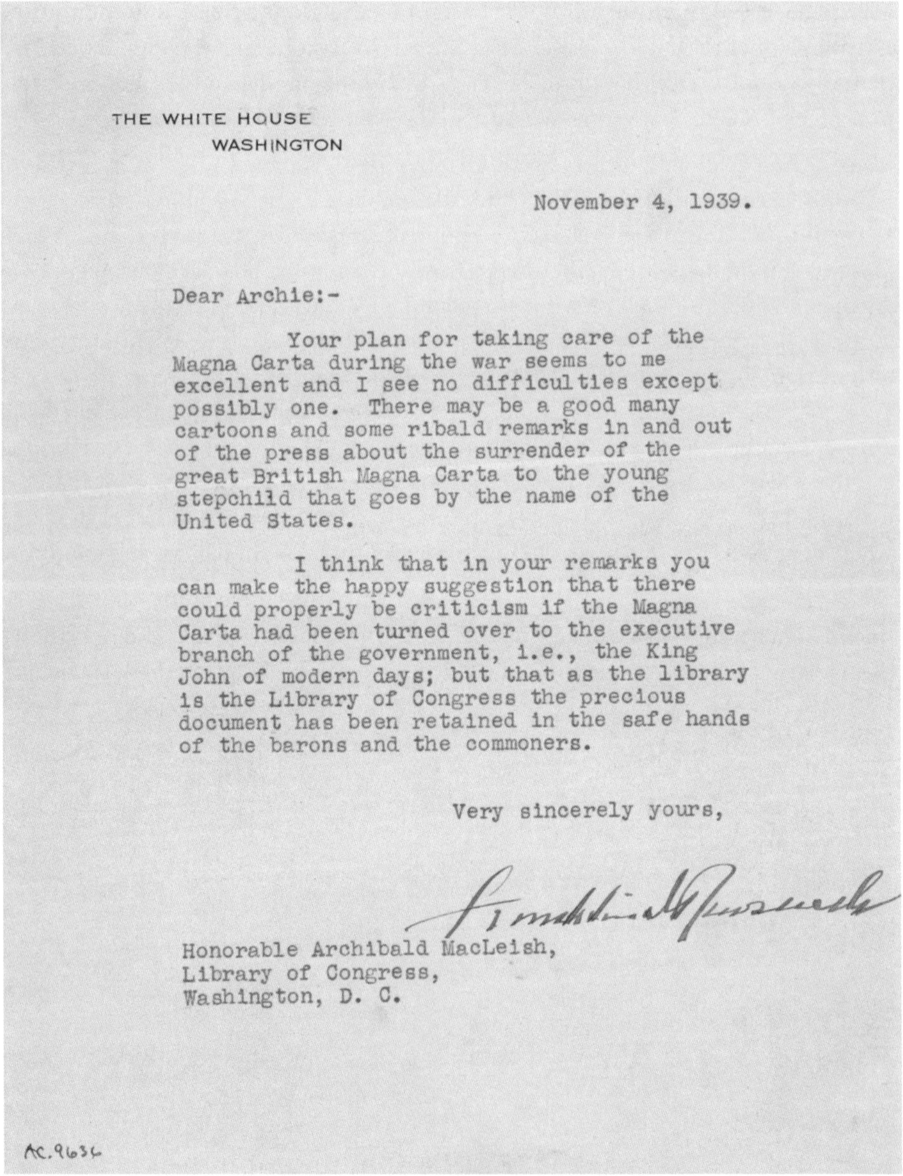

THE WHITE HOUSE
WASHINGTON

November 4, 1939.

Dear Archie:-

Your plan for taking care of the
Magna Carta during the war seems to me
excellent and I see no difficulties except
possibly one. There may be a good many
cartoons and some ribald remarks in and out
of the press about the surrender of the
great British Magna Carta to the young
stepchild that goes by the name of the
United States.

I think that in your remarks you
can make the happy suggestion that there
could properly be criticism if the Magna
Carta had been turned over to the executive
branch of the government, i.e., the King
John of modern days; but that as the library
is the Library of Congress the precious
document has been retained in the safe hands
of the barons and the commoners.

Very sincerely yours,

Franklin D. Roosevelt

Honorable Archibald MacLeish,
Library of Congress,
Washington, D. C.

AC.9636

Letter from President Franklin D. Roosevelt to Archibald MacLeish, Librarian of Congress, November 4, 1939. The president, who had a great interest in historical artifacts, was delighted that Magna Carta would be displayed at the Library. However, when MacLeish made his public remarks on its arrival, he did not use FDR's suggested commentary. LC Archive Central Files, Manuscript Division, Library of Congress

an equally artful note, Dean Mitchell recalled "the great debt of gratitude which Lincoln Cathedral owes to the citizens of the United States" for their "more than generous help" in funding projects to repair and restore the cathedral.[10] Thus, the presence of Magna Carta in America also served as a thank-you note.

When the fair closed at the end of October 1939, Britain had been in a state of war with Germany for two months; the Atlantic Ocean was becoming infested with German U-boats, and the British dared not risk sending Magna Carta home in such perilous conditions. Instead, they looked around for a suitable place of refuge. Congressman Sol Bloom (D-NY), who also served as a commissioner to the World's Fair, took up the matter with the British ambassador,[11] Philip Kerr, the eleventh marquess of Lothian, who in turn formally asked Archibald MacLeish, the Librarian of Congress, if the Library might take temporary custody of the charter for "safekeeping during the war."[12] MacLeish, who had only been on the job a few weeks, was thrilled to offer a safe haven. So was President Roosevelt, who told the Librarian that "[t] here may be a good many cartoons and some ribald remarks in and out of the press about the surrender of the great British Magna Carta to the young stepchild that goes by the name of the United States."[13]

Archibald MacLeish, the Librarian of Congress, shakes hands with Lord Lothian moments after the British ambassador formally deposited the Lincoln Cathedral original copy of Magna Carta in the Library, November 28, 1939. LC Archive Central Files, Manuscript Division, Library of Congress

For years, the two most important documents in American history—the Declaration of Independence and the Constitution—were on public view in the Library of Congress's Great Hall, on the mezzanine level.[14] The addition of Magna Carta directly opposite the country's founding documents brought together, as never before, a paper trail of milestones in the development of civil liberties. Its arrival at the Library certainly called for a ceremony. Shortly after 4 p.m. on November 28, 1939, Lord Lothian, red-faced from having just hiked up a small mountain of marble stairs,[15] formally deposited Magna Carta in the Library. A beaming MacLeish stood beside him. To those assembled, including Supreme Court justices, congressmen, and CBS Radio, Lothian asked, "Why all this fuss and trouble about a medieval relic?" The short answer was that "[t]he principles which underlay Magna Carta are the ultimate foundations of your liberties no less than ours." The ambassador then traced its influence on tea-tossing Bostonians and the efforts required of the current wartime generation "if Magna Carta is to come to its fruition."[16]

In some measure, the wry flex of history had turned back on itself that day in the Great Hall. A century and a quarter earlier, during the War of 1812, British troops torched the U.S. Capitol and destroyed the fledgling Library of Congress. Now that very institution was protecting, on behalf of a former foe, embryonic evidence of a shared democratic heritage. Not only that, but Thomas Jefferson, also a descendant of some Runnymede barons,[17] had drafted the Declaration of Independence, and was, as MacLeish pointed out, "the true founder of this library."[18] In 1815, the former president sold his extensive book collection to Congress to replace the material burned by the British.[19] MacLeish confidently expressed his belief that Jefferson "would have relished" seeing these documents exhibited together, finding it "just and fitting—an affirmation of the faith in which this nation was conceived."[20] After MacLeish finished his remarks,[21] the ambassador locked the Great Charter in its ornate display case and handed the key to the Librarian, who "dropped [it] into his right pants pocket and smiled."[22]

Magna Carta continued on display in the Great Hall, with a guard on duty at all times, as MacLeish had promised the ambassador.[23] There was considerable demand for the accompanying booklet the Library published[24] and for copies of the ambassador's and Librarian's remarks, as well as for photographs of the document itself. Requests came from congressmen, lawyers, small-town public libraries, and people nationwide who had read the news coverage or heard the radio broadcast from the Great Hall. From the start, the ambassador and the Librarian maintained a warm, easy-going relationship. Lothian was a thoughtful, forward-thinking fellow who had kept a low profile in high government places. He spent much of his tenure in the United States urging its citizens and government to provide more tangible support for defense against the impending fascist threat to world peace.

A crowd gathers around Magna Carta shortly after it went on public view in the Great Hall at the Library of Congress, November 28, 1939. The shrine housing the Declaration of Independence and the U.S. Constitution is in the upper background. Harris & Ewing, Prints and Photographs Division, Library of Congress (LC-DIG-hec-27725)

MacLeish, a former Yale varsity football player who served as an artillery captain in World War I, was a lawyer and a Pulitzer-prize winning poet.

Meanwhile, with their nation at war, British officials mulled over the expense of reopening their pavilion for the second and final season of the World's Fair. An editorial in the *Hartford Courant* cited the popularity of Britain's pavilion in general and Magna Carta in particular as reason enough for the exhibit to continue, but also noted that if the British decided not to return, "other European countries, belligerent and neutral, may well ask themselves why they should invest in American good will when Great Britain, with more to gain than any other nation, does not."[25] After careful deliberation and some financial maneuvering, the British announced in late February 1940 that they—and Magna Carta—would be back. In readying the charter for its trip to New York that spring, MacLeish told Lothian that "[t]he display of Magna Carta here has been of great service to a large number of visitors . . . and the Library would welcome an opportunity to exhibit the document again."[26]

On April 24, the charter left the Great Hall and headed north. The World's Fair, with a new slogan, "For Peace and Freedom," reopened on Sunday, May 11—the day after Germany invaded France, Belgium, Luxembourg, and the Netherlands.

The mood at the fair was noticeably different from the year before; many of the foreign pavilions were hosted by countries now under Nazi occupation or in danger of becoming so. In the British pavilion, the Hall of Metals, next door to Magna Carta Hall, was changed to War Exhibits.[27] The pavilion soon became a gathering place for supporters of the Allied cause and war relief meetings. On June 12, two days after Italy declared war on Britain and France, the British welcomed seven hundred guests in their pavilion garden to mark United Kingdom Day. Lord Lothian, who publicly noted the absence of the Italian ambassador, told his audience that "[i]t is perhaps appropriate at this moment, when the forces of tyranny and of liberty are grappled in war, that the central exhibit at the British Pavilion should be Magna Carta, one of the primary documents of human liberty."[28]

A few weeks later, as the United States celebrated its birthday on July 4, the very thing New York police and fair officials had fretted about, prepared for, and worked against came to pass. An electrician in the British Pavilion realized that a small canvas suitcase, which he had seen the day before, remained in the building's central ventilation room, only now it was ticking. He carried the case past hundreds of visitors to a pavilion officer. Incredibly, the two men then took it to Magna Carta Hall, where they showed it to another official. After some discussion, the case was taken outside to a nearly deserted area near the Polish pavilion. Two New York City bomb squad members arrived, examined it, and were instantly killed when the dynamite-filled bag exploded, leaving a five-foot-deep crater in the ground.[29] The tragedy was front-page news across the country. Hundreds of "agitators," German illegal aliens, and others were arrested, only to be released soon after, and the crime was never solved. Despite increased security measures, just three days later a small "mysterious box," with a message written in German, was discovered *sitting on* Magna Carta's case.[30] The box was harmless but the circumstances were unsettling.

If protecting Magna Carta at the fair had been a challenge that summer, so was defending its native land. The British home island was under direct assault. The Battle of Britain, culminating in September in the skies over London, coincided with an agreement that the United States would trade retired warships for the long-term right to lease military bases on British territory. It was to this deal that MacLeish referred when he wrote to Lothian on September 6: "As the days get cooler and the sky bluer, my mind turns to Magna Carta. Do you suppose it is to come back to us—not in exchange for fifty old destroyers but just back?"[31] Lothian was charmed. "Of course Magna Carta will ultimately return to its American home in the Library, for the duration," he replied.[32]

When the World's Fair permanently closed at the end of October 1940, Magna Carta's next port of call was still under discussion. Several interested parties had approached both the ambassador and the Librarian about putting the Great Charter on a tour of major American universities, and MacLeish was eager that such an exhibit should include "other manuscript treasures" from the Library's collections. But as he explained to one potential organizer, a Magna Carta tour for British war relief efforts in the officially neutral United States could not be associated with the Library, a federal institution, as that would be considered a "propaganda gesture."[33] He much preferred an educational approach that would prompt college students "to recall . . . the length, the vitality, and the vigor of the democratic tradition."[34] Plans then focused on an American-sponsored tour, with accompanying Library documents. MacLeish asked an outside planning committee about finding $25,000 to support a six-month tour while he "worked out the problem of sending manuscripts" on the road since "the entire tradition of the Library of Congress—or its rules and practices—are opposed to any such procedure."[35]

In the meantime, the British Embassy was hoping to send Magna Carta to the Cleveland International Exposition, where featured items from the New York World's Fair would make a two-week encore appearance in January 1941.[36] While the Librarian was still navigating his way around tour obstacles, he made arrangements for himself and Lord Lothian to record their still-in-demand speeches from the previous year when the ambassador was scheduled to redeposit the charter.[37] Lothian's sudden death on December 12 put everything on hold. Shortly after Christmas, the British embassy's chargé d'affaires brought Magna Carta to the Library, and it was placed in the Librarian's safe, its display case with the fleur de lis motif having been shipped to Cleveland the day before. Library staff later took front-and-back photographs of the charter, which were then sent to the exposition to be shown inside the case.

As plans for a tour fizzled, Magna Carta remained in Washington, D.C., so that it would be on display for Inauguration Day, January 20. That afternoon, on the East Portico of the U.S. Capitol, President Roosevelt was sworn in for his third term. In his address he recalled that "[t]he democratic aspiration is no mere recent phase in human history. It is human history. It permeated the ancient life of early peoples. It blazed anew in the middle ages. It was written in Magna Carta."[38] At that moment, Magna Carta was not some abstract, rhetorical notion tucked into FDR's speech. As an actual human artifact, in parchment and ink, it was currently on public view in the Library's Great Hall, directly across the street from where the president spoke.

With the decorative Magna Carta case in Cleveland, the charter was housed in the case normally used to display the Gutenberg Bible, which was relocated to the Library's vault.[39] There were numerous requests for copies of the photographs delivered to the exposition, and MacLeish sent a set of prints to Dean Mitchell at Lincoln Cathedral. The accompanying exhibit booklet was updated to include photographs and new information, and to dispel the idea that because King John sealed, rather than signed, Magna Carta, he must have been illiterate. Library staff also spent the early part of the year attempting to retrieve the document's display case and Washington's pedigree chart from a Cleveland warehouse, where the items languished after the exposition due to the organizers' nonpayment of shipping charges. Once the Library bailed out the case, the staff was dismayed to see the condition it was in. They reported that "we found the left side of the bronze case bent; reflectors have been removed; the case is locked with two padlocks but no keys found; the front glass is missing;" and its clover-leaf ornaments now drooped, along with other damage.[40]

By mid-March Magna Carta was back in its repaired display case. The next month, MacLeish was writing to Treasury Secretary Henry Morgenthau about possible storage space at Fort Knox, home of the nation's Bullion Depository of the U.S. Mint, should the country go to war and the Library need to evacuate its most important holdings. The Smithsonian Institution, the National Gallery of Art, and other cultural institutions were making similar preparations, just as their British and French counterparts had done in the late 1930s. Morgenthau and MacLeish's staffs continued to make storage space calculations, and by July the Library ascertained that it would need about 40,000 cubic feet to house its most significant and irreplaceable objects. Fort Knox, however, anticipating an influx of gold deposits, offered just a tad over 60 cubic feet. This was a generous upgrade. Originally, Morgenthau thought only 10 cubic feet would be available.[41]

American entry into World War II in December 1941 jolted the nation out of its isolationist mindset and the country instantly became a co-leader in the Allied cause. Washington, D.C., scrambled to mobilize, and the eastern seaboard went on alert for Axis submarines and saboteurs. On Friday morning, December 26, MacLeish told the new British ambassador, Lord Halifax, that he planned to send the Library's "priceless documents" to another part of the country for safe-keeping. In his notes of their conversation, MacLeish recorded that "I told Lord Halifax that I should like to include the Lincoln Cathedral copy of the Magna Carta, now entrusted to my care. I informed [him] that the responsibility was mine and that I did not ask him to share it but that I did not wish to take action without informing him. . . . [He] authorized me to say that he was prepared wholeheartedly to back my judgment."[42]

The next stage in Magna Carta's American adventure was now under way. That afternoon, Library staff removed the charter from its display case, brought it to the Rare Book Room, and placed it in a copper-lined oak case along with President Lincoln's second inaugural address and two drafts of the Gettysburg Address written in his hand. The Articles of Confederation and the three-volume Gutenberg Bible were packed in two similar cases, and the Declaration of Independence and the Constitution were bundled into a separate, customized container. All the items, under armed guard and Secret Service protection, were then loaded into an armored truck and delivered to Union Station. At 6:30 p.m., the National Limited departed Washington, D.C., and arrived the next morning in Louisville, Kentucky, where it was met by a small convoy that included more Secret Service agents and members of the Thirteenth Armored Division. Just after noon, all four hermetically sealed cases were locked in a vault at Fort Knox. There they would remain for nearly three years.[43]

Shortly after the Library's goods were securely ensconced, MacLeish contacted Morgenthau to express his "inexpressible gratitude" for their safe transfer and accommodation. "I think you can appreciate what it means to bear responsibility for the safety of these documents in this time," he told the secretary. "The responsibility had weighed heavily upon me for many months, but never as heavily as on the night when the shipment left the Library of Congress. I suppose it is quite literally true that no shipment of a value even remotely approaching the value of this shipment was ever made in this country. Here in one small group of containers was the documentary history of freedom in our world."[44]

When MacLeish wrote to Lincoln Cathedral's dean of his decision to send Magna Carta into hiding, he did not tell him where it had gone "since I should prefer not to entrust this information to the mails."[45] However, he assured Reverend Mitchell that "[t]he British ambassador knows of the location of Magna Carta, and receipts from the present depository are on file in original in the Library of Congress and in photostat with the United States Secret Service in the Treasury Department."[46] The dean graciously responded that he had full confidence in MacLeish and was "most grateful for the care and trouble you have already taken."[47]

Although Library staff no longer worried that an air raid on the capital might destroy the documents, air itself and insects could do just as much damage in Kentucky. Even before the documents were deposited at Fort Knox, Library staff had studied weather and atmospheric conditions both in the vault and outdoors. While the treasures were in residence, the vault was regularly inspected to measure environmental conditions and the items were checked for signs of mold or other deterioration. But even inspection posed risks, since repacking the documents afterward in good conditions could lead to problems later if the vault temperature should change. Verner Clapp, the Library's director of acquisitions, kept track of the documents' vitals and visited the site himself to see what effects humidity, air-conditioning, and calcium chloride dryers were having on sling-psychrometer and hygrometer readings.[48]

Dr. Luther Evans, Librarian of Congress, and British Minister John Balfour, third and fourth from left, respectively, oversee Magna Carta's removal from its exhibition case in the Great Hall in preparation for its return to Britain. A tinsmith, far right, with the metal traveling case at his feet, soldered the container shut before it was handed over to the British, January 11, 1946. LC Archive Central Files, Manuscript Division, Library of Congress

Col. Ian Ferguson MacLeod MacAlpine accepts Magna Carta from a U.S. service-man outside the Library of Congress, January 11, 1946. LC Archive Central Files, Manuscript Division, Library of Congress

In the strong-room aboard the *Queen Elizabeth*, Master-at-Arms William Peters, British Consul-General Sir Francis Evans, and Commodore James Bisset try unsuccessful-ly to squeeze Magna Carta into one of the ship's large safes, January 18, 1946. New York World Tele-graph and Sun, Prints and Photographs Division, Library of Congress (LC-DIG-ppmsca-38459)

In Europe, Allied forces began landing in France on D-Day, June 6, 1944, initiating the western drive toward Germany. Later that summer the president and Joint Chiefs of Staff gave the Library the all-clear, confirming that military officials believed Washington and the East Coast were no longer in danger. With that, Clapp made his last trip to Fort Knox on September 19, carrying with him the Library's receipt for its belongings. (He also returned home with the sling-psychrometer and the hygrometer.) MacLeish, of course, was already planning a homecoming celebration, and in late September he issued invitations. Plans to put Magna Carta on tour were briefly revived then quashed when Secretary Morgenthau, citing domestic travel and security concerns, asked that the idea be dropped for the time being.[49]

On Sunday morning, October 1, Magna Carta, the Declaration, and the Constitution were once more in the Great Hall, as was the Gutenberg Bible and, temporarily, their other traveling companions and vault-mates. A new Marine honor guard, comprising men who had seen active service during the war, was installed to watch over the displays. The Library announced later that month that its exhibition halls would open at 11:30 a.m. on Sundays—two and half hours earlier than usual—to allow defense workers and military personnel greater opportunity to see the documents.[50] All that was left now was for Magna Carta to ride out the closing months of the war and MacLeish, his responsibility nearly at an end, to wind up his days at the Library and join the State Department. Congressman Sol Bloom, however, had edited and promptly returned his invitation to the Magna Carta ceremony, opening up a new field of research.

"My dear Archie," began the congressman's missive to MacLeish, wondering if the Librarian had not erred in referring to Magna Carta as "the Magna Carta." "This is only one mistake that I find in your invitation and I would suggest that the Librarian of Congress be a little bit more careful. How about it?"[51] Bloom's enclosed invitation showed that he had crossed out the definite article preceding the document's name. As a New York World's Fair commissioner and longtime history buff, he was well aware that the British omitted the definite article at Magna Carta Hall.[52] In another message, he shot down MacLeish's logic, saying that "when you use 'Magna Carta' you cannot use 'the'. Am I right? Yes."[53] Although using 'the' sounded natural, especially to American ears, the rationale was that since *magna* was Latin, which did not use definite articles, 'the' should not be used with Magna Carta. MacLeish himself had used both styles, but with an army of librarians at his disposal, he giddily took up Bloom's challenge and asked David C. Mearns, the director of reference, "Want to help me spank him?"[54]

Within two days, Mearns and his assistant, Mortimer Taube, had compiled a list of references to "the Magna Carta" in a variety of legal, government, and

Magna Carta enters Lincoln Cathedral for only the second time in its 730-year history following its seven-year sojourn in the United States, January 24, 1946. On April 5, the cathedral
held an official ceremony in its chapter house to welcome the document back. LC Archive
Central Files, Manuscript Division, Library of Congress

academic publications. "In the first place," reported Taube, "it is permissible to use the article 'the' with Latin names and phrases . . . . Jespersen, the greatest authority on English grammar, leaves the use of the article in most cases a matter of preference."[55] In his memorandum to the Librarian, Mearns cited examples found in a landmark House of Commons report,[56] which he said provided "further evidence of the authorized use of the definite article in referring to a charter as a physical object."[57] Delighted with the research results, MacLeish summarized the findings in a letter to Bloom,[58] concluding that "our invitation was correct. You may send the roses over any time you please."[59]

MacLeish resigned his position in November to become assistant secretary for public and cultural affairs at the State Department. His replacement had not yet been named when Germany's surrender in May 1945 ended the war in Europe. Dr. Luther Evans, who had served as MacLeish's chief assistant, became the new Librarian in July as Magna Carta's unexpected exile in the United States was nearing an end. According to the British Foreign Office, Lincoln Cathedral was eager to have its charter back "as soon as convenient."[60] But even as plans were made to return it, Evans sought to get another Great Charter to grace the Great Hall. He hoped that its acquisition during peacetime, rather than out of wartime necessity, would further "illustrate the great tradition of Anglo-American friendship and freedom."[61]

The Lincoln Magna Carta remained on display at the Library of Congress until early 1946. On January 11, the Librarian, the British minister (John Balfour, stepping in for Lord Halifax), and the dean of Lincoln Cathedral (who participated via CBS and BBC radio hookup from England), oversaw the charter's change in custody. "This is a family occasion," said Evans, referring to "our British cousins." In handing back the charter, he noted that "[w]e are returning to you a document, but we retain a doctrine."[62] From 3,600 miles away, the voice of Dean Mitchell reached the Library, telling the American audience that "if any of you who are listening tonight should chance in your travels to come this way, you may always be

At Lincoln Cathedral, the staff pries open the sealed box containing Magna Carta, January 24, 1946. LC Archive Central Files, Manuscript Division, Library of Congress

assured of the warmest welcome in Lincoln Cathedral."[63] As the dean spoke, the charter was placed in a copper-lined wooden box with a zinc case and soldered shut in the Great Hall. American servicemen escorted it outside where a British soldier, the kilted Col. Ian Ferguson MacLeod Macalpine of the Royal Highland Black Watch Regiment, accepted it on the front steps.[64]

From the British embassy in Washington the weighty box traveled to the consul's office in New York to await transfer to the *Queen Elizabeth*. A week later, Sir Francis Evans, British counsel-general, delivered it to the ship, and Commodore James Bisset was asked to sign a receipt for "One Tin Box containing the Magna Carta."[65] Taking the box to the ship's strong-room, Bisset discovered that it would not fit inside the largest safe on board. Thus, despite all the pomp and ceremony given the Great Charter in America, it made the voyage home stowed under the commodore's bed.[66] Once it reached its native shores at Southampton, the document was taken to London and the next day, January 24, it entered Lincoln Cathedral for the second time in its 730-year history. A can opener was used to get through the sealed zinc case containing the document's heavy wooden box. Later that spring, the Library shipped Magna Carta's display case to the cathedral's dean and chapter, which they regarded as a "much valued and interesting reminder"[67] of their charter's American escapades.

In the meantime, Evans continued pursuing a long-term Magna Carta loan, but under very different, and more formal, circumstances. The deed for the two 1215 charters at the British Museum did not permit them to travel. As it happened, a Magna Carta original copy issued by Henry III in 1225 had suddenly come to public attention. In the summer of 1945, Matilda Talbot announced that she would donate what became known as the Lacock Abbey Magna Carta to the British Museum. Until then, hardly anyone had known of this copy's existence.[68] For centuries it had been squirreled away in a nunnery located in a village owned by the Talbot family. During the war she had kept the charter hidden in an air raid shelter beneath her house. It was well preserved, with the king's huge royal seal still attached. The document would have fetched an extraordinary sum had she sold it; that she did not won her praise in both the press and Parliament. Perhaps, the British Foreign Office suggested, the Library might be interested in exhibiting the Lacock charter?

The possibility of borrowing the recently revealed Lacock Abbey Magna Carta excited Evans. He also thought this 1225 charter would be especially interesting to Americans, because it was this version that judge and legal scholar Sir William Blackstone had used in his book *The Great Charter and Charter of the Forest* (1759). "Blackstone," Evans told the Foreign Office, "was gospel to the group of American lawyers of the eighteenth century, from whom our founding fathers were drawn."[69] Talbot happily supported the idea, but once the document was in the British Museum, the endeavor would require Parliament's consent. In the spring of 1946 a bill was proposed authorizing the museum to loan the Lacock charter to the Library of Congress for a two-year exhibition. Although the outcome was never really in doubt, a lively debate ensued.

One of Parliament's most important considerations, it turned out, was how to spell *Magna Carta*. "I am making no complaint about our treasures going abroad," said Sir Patrick Hannon, "but if this document goes abroad I want it to be spelt correctly."[70] At issue was whether to use the letter *h*, since Magna Carta was often rendered *Magna Charta*, and that was the spelling used in the very bill that Parliament was considering. In the House of Lords, Viscount Simon admitted to offering "a little display of pedantry," having only a half hour before looked up the terms in Latin and Greek dictionaries. His findings: *magna* was Latin, as they all knew, but the English word "charter" derived from Greek. Viscount Samuel responded that "the term is itself a most horrible hybrid, and the sooner we alter it one way or the other the better." There followed discussion on the spelling habits of Cicero, Catullus, and Pliny. Ultimately, after an extensive recitation of the Great Charter's history, the lords determined that "the 'h' crept in . . . through some careless scribe in medieval times or perhaps rather earlier" and it should be done away with.[71] Over in the House of Commons, David Eccles was relieved to know that his counterparts had excised "the offending aspirate, the vulgar interloper in the word 'Carta.'"[72]

On December 15, 1946, less than a year after the Lincoln Magna Carta had departed the Library's Great Hall, the Lacock Abbey Magna Carta appeared in its place. The charter itself, with its ornate script and bold seal, was a bit flashier than the Lincoln copy, but its simple white display case championed postwar austerity compared with its flowery World's Fair predecessor. Lord Inverchapel, the British ambassador, officially presented it to the Library, and Matilda Talbot made some remarks, with scholars, cabinet members, Supreme Court justices, and members of Congress in attendance.[73] The Library produced an accompanying booklet written by Arthur Jeffries Collins, deputy keeper of manuscripts at the British Museum, who tended to the charter as it traveled to and from the United States.[74] After two years, the document returned home and for one of the few times in nearly a decade, there was no Magna Carta in the Library's enthusiastic custody.

The American and British tendency to inspire and fascinate each other continued. Librarian Evans attempted to obtain a third Great Charter on a long-term loan, but the rarity of such documents precluded another acquisition during his administration. Meanwhile, Magna Carta's popularity in the United States

Visitors to the Library of Congress line up to see the Lacock Abbey Magna Carta (1225), which went on display on Bill of Rights Day, December 15, 1946. It remained on exhibit through 1948. LC Archive Central Files, Manuscript Division, Library of Congress

prompted the dean and chapter at Lincoln Cathedral to permanently display their charter publicly, whereas before it was only on view to those who found their way to the narrow library in the cloister. When the Lacock charter arrived back in London, it, too, received a prominent display in the British Museum. In a letter to the Librarian confirming his and the charter's safe return after a stormy sea voyage, Collins wrote, "The publicity given to it on your side has followed it here; in consequence, it is attracting a crowd of visitors to my galleries."[75]

The barons and churchmen at Runnymede, the clerks in their uncatalogued libraries, the antiquarians with their private archives could hardly have envisioned that the charters passing through their hands would one day draw such attention around an exhibit case. Perhaps it was not until those documents' surviving and evolving sentiments were inscribed in statute books and chiseled on courthouse pediments—or threatened by world war—that viewing their tangible origins resonated so strongly. "It is natural that men should value the original documents which guarantee their rights," wrote Archibald MacLeish in 1939. "The great constitutions and charters are not mere records of something already accomplished. They are themselves its accomplishment."[76] And given the opportunity, people wanted then—and still do now—to see them, whether in a museum or at the fair.

WILLIAM MARSH... THE ELDER
EARL OF PEMBROKE

REBELLION
AND THE
GREAT
CHARTER

WILLIAM MARSHAL,
EARL OF PEMBROKE (ca. 1146–1219)
The Right Honourable The Lord Igor Judge

William Marshal, Earl of Pembroke, is the hero of the convoluted events which culminated in the creation and survival of Magna Carta. None of his contemporaries played such a pivotal role. Without him the Charter of 1215 (not entitled Magna Carta) would have been the only charter rather than the first of four, and would have been relegated to a minor note in history, one more charter in an age of charters, annulled by the Pope almost as soon as it was sealed by King John, and revoked by King John at the first available opportunity. Yet, apart from professional historians of the period, William Marshal is virtually unknown today.

Few remember Marshal's contribution to the protracted negotiations which culminated in the sealing of the Charter. Yet the Charter itself acknowledges his importance by listing him as the first of the non-clerical individuals who advised the King. Perhaps more significant, few remember that after the annulment of the Charter by the Pope and its revocation by the King, and in the middle of the subsequent civil war, the King died leaving an infant son to succeed him. Marshal was elected regent of the infant King Henry III, and then rapidly reissued and distributed a new version of the Charter in 1216 in his own name and under his own seal, and again reissued it in 1217. Finally, few remember that in that same year, by then seventy years or so old, he returned once more to the battlefield and defeated an invading French army at the Battle of Lincoln, bringing to an end the serious prospect of a Capetan dynasty replacing the Plantagenet dynasty in England. The potential consequences were not merely dynastic: the political and constitutional developments which took place over succeeding centuries might well have been significantly different.

Marshal is one of the forgotten men of history. His immediate contemporaries appreciated his life far more than we do. On his death in 1219 he was given the

Effigy of William Marshal (1146-1219), 1st Earl of Pembroke, in the Round Church, Temple Church (before the damage of 1941). The unsheathed sword pierces a lion's head

equivalent of a modern state funeral. In his funeral oration the Archbishop of Canterbury described Marshal as "the greatest knight that ever lived". It was an apt summary of the admiration and respect in which his contemporaries held him.

Within a very short time the story of Marshal's life was being told in *Le Histoire de Guillaume le Mareschal*, the first, and with the exception of an autobiographical effort, the only known or surviving "lay" or story of the life of an individual who was not a monarch or, in our language, Head of State. Discounting the risk of hagiography and the danger of over-romanticising the life of the hero of the story, by checking the assertions in the *Histoire* against facts which can be established independently of it, a remarkable story of a towering figure of medieval history emerges.

Yet Marshal's start in life was hardly propitious. He was the fourth of his father's sons, and although his father John enjoyed the hereditary office of "Mareschal" (from which his sons drew their surname), he was not and would not have been regarded as a grandee. Young William had to make his own way in the world. One way to advancement from humble origins was through the Church. Another was to make an impact as a warrior. Marshal's talents in this direction were unsurpassed. As his reputation burgeoned, he had the good fortune to encounter and impress Eleanor of Aquitaine, the wife of Henry II. Through her influence he entered the hazardous service of the royal Plantagenet family. The level of dysfunction in that family is notorious. Henry II imprisoned his wife for well over a decade. At different times each and sometimes more than one of his sons was in open rebellion against him. They warred against each other. John was almost certainly complicit in the murder of his older brother Geoffrey's son Arthur, then a teenager with, on primogeniture grounds, a better claim to the throne. In this venomous atmosphere contemporaries gradually came to be struck with the unswerving loyalty of Marshal to his oath of fealty, not least at times when others saw that over-enthusiastic allegiance to this principle might create an obstruction to advancement.

Taking it very briefly, backed by Eleanor, at the request of Henry II, Marshal assumed responsibility for their oldest son, Henry, who although crowned as the Young King, predeceased his father. When he died, it was Marshal who fulfilled the Young King's vow to go on crusade to the Holy Land. On his return he re-entered the service of Henry II. We can see evidence of his gradual assimilation into the group of close advisers of the king in some of the records towards the end of this reign. For example, in 1186 Marshal's name is included as a witness to the termination of a dispute between the Bishops of Hereford and Worcester. Among the list of witnesses, plain, untitled William Marshal comes a very long way behind the Archbishop of Canterbury, and a variety of named bishops and earls, at that time the highest rank of the nobility in England.[1] Less than twenty years later, now vested with the dignity and title of Earl of Pembroke, he appeared as the first great noble of the realm witnessing Magna Carta. That, however, was for the undecided future.

In the war which erupted between Richard and his dying father, Marshal remained loyal to Henry II until the very end. Indeed shortly before his death, Marshal encountered Richard, whom he had trained in the skills of war in the field, reconnoitring Henry's defences. Marshal spared Richard's life, but humiliatingly for Richard, he killed his horse under him.

When Henry II was dying, Marshal remained with him to the end. His career prospects thereafter cannot have seemed very bright. Nevertheless when he offered his fealty to Richard, no doubt bearing in mind that as well as his loyalty to his father, Marshal had also demonstrated conspicuous loyalty to his first patron, his mother, Eleanor, Richard accepted it. Moreover when he went on his own crusade, Richard appointed Marshal to be the first of the co-justiciars to William Longchamps, the Archbishop of Canterbury. Among the burdens falling on Marshal and his co-justiciars was a siege of the troublesome John at Windsor Castle. A burden of a different kind which fell on the illiterate Marshal was sitting as one of the judges in Westminster Hall.[2] Perhaps he was happier on the battlefield. His standing with Richard on his return from captivity would have been undiminished by his stupendous folly in leading the way up the scaling ladder and knocking out the constable of Beauvais Castle when it was under siege by Richard in 1197. As a public acknowledgment of Marshal's increasing standing, he was allowed to marry the heiress, Isabel of Striguil (Chepstow), a notable heiress, with vast interests in Wales and Ireland. In stark terms of career progress, this represented significant public recognition.

In 1199, Richard died, without issue, naming John as his heir. It is an indication of how close Marshal had arrived at the inner circle of power that he was immediately consulted about the succession by the Archbishop of Canterbury. William recommended that in accordance with Richard's last wishes, John, rather than Arthur, should become king. Shortly after John's coronation, William was invested as the Earl of Pembroke in his own right.

At the outset of the new reign Marshal's fortunes continued to flourish. Perhaps inevitably in any working relationship with John, things changed, and in 1205 Marshal left the court in England and went into political exile in Ireland. The main area of dispute was relevant to the issues which came to be resolved in

1215. John was determined to recover land in Poitou, France. Marshal refused to join the expedition as this would contravene the fealty he owed in France to Philip Augustus. John alleged that this was treasonous, but when William elected trial by battle, his reputation as a warrior meant that no one took up his challenge to fight. Perhaps more important, whether or not Marshal's refusal was a form of special pleading, or a principled adherence to his oath of fealty, the issue was very public, and a few years later, rebel barons would have recollected Marshal's refusal to serve the king abroad, and it would have provided the basis for their contentions that they should have no liability for "scutage" to replace service to the king outside England. Clauses 12 and 14 of the 1215 Charter may have had many progenitors, but as Marshal conducted negotiations on John's behalf in those turbulent months, he may well have had some sympathy with the determination of the rebel barons that the consent of the Council should be a pre-requisite of liability for scutage. This is a very long way from "No taxation without representation", but it is not too fanciful to discern the link between the requirement of formal consent to the raising of royal revenue which became the foundations both for the constitutional struggle in seventeenth-century En-

Christopher Saxton (b. 1540). London area map in An Atlas of England and Wales. London, 1579. Geography and Map Division, Library of Congress

gland, and the assured defiance of London by the colonists in eighteenth-century North America.

His time in Ireland, where by virtue of his wife's descent from King Dermot of Leinster, Marshal and his wife had many interests and responsibilities and troubles, proved to be a training ground for the future Regent. "In his Irish policies we can at last see the Marshal as ruler rather than courtier and soldier".[3] Ireland was not overlooked when the Charter later came to be reissued by Marshal in 1216 and again in 1217, when he required that they should be distributed in Ireland on the basis that Irish subjects should enjoy the same liberties as those of England (a promise which was not fulfilled, but which supplied Edmund Burke with his powerful reasoning in support of the proposition that the American colonists were entitled to the same rights as the King's subjects in England).

John's reign became increasingly turbulent. In 1207 England was placed under a papal interdict, with all ecclesiastical offices save for baptism and deathbed confession banned. In 1209 John was excommunicated. By 1212 two senior barons were accused of conspiracy to murder the King, and fled the realm. In January 1213 the Pope pronounced a sentence of deposition on John, and authorised Holy War against him. Unsurprisingly, John was virtually bereft of any allies. By a process of reconciliation which began in 1212, Marshal responded to the King's summons to return to England in May 1213. There were now almost exactly two years to go to the meeting at Runnymede.

With others, Marshal advised John to reach an accommodation with the Pope, which John eventually did in sufficiently sycophantic terms for the Pope to embrace him as the returning prodigal son. John then embarked on the disastrous expedition to France which culminated in the Battle of Bouvines. This constituted not simply a defeat, but utter humiliation for John, whose treasury was empty. After Bouvines Marshal organised the mustering of loyal troops (wherever they could be found) and the preparation of defensive royal positions. Although John was the anointed King, and the vassal of the Pope who would stand behind him, and had the support of a formidable and tried military campaigner in Marshal, his vulnerability could not be disguised. And so negotiations began with Marshal as John's key envoy. The narrative of the negotiations which began at the Temple in the autumn of 1214 need not be repeated here. What matters is that Marshal was the only civilian (as opposed to clerical) guarantor of John's good faith during these meetings. At the risk of stating the obvious it follows that he must have been a very close, if not the closest adviser of the King, not a comfortable role for an individual of marked integrity who was as well aware as anyone of the unpredictable nature of the royal personality. Nevertheless he was sufficiently influential to give dispassionate and unpalatable advice. Indeed it has been suggested that he was the joint author of the terms of the Charter, a suggestion which modern historians regard as improbable,[4] but which does serve to underline how very close to the heart of the negotiations he must have been when the Charter was eventually sealed at Runnymede in June 1215. As already noted, it is certain that the first "illustrious", that is, non-clerical, magnate from the baronial class to be named in this Charter was Marshal. After it was sealed he was given the responsibility of informing London, still hostile to the King, of its terms.

To no avail: the 1215 Charter was buried under the turmoil of civil war. John appealed to the Pope for its annulment, which duly followed, and the rebel barons, despite the "security" clause, could not enforce its terms. Forces from France invaded England. The rebel barons offered the throne to the future King of France, Louis VIII. Military action continued. Marshal himself was first committed to action in Wales, and then sent as an emissary to France to seek, without success, to dissuade Philip Augustus from supporting his son's claim to the throne of England. As 1216 was drawing to a close, the outcome of the civil war and the French invasion was uncertain.

Marshal was at Gloucester when John died in October 1216. That was a most fortunate incident in the history of Magna Carta. Some contemporary material suggests that on his deathbed John nominated Marshal as the guardian for his infant heir, Henry III. The evidence to support this suggestion is problematic. What mattered was that Marshal took urgent action to secure the Plantagenet succession by summoning the barons loyal to the King to Gloucester Abbey and arranging for the young king to be conveyed there. Westminster Abbey itself was unavailable for the coronation as it was under the control of French forces.

Marshal knighted the boy who was then crowned King in the presence of the Papal Legate, Guala. After obtaining the consent of the Earl of Chester, the most senior nobleman in England, Marshal accepted the office of Regent (*Rector noster et Regni nostri*), a new title and office. In effect and in practice he became Regent or Protector, and the ruler of the country.

> All those in the abbey's vast crowd would have realised that this was a dreadful way to start a reign. The most uncertain transfer of power seen for nearly a century was placing the crown on the head of a child. . . . Henry III was fortunate to have around him a group of supporters committed to not seizing power for themselves, but to maintain the fragile office of kingship as his predecessors had created it. . . . It was not just to the solemn nine-year-old Henry's advantage that (Marshal's) attitude prevailed among a few good men in England. The future of the dynasty depended on it.[5]

The undoubted leader of this small loyal group was William Marshal.

With Marshal's new authority, within less than a month of John's death, and notwithstanding John's repudiation and the Pope's annulment of the Charter, it was reissued in the name of the king, but under Marshal's personal seal and that of the Papal Legate. By contemporary standards this was a remarkably rapid response. The reissue included a number of revisions, no doubt reflecting the reality that civil war was continuing and French invaders were still present in England. The objective seems clear. It was a gesture towards reconciliation with the rebel barons. The omission of clauses restricting the authority of the King may have reflected the exigencies of the civil war and the need to secure the throne, and perhaps, just because the monarch was a boy, a belief that he should not suffer in the event of misconduct by the Regent. Significantly however, in the final clause, reference was made to the resolution of outstanding issues when fuller council would be possible, so as to do what was best for the common good and the peace of the kingdom. By way of further encouragement, this reissue was accompanied by a threat of excommunication for those who rejected its terms. This effort to achieve peace failed.

The war continued. Next year, the rebel army, backed by Louis of France, besieged loyalist troops at Lincoln Castle. Marshal was now seventy or so years old. Nevertheless, he was at the forefront both of the battlefield tactics and the very fighting itself. Anxious to take advantage of the unfolding military situation, he forgot to wear his helmet. His supporters reminded him to wear it: just as well. During the hand-to-hand fighting it was dented in more than one place. The end result was a great victory, in which forty-six of the rebel barons were captured. The French invasion nevertheless continued until Louis was defeated shortly afterwards in a sea battle off Sandwich.

That brought the civil war to an end and culminated in the departure of the defeated French. In the peace

Effigy of William Marshal (1190-1230, eldest son of the 1st Earl), 2nd Earl of Pembroke, in the Round Church, Temple Church (before the damage of 1941). He sided with the barons at Runnymeade, and was one of the Twenty-Five "who with all their might are to observe, maintain and cause to be observed the peace and liberties which we have granted by this our present charter" (Magna Carta, Clause 61)

treaties, Louis abandoned his claim to the throne of England, the rebel barons renewed their homage and were absolved from excommunication, and Marshal, together with the Papal Legate, undertook that the liberties demanded by the rebel barons would be restored. And so as part of what we today would describe as the peace process, after a meeting of the Council, an undated Charter was reissued in November 1217, again in the name of the King, but again under the seal of Marshal and the Papal Legate. Significantly, this Charter was sealed not under the pressure of military weakness which led John to seal the 1215 Charter, nor in the desperate need to secure the succession of the Infant King, as in 1216, but with the confidence of victory in battle. Indeed in his endeavours to secure this peace and bring to an end a civil war which it is apparent from the *Histoire* he loathed, Marshal made concessions which a later generation, led by Henry III himself, regarded as a virtual betrayal. Victory, they believed, should have been crowned in brighter garments. That was the perspective of hindsight, easily asserted by those contentedly basking in the peace which had been secured during Marshal's rule. Henry III was later to learn the bitter price to be paid for civil war. Perhaps, however, for this reason, and perhaps, because somewhat surprisingly given the large number of healthy sons born to him, Marshal's immediate line died out very quickly, his name gradually faded into obscurity.

Yet in the few short years between his return from Ireland in 1213 and his death in 1219, at the very least, Marshal had been at the heart of all the negotiations which culminated in John's reluctant sealing of the first Charter in 1215; he had himself reissued new charters during 1216 and 1217, and thus countered the annulment and revocation of the 1215 Charter; he had saved the Plantagenet dynasty; driven out a powerful invading French army, and brought a civil war to an end; and his method of government, using councils and assemblies during his regency, produced a period of "proto-parliamentary government, opening the way for the emergence of parliament".[6] Many more famous names in history have achieved significantly less.

William Blackstone (1723–1780).
The Great Charter and Charter of the Forest, with Other Authentic Instruments: To Which Is Prefixed an Introductory Discourse, Containing the History of the Charters.
Oxford: Clarendon Press, 1759.
Law Library, Library of Congress

VARIAE LECTIONES·

hun comite Hereford' et Eſſex' Guydone de Bello Campo comite Warr' Ricardo filio Alani comite Arundel' Reginaldo de Grey Johanne de Haſtinges Henrico de Percy Hugone le Deſpenſer Hugone de Veer Roberto de Tateſhale Hugone Bardolf Hugone de Curteney Johanne de Segrave Henrico de Grey Willielmo { le. D,Inſp.O. } Ros de { de. T28. . . } Helmeſleye Alano la Zuſche Roberto de Tony Ro-

berto de Monte Alto Willielmo de Breus Thoma de Furnival Johanne { Engayne. D,Inſp.O. } Pe- { Engaigne. T28. . . } tro Corbet Willielmo de Leyburne Willielmo le Latimer Waltero de Bello Campo ſeneſcallo hoſ- pitii noſtri Waltero de Huntercumbe et aliis Dat' per manum noſtram apud Weſtmonaſterium vice- ſimo octavo die Martii anno regni noſtri viceſimo octavo. D,Inſp.O.T28.

fide et fine malo ingenio obſervabuntur Teſtibus ſupradictis et multis aliis Data per manum noſtram in prato quod vocatur ⁸Runingmed' inter ⁹Windeleſorum et Stanes quinto decimo die Ju- nii anno regni noſtri ſeptimo decimo. ⁴

VARIAE LECTIONES.

⁸ Runigmed. R.   ⁴ Et ne huic forme predicte aliquid poſſit addi
                                   vel ab eadem aliquid poſſit ſubtrahi vel minui huic
⁹ Windeleſore. R.   ſcripto ſigilla noſtra appoſuimus. R.

CONFIRMATIONS BY KINGS AND PARLIAMENT

From the Design for the Cartoon in the Royal Exchange.

Andra & Sleigh, Limited, Bushey, Herts.

KING JOHN GRANTING MAGNA CHARTA.

By ERNEST NORMAND.

MAGNA CARTA'S ENACTMENT
William C. Koch, Jr.[1]

King John and the barons met at Runnymede in June 1215 to strike a political compromise. The barons were in open rebellion against the crown because of King John's accumulation and abuse of royal power.[2] The king had been increasing the weight of the barons' feudal obligations and had been infringing on their accustomed feudal jurisdiction. Accordingly, the barons were goaded into action, not by any altruistic notions of the common good, but rather by their own personal and class interests.[3]

For his part, King John could ill-afford prolonged civil strife at home so soon after a losing war with the King of France and a protracted dispute with Pope Innocent III.[4] To restore peace at home, he agreed to meet his rebellious barons in a meadow on the south bank of the Thames between Windsor and Stains to strike a bargain that would win back their loyalty.[5] Magna Carta was the price King John paid for the barons' renewed fealty and allegiance.[6]

The barons' purpose at Runnymede was to restore the customary limits on the king's power.[7] They did not demand new rights but rather the king's formal recognition of their existing rights. Thus, Magna Carta is in the form of a declaration of the fundamental rights possessed by landholders at the time.[8] Its substance embodies the common law and the ancient customs of the realm.[9] Its purpose was to define the rights that had heretofore been vaguely understood and, thereby, to make it more difficult for the king to ignore or evade them.[10]

King John's Charter was written in Latin using a form borrowed from the feudal lawyer's book of styles for conferring title to landed estates.[11] It was written rapidly, but carefully, at Runnymede, and then copies were made and distributed after it was signed. None of the four extant original copies were divided into the now familiar preamble and sixty-three chapters.[12] These divisions were added later for convenience of reference.

The signing of Magna Carta illustrated in *Cassell's History of England,* Volume 1. London: Cassell, 1903. General Collections, Library of Congress

No provisions of the Charter of King John would have more impact on later American constitutions than Chapters 39 and 40. In Chapter 39, King John agreed that

> No freeman shall be taken or imprisoned or disseised or exiled or in any way destroyed, nor will we go upon him nor send upon him, except by the lawful judgment of his peers or by the law of the land.[13]

Similarly, King John agreed in Chapter 40 that

> To no one will we sell, to no one will we refuse or delay, right or justice.[14]

Together, these two chapters have provided the basis for the commonly accepted understanding that our federal and state constitutions provide everyone the protections of law, liberty, and good government.[15] Much, however, has been read into these chapters over the centuries that would astonish the barons who drafted them in 1215.[16]

Chapters 39 and 40 can only be understood in the context of their historical antecedents. Two of the most powerful political forces at work in early English history were the establishment of a strong monarchy that centralized control and brought stability to the realm and the concomitant establishment of safeguards to protect the public against the monarch's unrestrained tyranny.[17] Chapters 39 and 40 represent efforts by the barons to restrain King John's abuse of the judicial machinery in existence at the time.

England did not have a strong monarch until 1066. William the Conqueror created a centralized authority unlike any other that had existed in medieval Christendom.[18] While he and his Norman successors[19] provided order, their reigns were punctuated by continuing strife with the barons. On one hand, the monarchy sought to eliminate local anarchy, while on the other hand, the barons sought to preserve local autonomy from erosion by centralized autocratic power.[20]

Nowhere was the tension between central control and local autonomy more evident than in the courts. Dispensing justice to the nation as a whole was not considered a royal responsibility or prerogative.[21] Feudal justice consisted of many local jurisdictions; in fact, practically every land owner provided a court for the persons residing on his domain. These local courts competed with each other to expand their spheres of influence and to increase their fees.[22]

William the Conqueror established the Curia Regis, a judicial body that followed him from place to place as he traveled throughout the kingdom.[23] The king, like any other feudal lord, was expected to dispense justice among his tenants, and thus the king's court was merely one among many feudal courts. William never intended the Curia Regis to dispense justice for the entire nation.[24] Persons seeking royal justice were required to follow the king's court from place to place. The King's justice was thus slow, costly, and not widely available.

The first royal efforts to centralize the judicial system began during the reign of Henry II, the first of the Plantagenets.[25] Henry of Anjou set out to overthrow the feudal jurisdictions by converting the county courts into royal courts and by undermining the significance of manorial or private courts by diverting pleas to his own courts.[26] By his Assizes of Clarendon and Northampton, he opened the royal courts to ordinary freeholders who could pay for a royal writ.[27] And so began the process by which royal courts became the preferred source of justice in England.

Pieter van der Banck (1649–1697), engraver. *King Iohn* [King John]. Engraving, ca. 1697. Prints and Photographs Division, Library of Congress (LC-DIG-ppmsca.37770)

Access to the royal courts was tightly controlled by a complicated system of writs. Each crime and complaint had its own writ. Persons seeking to present a claim to the royal courts were required to purchase the appropriate writ. Individuals who did not purchase a writ or who purchased the wrong writ had no remedy in the King's courts. Writs could occasionally be purchased for a fixed fee, but their price in a particular case could also be set by the Crown depending on the facts of the case.[28]

The system of royal writs had emptied the seignorial courts of their business by the time of King John's reign.[29] Not only had the barons lost the fees they had once collected from their courts, but they also were now subjected to the King's justice if they were amerced or accused of a criminal offense.[30] Henry's reforms had, without question, shifted the balance of judicial powers from the barons to the Crown.[31]

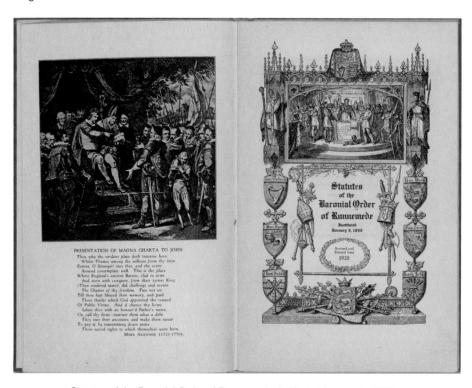

Statutes of the Baronial Order of Runnemede, Instituted January 8, 1898.
Philadelphia: J.E. Caldwell & Co., 1928. Law Library, Library of Congress

The barons' concern over the shift in the balance of power was exacerbated by King John's abuse of the judicial process. The King customarily placed or threatened to place his personal and political rivals under arrest before judgment[32] and ignored the feudal tradition that persons were to be judged by their equals by using royal tribunals to exile and deprive his enemies of their estates and money.[33] The King also viewed royal writs as a source of revenue and frequently increased the price of the writ in proportion to the value of the claim or the wealth of the person seeking the writ.[34] Magna Carta was thus one of the barons' last efforts to stem the Crown's encroachment on feudal justice.[35]

The barons' purpose at Runnymede was to protect themselves and their friends from King John. The King had been using the machinery of justice to transfer their land and money to his treasury, and so the barons intended to use Magna Carta to prevent him from taking the law into his own hands.[36] By seeking the King's agreement to Chapters 39 and 40, the barons intended: (1) to prevent him from placing execution, imprisonment, or banishment before judgment,[37]

(2) to return to the ancient custom of trial by equals,[38] (3) to require that judgments be consistent with the "law of the land" instead of the King's whim,[39] (4) to prevent the King from substituting violence for legal process,[40] and (5) to redress the abuses of the writ system.[41]

King John accepted the Charter unwillingly and insincerely[42] and set out to undermine it soon after it was signed. On August 24, 1215, Pope Innocent III declared that the Charter was null and void and threatened excommunication to anyone who observed or attempted to enforce its terms.[43] The original Charter had lasted a mere sixty-six days. With the Pope's blessing, John moved to regain control of his kingdom by force. He had reconquered most of the country except London when he died suddenly from dysentery on October 19, 1216.[44]

Henry of Winchester was crowned at Gloucester on October 28, 1216.[45] He was only nine years old,[46] and in order to rally support for the young king, his regent and advisors decided to reissue King John's Charter as a sign that Henry III intended to recognize the feudal rights of his subjects.[47] The Charter reissued in Henry III's name on November 12, 1216,[48] differed from the Charter acceded to by King John the year before. It did not contain twenty-two chapters dealing with either specific circumstances at issue at Runnymede[49] or with temporary provisions that were no longer needed.[50] Other notable changes included: (1) the omission of the restraints on the Crown's taxing power, (2) the omission of the chapter granting subjects the right to leave and return to the kingdom without the King's consent, and (3) the deletion of the

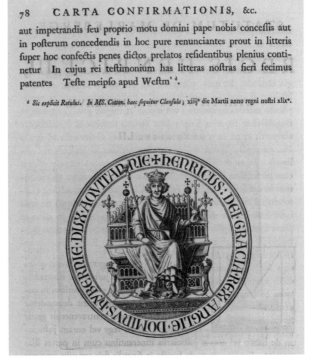

William Blackstone (1723–1780). *The Great Charter and Charter of the Forest, with Other Authentic Instruments: To Which Is Prefixed an Introductory Discourse, Containing the History of the Charters.* Oxford: Clarendon Press, 1759. Law Library, Library of Congress

provision empowering the church to supervise the distribution of the chattels of persons who died intestate.[51]

The revisions contained in Henry III's first reissue of the Charter dealt primarily with matters of private law. The King's advisors were not attempting to devise a machinery of government or to construct safeguards for national liberties.[52] Unlike his predecessor, Pope Honorius III ratified the Charter of 1216.[53]

The Treaty of Lambeth in September 1217 ended two years of hostilities between Henry III and Louis of France. It marked the final acceptance of Henry III's advisors that the substance of the Charter would be the permanent basis for government in England during times of peace.[54] Henry III made good on his commitment on November 6, 1217, when he issued his "Carta de libertatibus" or Charter of Liberties and his "Carta de foresta" or Charter of the Forest.[55] These two charters contained more detailed legal procedures and revived and strengthened the system of local government and administration.[56] Henry III emphasized his commitment to the

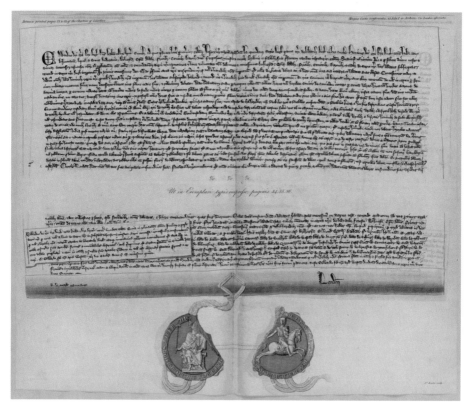

Edward I's re-issue of Magna Carta in *Statutes of the Realm*, Vol. 1.
London: G. Eyre and A. Strahan, 1810. Law Library, Library of Congress

Charter of Liberties in February 1218 by directing that copies of the Charter be distributed to the sheriffs with directions that the Charter be published and enforced.[57]

Pope Honorius declared Henry III to be of full age in April 1223. Less than one year later, Henry was called upon to confirm the Charter of Liberties and the Charter of the Forest that had been issued in his name in 1217.[58] Henry demurred. Later, in December 1224, he demanded that all freeholders contribute one-fifteenth of their movables to enable him to deal with Louis of France's plot against the remaining Angevin provinces on the Continent.[59] Henry's need for funds provided the barons with an opportunity to renew their demand for the confirmation of the Charter of Liberties which had become known as Magna Carta.[60]

King Henry complied with the barons' demands and reissued Magna Carta on February 11, 1225. This reissue marks the final form that Magna Carta was to take.[61] The Charter now contained thirty-seven chapters.[62] Henry III's revisers combined Chapter 39 and Chapter 40 of King John's Charter because they considered Chapter 40 to essentially supplement Chapter 39.[63] Accordingly, Chapter 29 of the 1225 Magna Carta read as follows:

> NO freeman shall be taken or imprisoned or disseised of any freehold, or liberties, or free customs, or outlawed, or banished, or in any other way destroyed, nor will we go upon him, nor send upon him, except by the legal judgment of his peers or by the law of the land. To no one will we sell, to no one will we deny, or delay right or justice.[1]

While the evolution of Magna Carta's language ended in 1225, the evolution and growth of its significance has continued through the centuries into the present time. Magna Carta was the first manifestation of the fundamental principle that both the governor and the governed are subject to the rule of law.[65] Its history has been one of reinterpretation,[66] and thus its importance lies not in the literal intent of the men at Runnymede but rather in the meaning that future generations have read into its words.[67] Over the centuries, Chapters 39 and 40 of King John's Charter and Chapter 29 of the Magna Carta of 1225 have evolved into two of the most dominant themes in Anglo-American jurisprudence—the principles of due process of law[68] and the universal guarantee of equal justice for all.[69]

KING JOHN
IN HISTORY AND MEMORY

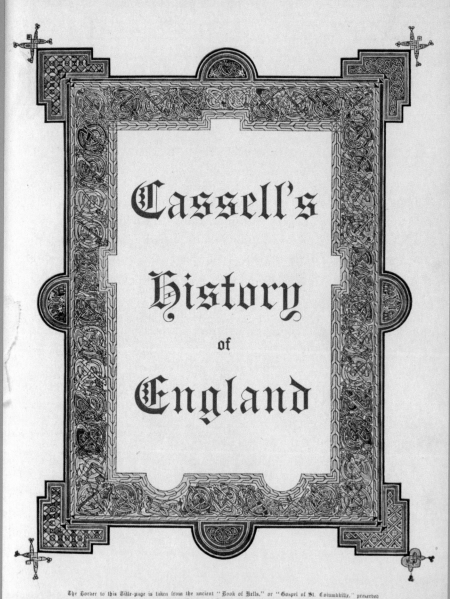

Cassell's

History

of

England

The Border to this Title-page is taken from the ancient "Book of Kells," or "Gospel of St. Coiumbkille," preserved
in the Library of Trinity College, Dublin.

MAGNA CARTA AND RELIGION FOR THE HONOR OF GOD AND THE REFORM OF OUR REALM

Robin Griffith-Jones

Master of the Temple at the Temple Church, London[1]

The Temple in London is today an oasis of calm between two of the city's major thoroughfares. Courtyards, gardens, fountains and ancient buildings evoke an earlier and less frenetic age. The Temple is the home of Inner and Middle Temple, two of England's four historic legal colleges, the Inns of Court. Every barrister—that is, almost every litigating attorney—in England and Wales is to this day a member of one of the Inns. The Temple houses the chambers or offices of some four thousand barristers and their staff. The Royal Courts of Justice are just yards to the west, across the Strand; the Central Criminal Court of the Old Bailey is less than a mile to the east, towards St Paul's Cathedral; the Supreme Court is twenty minutes' walk away along the bank of the Thames. The Temple is at the heart of legal London; and at its centre stands the Temple Church. The Church is a collegiate chapel within the Church of England, owned, financed, and run by these two Inns of Court. The land of the Temple was granted to the Inns by James I in 1608 on condition that the Inns would accommodate and educate those studying and working in the law; and that they would maintain the Temple Church for the celebration of divine service. They have done so, ever since. The Church itself, however, predates the Inns by centuries; its western end, the Round Church, was already fifty years old when Magna Carta was sealed.

The Temple was one of King John's safe havens in the crisis of 1214–15. On 21 November 1214 he issued from the Temple the charter that granted freedom of cathedral and conventual elections; it was reissued, again from the Temple, on 15 January 1215. This developed into Magna Carta's opening clause, on the freedom of the English church. On that visit early in 1215 the

Cassell's History of England, Volume 1. London: Cassell, 1903. General Collections, Library of Congress

King was confronted by a delegation of barons who demanded for the first time that the King declare his own fealty to a charter. The King was to be subject to a written law, in the terms of his own prior oaths but imposed and sustained by his own subjects. This demand took shape as Magna Carta's Security Clause. In May 1215 he was back, and issued from the Temple the charter granting free mayoral elections to the City of London. (There was one condition: new Lord Mayors must present themselves to the Sovereign's Chief Justice. This is still the function of the annual Lord Mayor's Show, the Mayor's procession from Mansion House to the Royal Courts of Justice.) In the Temple Church itself, three of Magna Carta's protagonists were buried, two with effigies that lie there still. This is the only surviving building that played a part in the Charter's creation; and its setting is still, eight hundred years later, at the centre of England's legal and constitutional life. This is a powerfully symbolic building, where history, topography, and the ongoing life of the Common Law world converge. It is aptly famous as the mother-church of the Common Law.

Magna Carta can be read as a historical, constitutional, or legal document. But it was first and foremost a *religious* document.[2] The King sealed the Charter of 1215 'from reverence for God and for the salvation of our soul and those of all our ancestors and heirs, for the honour of God and the exaltation of Holy Church and the reform of our realm'. His advisors included two archbishops, seven bishops, and Aymeric de Saint Maur, Master of the Temple. Archbishop Stephen Langton was resolute in the promotion of the Church's interests, most conspicuously in clause 1 itself:

> In the first place we [the King] have granted to God, and by this our present charter confirmed for us and our heirs forever that the English Church shall be free, and shall have her rights entire, and her liberties inviolate. [3]

This guarantee to the Church was made to God, and so was inviolable. It was made freely and by a promise undertaken before the dispute between John and the barons, and so was conscionable. And it was commended to the king's heirs, and so was (designed to be) irrevocable. This clause had surely been formulated by or for Archbishop Langton himself.

The liberty of the 'holy Church of God' had been guaranteed by the Coronation Charter of Henry I (1100). It had become an issue of burning importance since the Constitutions of Clarendon (1164), when Henry II sought to recover what he claimed had been the customs of his ancestors. He demanded that the bishops put their seal to the Constitution's sixteen chapters. Some of these en-

The Temple Church, London

croached directly on the Church's freedom, and were condemned by the pope as contrary to her canons and liberty: the King would have significant control over the foreign travel of bishops, over the excommunication of the King's ministers and tenants in chief, and over episcopal and abbatial elections.[4] At one clause in particular, on the trial of clergy ('criminous clerks'), the clash between Henry and Archbishop Thomas Becket was irresoluble and bitter. Justice, ecclesiastical law and the Church's freedom: these were linked and recurring themes in Becket's correspondence with the pope. Moments before the knights drove their swords drove into his head, Becket told his murderers, 'I am prepared to die for my Lord, so that in my blood the Church may find liberty and peace.'[5] No wonder his successor, Stephen Langton, who revered and modelled himself on Becket, ensured as a condition of his own return from exile that the English Church would be allowed its ancient liberties. We have heard of the Charters issued here at the Temple promising to the Church free elections. John had Henry I's charter in front of him, with its promise of a free Church, when he added his own concessions to the 'Unknown Charter'.[6] It is only striking that the Church's freedom is not mentioned in the Articles of the Barons, probably sealed by the King just days before Magna Carta itself.[7] Langton must have stepped in, at the last moment, to ensure its inclusion. The character and extent of such freedom, as intended and as realised in 1215, remains open to question. The disputes of the previous fifty years—over episcopal elections free from royal interference, special privileges for the clergy, and the areas of life to be left to the judgment of the Church—were being settled in the Church's favour.[8]

In the crisis of 1214–15, however, Langton saw far more at stake than the Church's own independence. The Archbishop returned from exile in summer 1213, aadmonished by the pope to do all he could to secure the safety and peace of the king and the realm.[9] At Winchester on 20 July he absolved the King from his excommunication, in return for the King's renewal of (some form of) his coronation oath; John swore to abolish evil laws, establish good laws, judge all his subjects by the just sentences of his courts, and render every man his rights. The King was now openly bound by the terms of an oath to which the recalcitrant barons could quite properly appeal. Langton had extracted the oath, and it was natural for any malcontents to turn to Langton for support.[10] On 25 August, according to Roger of Wendover, the day on which Langton preached to the people at St Paul's Cathedral and relaxed the rigor of the interdict, he produced a copy of Henry I's Coronation Charter before the barons gathered there and had it read in their midst. The barons swore to defend the liberties that Henry I had granted, Langton vowed to support them.[11]

In September John threatened a punitive expedition against his northern opponents; Langton invoked those recent oaths to insist, on pain of renewed sanctions, that the King proceed against them only by judgment.[12] Langton was yielding nothing; the pope had good reason to recall later that opposition to the King had broken out on Langton's return from exile.[13]

By 1214 King John was faced with a coordinated demand for the confirmation of the laws of Edward the Confessor and that Charter of Henry I. He resorted by 6 January 1215 to the safety of London's Temple. Here a delegation of barons, armed and ready for war, encountered him. They demanded the confirmation of the oath taken at Winchester in 1213. Rebellion was not unusual, but there was in 1215 no obvious rival to claim or to place on the English throne. The barons were rallying instead round a charter, a set of written, practical demands raised to the level of principle. The King saw the threat to his own power. Such a charter would be a rival centre of allegiance and of sovereignty. He demanded that the barons swear fealty to himself, renounce any charter and undertake in writing never to seek such liberties again. The barons gave him warning: they pledged themselves to sustain the house of the Lord and stand fast for the liberty of the church and the realm. The King sought refuge in delay. The course was set by both sides that would lead them, six months later, to Runnymede.

Langton remained loyal to the beleaguered king; but urged him to meet the barons' demands for a charter of rights and liberties. He was mediating, in a time of deepening turmoil. It remains unclear how much leadership he was providing for the barons, and indeed how much of the Great Charter's wording was due to him or to his influence. His role was central to the drama, and extraordinarily delicate. It is time to do justice to the principles underlying his actions. He had been perhaps the most prestigious of all lecturers on the Old Testament in Paris. John Baldwin has shown in a series of articles how important to Langton were the story and covenant of Deuteronomy.[14] Generating and shaping the Charter itself was Langton's desire to create a biblical, covenantal kingship in England; and this needed a new law, a new Deuteronomy for England. At the selection of Saul as king, 'Samuel declared to the people the law of the kingdom and wrote it in a book and deposited it in the presence of the Lord' (I Sam. 10.25).[15] The law, argued Langton, was written down to prevent the king from demanding more power than had been agreed. Deuteronomy 17.18–20 prescribes the duties of the king: 'After he has sat down on the throne of his kingdom he will write out for himself the Deuteronomy of this law in a book, taking an exemplar from the priests of the levitical tribe; and he will have it with him and will read it all the days of his life so that he might learn to fear the Lord his God and observe his words and ceremonies which are written in the law and so that his heart may not be raised into pride over his brothers nor veer to the right or to the left' (Deut. 17.18–10). Centuries later under King Josiah the book of the law was rediscovered in the Temple in Jerusalem; the king read it and was warned by the prophetess Huldah of the destruction threatening his kingdom. Josiah pledged loyalty to the book of the law, and secured a similar pledge from all his subjects (2 Kings 22, 2 Chronicles 34). Langton in his commentary on Chronicles drew attention to Josiah who rent his garments on reading the book of Deuteronomy; Langton contrasts him with modern princes who only rarely hear the word of God preached.[16] The Archbishop surely had this discovery of the law in mind, when he produced the Coronation Charter of Henry I in St Paul's in August 2013.

All this is general. Just as telling is the likely influence of Langton's circle on the details of Magna Carta. Richard Helmholz has found, in several clauses that seem alien to feudal law, close parallels in canon law. This may reflect no more than the predispositions of some canonists among the Charter's draughtsmen.[17] But Langton had good reason in principle to promote the Church's law. The freedom of the Church (Magna Carta, clause 1) had unsurprisingly become a refrain of canon law; so were the rights of widows (clauses 7, 8; James 1.27) and the proportionality of punishment (clause 20). The principle that the King should take counsel (clause 12) was a commonplace; particularly prominent, however, were demands in canonical texts that churches, popes, bishops, and elections be guided 'by the [common] counsel' of the priesthood and brethren, and that proper deliberative procedures be followed (clause 14). The guarantee that justice would not be sold (clause 40) is foundational but prime facie baffling, since litigation had never been cost-free; the canonists help us to see its sense, in their persistent demand that judges take no gift for their judgment.[18]

Langton in exile and canon law: these broaden our horizons, far beyond England itself and into Continental Europe. Sir James Holt and Richard Helmholz have both emphasised the spread of charters in Europe. Helmholz shows how Magna Carta stands alongside the Hungarian *Golden Bull* (1222) and Frederick II's *Constitutions of Melfi* (1231) for the kingdom of Sicily, and—from later in the century—the French *Établissements de Saint Louis*, the Spanish *Fuero real* and Alfonso X's *Siete Partidas* in Castile. The *Constitutions of Melfi* (in the *Liber Augustalis*) contained titles for protection of the church's interests, guarantees of trial by peers, promises of learned and upright judges, and provisions to guarantee honest weights and measures. (It also gives permission for criminal defendants to be represented by lawyers, an advance in civil rights not reached in England for many centuries.)[19] In the *Golden Bull,* Andrew II committed himself and his successors to hold a court at a fixed time and place every year, not to seize any noble nor destroy him out of favour to any powerful person unless he shall first have been summoned and convicted according to law, to confer no offices on foreigners who come into the kingdom 'without the consent of the council, to degrade, dismiss and require restitution from any lord-lieutenant who shall not conduct himself in accordance with the dignity of his office or who shall despoil the people under his authority' . The *Golden Bull* ends: 'We also ordain that if we or any of our successors shall at any time contravene the terms of this statute, the bishops and the higher and lower nobles of our realm, one and all, both present and future, shall by virtue thereof have the uncontrolled right in perpetuity of resistance both by word and deed without thereby incurring any charge of treason'.[20] Magna Carta was part of a larger movement towards the definition of rulers' rights and duties. So it can become, in modern retrospect, less exceptional but still more important. Here is a plant characteristic of Europe's thirteenth century that, unlike any others, has grown into a tree providing shade for a large part of the world's population in the twenty-first.

Looking back on this whole movement, today's churches have good reason to take pride in the Church's own role.[21] It has long been recognised that a 'papal revolution' in the twelfth and thirteenth centuries transformed the governance—increasingly centralised, sophisticated, and *codified*—of both church and state. 'The church borrowed secular ideas just as the state borrowed ecclesiastical ones; the church had to become half a state before the state could become half a church. Moreover, some of the secular ideas that the church assimilated were not taken over from the contemporary medieval world but from ancient classical civilization. . . . For the twelfth century these "areas of interaction" can best be studied in the works of the church lawyers. . . . Their work as teachers, prelates, administrators touched the life of their world at many points; and, as Maitland wrote, "in no other age since the classical days of Roman law had so large a part of the sum total of intellectual endeavour been devoted to jurisprudence."'[22] Langton's predecessor at Canterbury, Hubert Walter (Archbishop, 1193–1205), gives some indication of such roles. He is viewed as one of the great administrators in England's history. He was Chief Justiciar (1193–98) and Lord Chancellor (1199–1205), established new systems of local justice, was ably served by a team of canon lawyers, and may have had a part in the production of the treatise on English law known under his uncle's name, *Glanvill*. Matthew Paris tells of his sermon at John's coronation, 27 May 1199: it was the last time that a king was reminded on such a day that he became king not be heredity but, like Saul and David, by election.[23] Larry Siedentop has recently made the strongest of claims for the wider role of the Church in the search for her own liberty.[24] The Gregorian Church-reformers of the eleventh and twelfth centuries were seeking the Church's autonomy from a weakening empire; such liberty would be the essential counterpart of that equal Christian liberty of individuals which had been conceived and expounded by the Church fathers. This Christian liberty stood in stark contrast to the inexorable hierarchies in the pagan world of creation, nature, and society. Such equality, Siedentop argues, directly gave rise to the notion of equal subjection under law. Objective right was now joined in the legal thought by subjective rights. (We might remind ourselves that the vast structure of canon law expounded in Gratian's *Decretum* is built on his opening statement of the Golden Rule, Do unto others as you would have them do unto you.) In this perspective Magna Carta is one outstanding moment, the fruit of England's particular and tumultuous areas of interaction, in a vast progression of specifically Christian thought and life throughout Europe. We are all its heirs.

We do not need, then, to make any exaggerated claim that Archbishop Langton was the first to link these areas or alone, in 1214–15, in deepening them. On the contrary. Lord Judge has written forcefully of life in the thirteenth century as fundamentally informed by Christian convictions, hopes, and fears.[25] Principles of polity, justice, and due process had for centuries been drawn from scripture and reiterated by churchmen with all the political and supra-mundane authority at their command. The theme takes us beyond churchmen themselves. The barons who confronted John in the Temple in January 1215 declared (if Walter of Coventry is to be trusted) that they were putting themselves in opposition to him 'as a wall for the house of the Lord' and were standing for the liberty of the church and the realm. They were recalling Ezekiel's false prophets who cried 'Peace' when there was no peace, who put up no wall for the house of Israel nor stood in battle on the day of the Lord (Ezek. 13.5). Robert fitz Walter , a leader of the baronial opposition to John, hereditary castellain of the City of London and one of the Charter's Surety Barons, was by May 1215 styling himself Marshal of the Army of God and Holy Church. Confederation round the demand for a charter—an impersonal, bloodless focus of loyalty focused on no human king—may itself have drawn strength from those loyalties to ideas and ideals which informed the Crusades. Langton's was just one voice within one—exceptionally anti-monarchical—tradition within the theology and politics of Christian Europe. Our claim for Langton can be proportionate and qualified, and can still be a source of inspiration.

We look back on the Charter as a moment of—fragile but long-term—triumph. It is easy to forget how revolutionary it was, to have imposed such restraints upon a king. The Pope was, in his own terms, right: the barons had constituted themselves both judges and executors of the judgment in their own suit against the King, and had (drastically) impaired his royal rights and dignity. Verses in the thirteenth-century *Melrose Chronicle* lament both the King's tyranny and its consequences; the disease had been fatal, its cure almost unimaginable.

> England has sanctioned a topsy-turvy order.
> It is astonishing, even in the telling; who has heard of such a thing?
> For the body has aspired to be preeminent over the head;
> The people have sought to rule their king!
> But the cause was complex, that brought this about.
> The King corrupted the best customs of the realm,
> Its rights and laws which he subverted. He did not govern rightly.
> Whatever gave him greatest pleasure he believed to be the greatest law.[26]

Magna Carta, 1215–2015

This is an inspiring but an ancient story. As we celebrate the Charter and its principles, we should certainly acknowledge the centrality of the Church, its Archbishop and the biblical principles which informed and animated his

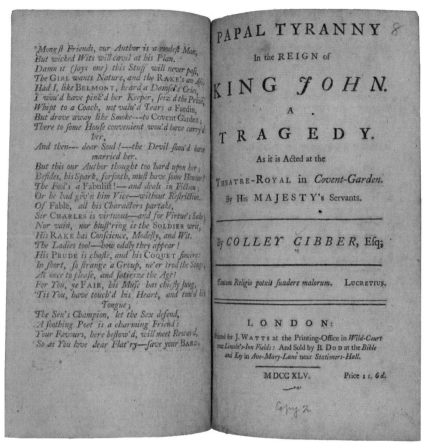

Colley Cibber (1671–1757). *Papal Tyranny in the Reign of King John.*
A Tragedy. London: J. Watts, 1745. Rare Book and Special Collections
Division, Library of Congress

contribution. But the thirteenth-century universal Church under papal control is as alien to us now as medieval kingship and baronage. Langton secured for his English Church extensive privileges of jurisdiction; most of us will be relieved that these privileges have been lost. Magna Carta's opening clause is still in force as English law; but equality before and under the law has trumped the Church's ancient claims, and the courts are ever less sympathetic to the exemptions and opt-outs that survive.

This trajectory has, however, a curious consequence. Other chapters in this book speak eloquently of such equality before the law, of representation before taxation and of restraints upon the executive. In each case, the route from 1215 to the present day may well be circuitous; our fundamental understanding of the state, the individual, rights, and laws has evolved over the centuries beyond all easy recognition. But we can nonetheless trace that route from those guarantees of 1215 to their constitutional and legal expression today. We can speak without artifice or strain of the Charter as a foundation on which our present polities are built.

Today's churches and religion, by contrast, are isolated from their medieval role by unbridgeable gulfs. The secularism of the United Kingdom and Continental Europe has marginalised the churches. Freedom of religion in the United States has since the eighteenth century programmatically disestablished religion from the state. Langton sought freedom of the Church from the crown's control; our age expects the legislature, executive, and courts to be free in their decisions from any imagined contamination by religion. 'In King John's day', wrote Arthur Sullivan at the Charter's 750th anniversary, 'and for centuries after him, the problem of relation between lay ruler and Church was how governing power should be shared between them. Somehow it has come about that in our time a problem of government is the means for excluding from all religious influence whatever from the business of governing'.[27] The news that reaches the West of the theocentric political and legal systems of Islam tends (whether justly or not) to reinforce the West's commitment to representative, constitutional governance in which all residents are free and equal before and under the law, and the conviction that the only real prospect of such governance lies, in practice, in the life of a secular, democratic polity.

I am writing in England. All our faith-communities and their leaders are expected by Government and the media to promote civil harmony, cohesion, and good-will. But the law does not acknowledge any text or doctrine of any religion to be the basis of our polity. Historians may point to the influence of Judaeo-Christian teaching (asserting equality and dignity before God) on modern human-rights principles (asserting equality and dignity before the law); but that ancestry carries no weight in law or litigation. The custodians of ancient traditions and principles that have for centuries undergirded our polity do not earn respect or attention through that wardship alone; and the conservatism natural to religious institutions and their role can more readily stir the derision or anger of a present age that readily sees in them a recalcitrant, unregulated home of prejudice and malpractice.

In 2012 the Prime Minister, David Cameron, embarrassed himself on an American talk show by being unable to translate the term 'Magna Carta'.[28] By April 2014 he was calling for Magna Carta to be taught in every school. He particularly wanted children in Muslim faith schools to be taught expressly about Magna Carta and the place of its intrinsic values at the core of modern Britishness.[29] He was responding to the reports that Muslim children in some schools are the object of moves—or even of a coordinated 'Trojan Horse' conspiracy—by Islamic fundamentalists to indoctrinate and isolate these children through their schooling. It was surely no coincidence that in the same month, just before Easter 2014, the Prime Minister was reaffirming the centrality of Christianity to Britishness in a church newspaper.[30] Here in microcosm is the dichotomy from which we cannot escape. The Charter is a convoluted, practical document of the distant, specifically Christian past; it is also part of our febrile, contested present. It is an icon of the benefits inherited from that past by all citizens in the multinational, multicultural, inter-religious Common Law world; but readily becomes a slogan of partisan national politics.

Within days of the Prime Minister's article, Lord Williams, until 2013 the Archbishop of Canterbury, was invited to respond in an interview for the (right-leaning) *Sunday Telegraph*. Lord Williams spoke judiciously and with characteristic care of post-Christian Britain, in which the cultural memory and presence is still 'quite strongly Christian'.[31] Recent surveys by Baroness Hale of the UK Supreme Court and by Lord Justice Etherton of the Court of Appeal[32] have told of the inexorable dissolution of the special consideration historically enjoyed by Christians and in particular by the Church of England. We have moved a long way since Sir Matthew Hale famously declared in 1676:

> . . . to say religion is a cheat is to dissolve all those obligations whereby the civil societies are preserved, and Christianity is a parcel of the laws of England: therefore to reproach the Christian religion is to speak in subversion of the law.[33]

The Church of England still, however, by bishops' places in the House of Lords, has a presence in the legislature. The Church can claim that such bishops represent the concerns of all Christians or of all faith-communities or indeed of all those whose quiet concern for the nation's fundamental standards needs a voice in Parliament. It is not always clear by what right these unelected leaders of a particular religion speak for so many citizens who do not share that religion and who indeed by their own account espouse no religion at all. In the debate in the House of Lords on the Assisted Dying Bill, 18 July 2014, the Archbishop of York said:

> The present Bill is not about relieving pain or suffering. . . . The Bill is about asserting a philosophy, which not only Christians but also other thoughtful people of good will who have had experience in care for the dying must find incredible—that is, the ancient Stoic philosophy that ending one's life in

circumstances of distress is an assertion of human freedom. That it cannot be. Human freedom is won only by becoming reconciled with the need to die, and by affirming the human relations we have with other people. Accepting the approach of death is not the attitude of passivity that we may think it to be. Dying well is the positive achievement of a task that belongs with our humanity. It is unlike all other tasks given to us in life, but it expresses the value that we set on life as no other approach to death can do.[34]

The ancient Stoics are admired in some of the finest modern moral philosophy;[35] and it is an open question now whether a modern Stoicism is growing in strength. At issue in such Stoic discipline is not a shallow or ill-informed evasion of human life and dignity, but a modern version of an anthropology as ancient and arguably as deep at Christendom's. The Bill concerned as deep and painful a question as any confronted by Parliament in many years. In such consultation, who speaks for whom? What role is justifiably played by the leaders of which faith-communities, and in the name of what community or higher law?

If Christianity's role in our polity is being diluted, where do other religions stand?[36] It was Lord Williams, as Archbishop of Canterbury, who raised this question to prominence in the lecture that in 2008 he delivered for the Temple Church on sharia law. As we look back with respect on the Church's role in Magna Carta, we do well to acknowledge how Muslim jurists are struck by the West's secularization of law and its administration. Such deracination of the law is quite alien to Islam. There is in consequence a danger of real misunderstanding between the jurists of two great legal systems; Western and Islamic tribunals are approaching the same problems from drastically different viewpoints. Classical Islamic constitutionalism confronted a basic question: who was qualified—and by what character of learning and insight—to understand, expound, and legislate for God's will? Creation belongs to the God who made it; God therefore is the sole legislator, and it is with him and him alone that sovereignty lies. The sharia is the temporal and spatial expression of God's law and will, which stands above all else, especially above all political structures and any form of political organization. Authority is invested in the judges qualified to expound God's will. This does not yet address the question to which any Westerner will turn: What are the checks and balances that will prevent abuse of such fundamental authority? But it reminds us that 'law' in the West and in classical Islam may be denoting two quite different constructions with quite different premises and roles. An English court cannot (and should not) attempt to answer the question asked by one petitioner who rang an Islamic tribunal to ask for a simple way of getting to paradise.[37]

The danger of misunderstanding extends beyond England's domestic courts. Among the judgments of the European Court of Human Rights (ECtHR), two stand out. In *Refah* the Grand Chamber declared Sharia to be incompatible with democratic pluralism, the constant evolution of public freedoms or the values of the European Convention on Human Rights with regard to criminal law and procedure. In *Lautsi* the Grand Chamber accepted the argument that only Christianity, thanks to the priority of love over faith, overcomes the 'logical mechanism of exclusion of the unbeliever inherent in any religious conviction'. The judgment in *Lautsi* impugns by implication the administration of justice itself in Islam as incapable of offering equal dignity to all litigants of all religious and cultural backgrounds. At issue here are not the particular circumstances of each case, but the Court's understanding of the deepest principles of justice in Islam. To a Muslim, the ECtHR may seem to be denying justice to Muslims in the name of justice itself.[38]

And what, conversely, can religions and their leaders offer to our public life? Lord Dyson, Master of the Rolls, suggests that the equality of all religions under the state's secular law is the best guarantee, in a secular society, of equal freedom for each religion and its adherents.[39] Faith-communities, with little leverage in Parliament, may pragmatically accept this. (It has perhaps become easier for Church leaders to extol humility as the Church's own position has weakened.) But faith-leaders are expected to promote such equality under the law not concessively or opportunistically but as a fundamental and indispensable social good; and this can be a 'tone' far harder for leaders to maintain with integrity and confidence.[40] Leaders convinced of their religion's God-given fidelity to God's own will are likely to chafe under legal systems that are sustained without reference to God. Garth Fowden has recently argued that law, Judaism, Christianity, and Islam are all 'exegetical cultures'. But in an England without a written constitution, the jurists' foundational texts, including Magna Carta, are unambiguously manmade and subject (not just to exegesis but) to the decisions of Parliament; and the courts can urge Parliament to re-assess and change the law. These emendable statutes are not sacred texts to our polity as sacred scriptures are to our religions. The American readers of this book will be far better equipped than I am to describe the standing of the Constitution. It is often remarked that Americans are more deeply engaged than the English with Magna Carta; America has, ever since Massachusetts 'framed a body of grounds of law, in resemblance to a Magna Carta, which should be received for fundamental laws', perhaps given greater weight than England to constitutional documents.[41]

As society, religion, and law have changed; so has their use of the Charter. There is, then, no prescription to be offered for the future. Society, religion and law will continue to change; so will the deployment of the Charter's principles. Archbishop Langton's role, however, lit one inextinguishable torch, handed on from generation through generation to our own: the axiom that the Church is committed to the principled and active betterment of society as a whole. Siedentop urges us to recover the history of Christendom's moral intuition that the individual subject, beloved by God and offered salvation in Christ, is the basic unit of human value and dignity. Modern praise of the Renaissance and the Enlightenment has blighted the twelfth and thirteenth centuries—and their Church—with a reputation for little more than feudal tyranny and theocratic ignorance. Their real achievement must be rediscovered and revalued. Only then can Christendom be given the respect it deserves in today's 'conversation of the world'.

As Sir James Holt demonstrated, Magna Carta helped to create a *society*:

> The men who were responsible for the Great Charter of 1215 asserted one great principle. In their view the realm was more than a geographic or administrative unit. It was a community. As such, it was capable of possessing rights and liberties . . . which could be asserted against any member of the community, even and especially against the King.[42]

And among those men, Archbishop Langton stands tall.

Church And State, 1215: Archbishop Langton And 'The Greatest Knight That Ever Lived'

Close ally of Stephen Langton and hero of the hour at Runnymede was William Marshal, Earl of Pembroke; as Regent he re-issued the Charter in 1216 and 1217 under his own seal and so ensured its survival. These reissues omitted the Security Clause; the Regent guaranteed by his own seal the conformity of the young King on his deathbed. William summoned Aymeric, Master of the Temple, to prepare for William's own admission to the Templars. William's almoner Geoffrey, a Templar, brought him the Templar cloak which had secretly been made for him a year before. William had arranged to be buried in front of the rood-screen in the Temple Church; Aymeric predeceased the sick Marshal by just a few days, having asked to be buried next to him. 'For I greatly loved his company on earth; may God grant that we be companions in the life eternal'. It is a measure of William's achievement that his cortege was led to the Temple Church by former rebels, now pacified. The Archbishop of Canterbury and the Bishop of London presided when William was laid to rest here on 20 May 1219. Archbishop Langton described him as 'the greatest knight that ever lived'.

William's effigy lies in the Temple Church to this day. William's heir, William Marshal 2nd Earl of Pembroke, was one of the twenty-five Surety Barons commissioned by the Security Clause at Runnymede to ensure the King's conformity to the Charter. In 1225 Henry III issued the Charter again, in the form in which it was eventually enrolled in England's statutes. The younger William Marshal married the sister of Henry III and was buried (1231) in the Temple Church; his effigy lies beside his father's. Ten years later the Templars rebuilt their Chancel, east of the Round, to be the funerary chapel of Henry III and his Queen. A Church built as a shrine to Jerusalem and the Crusades had within eighty tumultuous years become a shrine to the heroes of England's fragile constitutional settlement.

Langton's work in 1214–15 can be seen, in the short run, as a failure: the Charter was quickly annulled, the country lurched again into civil war. We may wonder, however, if the Langton who at St Paul's had produced the Coronation Charter of Henry I would, even in the darkest weeks of 1215–17, quite have admitted defeat. Magna Carta *had* been sealed; its instantiations were still there to be brought out, revised, reissued, and re-implemented. And thanks to William Marshal, they were. The Charter became the Coronation Charter of Henry III in 1216, was issued again in 1217, and again in 1225. In 1225 all doubts over the Charter's standing were laid to rest: the King sealed it 'of his own spontaneous and good will'. In place of the Security Clause the bishops issued, at the King's own instigation, an excommunication against anyone who broke the Charter's terms.[43]

Over and again in the thirteenth century the Charter was invoked as a counterweight to the king's demand for taxes: the king could levy tax if and when he confirmed the Charter. The meeting of the Great Council in 1237 that demanded this confirmation was described as a 'Parliament', the first such usage recorded in the language of England's constitution. The Charter, inextricably interwoven with the Church, was already more than a sequence of laws; it had become a settling element in England's unstable and ever-evolving balance of powers.

The bishops reissued the threat of excommunication in 1237 and 1253. The sentence of 1253 was pronounced in Westminster Hall by Archbishop Langton and thirteen bishops, with conspicuous ceremony. The sentence was then pronounced in every parish church of the country; in Lincoln and London priests visited county courts too to fulminate the anathema. The sentence was confirmed in 1254 by Pope Innocent IV, who commissioned the Dean of Lincoln to publish it. Bishops were to have it pronounced in every church of the country and in all public assemblies, in English and in French. So began the tradition of the Charter's reiteration, with the sentence of excommunication, in parish

William Marshal, 1st Earl of Pembroke (near side), and his eldest son
William Marshal, 2nd Earl of Pembroke (far side)

churches. There was, as ever, self-interest in the measure. In 1253 the bishops distinguished between the Church's (seemingly intrinsic) right, the Church's liberties and free customs contained in Magna Carta and the Charter of the Forest, and such liberties and customs granted to the earls, barons, knights, and other freeholders. The Church stood to gain significantly from the taxes legitimated by the Charter's confirmation. We can be grateful for the Church's role without being naïve.[44]

The Temple Church still stands at the centre of legal London. The effigies of William Marshal, father and son, still lie beside each other. The Chancel built here for Henry III is still one of the simple glories of London. We must work harder now, than churches had to in the past, to serve our community. We have honoured the Jewish lawyers persecuted under the Third Reich; among them were some young men who rose to the greatest heights in our judiciary and universities. We have gladly sustained many years' work on Islam and English law, to bridge some of the gulfs between Christendom and Islam that the Church itself was built to represent and deepen. Few places are now more closely linked than we are to Magna Carta, religion, and the history of the rule of law.[45] It is still to be seen what part shall be played by the churches at large and by this church in particular in the twenty-first century. It is for us to imagine and to realise the roles in our secular, democratic, and unsettled polity which all religions and their leaders have the moral mandate and the resources to fulfil. We have buildings and effigies before us. We have as well the example of Archbishop Langton, his deep biblical scholarship, his vision of a nation governed justly under God, and the resolutely courageous, careful work with which he sought to realise that vision in the turmoil of thirteenth-century England.

INTERPRETING
THE RULE OF LAW

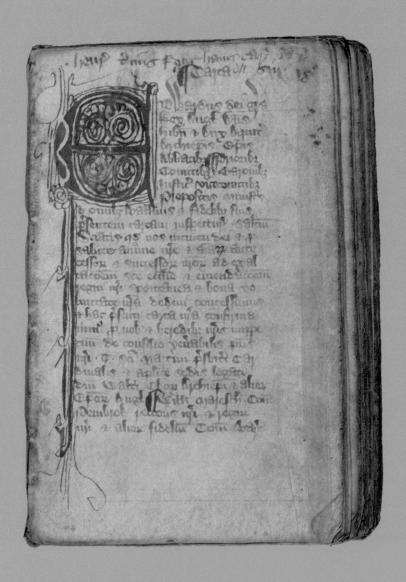

THE LEGAL FORCE AND EFFECT OF MAGNA CARTA

Sir John Baker

It is a tenet of legal and political discourse that Magna Carta is one of the world's great documents, worthy to be written in letters of gold, inscribed on the walls of law schools and courts, taught to all schoolchildren, and so forth. There is no doubt that it has had an immense influence on hearts and minds. Yet it is not always understood that this influence has been achieved more by magic than by operation of positive law. Whether it has been incorporated into law in the United States is for others to say. But the position in England is surprisingly murky. It is not altogether clear that it was ever a statute. Even if it was, no one is sure how much of it, if anything, is still in force. If it was not a statute, then surely it was at least a grant of liberties. But can such a grant have any legal effect without specific grantees? If it is assumed that it did take effect in some way, there is then the central question of what the words mean. Most of it was obsolete or obsolescent five hundred years ago, and what remained was difficult even for the lawyers of those days to comprehend. Moreover, no remedies were provided in case the words were not observed. The present essay is an exploration of these difficulties from a lawyer's point of view. It is not concerned with the struggles of 1215, or with the original intent, but with the legal questions which the wording posed for future generations, concentrating in particular on chapter 29.[1]

1. Was It A Statute?

The charter of 1215 was clearly never a statute. Not only was there nothing resembling Parliament at that time, but only a few weeks after it was sealed the charter was repudiated by King John, with the pope's blessing. The king, on good legal grounds, regarded it as void for duress, while the pope did not want kings giving away their absolute power and actually forbade John on pain of eternal anathema

Magna Charta cum Statutis Angliae [Miniature Magna Carta with the Statutes of England]. Bound manuscript on vellum, fourteenth century. Law Library, Library of Congress.

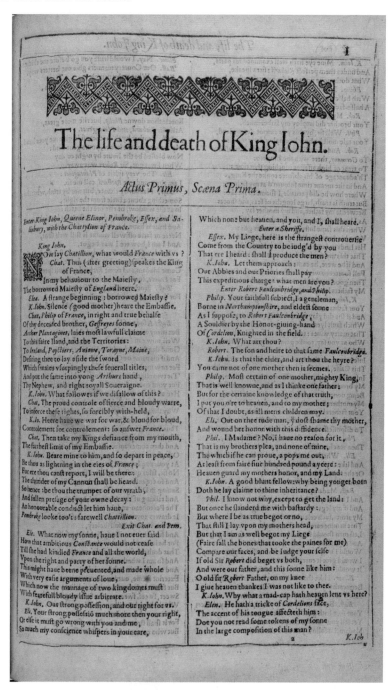

William Shakespeare. *The Life and Death of King John* in *Mr. William Shakespeare's Comedies. Histories, and Tragedies* (First Folio). London: Isaac Jaggard and Edward Blount, 1623. Rare Book and Special Collections Division, Library of Congress

to presume to observe it.[2] The importance of the 1215 document was not that it ever had any legal effect itself but that it inspired the extraction of modified versions from King Henry III and King Edward I. For many centuries Magna Carta was commonly understood to be the charter which Henry III granted in 1225 and which Edward I and subsequent kings confirmed. The despicable King John could hardly be given credit for something which had turned out so well, particularly since he was against the very idea of it. When Shakespeare wrote a play about King John—first published in 1623—he did not see fit to mention the episode at Runnymede at all.

There are also difficulties in the way of treating the 1225 charter as a statute. There was still not a Parliament as historians see it. And the king was a minor at the time, age seventeen. Those were not, however, problems which troubled lawyers very much in the past. Many things were done in the name of infant kings. If explanation were needed, the early-modern solution was to say that the king had two bodies, and in his 'politique capacity' (as Coke put it) he was deemed always to be of full age. And the charter seemed on its face to have been more than a unilateral act by the king alone. The expressed consideration for it was a fifteenth granted to the king by the bishops, abbots, priors, barons, knights, freeholders, 'and all those of our realm' (*et omnes de regno nostro*), comprehensive words which seemed in the past, and with some justice, to imply a major assembly in which everyone in the realm was somehow represented. At any rate, it was close enough to the concept of parliamentary legislation for it to be received, as a matter of law, as the first statute in the notional 'statute-book'. What is more, the charter was confirmed many times by undoubted parliaments, beginning with that held at Marlborough in 1267, and that would have given it statutory force anyway. Oddly enough, however, it is the royal confirmation of 1297 which is now treated as the official version of the few parts that remain, although that instrument makes no mention of Parliament. It is in the usual form of an *inspeximus* charter, setting out a transcript of the 1225 text, and concluding with words of grant, confirmation, and renewal, 'willing and granting for our self and our heirs that the aforesaid charter shall be firmly and inviolably observed in all its articles for ever'. The king himself was at Ghent, in Flanders, when the charter was sealed on the authority of his regency council, possibly against his wishes, and witnessed by his thirteen-year-old son Prince Edward. Although the regency council had summoned a parliament to discuss the reissue of the charter, there is no indication in the charter itself or in any other record that it was an act of Parliament. Its primacy as a text presumably resulted from its being the first version of Magna Carta to be enrolled in Chancery. And that seems to have misled some

Victorian lawyers, who were usually very punctilious about matters of history. The Statute Law Committee, which in 1870 produced the first edition of the chronological table of statutes, showing whether they were in force or repealed, considered the Statute of Merton 1235 to be the first act of Parliament and therefore omitted the 1225 charter from the table. The decision was not explained and is difficult to understand, given six centuries of previous legal tradition. Probably it was based on current thinking about the origins of Parliament. But the assembly at Merton in 1235 was just as remote from the present Parliament as that which negotiated the confirmation of Magna Carta in 1225. To treat these ancient meetings as being organically connected to the Parliament which still continues to possess legislative sovereignty in the United Kingdom is, on any view, a whopping legal fiction. But it is the fiction upon which sovereignty of Parliament rests. The Statute of Treasons 1350, which (though written in French) still governs the most serious of criminal offences, is no less a statute because the parliaments of Edward III look very unlike those of Elizabeth II.

The piecemeal repeal by Parliament of various parts of the 1297 *inspeximus* has seemingly left three chapters in force (1, 9, and 29); even the opening words of grant in the 1297 charter have been repealed, though the words of confirmation and renewal at the end have been retained as 'chapter' 37. The 1225 charter, on the other hand, has escaped repeal and may still arguably be a complete statute. But the conundrum is of little consequence, since the chapters which have supposedly been repealed—over ninety per cent of the text—had already been rendered obsolete by implied repeal, and implied repeals must by their nature extend to each and every statutory version. The charter lives on so vigorously in the imagination that no one is really interested in the question whether or not it is still in force.

2. Was It Effective As A Grant?

The 1225 charter was granted to the archbishops, bishops, abbots, priors, earls, barons, 'and everyone of our realm of England, in perpetuity'. At the end were the words 'We have also granted to the same, on behalf of our self and our heirs, that neither we nor our heirs will seek to do anything whereby the liberties contained in this charter would be infringed or weakened, and if anything of the kind is attempted it shall be taken as null and void'. The language was similar to that used in granting franchises to corporations or individuals. But could a grant of liberties enure, as a matter of property law, to all of the people? The strict legal answer would have to be no. Many of the provisions of the charter were not liberties, or even analogous to liberties, as understood in the law of property. Some even took away previous rights. And a grant could not be made to a fluctuating body unless it was first incorporated. In the thirteenth century the law of corporations was in its infancy and this problem would not have been understood. In the two succeeding centuries it became clear that if the king granted liberties to the inhabitants of a place, they would be impliedly incorporated for the purpose of taking the grant. No one, however, ever suggested that all the people of England were a corporation capable of suing for their liberties and being sued. The matter was not even discussed by the readers on Magna Carta in the inns of court.[3] A similar point was made, however, in the readings on chapter 1 (*Concessimus Deo*), which granted liberties to God and the English Church.[4] Those who glossed these words accepted that they were a formula current in the thirteenth century but questioned their legal efficacy. God was certainly not a corporation, and it was plainly absurd for creatures to grant anything to their creator. More to the point, the English Church was not a corporation either, any more than the universal Church was, and therefore it could not own property (such as a liberty) or appear as a litigant in the courts. A grant of liberties to all the people of England was therefore an exercise in rhetoric rather than a meaningful piece of conveyancing. The learned men of the inns of court accordingly treated the charter, not as a constitutional document, but as a statute like any other, confirming or clarifying numerous particular rules of law.

3. What Does It Mean?

Even in medieval times Magna Carta was not easy to interpret. Parliament was sometimes asked to explain it,[5] usually without result, while the law schools tied themselves in knots exploring its intricacies. The three chapters considered still to be on the statute book are among the most problematic. Perhaps, indeed, they survived extinction precisely because they have no very clear meaning. Chapter 1 granted that the English Church (*ecclesia anglicana*) should be free and should retain its liberties inviolate. Given that the Church was not a corporation, it was deduced by legal commentators that this grant must have been intended to apply to individual churches, including religious houses, and to clergymen, and was perhaps chiefly about benefit of clergy—the exclusion of clerks in Holy Orders from secular criminal justice in respect of murder and felony. That was not too far-fetched, since the Becket affair was not so long in the past. Benefit of clergy, extended by fiction in the following two centuries to laymen, became built into the system of criminal justice and even reached the New World, but it became an absurdity and was abolished centuries ago. It was, in any case, common law and needed no statutory confirmation, especially such an obscure one, for purely legal purposes. Whatever chapter 1 meant in the thirteenth century, if it is thought to have retained any meaning which might justify its retention today, it has to be reinterpreted anachronistically to confirm the status of the Church of England, finally liberated in the 1530s from interference by foreign potentates. But whether it really means that is a matter of no legal consequence, since the constitution of the Church of England rests on immemorial custom, royal prerogative, and later acts of Parliament, not on Magna Carta.

Chapter 9 confirmed the liberties and free customs of the city of London, and likewise of other cities, towns, and ports. A few of those liberties have survived, such as market rights, and the unique constitution of the city of London (as distinct from Greater London), which is proudly preserved. Most have been overtaken by law reforms. The latest immemorial London custom to disappear was that every shop in the city was a market for the purposes of the law of market overt, meaning that if goods were sold openly the buyer would acquire good title whether or not the seller had any title to sell. This custom inevitably ended with the abolition of market overt in 1994, and so there was no need to abrogate the custom itself. Most civic and municipal customs have similarly disappeared as an indirect result of general changes in the law of the land, though there is no question but that Parliament could abolish them specifically if it so desired. What, then, was the legal effect of confirming such customs in Magna Carta? The courts took the view in the fifteenth century that the charter only confirmed lawful liberties, and therefore an alleged liberty or custom of London was not immune to challenge; if it was unreasonable it could not in law exist and could not therefore have been confirmed. On the other hand, reasonable immemorial local customs and privileges were perfectly good in law without royal or statutory confirmation and could only be abrogated by act of Parliament. This was as true of the customs of the manor of Piddletrenthide as of those of the city of London. Chapter 9, therefore, though jealously guarded by generations of lord mayors and aldermen, has been meaningless for at least five centuries.

The most important of the three surviving provisions is chapter 29 (*Nullus liber homo*), which originated in clauses 39 and 40 of the 1215 charter:

No free man shall be taken or imprisoned, or disseised of any freehold, or of his liberties or free customs, or outlawed, or exiled, or in any way destroyed, nor shall we go upon him or put upon him, except by the lawful judgment of his peers (*per legale judicium parium suorum*) or (*vel*) by the law of the land (*per legem terrae*); to no one shall we sell, to no one deny or delay, right or justice.

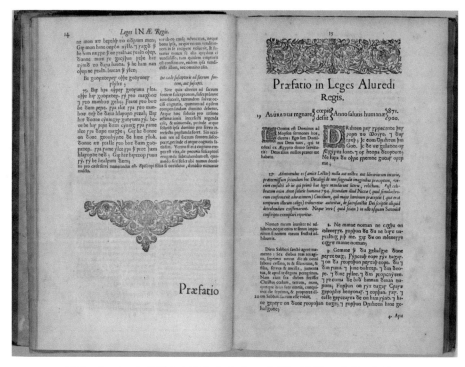

William Lambarde (1536–1601). *Archaionomia* [The Old Laws]. Cambridge: Roger Daniel, 1644. Law Library, Library of Congress

Anyone who reads these resounding words instinctively understands what they are about. And yet their legal meaning has caused much perplexity to lawyers since at least the fourteenth century. To whom did this chapter apply? It begins as a general prohibition in the passive voice—'No free man shall be taken …'—which would apply as well to a private imprisonment as to action by the king. But then it turns active and adopts the royal we—'Nor shall *we* go or put upon him …'. Was it therefore intended to make distinctions between private and governmental action? Such a conclusion seems to be ruled out by a provision at the very end of the charter that all the provisions to be observed by the king were to be observed by everyone in the realm, including the clergy, with respect to their own men (*erga suos*). This was not, however, a comprehensive solution. The words 'erga suos' presupposed a feudal relationship, the usual context for imprisoning and putting upon people. They meant, for instance, that the clergy were bound by the provisions as feudal lords, whereas the Church as an institution was not bound to observe due process in exercising its canon-law jurisdiction. The scope of chapter 29 was widened in 1354 by avoiding the royal 'we' and making the whole provision passive: 'no man … shall be put out from land or tenement or arrested, imprisoned or disinherited or put to death without being brought to answer by due process of law' (28 Edw. III, c. 3). This brought all inferior forms of authority under the same regime, whether or not the authority had been conferred directly by the king, and whether or not it was derived from lordship over men. But it was only in the seventeenth century that lawyers would stretch the clause to apply to the Church as well, on the grounds that the king was the temporal supreme head of the Church.

Another question as to the scope of chapter 29 arose from the words 'free man'. It was always clear that 'man' included women, but what about unfree men and women, the villeins? There must have been a doubt about this, because the statute of 1354 changed the wording to read 'no man, of whatever estate or condition he be'. The alteration may have reflected changed social conditions after the Black Death. But later medieval lawyers considered the alteration to have been unnecessary, except in the case of the king's villeins, because villeinage

Edward Coke (1552–1634). *The Second Part of the Institutes of the Lawes of England . . . .* London: Thomas Basset, 1681. Rare Book and Special Collections Division, Library of Congress

was relative; a man might be unfree against his own lord, but he was free against everyone else, including the king. On the other hand, lords could continue to imprison their own villeins: that was the law of the land. The great charter of liberties could not grant liberty to anyone who was unfree. It was not in the power of the king to do it. Indeed, in 1381 the Lords and Commons agreed with one voice to confirm the annulment of all charters of freedom granted by the crown to villeins during the Peasants' Revolt. Granting freedom to villeins was a disinheritance of their lords and therefore unlawful without their agreement, which agreement (they said) they would never give to their dying day.[6] This might seem to have been England's *Dred Scott* moment, but it was not. The objection was to taking away property by executive action, in a time of crisis, rather than by act of Parliament. As it turned out, the eventual ending of villeinage was not the work of Parliament either.

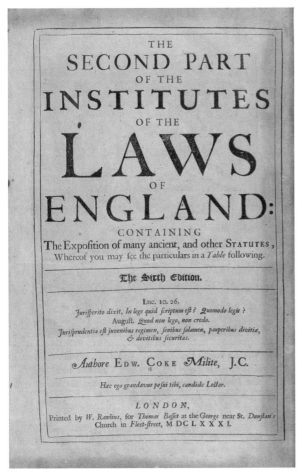

THE

SECOND PART

OF THE

INSTITUTES

OF THE

LAWS

OF

ENGLAND:

CONTAINING

The Expofition of many ancient, and other STATUTES, Whereof you may fee the particulars in a *Table* following.

The Sixth Edition.

Luc. 10. 26.
Jurifperito dixit, In lege quid fcriptum eft ? Quomodo legis ?
Auguft. *Quod non lego, non credo.*
Jurifprudentia eft juvenibus regimen, fenibus folamen, pauperibus divitiæ, & divitibus fecuritas.

Authore EDW. COKE *Milite*, J.C.

Hæc ego grandævus pofui tibi, candide Lector.

LONDON,
Printed by *W. Rawlins*, for *Thomas Baffet* at the *George* near St. *Dunftan's* Church in *Fleet-ftreet*, M DC L X X X I.

Far more difficulty arose from the phrase 'judgment of his peers'. In the seventeenth and eighteenth centuries this was often taken to mean trial by jury, an error which may have influenced the framers of the United States Constitution. But there was no trial by jury in 1215, in criminal cases, and until well into the seventeenth century the word 'peers' here was taken to mean temporal lords of Parliament. That opinion was still espoused by Coke, despite Lambarde's suggestion in 1581 that it meant trial by jury.[7] Earlier attempts to argue that commoners were entitled to a jury of their social equals, so that knights should be tried by knights, might be evidence that this interpretation was far from new,[8] but the idea had not taken root.[9] Yet the restriction to lords of Parliament would have led to impossible difficulty if *vel* was construed conjunctively, as some modern historians have forcefully contended. Unless the whole chapter applied only to peers of the realm, which was negated by the words 'no free man', the phrase 'by the lawful judgment of his peers or by the law of the land' would have to be confined to going and putting on people, whatever that meant. But that would mean that no free man could be imprisoned or outlawed at all, even by the law of the land, which would be equally absurd. A plausible way out of the difficulty for the conjunctivists might be to read the words as meaning that judgments should always be given by subjects, not by the king in person, and that those giving judgment should apply the law of the land. As it happens, there was a provision in the 1215 charter (clause 45), not included in the later versions, that justices should know the law of land. But this interpretation never occurred to lawyers. Even Sir Edward Coke, who famously told King James I that he could not sit judicially in his own courts because he was not a lawyer, did not think of founding his advice on the *judicium parium* clause.[10]

The disjunctive interpretation therefore seems preferable. An arrest by a village constable involved no judgment of peers, and yet it was a taking allowed by the law of the land. The procedure of outlawry never (in civil cases[11]) required a judgment of peers, but no one suggested that outlawries were thereby invalidated. It is true that the disjunctive interpretation of *vel* might seem to carry the implication that judgment by peers was something apart from the law of the land. But it had to be *legale judicium*, a lawful judgment, not an arbitrary proceeding outside the law. Trial and judgment by peers was controlled by the common law. It was limited by the law to indictments of treason, murder, and felony, and was conducted in accordance with the law of the land. In other criminal cases, including appeals of felony, peers were subject to the same procedural law as commoners.[12] The phrase therefore added nothing of substance to *lex terrae*. Whatever *legale judicium* had meant to the draftsmen of 1215, by the fourteenth century it had come to represent nothing other than a vague and indirect confirmation of the common-law privilege of trial by peers.

The whole weight of chapter 29 thus fell on the words 'or by the law of the land' (*vel per legem terrae*). What, then, was the law of the land for this purpose? Did it mean that the common law as it stood in 1225, or perhaps as it had been in the golden age of St. Edward, was to be preserved forever? No one ever suggested that in succeeding centuries. By the end of the thirteenth century legislative sovereignty was vested in the king in Parliament. Parliament alone could change the law; and it followed that, if and when it did so, the law of the land was thereby changed. The common law too, though deemed to be immemorial, continued to change through judicial interpretation and through concentrated scrutiny and debate in the inns of court. It was never argued that conflicts between judicial opinions had to be resolved in favour of the earliest, or that *Glanvill* (being pre-1215) must be preferred to *Bracton* or Littleton; on the contrary, common lawyers have always followed the developing currents of professional understanding. No particular rules of law were considered to have been entrenched in 1225 or 1297. The law of the land could only mean the law in operation for the time being. Chapter 29 was therefore taken to be an expression of what is now called the Rule of Law. It was a restraint on the executive, not on the legislature. Governments could not act arbitrarily, disregarding or changing the law as they pleased, but had to operate within the law as it stood.

It has already been noticed that the important reformulation of 1354 replaced both *judicium parium* and *lex terrae* with the phrase 'due process of law'. Much has been made of this phrase in the United States, but it was not in 1354 a technical concept. It obviously did not mean that the legal procedures used in 1225 could never be altered. It was a compendious reformulation of the principle just mentioned, that people must not be treated arbitrarily but only in accordance with the regular legal procedures of the day; and it had been used in that sense well before 1354.[13] What qualified as due process varied with the context. Our village constable did not require written pleadings and representations by counsel before arresting someone for felony. The reason why 'due process' has acquired such significance in the United States is that the words were incorporated into the written Constitution and were later seized upon as imposing restrictions on the capacity of the legislature, restraints which may be policed by the Supreme Court. That did not happen in England, where acts of the High Court of Parliament could not be questioned by lower courts even if they seemed to infringe Magna Carta. The duty to observe due process was laid upon the government, not upon the representatives of the people.

An act of Parliament requires the royal assent, and so a solemn promise by the king, for himself and his heirs, to keep the provisions of Magna Carta inviolate, might on the face of it have prevented the royal assent from being properly given to any statute which threatened to contravene the great charter. A constitutional monarch, however, as later understood, must as a rule accept the advice given by the ministers who promote legislation, and any interference with that principle would run the risk of the monarch entering the judicial sphere by deciding what Magna Carta meant. It was never seriously proposed, even in earlier times. The coronation oath to govern according to law did not include stopping law from being made. What, then, of the provision in the charter itself that anything done contrary to the charter should be void? For the same reason, that could only be read (in a parliamentary world) as applying to governmental acts by the king and his ministers, not to legislative acts by the king in Parliament. But in 1368 Parliament itself declared that all statutes contrary to Magna Carta were void.[14] Did this not entrench the charter as a form of higher law? That may have been the intention, but it was not treated that way by lawyers. Coke held that it repealed some pre-1368 legislation which was inconsistent with the charter,[15] but did not attempt to reconcile this with the fact that many other pre-1368 statutes had unquestionably modified the law as stated in Magna Carta. When it suited him, as when speaking in the House of Commons in the 1620s, Coke would make very broad claims for the statute of 1368; but it has been persuasively argued

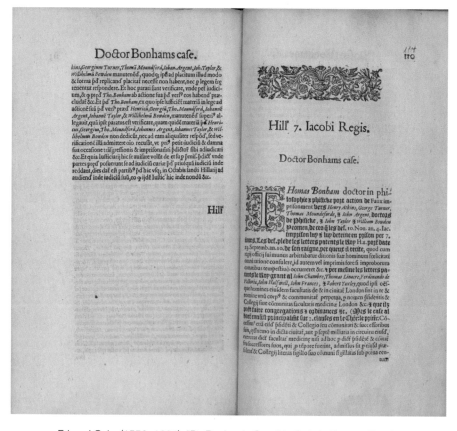

Edward Coke (1552–1634). "Dr. Bonham's Case" in *Coke's Reports*, Part 8. London: Society of Stationers, 1611. Law Library, Library of Congress

that these claims were rhetorical rather than legal. He was not maintaining that Parliament was unable to repeal provisions in Magna Carta, only that it could not be done without great danger.[16] It was also, perhaps, a principle of construction: 'A *general* law shall not take away any part of Magna Carta'.[17]

Any notion that statutes interfering with due process could be reviewed by reference to some fundamental law enshrined in Magna Carta received its final death sentence under the Cromwellian regime. Colonel Euseby Andrewes, in peace-time a barrister of Lincoln's Inn, was arraigned for his life before the inaptly named High Court of Justice, established by the Rump Parliament in 1650, without indictment by grand jury or any right to trial by petty jury. Relying on the statute of 1368, he submitted on his application for *habeas corpus* that the statute erecting the court was invalid because it was contrary to Magna Carta, and that he was entitled to be tried by his peers before a regular court of law. He was beheaded.[18] Three years later Colonel Streater, well known to legal bibliophiles as a law printer, sought release from imprisonment by order of Parliament on the ground that it was contrary to Magna Carta. His counsel, Edward Freeman of Gray's Inn, is said to have argued that all laws against the law of the land were void. Either he or the reporter evidently saw no inherent contradiction in this proposition; probably the reporter garbled what was said. But it was certainly his submission that a mere order of Parliament, as opposed to an act of Parliament, was not the law of the land. The court responded that 'an inferior court cannot control what the Parliament does. If Parliament should do one thing and we the contrary here, things would run around. We must submit to the legislative power'. The following year Streater was released, because Parliament had been dissolved and so the order had lapsed.[19] Ten years later the acts of the Rump Parliament would all be treated as void, for want of the royal assent. But the principle of parliamentary sovereignty has not otherwise been seriously questioned since. It is connected both with parliamentary privilege and with the doctrine of estoppel by record. The doings of the High Court of Parliament, even when not judicial in character, cannot be questioned in any other court.

Chapter 29 ends with the provision about selling and delaying right and justice. This was given a very limited meaning in the inns of court readings. How could the commitment not to sell justice be enforced? Given the prior requirement of due process, it could only mean not charging for the original writs by which litigation in the king's courts was duly commenced; but the Chancery had not given that up and was not going to give it up. Not that the point was overlooked. In 1381 a complaint was made in Parliament that charging fees for writs was against Magna Carta, but the king responded that he was not willing to abandon a source of revenue which had been enjoyed by all his forebears, both before and after the charter.[20] So 'right and justice' were interpreted in the inns of court to mean writs of right and writs of *justicies*, which alone were granted without fee. This had the perverse consequence that a seemingly fundamental rule of justice applied only to litigation in inferior courts.[21] The commitment not to delay justice was equally difficult to enforce. The principal ways in which the king might formally delay justice were aid prayer, writs of *non procedendo*, and writs of protection, none of which was inhibited in the slightest by Magna Carta, though the most dilatory aspects of aid prayer would be removed by statute in 1340.[22] In a case of 1311 a protection was objected to as being against chapter 29, but Bereford C. J. responded that, since the king had sent word that the defendant should be quit of all pleas, 'how can we, who hold pleas in his name, hold pleas against his command'.[23] And so the great Bereford C. J., with impeccable logic, condemned this part of chapter 29 to ineffectiveness for

Henry Care (1646–1688). *English Liberties, or, the Free-born Subject's Inheritance. . . .* Boston: J. Franklin, 1721. Rare Book and Special Collections Division, Library of Congress

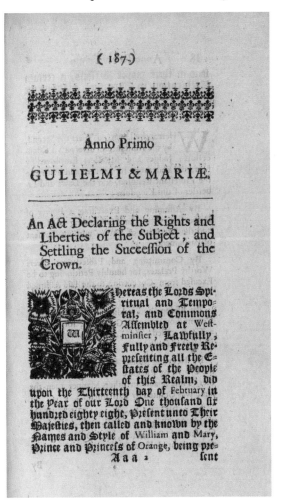

English Bill of Rights in *Anno Regni Gulielmi et Mariae, Regis & Reginae, Scotiae, Franciae [et] Hiberniae, primo. . . .* London: Charles Bill and Thomas Newcomb, 1689. Law Library, Library of Congress

over two hundred years. Protections continued to cause injustice until the sixteenth century, when Tudor judges began to take a bolder course in limiting their scope.[24] So likewise did the staying of suits by writs of *non procedendo rege inconsulto*, which as early as 1330 had been complained of as contrary to Magna Carta,[25] but which were not tackled head on until Coke's time.[26]

4. What Remedies Were Available For Infringement?

In the thirteenth century the enforceabilty of Magna Carta was viewed in political and military rather than judicial terms: according to the author of *Bracton*, the earls and barons, as the king's associates, could rein him in if he broke the law.[27] In the less turbulent fourteenth century it became more a matter of pressing the king in Parliament to grant repeated confirmations, lest he should forget what had been conceded by his forebears. But these were not legal remedies; they were not available to individual subjects in specific cases. The *Mirror of Justices*, written in about 1290, listed numerous 'abuses' in (or contrary to) Magna Carta, and one of them was that the charter itself provided no remedy if the Church or free men were deprived of their liberties.[28] This would also be a constant criticism in the readings in the inns of court. For example, the provision in chapter 6 that 'lords should marry off their wards without disparagement' did not provide a remedy; indeed, it was not even framed as a negative prohibition. The remedy came in 1236, when the Statute of Merton provided an action for damages. Likewise the provision for a widow's quarantine in chapter 7 was unenforceable before Merton provided a writ *de quarantina habenda*. But the most serious lacuna seemed to be in chapter 29. As the readers pointed out, no indication was given in the charter as to whether or how freedom from arbitrary imprisonment, or from the other less explicit forms of official oppression, could be protected by legal means. The king could not be sued in his own courts, and there was no possibility of an action for damages against a government department until the Crown Proceedings Act 1947. Did this mean that chapter 29 merely expressed an idea, an aspiration, rather than binding law? Worse than that, was it a mere figment of the political imagination to suppose that the king, as *Bracton* taught, was under the law at all?

Mere textual analysis might suggest defeatist answers to these questions. But this is where the common lawyers revealed their ingenuity, and the common law its innate strength. When the medieval benchers of the inns of court explored the limitations of Magna Carta as a document, they were very properly inculcating in their students a precise critical approach to words and statutory interpretation. Whatever the law schools taught, however, its graduates were equal to the challenge of finding practical solutions, and in due course the solutions would become retrospectively linked to Magna Carta so as to create a powerful illusion of cause-and-effect. Trial by jury was one of them. By the fourteenth century no one could lawfully be sentenced to death without a specific accusation followed by a trial before twelve sworn members of the public. Another was the petition of right. If a subject's property or money came into the hands of the crown, he could not sue the king but he could sue *to* the king for restitution, and the suit would be heard by judges applying rules of law. The king could only make out a title to property by matter of record, and therefore when facts occurred which gave him a right it was necessary to summon a jury to establish and record the facts, such as an inquisition *post mortem* after the death of a tenant in chief or an inquisition after an attainder for treason. It was possible for interested parties to 'traverse' such an inquisition, in the Chancery, alleging that the facts had not been truly found, or to admit the facts as found but show further facts establishing their own right (the 'monstrans de droit').[29] The Chancery would routinely call on the judges for advice in such cases, and it became the practice to send the cases to the King's Bench for trial of any disputed facts by jury. The many cases of this kind in the law reports show that the rights of the crown were frequently the subject of legal dispute, and that the judges were free to decide against the king. In later times a party could alternatively seek a 'declaration of right' against the crown, even if no other relief was claimed.[30]

Besides the assertion of rights there was the annulment of wrongs. The year books are full of judicial statements about things the king cannot do—for instance, the king cannot grant a franchise which would defeat justice,[31] or which would harm his people.[32] In such cases the remedy was simply to treat the grant as void. From this developed the fundamentally important principle that the

William Prynne (1600–1669). *The Petition of Right of the Free-holders and Free-men of the Kingdom of England* . . . . London, 1648. Rare Book and Special Collections Division, Library of Congress

(3)

THE

PETITION

OF

RIGHT

OF THE

Free-holders and Free-men

OF THE

Kingdom of England

In all humbleneſs ſhew unto the Lords and Commons now in Parliament aſſembled;

THat whereas the Lords Spiritual and Temporal, and Commons in Parliament aſſembled, in the third year of his Majeſties reign, that now is, did, in their moſt famous Petition of Right, among other things, claim theſe enſuing, as their and our undubitable Rights and Liberties, according to the Laws and Statutes of this Realm, *viz.* That no Free-man in *England* ſhould be compelled to contribute to make or yeeld any Gift, Loan or Benevolence, Tax, Tallage, or other ſuch like charge, without common conſent by Act of Parliament. That no Free-man may be taken or impriſoned, or diſſeiſed of his Free-hold, or Liberties, or free Cuſtoms, or be out-lawed or exiled, or in any manner deſtroyed;

A 2

or

king can do no wrong. Few principles of law have been more misunderstood, and yet it was a major reinforcement of the Rule of Law. It had nothing to do with the monarch's personal or political behaviour. Kings as human beings could obviously do wrong, and medieval kings were better placed to do wrong than most people. Nor was it about the immunity of the king from suit in his own courts, an immunity shared by every manorial lord. It meant rather that the king in his royal capacity could only, as a matter of law, do right. He could not lawfully do or command something legally wrong. If, therefore, a minister or official of the crown, high or low, claimed to be acting under the king's authority, any defence on that footing fell away if the command was one which the king could not lawfully have given. And it worked in other ways. The rule that the king could not be a disseisor meant that if the king seized another person's land without title, and then granted it to someone else by patent, the person entitled could lawfully enter upon the patentee or bring an assize against him to recover possession.[33] Similarly, according to all the judges of England advising the Chancery in 1483, if someone disseised a man to the king's use, the king was not a disseisor and would therefore not acquire an equitable interest.[34] None of this was attributed to Magna Carta, but it is easy to see how it could become linked to the words 'No free man shall be disseised'.

It was held in 1438 that the king could not send anyone to prison by his own discretion, because the king could not command anything without matter of record.[35] The remedy in such a case was not discussed, but it might well have been an action against the gaoler, on the principle just mentioned, since he would have had no lawful authority to detain his prisoner. A century later the remedy would be the writ of *habeas corpus*, which went to the gaoler rather than the king or the minister who had commanded the imprisonment. In either case the courts of law were enabled to consider whether the imprisonment was lawful, and in the latter could also decide whether bail should be allowed. During the sixteenth century *habeas corpus* was increasingly used to challenge imprisonment by ministers of the crown and by various courts.

It was only in the Tudor period that such remedies came to be associated with Magna Carta. From around 1501 the plea rolls contain a steady trickle of special trespassory actions founded on chapter 29, in which plaintiffs sought damages for arrest and imprisonment in proceedings before the conciliar courts for matters determinable at common law. The standard declaration in these actions recited that the plaintiff was *liber homo* and that 'according to the law and free custom of the realm of England every free man in common pleas ought to implead and be impleaded by original writs under the lord king's great seal' in the Common Bench or King's

Bench. About a dozen such cases have been noted, and a few others of like nature founded on the later statutes of due process.[36] At the same period Magna Carta became linked in a legal context with the Rule of Law. King Henry VIII, in the first year of his reign, issued nationwide commissions of oyer and terminer, which included for the first time offences 'against the form of the statute of the great charter of the liberties of England'.[37] In 1532, when a king's serjeant complained in the King's Council of having been arbitrarily imprisoned by the king's command, reliance was placed on chapter 29, 'whereby it appeared that the king may not use his subjects contrary to the law'.[38] In 1554 James Dyer attributed to chapter 29 the principle that every subject had access to the king's courts, 'whether bond or free, woman or infant, religious, outlawed or excommunicated'.[39] As chief justice of the Common Pleas under Elizabeth I, and a valiant champion of the Rule of Law, Dyer was later to create some of the precedents which inspired Coke. Then, in 1572, upon an application for *habeas corpus* to the mayor of Exeter, Edmund Anderson of the Inner Temple explicitly linked that remedy to chapter 29 of Magna Carta,[40] an association which soon became common currency. And in 1582 John Popham, the attorney-general, cited the same chapter in challenging (on behalf of the crown) a power of imprisonment claimed by a London livery company.[41]

Sir Edward Coke was prominent in tying all these strands together. Already by 1604 he was a devotee of chapter 29, maintaining that 'everything that anyone has in this world, or that concerns the freedom and liberty of his body or his freehold, or the benefit of the law to which he is inheritable, or his native country in which he was born, or the preservation of his reputation or goods, or his life, blood and posterity: to all these things this act extends.'[42] He dismissed the late-medieval doctrine that there was no way of enforcing its provisions. True it might be that no express remedies were mentioned, but every statute made against an injury, mischief, or grievance implied a remedy.[43] The statute was, moreover, simply a declaration of the common law, and so the common law could provide supportive remedies. Coke listed five of them in 1604: *habeas corpus*, actions of false imprisonment, actions on the statute, indictments on the statute, and writs *de homine replegiando*. He also attributed the recent decisions rejecting exorbitant writs of protection to the *nulli negabimus* clause of chapter 29.[44] At this period the writ of prohibition, used principally against ecclesiastical and conciliar courts, came likewise to be attributed to the same increasingly fruitful source.[45] And soon afterwards the new prerogative remedy of *mandamus* was found to be another of its progeny.[46]

Magna Carta is indelibly associated with the great debates in Parliament on the liberty of the subject early in the reign of Charles I, in which Coke spoke, and which culminated in the Petition of Right 1628. But it had already reached its apotheosis in the previous reign, when many common lawyers were worried by the Romanist legal inclinations of a Scottish king who considered monarchs above the law. Francis Ashley, reader of the Middle Temple in 1614, hailed chapter 29 as fundamental law: 'if it be the common law, it is the law of laws…. . But if it be a mere statute, it is the statute of statutes, for it hath begotten many of the like kind…. . And the Lord Coke saith in his Fifth Report it hath been confirmed thirty times; and thirty times thirty more I suppose it would, if it lay in the power of the subject to give any strength to it.'[47] The reason for its importance he proclaimed in terms which exceeded even Coke's expansive encomiums:[48]

> In brief, by virtue of this statute we have property in our goods, title to our lands, liberty for our persons, and safety for our lives. But … in the case between *Anderson* and *Warde*[49] it is further added another, and that justly, that by force of this statute every free subject may have remedy for every wrong done to his person, lands or goods. And not only so, for that would but give recompense for a wrong done; but this statute also *prevents* wrongs, for by virtue thereof no man shall be punished before he be condemned, and no man shall be condemned before he be heard, and none shall be heard but his just defence shall be allowed.
>
> … By this statute are condemned and prohibited all judgments without hearing the party and without trial, and all unlawful trials and all judgments by judges not lawfully authorised, and all manner of unlawful proceedings to judgment, and all unlawful executions.

Very little of this, of course, was in chapter 29 itself. But it was Ashley's understanding of Magna Carta, largely shared by Coke, which informed the debates of the 1620s and which has remained in the legal and popular consciousness ever since. It is not the words themselves which make the law, but the meanings which people heap upon them.

A LEXICOGRAPHIC LOOK
AT MAGNA CARTA

Bryan A. Garner

The phrase *Magna Carta* raises many tricky points for the lexicographer or encyclopedist who prepares an entry for the term. How is it predominantly spelled (*Carta* or *Charta*)? Has there been a shift in spelling over time? Are the variant forms pronounced the same or differently? Although we think of only one document, there were many confirmations of it in various forms; hence, what is the plural form? What is the best translation of the phrase? How did the name come about—that is, what explains the etymology? When did the phrase first appear in an English-language context? What synonyms have been used historically? As a matter of usage, does one refer to *Magna Carta* (as a proper noun without an article) or to *the Magna Carta*? Does the phrase have extended or figurative senses?

Then there are questions of substantive coverage and context. How much detail does a dictionary or encyclopedia entry merit? That is, is it better to summarize briefly the importance of the document or to explain it in great detail? Which king should be credited with first acceding to the document? (Believe it or not, King John was often overlooked in early dictionaries.) Is the place of signing preferably known as *Runnymede*, *Runimede*, or *Running Mede*—or any of several other variations? Why is it sometimes said to have 63 clauses and sometimes 37?

Finally, there are some literary questions. What did Geoffrey Chaucer, William Shakespeare, and Samuel Johnson have to say about Magna Carta? Did Johnson insert some characteristic aperçu in his *Dictionary of the English Language* (1755)? Has the phrase lent itself to humorous treatment in dictionaries?

Lexicographers have grappled with all these questions and others, not always successfully. They are worth considering in some detail, not just for what they disclose about Magna Carta and its history but also for what they might tell us about lexicography and its methods—and the art of relentlessly asking and answering questions. Very little about Magna Carta is simple or straightforward.

What Is The Predominant Spelling?

Originally, the predominant form was *Magna Charta*, which long held sway. At its height, *Magna Charta* was nearly ten times as common as *Magna Carta*. But the two spellings had a significant reversal of fortune in the late twentieth century. The following chart shows frequencies of occurrence for the two forms in published books (as calculated by Google Books):

Period Covered	Magna Carta	Magna Charta
16th century	1,140 sources	2,250 sources
17th century	1,050	5,610
18th century	1,580	15,200
19th century	34,700	255,000
1901–1950	109,000	227,000
1951–2000	274,000	130,000
2001–present	68,200	26,200

In 1926, when H. W. Fowler wrote the first edition of his *Dictionary of Modern English Usage*, he said: "*Magna C(h)arta*. Authority seems to be for spelling *charta* & pronouncing kar´ta, which is hard on the plain man. But outside of histories & lecture-rooms the spelling & pronunciation *charta* will take a great deal of killing yet."[1] In his 1965 revision of that book, Sir Ernest Gowers introduced an excellent update: "In a Bill introduced in 1946 authorizing the Trustees of the British Museum to lend a copy to the Library of Congress, *Charta* was the spelling used. But when the Bill reached committee stage in the House of Lords, the Lord Chancellor (Lord Jowitt) moved to substitute *Carta* and produced conclusive evidence that that was traditionally the correct spelling. The amendment was carried without a division; so *Carta* has now unimpeachable authority."[2] Jowitt had also spelled the term that way in his 1959 dictionary of English law.[3]

By its third edition of 1996, *Fowler's* (as it was now called) was essentially an all-new book by Robert W. Burchfield, the retired editor of the Oxford dictionaries. Burchfield misreported the American preference, though he hedged with *possibly*: "The recommended spelling of the second word is *Carta*, except in AmE, where *Charta* is possibly the dominant form."[4] Robert Allen's 2008 pocket edition of *Fowler's* added that "*Charta* and *Carta* are both valid forms in Latin."[5]

That is correct: Latin allows either spelling, although the *-h-* is typical not of Classical Latin but of Late Latin, from the Middle Ages. Hence it was not quite true what Eric Partridge wrote in 1942: "*Charta* is neither Latin nor English."[6] By 1965 Partridge had corrected the entry: "*Magna Charta; Magna Carta; The Great*

Charter. all three are correct."[7] But that correction was both too little and too late—the error had already been copied into at least two other books on English usage.[8] In any event, the correction might have noted that *Charta* was limited to medieval Latin (the time, of course, when the document was created).

Most dictionaries were slow to adopt the switch to the Classical Latin *Carta*, despite the post-1951 tide. As early as 1949, the Funk & Wagnalls dictionaries had recorded *Magna Carta* as the only spelling for the main entry, with a notation at the end: "Also *Magna Charta,* the erroneous but common form."[9] But that was the exception. Random House didn't record *Carta* as the first listing until 1987,[10] and Merriam-Webster took until 1993 to do an about-face. At the New York office of Oxford University Press, the 1980 *Oxford American Dictionary* listed only *Charta,*[11] but in 2001 the *New Oxford American Dictionary* listed only *Carta.*[12] This slowness to reflect actual usage typifies what often happens in lexicography.

By 1987, *The Associated Press Stylebook and Libel Manual* was taking a firm anti-*Charta* stance: "*Magna Carta.* Not *Magna Charta.* An exception to Webster's."[13] By 1995, the *UPI Stylebook* had followed suit.[14]

Leading encyclopedias of the 1980s and 1990s preferred *Carta.*[15] But the trend for encyclopedias went back to midcentury: they seemed to be more heavily influenced by W. S. McKechnie's usage in his 1914 treatise *Magna Carta.*[16] Today the *Charta* spelling is almost universally treated as a secondary variant.[17]

Are The Variant Forms Pronounced The Same Or Differently?

The phrase is pronounced the same regardless of spelling: /**kahr**-tuh/. All the dictionaries that give a pronunciation record the *Charta* spelling as having a hard -k- sound, not a -ch- sound.[18] As the orthoepist W. H. P. Phyfe put it, "The digraph *ch* is pronounced like *k* in all Greek and Latin words."[19]

The modern trend to spell the phrase *Carta,* not *Charta,* may have been in part because the cognoscenti realized that English speakers had started mispronouncing the term. (As Fowler said in 1926, the exceptional pronunciation was "hard on the plain man.") After all, English speakers are notoriously prone to mistaken "spelling pronunciations," as with *comptroller*[20] and *schism,*[21] so the reversion to the spelling *Carta* after a long period of *Charta* made sense if English speakers hoped to keep the traditional pronunciation intact. The frequent listing of the phrase in pronunciation books reinforces the idea that mispronunciations had become common during the mid-20th century.

Perhaps the most surprising comment on pronunciation is the wrongheaded idea that the first syllable is preferably /mahg/, as opposed to /mag/. Only one usage guide contains this poor advice.[22]

What Is The Plural Form?

Historically, most dictionaries have not recorded a plural. Oddly, the second edition of the *Oxford English Dictionary* (1989) gives the macaronic *Magna Chartaes*, with one citation from 1643 in support. The more modern form is fully anglicized—the only unpedantic choice: *Magna Cartas*. [23]That was the form used by the British Library when it announced, on July 15, 2013, that three historic copies (including those of Lincoln Cathedral and Salisbury Cathedral) were to be displayed together at the Library.

What's The Best Translation Of The Phrase? What's The Etymology?

All the reputable authorities translate it as "the great charter." One treatise records the etymology as "a great piece of paper."[24] An Australian legal dictionary, however, inexplicably translates it as "the great counting."[25]

As for the reason for the name, there are no fewer than seven possible explanations. The most influential early writer on Magna Carta was Edward Coke, who in 1628 attributed the name to the statute's moral weightiness and importance:

> This parliamentarie charter hath divers appellations in law. Here it is called *Magna Charta*, not for the length or largenesse of it, (for it is but short in respect of the charters granted of private things to private persons now a days being *elephantinae chartae,*) but it is called the great charter in respect of [1] the great weightinesse and weightie greatnesse of the matter contained in it in few words, being the fountain of all the fundamentall laws of the realme; and therefore it may truly be said of it, that it is *magnum in parvo*. It is in our books called *Charta Libertatum, et Communis Libertas Angliae, or Libertates Angliae, Charta de Libertatibus, Magna Charta,* etc. And well may the lawes of England be called *Libertates, quia Liberos faciunt. Magna fuit quondam Magnae reverential Chartae.*[26]

But there are other theories. In 1704, John Harris advanced four others that are frequently mentioned in the literature: "The Reason why it is termed *Magna Charta,* was either for that [2] it contain'd the Sum of all the Liberties of *England,* or else because [3] there was another *Charter,* called *Charta de Foresta,* establish'd with it, which was the less of the two; or because [4] it contained more than many other *Charters,* or more than that of King *Henry* the First, or of [5] the great and remarkable Solemnity in the denouncing Excommunication, and direful *Anathema's* [sic] against the Infringers of it."[27]

In 1729, the estimable Giles Jacob added two more theories to the number: [6] "the Excellency of the Laws therein contained"[28] (really a version of Coke's weightiness point), and [7] there were "great Wars and Trouble in the Obtaining it."[29]

Most of these explanations are probably spurious—the stuff of "folk etymology." My guess, as someone who has worked with the history of words for many decades, is that the most plausible explanation is #3: It was contrasted with its contemporaneous counterpart, the Charter of the Forest, which was less than half as long. All the idealism was probably a projection on the document by later ages. Here is what the scholar's edition (1911) of *Encyclopaedia Britannica* says of Magna Carta:

> [I]t differs only in degree, not in kind, from other charters granted by the Norman and early Plantagenet kings. Its greater length, however, still more the exceptional circumstances attending its birth, gave to it a position absolutely unique in the minds of later generations of Englishmen. This feeling was fostered by its many confirmations, and in subsequent ages, especially during the time of the struggle between the Stuart kings and the parliament, it was regarded as something sacrosanct, embodying the very ideal of English liberties, which to some extent had been lost, but which must be regained. Its provisions, real and imaginary, formed the standard towards which Englishmen must strive.[30]

It became a hallowed document, much as the United States Constitution is in America.

If I am right about the etymology, many people will consider it a paltry basis for such an august name. But language often works that way.

When Did The Phrase First Appear In An English-Language Context?

The first edition of the *Oxford English Dictionary* (1908—that's the year when M first appeared as a full volume) credited Richard Grafton's *Chronicle at Large* (1569) with the first use of the phrase *Magna Carta* in English. The current online *OED* adds a citation to the 1472–1475 Rolls of Parliament: "Where by the laudable Statute of Magna Carta, amonges other, it is ordeyned." But there are other pre-Grafton English-language antedatings:

- Robert Redman, *Magna Carta in F.: Wherunto Is Added More Statutes than Ever Was Imprynted in Any One Boke Before This Tyme, with an Almanacke and a Calender to Know the Mootes: Necessarye for All Yong Studiers of the Lawe* (1508).

- Robert Wyer, *The Artycles of the Chartour and Lybertyes of England Called Magna Carta* (1531).

- Thomas Petyt, *The Great Charter Called in Latyn Magna Carta: With Divers Olde Statutes Whose Titles Appere in the Next Leafe Newly Corrected* (1542).

The *OED* also lists a Latin quotation incorporating the phrase from as early as 1218. But even in Latin, *Magna Carta* was not treated as a name (as opposed to a description) until the middle part of the thirteenth century—perhaps no earlier than 1253.[31]

What Synonyms Have Been Used Historically?

There are many:

- Charta Magna.[32]

- Carta Magna.[33]

- The Great Charter.[34]

- Charter of 1215.[35]

- The Great Charter of Liberties.[36]

- *Magna Charta Libertatum.*[37]

- *Charta Libertatum, et Communis Libertas Angliae.*[38]

- *Libertates Angliae.*[39]

- *Charta de Libertatibus.*[40]

- *Augustissimum Anglicarum Libertatum Diploma & Sacra Anchora.*[41]

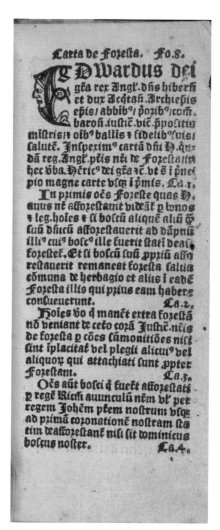

Antiqua Statuta [First printed Magna Carta]. London: Pynson, 1508. Law Library, Library of Congress

The greatest legal historian of the early twentieth century, F. W. Maitland, did not often use the normal term *Magna Carta*. In his *Constitutional History of England*,

Maitland refers to the document mostly as "the charter of 1215."[42] Although the index refers to "Magna Carta," most instances in the text are to the "charter of 1215." Maitland provides no index entry for "Great Charter" or "Charter of 1215."

Is It Better To Say *Magna Carta* Or *The Magna Carta*?

All the usage guides prefer omitting the definite article before *Magna Carta.*[43] The Merriam-Webster editors, perhaps unwilling to use the term *ignorant* or *uneducated*, put the matter delicately: "We suspect . . . that many Americans who are familiar with the term only from their school days use the definite article."[44] But it's not just Americans: the superfluous article often appears in the work of "writers outside England—even elsewhere in the U.K., in Commonwealth countries, and in former colonies, including the U.S."[45] Indeed, the disapproved usage crops up occasionally in surprising places, such as *The Oxford International Encyclopedia of Peace*, in which both references (by one article author) are to *the Magna Carta.*[46]

The traditional reason for omitting the article is twofold: (1) the name is being used as a proper noun, and (2) in Latin the phrase doesn't take an article, and early anglicizations followed the Latinate word pattern.

Does *Magna Carta* Have Extended Or Figurative Senses?

Yes. The first lexicographer to note this fact was the venerable Noah Webster in his huge two-volume *American Dictionary of the English Language* (1828). Note his sense 2 (what follows is the entire entry):

> MAGNA CHARTA, *n.* [L. great charter.] 1. The great charter, so called, obtained by the English barons from king John, A.D. 1215. This name is also given to the charter granted in the ninth year of Henry III. and confirmed by Edward I. 2. A fundamental constitution which guarantees rights and privileges.[47]

In a similar vein, nearly a century later the *Oxford English Dictionary* preceded a list of illustrative uses with the heading "*transf.* and *fig.*"[48] One of the early figurative uses was by the playwright Ben Jonson in 1630: "It is against my freehold, my inheritance, My Magna Charta . . . to drink such balderdash, or bonny-clabber."[49]

By the 1960s, specialized dictionaries were recording extended uses, as here: "Reformers have used Magna Carta to designate acts which seemed to advance their causes, thus referring to the Clayton Act as the Magna Carta of Labor, and the Seamen's Act of 1915 as the Magna Carta of the American Seamen."[50]

To Which King Should Magna Carta Be Credited?

To the nonhistorian this is really odd. Most of the early dictionaries give the year 1225—the ninth year of King Henry III—as the year for Magna Carta. Consider:

1607: "*Magna Charta,* called in English the great charter, is a charter con- teining a number of lawes ordained the ninth yeare of *Henry* the third, and confirmed by *Edward* the first." John Cowell, *The Interpreter* s.v. (1607).

1661: "*Magna Charta,* the great Charter, contains a number of Laws or- dained the ninth year of *Hen.*3 and confirmed by *Edw.*I." Thomas Blount, *Glossographia: Or a Dictionary* s.v. (2d ed. 1661).

1676: "*Magna Charta,* (The Great Charter) the most ancient of our written Laws, Granted by King *Henry 3.* confirmed by King *Edward* the first, and other Kings." Elisha Coles, *An English Dictionary* s.v. (1676).

1704: "MAGNA *Charta,* was granted the ninth Year of *Henry* the Third, and confirmed by *Edward* the First." John Harris, *Lexicon Technicum: Or, an Universal English Dictionary of Arts and Sciences* s.v. (1704).

1729: "Magna Charta, The Great Charter of Liberties granted in the ninth Year of King *Hen. 3.*" Giles Jacob, *A New Law-Dictionary* s.v. (1729).

1754: "*MAGNA charta,* lat. the great charter, granted by Henry III. in the 9th year of his reign, containing the grand privileges of the English na- tion." Benjamin Martin, *Lingua Britannica Reformata: or, A New Universal English Dictionary* s.v. (1754).

1765: "Magna Charta, The *Great Charter,* was granted the ninth year of *Henry* the Third, and confirmed by *Edward* the First." 2 Timothy Cun- ningham, *A New and Complete Law-Dictionary* s.v. (1765).

1815: "MAGNA-CHARTA, (*Magna Karta*) *s.* [Lat.] the great charter of the liberties and laws of England: its origin may be derived even from Edward the Confessor, and was continued by Henry I. and his succes- sors, Stephen, Henry II. and king John; but that more particularly meant by this word was granted in the ninth year of Henry III. since which, Sir Edward Coke observes, that even in this [his?] day, it had been con- firmed above thirty times." James Barclay, *A Complete and Universal En- glish Dictionary* 622 (1815).

1818: "*MAGNA CHARTA. n. s.* [Latin.] The great charter of liberties granted to the people of England in the ninth year of Henry the third, and confirmed by Edward the first." 3 Samuel Johnson, *A Dictionary of the English Language* s.v. (H. J. Todd ed., 1818).

1838: "MAGNA CHARTA. The great charter of liberties granted in the 9th year of King Henry III. King John had previously granted a similar one, but he broke it." Thomas Edlyne Tomlins, *A Popular Law Dictionary* 364 (1838).

1839: "Magna Carta. The Great Charter. The name of an instrument granted in the ninth year of Henry III., which secured to the English people many liberties which had before been invaded, and provided against many abuses which before rendered liberty a mere name." 1 John Bouvier, *A Law Dictionary* 85–86 (1839).

Only in 1803 did Thomas Potts[51] set things aright, from the modern point of view, by crediting King John in 1215. Noah Webster followed Potts's lead in 1828.[52] By the mid-nineteenth century, it was commonplace for King John to be credited (if that's the right word for someone being coerced) with Magna Carta in the year 1215.

Why does so much of the early credit go to King Henry III for the "third reissue"[53] of 1225? Because *that* version of Magna Carta is the one that became incorporated into British statute law. Here's how the thorough nineteenth-century lexicographer Alexander Burrill explained it: "This charter of Henry III. is the Great Charter which is always referred to as the basis of the English constitution; the charter of John being only remembered as a monument of antiquity. 1 *Reeves' Hist. Eng. Law,* 209, 231. The charter of Henry is the oldest printed statute now extant in England. 1 *Bl. Com.* 85. The original charter of John is still preserved in the British Museum."[54] King John's Magna Carta was declared a nullity by the pope just a little over two months after it was sealed.[55]

So the early legal lexicographers had reason to prefer citing the third reissue and crediting Henry III. But historians and schoolchildren alike care more today about the original 1215 date than 1225. That was the momentous year.

In its early history, Magna Carta sounds to have been in a parlous predicament. Perhaps the most succinct history of Henry III's relationship with Magna Carta was that of Sullivan, given in 1772:

This reign [that of Henry III] was as calamitous, as the preceding one, and rather more shameful; and, what added to the misfortune, it lasted three times as long. As soon as Henry came of age, he revoked *Magna Charta,* as being an act of his nonage, soon after he confirmed it, then broke it, then confirmed it by oath, with a solemn excommunication of all that should infringe it; then he obtained from the pope a dispensation of his oath, and broke it again. And thus he fluctuated for fifty years, according as his hopes or fears prevailed. However, in general, the charter was pretty well observed.[56]

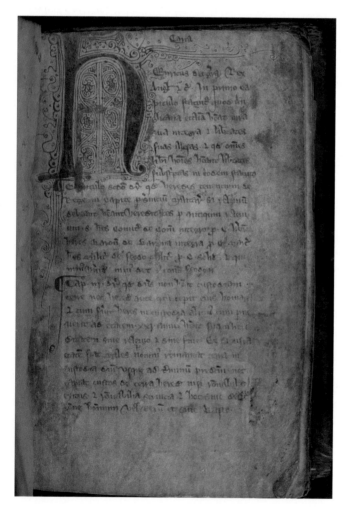

Statuta Vetera [Magna Carta and Other Statutes]. Bound manuscript, fourteenth-century. Law Library, Library of Congress

What Is The Precise Date Of King John's Magna Carta?

First, let's get the year right. One latter-day dictionary misrecords the year of signing as 1214,[57] perhaps misdirecting many a British law student in the 1930s. Although that is just a nonce error, it's a bad one.

Some dictionaries give the date as June 15, 1215.[58] Others give June 19, 1215.[59] This contradictory information counsels in favor of having lexicographers and encyclopedists avoid undue specificity. The *Oxford English Dictionary*, for example, says Magna Carta was "obtained from King John in 1215"[60] and leaves it at that. This may be a wise solution, since "The chroniclers give various dates to the settlement ranging from 18 to 23 June."[61] Only one major dictionary—the now-defunct *Funk & Wagnalls New Standard Dictionary of the English Language* (1943)—gives an account that seems to reflect the most reliable modern research: "dated June 15, 1215, but actually sealed (not signed) and delivered June 19, 1215, by King John, at Runnymede."[62] Except—except John probably did not seal the document either: that responsibility fell to a member of the Chancery staff.[63] But June 19 seems to be the best guess for the document's taking effect.[64]

How Do You Spell The Place Name Of The Meadow In Surrey Where Magna Carta Was Signed?

The usual spelling today is *Runnymede*, the secondary variant being *Runnimede*.[65] But there have historically been many variants, such as these:

- *Runimed* (1215).[66]
- *Renimed* (1607).[67]
- *Running-mead(e)* (1643).[68]
- *Runnemede* (1681).[69]
- *Running Mead* (1684).[70]
- *Rumney Mead* (1718).[71]
- *Runnimede* (1727).[72]
- *Runnymede* (1765).[73]
- *Runny Mead* (1787).[74]
- *Runemed* (1799).[75]
- *Runemede* (1860).[76]
- *Runningmede* (1860).[77]
- *Runny Mede* (1901).[78]

Why Do Different Dictionaries And Encyclopedias Attribute Different Numbers Of Provisions In Magna Carta?

Depending on which source you consult, you may read that Magna Carta comprises either sixty-three clauses or thirty-seven[79]—or perhaps sixty-one and thirty-eight.[80] Why such a great disparity? The confusion grows from the same root as that concerning the document's attribution: namely, the differences between the two significant versions of Magna Carta—the 1215 original granted by King John and the 1225 reissue granted by his son, Henry III. After John died in 1216, his nine-year-old son Henry's regents revised and reissued Magna Carta.[81] When Henry III came of age, the barons asked him to reconfirm the Charter. Henry was initially reluctant, but within a year certain exigencies forced him to demand contributions from those barons. The barons used this opportunity to strike a bargain exchanging the contributions for Henry's reconfirming the Charter. This third reissue was significantly revised, largely to record the circumstances under which Henry granted it. In the process, the original 63 provisions were reduced to thirty-seven—twenty-four were removed, four pairs were each consolidated into a single clause, and two entirely new clauses were introduced. This 1225 version ultimately became law. The 1215 charter is commonly reprinted with sixty-three clauses, but the 1225 (third reissue) with thirty-seven.

What Did Geoffrey Chaucer, William Shakespeare, And Samuel Johnson Have To Say About Magna Carta?

Nothing. Absolutely nothing. Chaucer, despite his knowledge of law, apparently didn't find it worth mentioning to his lay readers.[82]

The various Shakespeare concordances have no listing of *Magna Carta*. Somehow Shakespeare's play *King John* (1596) deals with baronial rebellion all the way through John's death without a whisper about Magna Carta. As the variorum edition of *King John* notes, the play contains "not the faintest allusion . . . to the constitutional struggle which ended in the grant of the Great Charter,"[83] adding: "Startling as it sounds to modern ears, it is almost certain that Shakespeare had small knowledge of that document, and a very inadequate sense of its importance."[84] This despite the playwright's extensive legal knowledge.[85] Perhaps this paradox can be explained partly by the low ebb that Magna Carta had reached in the 15th and 16th centuries.[86] Or the omission may have resulted from Shakespeare's dramaturgical strategy,[87] although some have suggested that *King John* is more subject to criticism by lawyers than any other play for precisely this reason.[88] One historian of the English Renaissance doubts that Shakespeare had even heard of Magna Carta.[89]

Samuel Johnson's *Dictionary of the English Language* (1755) has no entry for the phrase. Nor is there any reference to it in the entry for *charter*, although Johnson does say this: "*Charters* are divided into *charters* of the king, and *charters* of private persons." Not until Todd's revision of 1818, more than 40 years after Johnson's death, did an entry appear in an edition of Johnson's *Dictionary*. It read in full: "*MAGNA CHARTA. n. s.* [Latin.] The great charter of liberties granted to the people of England in the ninth year of Henry the third, and confirmed by Edward the first."[90]

Did Johnson discuss Magna Carta in any of the copious conversations recorded by Boswell? Apparently not. No reference appears even in his voluminous letters.[91]

Johnson does make an appearance in an erudite book by Anne Pallister. She says that Magna Carta "was, as Samuel Johnson picturesquely put it, 'born with a grey Beard.'"[92] But her footnote is to *The Second Part of the Confutation of the Ballancing* [sic] *Letter*, a book published in 1700 (nine years before Johnson's birth). Yet she was right in her citation (would that she had explained): it was an obscure clergyman Samuel Johnson (1696–1772)[93] who so spoke, not the illustrious lexicographer (1709–1784).[94] Confusingly enough, if you Google "born with a grey beard," you'll find many attributions to Samuel Johnson as if it were the better-known dictionary writer.

Is There Any Historical Humor Associated With Magna Carta?

Yes. In 1658, when Oliver Cromwell as Protector assessed a heavy tax, a fanatic refused to pay the tax, was imprisoned, and filed a petition for habeas corpus. Cromwell had him sent to the Tower of London, whereupon the judges of the King's Bench mentioned Magna Carta. Cromwell derisively insisted that "Magna Farta" would not control his actions.[95] About a decade later, when Magna Carta was cited to the notoriously arbitrary Kelyng C. J., he was said to have repeated, "with a loud voice, Cromwell's rhyme, MAGNA CHARTA—MAGNA ****A."[96]

Most dictionaries give a pretty sober-sided account of Magna Carta. But the irrepressibly sardonic Charles Pigott tried to inject some humor into his 1796 dictionary entry: "*Magna Charta.* An idle word, idly made use of by the populace, signifying a natural right of being governed by just laws, equally distributed, which they constantly suffer to be trampled on, and an inherent claim to the possession of those privileges which they have neither sense or spirit enough to possess."[97]

Few other lexicographers have been so wry. But one, named J. J. S. Wharton, allowed some vitriol directed at King John (whom he didn't deign to name): "It is mainly the solemn restitution of the ancient liberties of the realm, exacted from a profligate sovereign by our old warrior-barons, in consequence

Abbreviamentum Statutorum [Abridgement of Statutes]. London, 1482. Law Library, Library of Congress

of his abominable licentiousness, and the unendurable oppressions of his creature, the Chief Justiciary, Peter, Bishop of Winchester, an adventurous foreigner, who pandered to his master's villainies, and plundered the people of their own aggrandizement."[98]

Of course, the literature on Magna Carta is replete with passages that could spice up any dictionary entry that seeks to be exhaustive by including illustrative materials, as with the *Oxford English Dictionary* or, in its more recent incarnations, *Black's Law Dictionary*. The acidulous Jeremy Bentham, for example, scoffed at the idea that Magna Carta, unlike all other statutes, could be neither amended nor repealed—suggesting in fact it is rather constantly violated:

Justice shall be denied to no man, justice shall be sold to no man, says the first of statutes, *Magna Charta.* How is it under these later ones?—Denied, as we have seen, to nine-tenths of the people, sold to the other tenth at an unconscionable price. It was a conceit among the old lawyers, reported if not adopted by Lord Coke, that a statute made contrary to *Magna Charta*, though made in all the forms, would be a void law. God forbid, that by all the lawyers in the world, or for the purpose of any argument, I should ever suffer myself to be betrayed into any such extravagance: in a subject it would be sedition, in a judge it would be usurpation, in anybody it would be nonsense. But after all it must be acknowledged, to be in some degree unfortunate, as well as altogether singular, that, of an instrument deemed the foundation of all liberty, and magnified as such even still, to a degree of fanaticism, a passage by far the most important, and almost the only one that has any application now-a-days, should be thus habitually trodden under foot, without remorse or reclamation.[99]

Although Granville Sharp had declared in 1774 that "any attempt to repeal it would be treason to the State,"[100] Bentham was right about the repealability of Magna Carta.[101] Only four clauses (1, 9, 29, and 37) remain good law in England.[102] Much of it was repealed in 1874.[103] And many of the repeals have been quite recent: six clauses were repealed between 1965 and 1992.[104]

What Is The Shortest Definition Of *Magna Carta* On Record?

Noah Webster's small grammar-school abridgment from 1833 defines the phrase in but six words: "the great charter of English rights."[105] Another short one, by the legal lexicographer Thomas Tayler, is only eight words: "the great Charter; the bulwark of *English* liberty."[106] A modern abridged Oxford dictionary comes in at nine: "charter of liberty obtained from King John in 1215."[107] A close fourth is Thomas Sheridan's of 1789, at ten words: "The great charter, the basis of English laws and privileges."[108] The longer definitions run to thousands of words and many pages.[109]

What Is The Most Effusive Definition Of *Magna Carta* On Record?

The rhapsodic definition given in the third edition of *Ballentine's Law Dictionary* (1969) might seem at first to be extravagant:

Magna Charta. A charter of liberties, now found to be embodied in some form in every one of the American Constitutions; guaranteeing that every person shall be protected in the enjoyment of his life, liberty, and property, except as they may be declared to be forfeited by the judgment of his peers or the law of the land; issued by King John, at the demand of the barons, June 15, 1215, confirmed, with some changes, 9 Hen. III and 25 Edw. I.[110]

Every person? Life, liberty, and property? This seems fanciful at first look. Only two of the sixty-three clauses (#39 and #40) developed into our modern notions of liberty: "No freeman shall be seized or imprisoned, or stripped of his rights or possession, or outlawed or exiled or deprived of his standing in any other way, nor will we proceed with force against him, or send others to do so, except by the lawful judgment of his equals or by the law of the land" (39); and "To no one will we sell, to no one deny or delay right or justice" (40).

From the phrase *the law of the land* developed, through a Law French translation (*par due process de ley*),[111] our American idea of *due process of law*—the two phrases being essentially synonymous.[112] So in a sense, our most basic notions of legal fairness are indeed traceable to the great piece of paper that King John signed in 1215. Although some note that Magna Carta's protections extended only to the elite,[113] it's not too sweeping to say that Magna Carta has symbolically become "synonymous with responsible government and equitable justice."[114] But seeing it this way undoubtedly depends, as Philip B. Kurland once said, on "its exaltation beyond the realm of fact."[115]

Which Lexicographer Most Vividly Depicted The Scene At Which Magna Carta Took Effect?

Giles Jacob in 1729, but the description wasn't of King John at Runnymede. It was of Henry III late in life. It was the reaffirmation of Magna Carta in the thirty-seventh year of Henry III's reign—a down-the-line reissue of the Charter. The scene took place at "*Westminster hall*, and in the presence of the Nobility and Bishops, with lighted Candles in their Hands, *Magna Charta* was read; the King all that while laying his Hand on his Breast, and at last solemnly swearing *faithfully and inviolably to observe all the Things therein contained, as he was a Man, a Christian, a Soldier, and a King:* Then the Bishops extinguished the Candles, and threw them on the Ground; and every one said, *Thus let him be extinguished, and slink in Hell, who violates this Charter.* [Etc.]"[116]

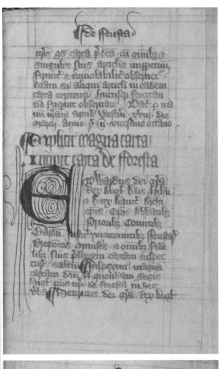

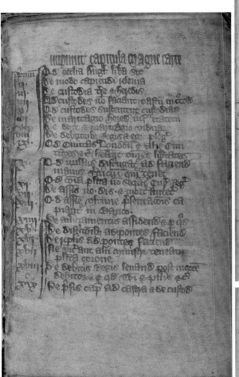

Magna Charta cum Statutis Angliae
[Miniature Magna Carta with the Statutes of England]. Bound manuscript
on vellum, fourteenth century. Law Library, Library of Congress

RIGHTS OF ENGLISHMEN
IN BRITISH AMERICA

The Excellent Priviledge of Liberty and Property

BEING A REPRINT AND FAC-SIMILE
OF THE FIRST AMERICAN EDITION OF

Magna Charta

PRINTED IN 1687 UNDER THE DIRECTION OF
WILLIAM PENN BY WILLIAM BRADFORD

PHILADELPHIA
Printed for The Philobiblon Club
MDCCCXCVII

MAGNA CARTA'S AMERICAN JOURNEY

*A. E. Dick Howard**

The First American Colonies

The first English colonists came to America for many reasons. Some sought refuge from religious intolerance; others simply sought a better life for themselves and their families. Each colony was grounded in a charter issued under royal authority.[1] The Virginia Company Charter of 1606 reflected the investors' hopes that the company's venture in the New World would turn a profit. The Crown, likewise, saw the colonies as a source of revenue, decreeing that it would get one-fifth of all the gold and silver found in Virginia.[2]

Nowhere does that early charter refer explicitly to Magna Carta. But the guarantees of the Great Charter of 1215 were borne to Virginia and to the later colonies all the same. The 1606 charter declared that the colonists and their posterity were to have and enjoy "all liberties, franchises and immunities" to the same extent "as if they had been abiding and borne" in England.[3] In other words, by settling in the New World, the colonists did not leave their rights behind. They carried those rights to the New World. The guarantees found in the Virginia charter were repeated in the charters of the other English colonies established in North America, from that of Massachusetts Bay (1629) to that of Georgia (1732) in language virtually identical to that found in the 1606 document.[4]

In some colonies, especially in New England, English laws were not the only source of governance.[5] In May 1636, the General Court of the Massachusetts Bay colony appointed a committee to draft laws "agreeable to the word of God," which would serve as the colony's fundamentals.[6] The result was the Body of Liberties of 1641. That statement of principles bore a striking resemblance to Magna Carta. The Body of Liberties began with the declaration that no one's life, person, or property be proceeded against save by virtue of "some expresse law of the Country"—an obvious

The Excellent Priviledge of Liberty and Property: Being a Reprint and Fac-simile of the First American Edition of Magna Charta; Printed under the Direction of William Penn by William Bradford. Philadelphia: Printed for the Philobiblon Club, 1897. Law Library, Library of Congress

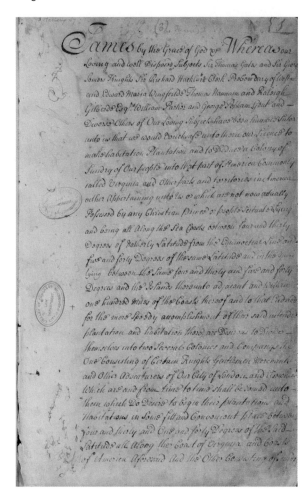

Charter of Virginia, 1606, in the Records of the Virginia Company. Thomas Jefferson Library Collection, Rare Book and Special Collections Division, Library of Congress.

descendant of Magna Carta's requirement that all proceedings take place according to the "law of the land," or what came to be called "due process of law."[7] Two hundred years later, the Supreme Court of Massachusetts observed that the Body of Liberties, even in its use of the term "liberty" in the sense of right, franchise, and privilege, drew directly on Magna Carta.[8]

The Body of Liberties did, however, contain a proviso that, for lack of a specific law, the proceedings would be according to the "word of God"—an open invitation for a judge to use his discretion.[9] Some persons in Massachusetts thought their rights were too uncertain. In 1646, some of the colony's freemen, led by Robert Child, submitted to the Governor and General Court a "Remonstrance and Petition." The petitioners said that they could not discern "a settled form of government according to the laws of England." They asked to be assured that they could enjoy their "lives, liberties, and estates" as was their due "as freeborne subjects of the English nation." Echoing the complaints of the barons of Runnymede, the petitioners complained of an "over greedy spirit of arbitrary power."[10]

The colony's magistrates were "much offended" by Child's petition, but they felt obliged to draw up an answer—the "parallels" of Massachusetts.[11] In one column, the General Court set down the "fundamental and common laws and customes of England, beginning with Magna Charta." In the other column, the magistrates outlined the "laws and customs" in force in Massachusetts.[12] At least one historian has found this bit of special pleading a tad "ingenious."[13] But what makes the "parallels" so interesting is that the colony's governors thought it necessary to declare that the rights given by Magna Carta and the common law were not being denied in Massachusetts.

Soon after the events of 1646, committees were appointed to undertake a comprehensive compilation of the laws of Massachusetts. As the project proceeded, the General Court ordered copies of six legal texts then in wide use in England. Three of those works—*Coke upon Littleton*, *Coke on Magna Carta*, and Coke's *Reports*—reflected the insights of Sir Edward Coke, the great expositor of Magna Carta and a leader in the seventeenth-century Parliament's battle against the overreaching of the Stuart kings.[14] The result of the drafting was the famous *Laws and Liberties of Massachusetts* of 1648. Historian George Haskins has called this "the first modern code of the Western world," antedating Colbert's project in France by twenty years.[15] Central themes drawn from Magna Carta appear in the *Laws and Liberties*. No punishments were to be meted out save according to "some expresse law of the Country"—an echo of Magna Carta's requirement that proceedings occur according to the law of the land. And every person in Massachusetts was to enjoy justice "without partialitie or delay"—the principle of impartial justice found in Magna Carta.[16]

Penn And Pennsylvania

William Penn had a personal hand in etching the lessons of Magna Carta on American constitutionalism. In 1670, Penn was put on trial at London's Old Bailey for the offense of "tumultuous assembly"—in fact, for his preaching of Quaker beliefs. Penn published his own version of the trial and explained that the judge had abused both the defendant and the jury. Penn declared that Magna Carta itself was on trial; the judge's "great charter" was "Will and Power."[17] Indeed, the judge, Sir John Keeling, was summoned to the bar of the House of Commons to answer the charge that, when a defendant had invoked Magna Carta, Sir John had called it "Magna Farta," a phrase attributed to Cromwell.[18]

In commenting on his trial, Penn cited a statute of Edward III that declared Magna Carta "be holden and kept in all points" and that statutes made contrary to the Great Charter "shall be holden for naught."[19] This suggestion of constitutional supremacy ultimately did not take root in England, where parliamentary sovereignty became firmly established.[20] But the idea took hold in Penn's mind. Several years after his trial, Penn arbitrated a dispute between two other Quakers over proprietary rights in New Jersey. Soon thereafter, Penn and Edward Byllinge drew up the *Fundamental Laws of West New Jersey* (1676). This remarkable document began with a declaration that the colony's legislature was "to make no laws that in the least contradict, differ or vary from" the *Fundamentals*.[21] It takes little imagination to see this notion of a fundamental law superior to ordinary statutes as anticipating the declaration in Article VI of the United States Constitution that the Constitution shall be the "supreme Law of the Land."

In 1680, Penn petitioned Charles II for a tract of land to be called Pennsylvania.[22] Now Penn had a colony in which he could put his ideas on religious and civil liberties to work. Setting sail for America in 1682, Penn carried with him his blueprint for Pennsylvania, the *Frame of Government for Pennsylvania*. In drafting this document, Penn drew deeply upon the tenets of Magna Carta. For example, the Great Charter's chapter 40 was replicated in the Pennsylvania admonition that "all courts shall be open, and justice shall neither be sold, denied, nor delayed."[23] Penn wanted Magna Carta's teachings to be widely understood in his new colony. Accordingly, he undertook the first publication in America of a commentary on the Great Charter. This appeared in 1687 under the title *The Excellent Priviledge of Liberty & Property Being the Birth-Right of the Free-Born Subjects of England*, published in Philadelphia. A preface to the reader expressed the hope that the publication of Magna Carta and other fundamental documents would bring American colonists to understand "that it is easier to part with or give away great Privileges, but hard to be gained, if once lost."[24]

Pennsylvania's Assembly followed Penn's lead when, in 1682 and 1683, it passed laws drawing heavily on Magna Carta and on Sir Edward Coke's writings about the Charter. For example, due process of law was guaranteed in language that was the virtual carbon copy of Magna Carta's chapter 39.[25] Pennsylvania's efforts to codify the rights of Englishmen in the late seventeenth and early eighteenth centuries ran into opposition in London. The Crown's advisors were concerned that the acts would interfere with the jurisdiction of the admiralty courts, where cases were tried by a judge sitting without a jury.[26] Indeed, England was beginning to move toward more centralized control over the colonies.[27] In 1719, the Lords of Trade declared that the plantations "will never be upon a right foot till the dominion of all the proprietary colonies shall be resumed to the crown."[28]

Toward Independence

In 1761, James Otis, representing Boston merchants, argued against the issuance by the Superior Court of writs of assistance.[29] The writs were being sought by royal officials attempting to enforce the Crown's customs laws and were therefore odious to merchants who looked to shipping for their income. Otis conceded that special writs—given upon oath to search specific houses—were acceptable. But general warrants would place "the liberty of every man in the hands of every petty officer," disregarding the principle that "a man's house is his castle."[30] Otis made the question one of fundamental law, asserting: "An Act against the Constitution is void: an Act against natural Equity is void … [and] the executive Courts must pass such Acts into disuse."[31] Otis lost the case. But John Adams, who had been in the courtroom to hear Otis argue, later said, "Then and there the child Independence was born."[32]

As support for his argument, Otis cited Coke's decision in *Dr. Bonham's Case* (1610). In that case, Coke had declared that if an act of Parliament "is against Common Right and Reason … the Common Law will control it, and adjudge such Act to be Void."[33] That famous decision might have encouraged English courts to review the constitutionality of statutes. But that is not where it led. Indeed, by the time Otis argued his case in Boston, Parliament was understood to have the last word. As Blackstone said in his *Commentaries*, which were published soon after the writs of assistance argument, if Parliament "will positively enact a thing to be done which is unreasonable, I know of no power that can control it."[34] In Boston, however, Otis continued to proclaim that natural equity and the British Constitution limited the powers of Parliament.[35] In his pamphlet, *The Rights of the British Colonies Asserted and Proved*, Otis asserted that "acts against the fundamental principles of the British constitution are void. This doctrine is agreeable to the law of nature and nations, and to the divine dictates of natural and revealed religion."[36]

As these events were taking shape in Boston, the Seven Years' War (1756–63) was changing the course of history, not only in Europe, but also in America. Great Britain was on the winning side, but it paid a heavy financial price for its victories. Having spent vast sums to secure the frontiers of the American colonies, the government in London looked to the colonists to pay part of the bill.[37] The first step was the Revenue Act of 1764, a measure that provoked petitions of protest by colonial assemblies.[38] A more severe test of the colonists' will was to come. In 1765, Parliament enacted the Stamp Act—the first direct, internal tax ever levied by Parliament in the American colonies (previous acts, such as the Revenue Act, had levied external taxes, such as customs duties).[39]

The colonists were quick to show their outrage over the Stamp Act.[40] In Boston, the "Sons of Liberty" sacked the homes of provincial officials, including the governor's residence. Colonial leaders put their case in constitutional terms. Virginia's legislature set the pattern. There the delegates declared that Virginia's original settlers brought with them and transmitted to their posterity the "Liberties, Privileges, Franchises, and Immunities" they would have enjoyed in England. They said, further, that the right not to be taxed without their consent was "the distinguishing Characteristic of *British* Freedom, without which the ancient Constitution cannot exist."[41]

The other colonies quickly followed Virginia's lead. The colonial assemblies voiced two main complaints against the Stamp Act—first, that it imposed taxes without the colonists' consent, and, second, that it contravened the right to trial by jury. The resolutions anchored both of these rights in Magna Carta. Massachusetts declared that the "essential Rights, Liberties, Privileges, and Immunities" of the people of Great Britain—among them, the right not to be taxed without consent—had been "fully confirmed to them by *Magna Charta.*"[42] Regarding trial by jury, Pennsylvania's assembly unanimously resolved that the vesting of jurisdiction in courts of admiralty to hear cases arising under the Stamp Act was "highly dangerous to the Liberties of his Majesty's *American* Subjects, contrary to *Magna Charta*, the great Charter and Fountain of *English* Liberty, and destructive of one of their most darling and acknowledged Rights, that of Trials by Juries."[43]

Massachusetts called for her sister colonies to combine their efforts. Foreshadowing the later Continental Congress, the resulting Stamp Act Congress brought some of the colonies' leading figures together in New York.[44] Among them was Pennsylvania's John Dickinson. Some years later, Dickinson was to write that it fell to Americans to preserve the ancient rights secured from King John in the thirteenth century and from the Stuart kings in the seventeenth century: "*England* must be saved in *America*. Hereafter, she will *rejoice* that we have *resisted*— and *thank* us for having *offended* her."[45] Acting on resolutions drafted by Dickinson, the Stamp Act Congress, like the individual colonies, affirmed that the colonists were entitled to "all the inherent Rights and Liberties" enjoyed by the King's subjects in England. Chief among these were the right to tax themselves and the right to trial by jury—rights "confirmed by the Great CHARTER of *English* Liberty."[46]

Yet while colonial discontent grew stronger, the road to revolution was not inevitable. There was a vast reservoir of goodwill in America toward the mother country. In 1770, George Mason voiced a widely held view: Americans, he said, had "the strongest attachment to the British government and constitution; they have experienced its blessings … [and] while they are protected in the enjoyment of its advantages they can never wish to change."[47] Until the end of the Seven Years'

War, they had enjoyed a freedom from interference in local affairs that colonists of France or Spain might have envied. For this goodwill to dissipate, there had to be, as John Adams put it, a revolution in the "minds and hearts of the people."[48] David Ramsay, an early historian of the American Revolution, pointed to the arguments of colonial leaders as an important catalyst in revolutionary thought. "In establishing American independence," Ramsay wrote, "the pen and the press had merit equal to that of the sword."[49]

Illustrative of the pamphlets written in response to British policies in the 1760s was Richard Bland's *Inquiry into the Rights of the British Colonies*. Bland adhered to a Whig view of history, admiring the virtues of a supposed golden age of liberty in Anglo-Saxon England. Bland's argument was eclectic. Looking to the colonial charters, the British Constitution, and natural law, he argued for the colonists' right to enact their own internal law.[50] In his rather scholarly essay, *Dissertation on the Canon and Feudal Law*, John Adams, too, saw something like Norman encroachments on Saxon liberties—what Adams called "a direct and formal design on foot to enslave all America." Adams attacked the Stamp Act as "renouncing the transactions at Runing Mede (the meadow, near Windsor, where Magna Charta was signed)."[51]

The Boston Tea Party brought a showdown. The Sons of Liberty, protesting the Townshend duty of 3*d.* per pound on tea, scurried aboard ships of the East India Company and dumped quantities of tea into the harbor. In response, Lord North's government set out to punish Boston. Some members of Parliament defended the American perspective. Edmund Burke protested the Boston Port Bill, which placed Boston under a kind of blockade. He hoped to see America governed by a plan "not founded upon your laws and statutes here, but grounded upon the vital principles of English liberty."[52] Yet despite Burke's dissent, the Boston Port Bill became law, as did other acts—labeled the "Coercive" or "Intolerable" Acts by colonists—providing for the quartering of British troops in private houses and the governor's appointment of a Council to replace the body elected by the Assembly.[53]

The other colonies rallied to support Massachusetts. Virginia's House of Burgesses set aside the day that the hated statutes went into effect as a day of fasting and prayer. Two days later, Governor Dunmore dissolved the Assembly.[54] Before leaving Williamsburg, the Burgesses met in the Raleigh Tavern and formed a committee, which recommended that each colony appoint delegates to a general congress.[55] The colonies concurred in Virginia's proposal. There remained hopes, as Delaware's resolution put it, that the people of Great Britain and America should remain "one people."[56] But the colonies agreed that concerted action was required.[57]

When the Continental Congress met in September 1774, the delegates agreed on a set of resolves. Among them was the declaration that the colonists' ancestors, emigrating to America, carried with them "all the rights, liberties, and immunities of free and natural-born subjects, within the realm of England."[58] The resolves spelled out what the members of the Congress believed those rights to be. These included, among others, "a free and exclusive power of legislation" in taxation and internal polity, the privileges of the common law (especially trial by jury), the rights of peaceable assembly and of petition for redress of grievances, and the right to consent to standing armies in time of peace.[59]

What place did Magna Carta have in the colonists' case against British policies? Was their case grounded in the British Constitution, which included Magna Carta? Or was the appeal ultimately to natural law and natural rights? In 1789, David Ramsay published his *History of the American Revolution*. Ramsay maintained that the colonists thought not about Magna Carta, but about the word of God:

> Many of them had never heard of Magna Charta, and those who knew the circumstances of the remarkable period of English history, when that was obtained, did not rest their claims to liberty and property on the transactions of that important day. They looked up to Heaven as the source of their right, and claimed, not from the promises of Kings but, from the parent of the universe.[60]

There is no doubt that advocates for colonial rights often put their arguments on the plane of natural law. In his *Address to the Committee of Correspondence in Barbados* (1766), John Dickinson declared that the Americans claimed their rights "from a higher source—from the King of kings, and Lord of all the earth." According to Dickinson, the colonists' rights had not been "annexed … by parchments and seals." Rather, they had been "created … by the decrees of Providence, which establish the laws of our nature." Those rights, Dickinson averred, were "founded on the immutable maxims of reason and justice."[61]

At the Continental Congress in 1774, much of the debate focused on just how the colonists' rights should be articulated. Richard Henry Lee, of Virginia, believed that those rights rested on several grounds—natural law, the British Constitution, colonial charters, and immemorial usage.[62] New York's John Duane preferred that the Congress ground the colonists' rights squarely on "the Laws and Constitution of the Country from whence we sprung"—on the "Birthright and Inheritance" of Englishmen.[63] Joseph Galloway, of Pennsylvania, agreed: "I have looked for our Rights in the Laws of Nature—but could not find them … . I have looked for them in the Constitution of the English Government, and there found them."[64] Ultimately, a spirit of eclecticism prevailed. Samuel Ward noted in his diary that the committee appointed to draft Congress' resolutions agreed to found the colonists' rights "upon the laws of Nature, the principles of the English Constitution, and charters and compacts."[65]

Appeals to natural or divine law and to Magna Carta and the British Constitution found a measure of common ground in the arguments of the revolutionary era. An example is an early pamphlet written by Alexander Hamilton, *A Full Vindication of the Measures of the Congress* (1774). Hamilton began with natural law: "All men have one common original: they participate in one common nature, and consequently have one common right." He then reinforced his argument by invoking the British Constitution: "Besides the clear voice of natural justice in this respect, the fundamental principles of the English constitution are in our favour." Hamilton then invoked yet another source of right—the colonial charters: "Nor is this all, our charters, the express conditions on which our progenitors relinquished their native countries, and came to settle in this, preclude every claim of ruling and taxing us without our consent." Then came a clean recapitulation—the argument that Parliament's pretensions were contradictory to "the law of nature, subversive of the British constitution, and destructive of the faith of the most solemn compacts."[66] Lawyer Hamilton thus summarized his arguments to the jury and rested his case.

The Early American State Constitutions

On May 15, 1776, Virginia's convention, meeting at Williamsburg, instructed their delegates in Philadelphia to introduce a resolution for independence. On the same day, the Virginians set to work on drafting a constitution for the new state. Then, as now, the country from which the Americans were breaking had no written constitution. Nor did it feel the need of one; custom, tradition, and convention would do the job. Americans, however, instinctively believed that the creation of a new society required writing a constitution. Actually, the Williamsburg delegates undertook two documents—a declaration of rights and a frame of government. Americans of that day were steeped in the philosophy of John Locke and the notion of a social compact. It was natural, therefore, that there were two steps—first, a statement of rights thought inherent in the human condition and, only then, the drafting of a frame of government.[67]

George Mason was the principal architect of Virginia's Declaration of Rights. In 1766, Mason wrote a letter to the Committee of Merchants in London in which he said that the colonists claimed "nothing but the liberties and privileges of Englishmen." Those rights, he declared, had been received from the colonists' ancestors, and "we will transmit them, unimpaired, to our posterity."[68] Mason had reason to know something about those rights, as he had been educated by an uncle who had a large library of over five hundred volumes, rich in law and

"North-Carolina" in *The Constitutions of the Several Independent States of America, the Declaration of Independence, the Articles of Confederation between the Said States, … .* London: J. Stockdale, 1782. Law Library, Library of Congress

history. In 1774, Mason wrote the Fairfax County Resolves, aimed at forming a militia ready to defend "the just rights and privileges of our fellow subjects, our posterity, and ourselves, upon the principles of the English Constitution."[69]

Mason's Declaration of Rights is vivid evidence of the way in which his generation of Americans blended natural rights and the legacy of British constitutionalism. The Declaration opens with statements of principle squarely in the tradition of John Locke:

That all men are by nature equally free and independent and have certain inherent rights, of which, when they enter into a state of society, they cannot, by any compact, deprive or divest their posterity; namely, the enjoyment of life and liberty, with the means of acquiring and possessing property, and pursuing and obtaining happiness and safety.[70]

112

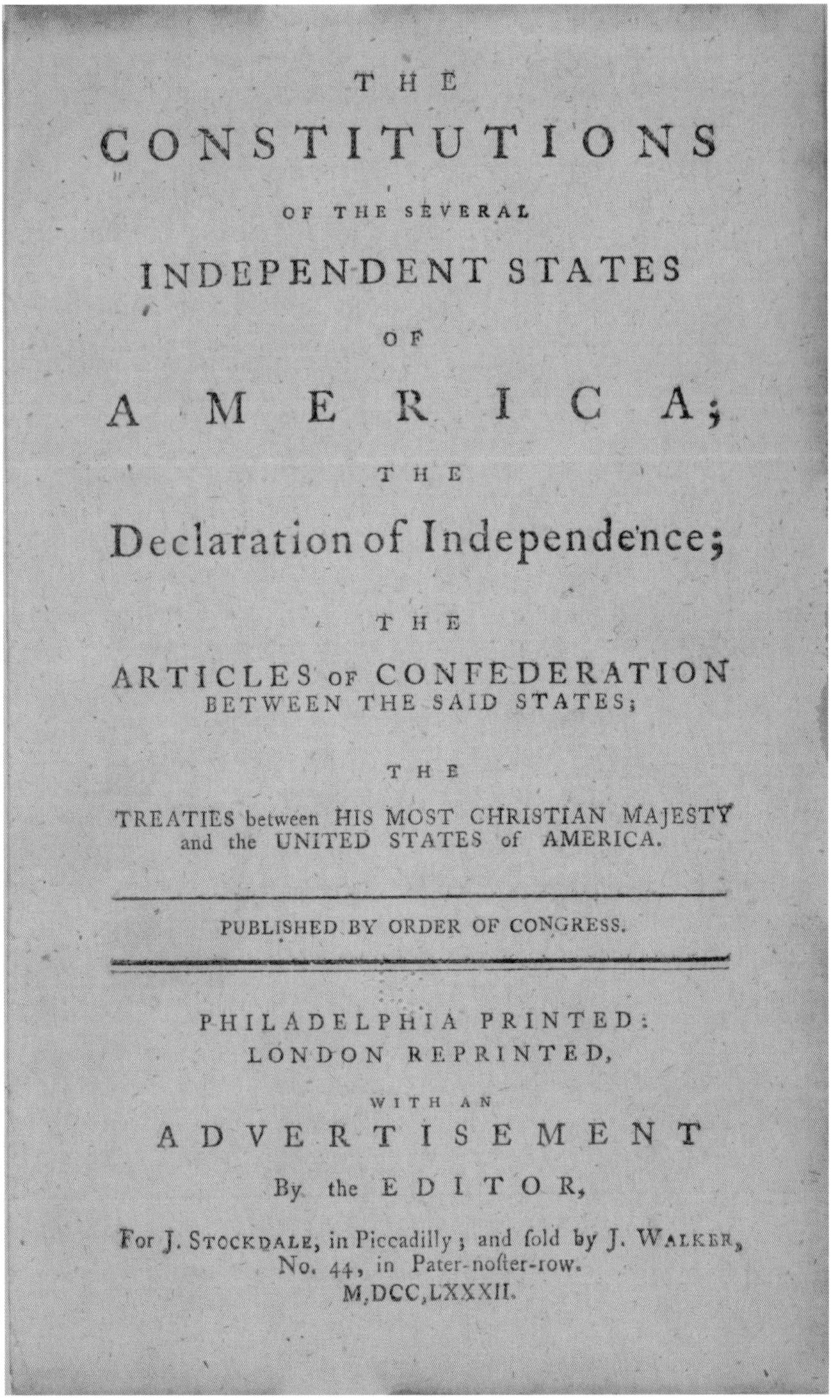

THE
CONSTITUTIONS

OF THE SEVERAL

INDEPENDENT STATES

OF

AMERICA;

THE

Declaration of Independence;

THE

ARTICLES OF CONFEDERATION
BETWEEN THE SAID STATES;

THE

TREATIES between HIS MOST CHRISTIAN MAJESTY
and the UNITED STATES of AMERICA.

PUBLISHED BY ORDER OF CONGRESS.

PHILADELPHIA PRINTED:
LONDON REPRINTED,

WITH AN

ADVERTISEMENT

By the EDITOR,

For J. STOCKDALE, in Piccadilly; and sold by J. WALKER,
No. 44, in Pater-noster-row.
M,DCC,LXXXII.

John Locke was, of course, English. But an Englishman of Mason's generation—living in an age in which Blackstone had decreed parliamentary sovereignty—would have been hard pressed to find the principle articulated in the Virginia Declaration of Rights in *his* basic law. Likewise, a distinct step beyond the old country's constitutionalism was the further statement in the Virginia declaration: "That all power is vested in, and consequently derived from, the people.[71] And what do you think George III made of the declaration that "whenever any government shall be found inadequate or contrary to these purposes, a majority of the community hath an indubitable, inalienable, and indefeasible right to reform, alter, or abolish it, in such manner as shall be judged most conducive to the public weal"?[72]

Following closely upon these principles in the Declaration of Rights drawn from natural law are provisions manifestly derived from Magna Carta and other English "liberty documents." Historian Allan Nevins believed that Virginia's Declaration of Rights and the other bills of rights that followed were in good measure restatements of English principles—"the principles of Magna Charta, the Petition of Right, the Commonwealth Parliament, and the Revolution of 1688."[73] And, indeed, that is just what one finds in the Declaration of Rights. From the principle developed in England from Magna Carta through the Petition of Right and the Bill of Rights came the Virginia provision that the people could not be taxed "without their own consent, or that of their representatives duly elected."[74] The first section of the English Bill of Rights finds its replica in the Virginians' declaration that laws shall not be suspended by any authority without the consent of the people's representatives.[75] Standing armies, thought to be a danger to liberty, are warned against in the 1776 document, recalling the 1689 Bill's prohibition against standing armies in peacetime without consent of parliament.[76]

Procedural rights (always a conspicuous feature of Anglo-American jurisprudence) are guaranteed in the Virginia Declaration of Rights. Trial by jury, which Coke and Blackstone had traced to Magna Carta, is assured.[77] The most tangible link to Magna Carta is found in Virginia's declaration that no one shall be deprived of life, liberty, or property "without due process of law"—echoing the Great Charter's requirement that proceedings occur according to the "law of the land."[78] The tenth section of the English Bill of Rights becomes, word for word, the ninth section of Mason's Declaration: "That excessive bail ought not to be required, nor excessive fines imposed, nor cruel and unusual punishments inflicted."[79]

Thomas Jefferson complained bitterly that Virginia's 1776 Constitution, adopted by the same body that enacted ordinary laws, was not fundamental law. He said that a convention, elected by the people, should be called, in order to put the Constitution on a firm basis.[80] Over time, however, Virginia's courts treated the Constitution of Virginia as in fact being superior to statutes, thus anticipating John Marshall's 1803 decision in *Marbury v. Madison*.[81]

In 1780, Massachusetts took the step that Jefferson's Virginia did not. Massachusetts's General Court began the process of writing a state constitution, but vocal opponents in the western part of the state objected that, in a free government, "there is an essential Distinction to be observed between the fundamental Constitution, & Legislation."[82] In 1779, the General Court issued a call for the election of delegates to a state constitutional convention. Meeting in September, the convention put the drafting job in the hands of a three-man committee composed of James Bowdoin, Samuel Adams, and John Adams. They, in turn, left the work largely to John Adams. The result was the Massachusetts Constitution of 1780.[83]

In his inaugural address as president of the American Historical Society in 1914, Andrew C. McLaughlin said that if he "were called upon to select a single fact or enterprise which more nearly than any other single thing embraced the significance of the American Revolution ... ," he would choose the Massachusetts Constitution of 1780.[84] Like George Mason's Declaration of Rights, the

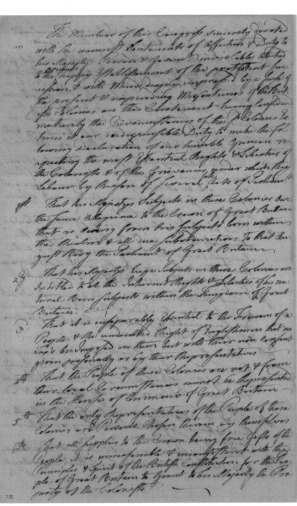

William Samuel Johnson (1727–1819). "Declaration of Rights and Grievances," October 19, 1765. William Samuel Johnson Papers, Manuscript Division, Library of Congress

Massachusetts Constitution shows on its face how natural law met the legacy of Magna Carta and British constitutionalism in America's founding era. Moreover, it merges two complementary insights—the notion of social compact and covenant theology. In its preamble, the Constitution uses "compact" and "covenant" interchangeably. "The body politic," it says, "is a social compact by which the whole people covenants with each citizen and each citizen with the whole people that all shall be governed by certain laws for the common good."[85]

We have seen how, in early colonial days, the word of God, as understood by public magistrates, might have seemed in tension with rights flowing from Magna Carta and the English common law. The drafters of the 1780 Constitution explicitly invoked God's blessings in drafting a constitution for the Commonwealth. The document's preamble acknowledges the "goodness of the great Legislator of the universe" in affording the people of Massachusetts the opportunity "of entering into an original, explicit, and solemn compact with each other, and of forming a new constitution of civil government for ourselves and posterity."[86] The Massachusetts Constitution further mingles the secular and the religious in its Declaration of Rights. The legacy of Locke and social compact is evident in the very first article. In language virtually identical to that penned by Mason in Virginia, the Massachusetts document declares, "All men are created free and equal, and have certain natural, essential, and unalienable rights," specifically, life, liberty, and property—"in fine, that of seeking and obtaining their safety and happiness."[87]

The Massachusetts Declaration places religion squarely at the base of the civil and political order: "It is the right as well as the duty of all men in society, publicly and at stated seasons, to worship the Supreme Being, the great Creator and Preserver of the universe."[88] Citizens are assured that they may worship according to the dictates of their conscience.[89] But the Declaration puts the power of the state behind religion, stating that the legislature shall require towns and other bodies to provide "for the institution of the public worship of God and for the support and maintenance of public Protestant teachers of piety, religion, and morality in all cases where such provision shall not be made voluntarily."[90] Separation of church and state, as we understand it today, had to await such further developments as Virginia's adoption, in 1786, of Thomas Jefferson's Statute for Religious Freedom, the First Amendment's Establishment Clause, and modern Supreme Court cases.[91]

Alongside its grounding in religion and morality, the Massachusetts Constitution of 1780 draws heavily on the legacy of Magna Carta. The Great Charter's requirement that proceedings occur according to the "law of the land" has its counterpart in Article X's assurance that each person is to enjoy the protection of life, liberty, and property "according to standing laws"—language that also recalls the requirement of the Body of Liberties of 1641 that proceedings be according to "some expresse law of the Country."[92] Article XII of the Constitution, in language virtually identical to that of Magna Carta's chapter 39, states that, in criminal proceedings, no one is to be "deprived of his life, liberty, or estate, but by the judgment of his peers, or the law of the land."[93] The King's promise, in chapter 40 of the Great Charter—"To no one will We sell, to none will We deny or delay, right or justice"— is more fully explicated in the Massachusetts Constitution:

> Every subject of the Commonwealth ought to find a certain remedy, by having recourse to the laws, for all injuries or wrongs which he may received in his person, property, or character. He ought to obtain right and justice freely and without being obliged to purchase it; completely, and without any denial; promptly, and without delay, conformably to the laws.[94]

The teachings of the English Bill of Rights also appear in the Massachusetts Declaration of Rights. These include the right to petition for redress of grievances, the ban on executive suspension of the laws, legislators' freedom of speech and debate, frequent legislative sessions, no taxation without consent, no excessive bail or fines, and the ban on cruel and unusual punishment.[95]

The extent to which John Adams looked to Magna Carta and other English sources as he worked up a draft of the Declaration of Rights is made clear when one considers how the relevant provisions are grouped. Near the beginning of the Declaration are three consecutive articles (X, XI, and XII) where Adams put into Massachusetts law principles drawn from Magna Carta's chapters 28, 39, and 40. Articles based on the Bill of Rights of 1689 likewise are grouped in Articles XIX, XX, XXI, XXII, XXIII, and XXVII. Toward the end of the Declaration, in Article XXVII, one finds a single provision drawn from the Petition of Right of 1628 (the ban on quartering troops on the populace in time of peace). And there is one provision (Article XXX) based on the Act of Settlement of 1701, which provides for an independent judiciary.

Picture the scene. John Adams sits alone, his fellow committee members James Bowdoin and Samuel Adams having decamped to a local tavern. Spread out on the table before Adams are an assortment of sources—Magna Carta, the English Bill of Rights, Locke's *Second Treatise*, Mason's Declaration of Rights, and other tomes. Deeply read in English and American constitutionalism, Adams knows these works intimately. He works briskly, turning first to one, then another, of the books before him. The result is perhaps as neat a distillation as one might ask of the era's constitutional principles, combining the rights the colonists claimed in the 1760s and 1770s with the rights Americans held basic to the formation of free governments.

The Federal Constitution And Bill Of Rights

In 1787, Congress issued a call to the states to send delegates to a convention to consider revising the Articles of Confederation. The men who assembled in Philadelphia in May were a remarkable group (young, too—five were under age thirty). They included most of the public figures who, during the nation's formative years, had made the most substantial contribution to thinking about how a free people should govern themselves.[96] In the four months they sat, the delegates achieved a fair measure of compromise between conflicting positions, reconciling the interests of large and small states and the competing views of nationalists who wanted a stronger central government and those who feared over-weaning national authority. The result was a mix of devices—federalism and checks and balances among them—designed to forge a "more perfect Union" while also securing the "Blessings of Liberty."

The delegates at Philadelphia were charting a course undreamt of by the barons of Runnymede. Charles Pinckney, of South Carolina, called the British Constitution "the best constitution in existence."[97] But he went on to say that the British model was "one that will not or cannot be introduced into this Country." Pinckney admired the balance among Crown, Lords, and Commons, but it was obvious that such a structure had no place in a country having neither Crown nor Lords.[98] Elbridge Gerry, of Massachusetts, warned his fellow delegates that "maxims taken from the British constitution were often fallacious when applied to our situation which was extremely different."[99]

Magna Carta was hardly relevant to the issues being thrashed out in Philadelphia. So far as the notes of the debates reveal, Magna Carta may never have been mentioned at all. The delegates at the 1787 convention were creating a new government. For such a project, Magna Carta offered little guidance. The barons and their allies did not seek to substitute one form of government for another; they wanted assurances against the Crown's arbitrary acts. The document agreed to at Runnymede could not be a blueprint for the delegates at Philadelphia.

The lessons of Magna Carta, however, held the hazard of derailing the proposed new Constitution. The Great Charter may not have attempted to craft a new government structure, but it was concerned with power and its limits. The delegates at Philadelphia were not unconcerned with individual liberty, but when they rejected the proposal to include a bill of rights in the proposed Constitution, they planted the seed of controversy that helped make ratification such a close contest. It was during those arguments over how best to protect the rights of Americans that Magna Carta appeared once again in the debate.

Among the proponents of the new Constitution were respected national leaders like George Washington and brilliant thinkers like James Madison and Alexander Hamilton. But the opponents of ratification packed a punch, too, led by such spokesmen as Patrick Henry, Richard Henry Lee, and Luther Martin. The opposition's case focused on the dangers of centralized power and, in particular, the proposed Constitution's lack of a bill of rights. In rebuttal, the proponents of ratification drew a contrast between America and Britain when arguing that a bill of rights was unnecessary. Oliver Ellsworth, who would later become Chief Justice of the United States, said that documents like Magna Carta were a function of disputes between kings and subjects, whereas, in America, "all the power government now has is a grant from the people."[100]

At Pennsylvania's ratifying convention, James Wilson conceded that England's Magna Carta was "an instrument of high value to the people of that country." Wilson held Magna Carta to be a grant from the king. In America, however, "the fee-simple remains in the people at large, and by this Constitution they do not part with it." For the Federalists, a bill of rights was not only unnecessary, it was imprudent. They reasoned that any attempt at an enumeration of rights would imply that anything not enumerated was within the power of the federal government.[101]

The Federalists sensed that, to achieve ratification, they had to yield some ground. A straw vote at the Massachusetts convention showed a majority of members prepared to vote "no." To secure a favorable result in Massachusetts, the Federalists agreed that, after ratification, a bill of rights should be added to the Constitution. Massachusetts then ratified, but the margin (187 to 168) was hardly overwhelming.[102] Greater tests lay ahead. Even though the Constitution went into effect with the ratification of the ninth state (New Hampshire), the important state of Virginia had not yet acted. There, it was a contest of giants: James Madison, John Marshall, and Edmund Randolph spoke for the Constitution, while George Mason and Patrick Henry led the opposition. In no state did the issues surrounding the new Constitution receive a fuller airing. Ultimately, the Federalists carried the day, and Virginia ratified by the close vote of 89 to 79.[103]

One doubts that some of the more reluctant states, notably New York and Virginia, would have ratified had there not been at least a tacit understanding that amendments to the Constitution would be proposed. Virginia's ratifying convention appointed a committee to draft proposed amendments. Chaired by the learned George Wythe, America's first professor of law and Thomas Jefferson's law teacher, the committee included an array of talent. Both Federalists and Anti-Federalists were well represented with Madison, Marshall, Henry, and Mason among the members. The committee reported a declaration of rights and a list

[Alexander Hamilton (1755–1804)]. Number 84 in *The Federalist: A Collection of Essays, Written in Favour of the New Constitution, As Agreed upon by the Federal Convention, September 17, 1787*, Vol. 2. New York: J. and A. M' Lean, 1788. Thomas Jefferson's Library, Rare Book and Special Collections Division, Library of Congress

of proposed constitutional amendments.

The declaration blended the precepts of natural law with traditions drawn from Magna Carta and the British Constitution. The declaration of rights articulated Locke's compact theory of government and the natural rights of life, liberty, and property. On this foundation of natural law, the declaration added provisions drawn from Magna Carta, including the glosses that centuries of constitutional usage had placed on it. Magna Carta's "law of the land" provision (chapter 39) was restated almost verbatim. The Charter's chapter 40 appeared in the proposed amendment insisting that justice not be denied or delayed. Other provisions reflected the legacy of the Bill of Rights of 1689. These included a ban on suspending the laws, a decree against excessive bail, excessive fines, a prohibition against cruel and unusual punishment, the right peaceably to petition for redress of grievances, and a warning against standing armies.[104]

James Madison steered proposed amendments to the Constitution through the first Congress, winnowing out those he thought dangerous and producing a final twelve. Ten of these were ratified, giving us the Bill of Rights.[105]

Throughout the colonial period, Americans had repeatedly invoked Magna Carta, especially in their resistance to British policies in the years leading up to the revolution. But independence and American constitution-making lent a new perspective. Americans might have learned from Britain, but they had greater goals in mind. Magna Carta might be admired, but it could not do all of the work for the new country. Yet the American debt to Magna Carta remains considerable. In his book *The American Commonwealth*, Lord Bryce praised the United States Constitution. But he added:

> The American Constitution is no exception to the rule that everything which has its power to win the obedience and respect of men must have its roots deep in the past, and that the more slowly every institution has grown, so much more the enduring is it likely to prove. There is little in this Constitution that is absolutely new. There is much that is as old as Magna Charta.[106]

Innovation and tradition: each has played a part in shaping constitutionalism in America. Innovation may perhaps be most obvious in such American devices as federalism and judicial review. The modern world sees a range of variations on American federalism, among them devolution and subsidiarity. As to judicial review, perhaps no American contribution to global constitutionalism has been more important. Judicial review, a rare phenomenon before World War II, is today a common practice in an age of human rights.[107]

Tradition is more obvious in the state and federal bills of rights. It is in those documents that we find the bridge between Magna Carta in England and the Charter's legacy in America. But there are other legacies as well. When we celebrate the rule of law, we mark a concept that traces back to Magna Carta. When we search for limits on government power, we walk in a pathway marked out by the parties at Runnymede. When we find manifold meanings in due process of law, we add new layers to Magna Carta's "law of the land." We don't live in feudal times, and in America we are not concerned about the pretensions of monarchs. But Magna Carta remains with us as we seek the promise of ordered liberty.

AMERICAN STATE CONSTITUTIONS AND THE THREE FACES OF MAGNA CARTA

G. Alan Tarr

Magna Carta has three "faces": an historical face, a legal face, and a symbolic face. The historical face of Magna Carta refers to the events that culminated in the fabled meadow at Runnymede, where in June 1215, King John agreed to the document prepared by his rebellious nobles, who sought to recover their traditional liberties. Magna Carta in actuality did little to restrain King John. He was able to persuade Pope Innocent III to annul Magna Carta as having no legal force, because it was signed under duress, and he violated the document within months after signing it. Yet a year after King John's death in 1216 and the accession of his nine-year-old son to the throne, Magna Carta was reissued with the approval of the new king's guardian and the papal legate, and it thereafter had a significant effect in regulating and restraining monarchial power. In any event, the immediate historical outcome was not decisive for the legal or symbolic faces of Magna Carta, as "its utility in the constitutional domain has been largely dependent upon its exaltation beyond the realm of fact."[1]

The legal face of Magna Carta refers to the legal restraints it imposed on monarchial power, which were incorporated into English law. Not all of the provisions of Magna Carta lent themselves to becoming legal standards. Some, such as clause 33, which required the removal of all fish-weirs from the Thames and the Medway, and clause 50, which required the removal from their offices of the relatives of Girard d'Athee, were tied to the particulars of the situation in 1215 and had no bearing on subsequent legal development. However, other provisions, such as the prohibition of taxation without consent and the requirement that no person be punished "save by the lawful judgment of his peers and by the law of the land," announced principles of broad and lasting significance.[2] The process of conversion of these latter restraints into law occurred through the processes of the common law, as judges elaborated, adapted, and applied the principles contained in the Great Charter. In doing so they confirmed that government was subject to law and that Englishmen possessed rights that the government could not violate. Thus, as John Phillip Reid has observed, "Magna Carta, a reservation of feudal privileges to the great barons and churchmen of the realm, was slowly transmuted by centuries of litigation and countless refinements into a popular document revered as the legal cornerstone protecting the personal liberties of average citizens."[3] Here the influence of Sir Edward Coke was decisive. His *Institutes*, which provided a commentary on the common law and in doing so highlighted Magna Carta's central place in English law, was the most widely read legal treatise in both England and America until the publication of Blackstone's *Commentaries*, and its invocation of Magna Carta influenced generations of law students and lawyers.

Finally, the symbolic face of Magna Carta refers to what the Great Charter has come to stand for. Invocation of Magna Carta has become shorthand for legal and political principles such as limited government, the rule of law, due process of law, and restraints on executive overreaching. By the early seventeenth century, "the very words 'Magna Carta' and 'Great Charter' had acquired an almost mystic incantatory quality."[4] These principles have had resonance beyond the British Isles, wherever English law has operated. Moreover, those invoking Magna Carta in support of those principles have had the signal advantage of being able to point out that the principles are of long-standing and of recognized authority, so that arguments against them can be seen as a denial of the English heritage of liberty.

Of these three faces of Magna Carta, the latter two—the legal and the symbolic—have had a major influence on American state constitutions, especially during the eighteenth century.[5] The reasons why Magna Carta was important to Americans as law and symbol during the seventeenth and eighteenth centuries and why it has declined in importance since then provide the focus for this essay.

Magna Carta In America Before The Revolution

Magna Carta influenced law and government in the North American colonies even before the drafting of the first state constitutions. The charters issued to those colonizing the new world guaranteed various rights—for example, the charter granted by King James I to the Virginia Company declared that all inhabitants of the colony "shall have and enjoy all liberties, franchises, and immunities . . . as if they had been abiding and borne within this realme of Englande"—and the liberties referred to in these royal charters were the traditional liberties recognized at common law, which itself drew inspiration from Magna Carta.[6] Most colonies from the outset established legal systems rooted in the common law, and even those like Massachusetts that initially grounded their law on the Bible incorporated the common law by the late seventeenth century. In adopting the English common law, the American colonies also imported Magna Carta. Indeed, "the most profound effect of common law was . . . to generate the core of their bills of rights: the right to trial by a jury of one's peers; the right to a speedy trial; prohibition of bills of attainder, ex post facto laws, and cruel and unusual punishment; the guarantee of habeas corpus; the rights of widows and the poor; the right to compensation for the taking of private property; and equal protection under the laws."[7]

Magna Carta was also reflected in documents drawn up by the colonists themselves, which were the antecedents of the later state constitutions and state declarations of rights. For example, the Mayflower Compact (1620), the Fundamental Orders of Connecticut (1639), and Penn's Charter of Liberties (1682) all elaborated the colonists' fundamental values and imposed restrictions on the discretion of governmental officials. Of particular note was the Massachusetts Body of Liberties (1641), arguably the first bill of rights ever crafted, which drew some of its provisions, such as the guarantee of due process, directly from Magna Carta.

The colonists from the outset saw themselves as Englishmen and the king's free subjects, and so when they had complaints about royal governors or the authorities in England, they tended to frame them in terms of Magna Carta. For example, when conflicts arose between governors and the people's representatives in lower houses of colonial legislatures, often over raising revenue, the legislators insisted that Magna Carta guaranteed the principle of taxation by statute. When in the decade prior to independence the American colonies protested against royal usurpations of their liberties, Magna Carta played an important role, just as it had in England during the seventeenth-century conflicts between king and parliament. Reinterpreting the barons at Runnymede as champions of popular liberty, the colonists regularly cited the "ancient and unalienable rights and liberties" of Magna Carta in pamphlets and in speeches, in courtrooms and in the streets, when arguing that they be accorded "the rights of Englishmen."[8] Doing so had the advantage for the colonists of appealing to a standard to which both they and the English recognized as authoritative. Magna Carta also served as an inspiration because it embodied the idea that political authority should be subject to law and the practice of forcing liberties from a reluctant king. Thus when Massachusetts created a state seal at the outset of the Revolutionary War, the seal depicted a militiaman with a sword in one hand and Magna Carta in the other.[9]

Magna Carta And The First State Constitutions

Even before independence was formally declared on July 4, 1776, three states—South Carolina, Virginia, and New Jersey—had already drafted constitutions; and after independence most states followed suit, although Connecticut and Rhode Island chose to retain their colonial charters as their fundamental law. Several things must be said about these eighteenth-century state constitutions. First, those who drafted them were concerned not only to establish new governments but also to justify the revolution that called them into being. Thus both the South Carolina Constitution of 1776 and the New York Constitution

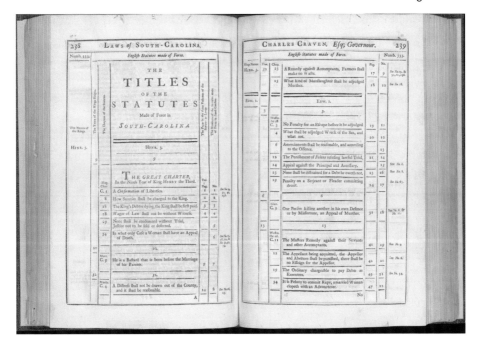

The Laws of the Province of South-Carolina, in Two Parts. . . . Charles-Town, South Carolina: Printed by Lewis Timothy, 1736. Law Library, Library of Congress

of 1777 began with a detailed inventory of the violations of rights that led to the break with England, implicitly invoking the catalogue of offenses found in Magna Carta. Second, several of these early constitutions were drafted in haste, given the exigencies of war. In New York, for example, the legislature was almost constantly on the run from British forces—two members wryly suggested that it might be better "first to endeavor to secure a State to govern before we established a form to govern it by"—and fear of invasion prompted the New Jersey legislature to frame and adopt a constitution in less than two weeks.[10] Third, the idea of creating written constitutions to establish and circumscribe governments was a new one, so those involved in drafting the constitutions had no experience in undertaking the task. As James Madison observed in The Federalist No. 47, the state constitutions "carry strong marks of the haste, and still stronger of the inexperience, under which they were framed."[11] As a result, it is hardly surprising that some states, like Massachusetts and New Hampshire, had difficulty gaining popular approval of their constitutions and that several states replaced their initial constitutions within a decade of their adoption.[12] Nor is it surprising that the inexperienced constitution-makers looked for guidance as to what should be included in their constitutions, and the Magna Carta served as an important resource, both directly and indirectly through its influence on the common law, for those crafting state declarations of rights.

More specifically, several clauses in Magna Carta served as inspiration for guarantees in state declarations of rights or, if the constitutions did not include declarations of rights, in the body of the documents themselves. The Pennsylvania Declaration of Rights of 1776, which was copied almost verbatim by constitution-makers in Vermont and Delaware, includes a right of free emigration from the state (Article XV), drawn from clause 42 of Magna Carta. It also includes a ban on the public taking of private property without just compensation (Article VIII), drawing on clause 28 of Magna Carta; a requirement of jury trial and judicial proceedings according to "the law of the land" (Article IX), drawing on clause 39 of Magna Carta; and a ban on excessive fines (Article XXIX), drawing on clause 20 of Magna Carta. Altogether nine states included law-of-the-land or due process guarantees in their early constitutions, and nine prohibited excessive fines.[13] The Massachusetts Declaration of Rights of 1780 includes jury-trial, law-of-the-land, and excessive-fines provisions (in Articles X,

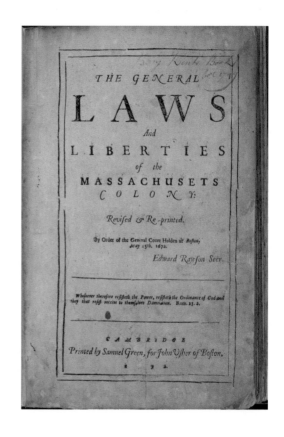

The General Laws and Liberties of the Massachusets [sic] Colony, by Order of the General Court, Holden at Boston, May 15th, 1672, Edward Rawson, Secr. Cambridge: Samuel Green, 1672. Law Library, Library of Congress

XII, and XXVI), but it also draws upon and elaborates clause 40 of Magna Carta in its Article XII: "Every subject of the commonwealth ought to find a certain remedy, by having recourse to the laws, for all injuries or wrongs which he may receive in his person, property, or character. He ought to obtain right and justice freely, and without being obliged to purchase it; completely, and without any denial; promptly, and without delay; conformably to the laws." Four other states also included right-to-a-remedy provisions in their declarations of rights.[14]

The Declining Influence Of Magna Carta

If the state constitution-makers of the eighteenth century were well aware of their debt to Magna Carta, the same cannot be said of their counterparts in the nineteenth and twentieth centuries. The constitutional convention debates of the nineteenth century contain few references to Magna Carta, and in the convention debates of the twentieth century (there are no twenty-first-century state constitutions), even those occasional references all but disappear. What accounts for the disappearance of Magna Carta from state constitutional discourse?

One major factor is the passage of time since American independence. The states that formed the Union in the eighteenth century all had the experience of British rule. They borrowed their legal systems from England and their legal principles as well: thus, the emphasis on Coke and on the common law. Because their legal sustenance was English, it was not surprising that the colonists, when disputes arose between them and the English government, tended to frame their arguments in terms of the British Constitution and to invoke Magna Carta as a key element of that constitution. As A. E. Dick Howard put it: "The story of Magna Carta in this country carries throughout the stamp of England."[15]

By the nineteenth century, the American connection with England was not lived experience but history. None of the new states drafting constitutions had been English colonies. Although the states retained the common law, it was not simply the common law as received from England but rather a body of law adapted to American circumstances, including American republicanism. As the New York Constitution of 1777 noted, "such parts of the common law of England . . . as together did form the law of the said colony on the 19th day of April, in the year of our Lord one thousand seven hundred and seventy-five, shall be and continue the law of this State." But it then added the proviso that "all such parts of the said common law . . . as may be construed to establish or maintain any particular denomination of Christians or their ministers, or concern the allegiance heretofore yielded to, and the supremacy, sovereignty, government, or prerogatives claimed or exercised by, the King of Great Britain and his predecessors, over the colony of New York and its inhabitants, or are repugnant to this constitution, be, and they hereby are, abrogated and rejected."[16] It also emphasized that the legislature could change or supersede the common law by statute.

Independent Chronicle and the Universal Advertiser (Boston), November 7, 1776 [with reprint of Pennsylvania Constitution from the *Pennsylvania Journal*, October 9, 1776]. Serial and Government Publications Division, Library of Congress

Moreover, the tasks facing constitution-makers shifted somewhat after the initial flurry of constitutional creation in the eighteenth century. Those early constitutions contained a listing of fundamental rights, and later constitution-makers for the most part simply added those lists to their constitutions, concentrating their attention on questions such as the franchise, legislative apportionment, and distribution of powers among the branches of government. With this shift in focus, state constitution-makers no longer looked to Magna Carta, which did not address such issues, but instead to a variety of American models. They could take their cues from the federal Constitution, or they could seek guidance in the constitutions of their sister states. Scholars have remarked on the ubiquity of constitutional borrowing, but it was always borrowing from American sources. There was no need to look beyond the nation's borders for guidance, and Americans believed that Europe had little to teach them about republican government. As Donald Lutz has observed: "In England the common law was the primary means of limiting governmental power, whereas in America the means was different. The idea of limited government does in part derive from it. But in the American constitutional tradition, what replaced common law was a new political technique, the written constitution."[17] Admittedly, in borrowing from those American sources, particularly for declarations of rights, the constitution-makers may have been very indirectly relying on Magna Carta. So as Americans' frame of reference shifted, so did the salience of Magna Carta.

Another factor was the replacement of Magna Carta by the Declaration of Independence as the primary source for political principle and political inspiration in the United States. This substitution of an American political document, memorializing an American revolt against arbitrary power, was facilitated by the striking parallels between the Declaration and Magna Carta. Both have an historical face, arising out of a particular series of political abuses detailed in the documents themselves. In the case of Magna Carta, these abuses produced an effort to constrain monarchial power; in the case of the Declaration of Independence, an effort to overthrow that power. Both documents have a legal face in that they spawned standards that became part of the legal structure of the society. In the case of Magna Carta, these legal principles were enshrined in the common law and in subsequent legal documents such as the Bill of Rights of 1689. The legal principles found in the Declaration—including the separation of powers, the independence of the judiciary, and the rights of the citizenry—were incorporated into constitutional documents and political practice. Finally, both documents have a symbolic function in that they stand for the principle of freedom from arbitrary power, although—perhaps unsurprisingly given its republican origins—the Declaration adds to that the equality of all human beings and their possession of natural rights. Put differently, Magna Carta served as a source of inspiration for American lovers of liberty until they developed their own Great Charter. This accords with the advice of Thomas Paine, who in *Common Sense* urged that a "continental conference" be called "to frame a CONTINENTAL CHARTER, or Charter of the United Colonies; (answering to what is called the Magna Charta of England)."[18] Yet even today, through the common law and through judicial rulings interpreting rights guarantees, Magna Carta continues to have an influence on American law, and through the Declaration of Independence, which it inspired, it continues to serve as a symbol of law circumscribing governmental power.

DUE PROCESS OF LAW

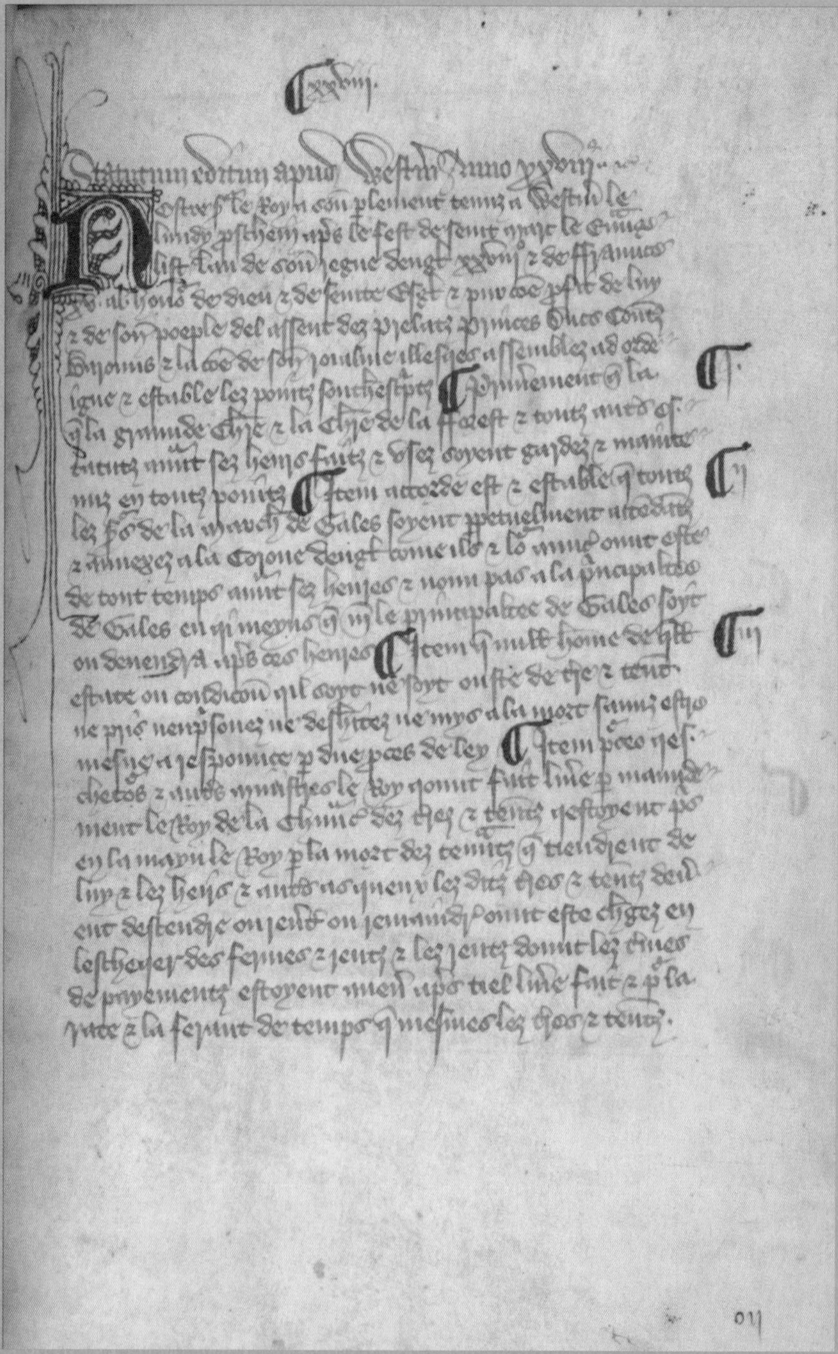

DUE PROCESS—OPEN COURT PROVISIONS / PROTECTION OF RIGHTS / REDRESS FOR INJURIES

William C. Koch, Jr.[1]

State courts are the chief protectors of their state's constitution[2] and thus are the chief expositors of the fundamental principles contained therein.[3] Their decisions express each state's unique constitutional culture.[4] Together, the state courts are engaged in a common search for the meaning of fundamental constitutional principles[5] and are now significant voices in the ongoing debate about the meaning of the rule of law in our country's democratic political order in the twenty-first century.[6]

The rights and powers of the people existed before the state constitutions were drafted.[7] The people possessed the inherent right of self-government[8] and had formed communities and governments before they set themselves to the task of drafting a constitution.[9] Thus, state constitutions are not the sources of the people's rights but rather the consequences of the exercise of their power.[10] Like their federal counterpart, state constitutions provide limitations and restrictions on government's authority.[11] They provide the framework of government and protect the people's pre-existing rights and powers.[12]

While each state constitution has its own unique history, all state constitutions share a common historical and jurisprudential heritage with other state constitutions.[13] Courts frequently rely on history[14] when called upon to interpret their constitution because constitutional freedoms vanish when their history is forgotten.[15]

It is against this backdrop that we will examine the development of open courts provisions in state constitutions. We cannot hope to understand their present meaning and application without understanding the past.[16] The inquiry begins in 1215 at Runnymede with King John's Magna Carta and proceeds through the reign of King

Due process statute in *Statuta Nova*, 1 Ed. III to 21 Richard II, 1354. Bound manuscript on vellum, fifteenth century. Law Library, Library of Congress

Henry III to the time of Sir Edward Coke. It then crosses the Atlantic Ocean to colonial America and the adoption of open courts clauses in the first state constitutions.

Magna Carta's influence was evident when the states began drafting their first constitutions and declarations of rights.[17] The colonists turned to the states to protect their rights and freedoms because the states were the most significant governmental institutions at that time.[18] After the Continental Congress advised the thirteen colonies to reorganize their governments based on "the authority of the people,"[19] each state began preparing documents patterned after Magna Carta.

On June 29, 1776, Virginia became the first state to adopt a permanent declaration of rights and constitution.[20] Five more states adopted constitutions in 1776.[21] Two more states followed suit in 1777,[22] and by 1784, all of the original states, with the exception of Connecticut and Rhode Island, had adopted constitutions.[23] The texts of these documents indicate that the bodies drafting the new state constitutions and bills of rights often imitated each other and that the form of the various states' bills of rights had fallen into a stereotyped pattern.[24]

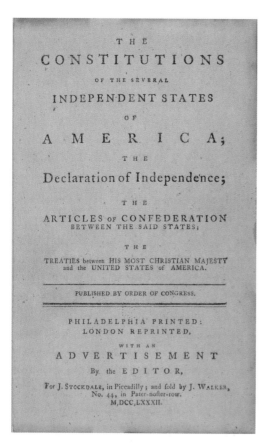

The Constitutions of the Several Independent States of America, the Declaration of Independence, the Articles of Confederation between the Said States, … . London: J. Stockdale, 1782. Law Library, Library of Congress

The constitutions in six of the original thirteen states contained "open courts" or "right to remedy" provisions derived from Chapter 40 of King John's Magna Carta and Chapter 29 of the 1225 Magna Carta. Four of these states paraphrased Lord Coke's explanation of Chapter 29.[25] Section 12 of the Delaware Declaration of Rights of 1776, for example, stated:

> That every Freeman for every Injury done him in his Goods, Lands or Person, by any other Person, ought to have Remedy by the Course of the Law of the Land and ought to have Justice and Right for the injury done to him freely without Sale, fully without any Denial, and speedily without Delay, according to the Law of the Land.[26]

The constitutions of Maryland, Massachusetts, and New Hampshire contained similar provisions.[27] Pennsylvania's 1776 constitution provided that "[a]ll courts shall be open, and justice shall be impartially administered without corruption or unnecessary delay."[28] North Carolina's 1776 constitution limited the remedy to persons who were restrained of their liberty.[29]

Vermont and Kentucky joined the union before Tennessee became a state in 1796. The constitutions of both these states contained an open courts clause. Vermont's provision was patterned after Part I, art. XI of the Massachusetts Constitution of 1780;[30] while Kentucky's provision was taken from Article IX, § 11 of the Pennsylvania Constitution of 1790.[31] In addition, Delaware amended its constitution and included an open courts provision resembling Pennsylvania's provision.[32]

Tenn. Const. art. I, § 17 actually embodies five discrete rights.[33] The "open courts" clause guarantees that "all courts shall be open." The "right to remedy" clause states that all persons "shall have remedy by due course of law" for injuries to their lands, goods, person, or reputation. In addition, Tenn. Const. art. I, § 17 guarantees that right and justice will be administered without sale, that right and justice will be administered without denial, and that right and justice will be administered without delay.[34]

In its earliest decisions, the Tennessee Supreme Court recognized that Tenn. Const. art. I, § 17 had been derived from Magna Carta.[35] Even though many of the provisions of the Bill of Rights, including Tenn. Const. art. I, § 17, were expressly addressed to the courts, the Court recognized that the judiciary was "required by the most solemn obligations, to see that, as to any and every citizen, they are not violated in one jot or tittle."[36] Accordingly, the Court reasoned that all branches of government are equally bound by the constitution.[37]

The prevailing view of the general applicability of the constitution to all branches of government was consistent with the specific interpretations of Tenn. Const.

art. I, § 17. In one of its earliest decisions of significant constitutional import, the Tennessee Supreme Court invoked the original version of Tenn. Const. art. I, § 17 to invalidate a statute restricting a plaintiff's ability to execute on a judgment. The Court explained:

> In Magna Charta this restriction [Tenn. Const. of 1796, art. XI, § 17] is upon royal power; in our country it is upon the legislative and all other power. We must understand the meaning to be that, notwithstanding any act of the Legislature to the contrary, every man shall have "right and justice" in all cases, "without sale, denial, or delay."
>
> In 1796, when the Constitution was formed, it could not have been apprehended that any other department of government, except that of the Legislature, would ever have weight enough to offer any obstruction. Experience from 1777 had fully demonstrated the imbecility of every executive office in the United States. From the executive no such offer could be anticipated. In 2d Institute, 55 my Lord Coke says the king is the speaker, and, in contemplation of law, is constantly present in all his courts, pronouncing the words of Magna Charta, *Nulli vendemus, nulli negabimus, aut differenemus justitiam vel rectum.*" In Tennessee every Legislature is in contemplation of law during the whole session, and the judge of every court during the whole term, in the constant repetition of the words "right and justice" must be "administered without sale, denial, or delay."[38]

Thirteen years later, the Tennessee Supreme Court reiterated its conclusion that Tenn. Const. art. I, § 17 was a restriction on the General Assembly when it struck down a statute intended to abolish a cause of action based on a pre-existing statute.[39] The Court adopted the chancellor's opinion striking down the 1831 statute which stated, in part:

> In England, the reason of riveting this barrier around the rights of the subject was well understood. Their sovereign was want to interfere in the administration of justice; "a remedy by due course of law" was often refused, under the mandate of men in power, and the injured man denied justice; they were ordered sometimes not to proceed with particular causes, and justice was delayed; and the obtainment of their rights was often burdened with improper conditions and sacrifices, and justice was sold. So anxious were they to stop this enormous evil, that a part of the official oath of a judge was that he would proceed to do right and justice, notwithstanding any letter or order to him to the contrary.[40] This clause of *Magna Charta*, why is it inserted in our Bill of Rights? Was it

from apprehension of our executive? We had left him no power. Whatever power is required as properly belonging to the executive department elsewhere is, by our institutions, conferred upon the legislature. It is the more important, therefore, and so the framers of our constitution decreed, that the judicial department should be independent and coördinate, and that the legislature should have no judicial power. Danger might justly be apprehended from this quarter. . . . If the legislature, possessing a large share of executive power, be permitted to exercise judicial power also, or control the action of the judges within their peculiar sphere, the liberty of the citizens, under the government of good legislators, would be in imminent peril, and under bad ones would be entirely destroyed.[41]

Thirty-eight state constitutions contain an open courts or right to remedy provision.[42] The provision first appeared in 1776 in Delaware's Declaration of Rights.[43]

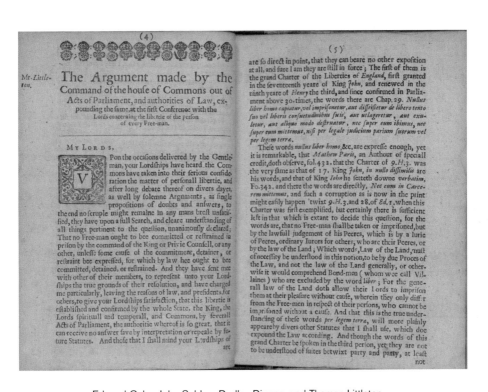

Edward Coke, John Selden, Dudley Digges, and Thomas Littleton. *A Conference Desired by the Lords and Had by a Committee of Both Houses.* London: M. Walbancke and R. Best, 1642. Law Library, Library of Congress

It was followed one week later by another formulation in the Pennsylvania Constitution of 1776.[44] The most recently enacted version of the provision appears in the Constitution of Arizona which was adopted in 1912.[45]

Most of these provisions reflect Lord Coke's elaboration of Chapter 29 of the 1225 version of Magna Carta.[46] They also reflect the concept that William Penn first introduced in 1683 in the Frame of Government of Pennsylvania that "all courts shall be open."[47] Thirty-six provisions, paraphrasing Lord Coke, guarantee justice without "sale, denial, or delay.[48] Thirty provisions contain language guaranteeing some form of a right to a remedy.[49]

Twenty-two provisions require that the courts of their state be "open."[50] In addition, one provision guarantees that "[n]o court shall be secret,"[51] and another provision declares that "[a]ll courts shall be public."[52] Five provisions specifically authorize the legislature to permit suits against governmental entities using language similar to a provision that first appeared in the Pennsylvania Constitution of 1790.[53]

State courts have been left to develop their own interpretations of their own state's open courts provision. It should not be surprising that these interpretations have not moved in lock step in the same direction. Differences in language and in each state's constitutional culture account for some of these differences.

Despite the lack of complete uniformity, the decisions of the various state courts construing their own open courts provision point to a growing consensus on a number of issues. First, most courts now agree that the open courts provision does not itself create new rights or causes of action.[54] They also agree that the open courts provision is not intended to protect the same rights and interests protected by the due process clause.[55] Thus, the open courts provision protects "jural rights," that is, the right to seek judicial redress for injuries or to protect rights and interests recognized elsewhere in the law.

Open courts provisions in state constitutions are a direct descendant of Magna Carta. They embody three of Magna Carta's most important principles: first, that all persons, including those in authority, are subject to the rule of law; second, that all persons are entitled to equal justice; and third, that all persons have the right to the protection of their person and property from injury or wrong. As later interpreted by Lord Coke, these principles coalesced into the fundamental guarantee that all Englishmen had the right to apply to the courts of justice for the protection of their rights and for the redress of injuries. American colonists considered this jural right—the right to a judicial remedy—to be one of their most precious rights as English subjects. Accordingly, they recognized and preserved this right in their early constitutions and bills of rights.

If the jural rights recognized in open courts clauses are to be preserved, judges must return to the fundamental principles that first prompted the inclusion of the open courts clause in state constitutions. Foremost among these principles is that the courts exist to provide an accessible forum for the resolution of disputes and the protection of rights and liberties. Returning to this fundamental principle not only insures the preservation and continuation of an important constitutional right but also serves as a reminder to the courts of their reason for being.

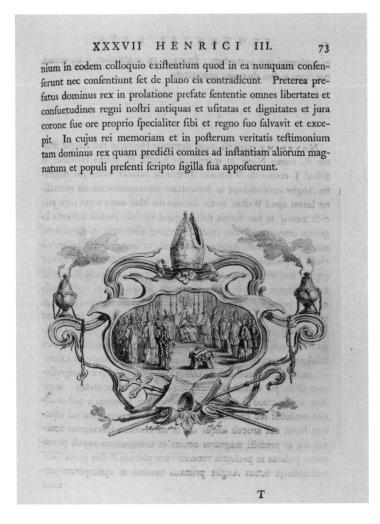

William Blackstone (1723–1780). *The Great Charter and Charter of the Forest, with Other Authentic Instruments: To Which Is Prefixed an Introductory Discourse, Containing the History of the Charters.* Oxford: Clarendon Press, 1759. Law Library, Library of Congress

RIGHT TO A JURY TRIAL

MAGNA CARTA AND THE RIGHT TO TRIAL BY JURY

Thomas J. McSweeney[1]

Magna Carta is often invoked as the primal source of the right to trial by jury. The influential English legal commentator Sir William Blackstone trumpeted Magna Carta's guarantee of trial by jury.[2] American constitutional debates regularly cited Magna Carta in connection with the right to jury trial. And linkages between jury trial rights and Magna Carta continue today. The United States Supreme Court wrote as recently as 2005 that in England, "the right to a jury trial had been enshrined since the Magna Carta."[3] Lawyers invoke Magna Carta's heritage in their briefs and summations in jury trials. Magna Carta is often identified as the origin of the right to a jury trial in popular writing as well.[4] Digging deeper into the history of Magna Carta, however, reveals a more complicated reality. Magna Carta's "judgment of his peers" language, which many associate with the jury trial right, did not guarantee trial by jury. The links between Magna Carta and the jury trial guarantee were actually forged centuries *after* the issuance of the original document in 1215.

The English Jury Before 1215

The history of the common law jury begins about fifty years before Magna Carta, during the reign of King Henry II (r. 1154–1189). Henry became king at the end of a long and destructive civil war, a time when one chronicler said that "Christ and his saints slept."[5] The memory of the civil war and the disorder it caused may have been in Henry's mind when he began the reforms of land law and criminal law that would ultimately come to be seen as the beginnings of the common law;[6] Henry proposed many of his reforms as a way to restore the

Medieval jury depicted in *Grand Coutumier de Normandie* [Customary Law of Normandy]. Illustrated manuscript on vellum, ca. 1450–1470. Law Library, Library of Congress

kingdom to its state before the civil war.[7] It is also possible that he was motivated to steal judicial business from the many local courts that existed throughout England.[8] Whatever the reason, Henry instituted new procedures for his royal courts, procedures which made the courts easier to use and more accessible, even to people at the low end of the social scale.[9]

On the civil side, Henry introduced new procedures called assizes. The first of these assizes was the assize *utrum*, which Henry probably authorized in 1164 as part of an ongoing fight he was having with his bishops. In that year, Henry issued a text called the Constitutions of Clarendon, which he claimed was a state-ment of the "customs, liberties, and dignities of his predecessors . . . which ought to be observed and kept in the kingdom" concerning the relationship between the crown and the Church.[10] Chapter nine of the constitutions dealt with the issue of land held by the Church. In the twelfth century, it was fairly common for landholders to donate land to the Church. Donations of land to Church bodies like parish churches or monasteries were thought to be good for one's soul and created a relationship with the parish or monastery that continued after the donor's death, as the priests and monks would remember the donor in their prayers. Certain types of land owned by the Church, known as land held as free alms, were exempt from the jurisdiction of the king's courts.[11] According to the Church's canon law, disputes concerning land held as free alms could not be heard in the king's court, only in the courts of the Church, which were extensive in the twelfth century.[12]

Henry recognized the Church's exclusive jurisdiction over land held in free alms. The question was, what happened when it wasn't clear whether the land was held as free alms or lay fee? Did the royal court or the ecclesiastical court get to decide who had jurisdiction? In chapter nine of the Constitutions of Clarendon, Henry answered that it was the royal court that had the right to decide. Chapter nine commanded that "If a dispute shall arise between a clerk and a layman, or between a layman and a clerk, in respect of any holding which the clerk desires to treat as free alms, but the layman as lay fee, it shall be determined by the recognition of twelve lawful men through the deliberation, in the presence of the king's chief justice, whether the holding pertains to free alms or to lay fee."[13]

The assize *utrum* (Latin for "whether," since the assize decides whether the land is held in lay fee or free alms) was the new procedure that Henry introduced to decide issues of lay fee or free alms. The assize was begun by royal writ, a tra-ditional tool of royal administration, and included a key role for laymen. Writs were essentially short documents issued by the royal chancery in the king's name that commanded one of the king's officials or subjects to do something. They had been used in England since Anglo-Saxon times. Instead of being an individualized command from the king, the assize *utrum* used a standard form. Any of the king's subjects could purchase a writ or command in this general form, and a clerk could fill in the specific information.[14] The writ took the following form:

> The king to the sheriff, greeting. If A. shall have given you security etc., summon, by good summoners, twelve free and lawful men of the vill of N. that they be before our justices at the first assize when they shall have come into those parts, prepared to recognize on oath whether ten acres of land with appurtenances in N. is the lay fee of the said A. or free alms belonging to the church of N. which B., the cleric, holds; and in the meantime let them view that land and cause their names to be recorded in writing, and summon by good summoners the said B., cleric, that he be there at the time to hear that recognition, and have there the summoners and this writ. Witness, etc.[15]

Writs such as these emerged as mainstays of the royal courts. By introducing the jury—the twelve free and lawful men who were commanded to come hear the case—into the assize *utrum*, the jury too became a mainstay of English law. Historians debate the origin of Henry's idea to use juries. Was the jury simply a continuation of trial procedures that had been used in England's county courts since Anglo-Saxon times? Or was it an institution of royal power that was transported from Normandy with the Norman Conquest? There is evidence for both points of view and it is possible that Henry drew inspiration from multiple sources.[16]

Fact-finding by small groups of people sworn to tell the truth, often called inquests, was commonplace in early medieval Europe.[17] Kings often used these fact-finding bodies to their advantage. Medieval kings had limited resources with which to extend their power. Generally, they could not afford to send royal servants into the counties to perform detailed investigations. The inquest was a way to draft local people into the fact-finding process. If the king wanted to know what rights he had over the people of a particular place, who owned a particular manor, or who had committed crimes, he could simply gather a group of local people together who were likely to know something of the local history of the place and make them swear an oath that they would tell the truth. Most notably, in 1086 William the Conqueror used the inquest to produce the Domesday Book, a survey of much of the land in England.[18]

The assize *utrum* orders the sheriff to summon "twelve free and lawful men of the vill." They were to come from the local community, and would be expected to know something about the dispute.[19] The twelve all had to be male; women only served on juries in very limited circumstances in the middle ages.[20] The twelve men all had to be free. A large proportion of England's population was unfree in this period. The unfree were subject to humiliating disabilities and were disqualified from service on inquests or juries and, in most cases, could not use the king's courts.[21]

The twelve men also had to be "lawful" (Lat. *legalis*). In this period, one meaning of the term "law," or *lex* in Latin, was "oath," and *legalis* essentially means "worthy of making an oath." Oath-worthiness was important in medieval England. Oaths were required in many social and legal contexts. A person who lost his status as a *legalis homo*, or law-worthy man, by breaking an oath or bringing a false claim in the king's courts, was subject to severe social and legal disabilities.[22] It was important that the twelve men be law-worthy, since the writ indicated that they were to be placed under oath.

These twelve men were known in documents of the time by several different names: the inquest (*inquisitio*), the recognition (*recognitio*; the writ says that they be "prepared to recognize"), the assize (*assisa*, after the statute-like documents, also called assizes, that first authorized their use), and, less often in the twelfth century than the thirteenth, the jury (*jurata*, from Latin *juramentum*, "oath").[23]

The basic elements of the assize *utrum*—the standard-form writ and the jury of twelve—were copied during Henry II's reign to create many new procedures for the king's courts, most of which decided questions relating to land. The assize of novel disseisin, which was probably authorized around 1166, called a jury of twelve to decide whether the person who was currently in possession of a piece of land had forcefully ejected the last holder.[24] The assize of mort d'ancestor, established in the Assize of Northampton in 1176, asked the jury whether the plaintiff was the nearest heir of the last person to die seised (essentially in possession) of a piece of land.[25] The grand assize was a procedure authorized in 1179 that allowed a person who otherwise would have to fight a judicial duel to determine his right to land to instead elect an assize of twelve men to decide the issue.[26] By the time Magna Carta was issued in 1215, juries had become the primary way of deciding land cases in the royal courts.

Henry II And Criminal Juries

At the same time he was introducing sworn groups of twelve men to decide land cases, Henry experimented with juries to deal with the problem of crime.[27] In 1166, Henry met with his barons at his hunting lodge at Clarendon and issued a text known as the Assize of Clarendon (not to be confused with the Constitutions of Clarendon). Through this document, Henry drafted local people into the royal administration to root out criminals. The assize ordered that "inquiry shall be

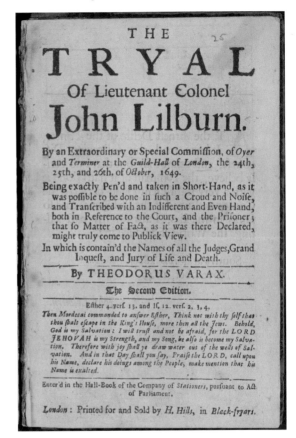

John Lilburne (1614?–1657). *The Tryal of Lieutenant Colonel John Lilburn. . . . the 24th, 25th, and 26th of October, 1649.* London: H. Hills, 1710. Law Library, Library of Congress

made throughout the several counties and throughout the several hundreds . . . whether there be in their hundred or vill any man accused or notoriously suspect of being a robber or murderer or thief, or any who is a receiver of robbers or murderers or thieves, since the lord king has been king."[28] This inquiry was to be made "through twelve of the more lawful men of the hundred and through four of the more lawful men of each vill."[29] Local people from the hundreds (subdivisions of counties) and vills (subdivisions of hundreds) would be called together to inform the king who had committed robbery, murder, or theft in their locality so they could be tried by the king's justices. The king's justices would periodically visit the counties and ask jurors from the hundred and the vill to present them with a list of suspected criminals. Forgery, treason, and arson were later added to the list of crimes the jurors were to present.[30]

These new juries were generally called juries of presentment, the ancestor of the modern grand jury. Their role was to present for trial people who were suspected of particular crimes. Although the juries of presentment did not decide the final issue of guilt or innocence, they played a role in determining who would go to trial. The trial itself would not be by jury. Instead, the accused were to "go to the ordeal of water."[31]

Judicial ordeals were a common way of trying suspected criminals in the twelfth century. Surviving ordeal liturgies paint a picture of ceremonies where a great deal of religious pressure was placed on the accused to confess.[32] An accused man heard a mass at which he was reminded that God would judge him justly. Before he took communion, he was reminded that he should not take it if he had "done or consented to or know who did this thing."[33] He took an oath, in the presence of a priest, that he had not committed the crime of which he was accused, and then was put to some kind of test. Monasteries often had ordeal pits that they blessed specially for the purpose of holding ordeals of cold water, but a stream could be used as well.[34] The priest entreated the accused

> by the Father and the Son and the Holy Spirit, by the day of terrible judgment, by the four evangelists, by the twenty-four elders, who with unwearied voice do not cease to praise God, by the twelve apostles, by the victory of the martyrs, by the invocation of your holy baptism, that, if you are culpable concerning this thing, either in deed or otherwise, with a heart hardened by the suggestion of the devil, do not presumptuously come to this judgment; the water will not accept you, and in this sign of the cross of Christ your malice will appear, and the virtue of almighty God will be manifested.[35]

By that point, if the accused had not confessed, he would go into the water. If he sank, he was adjudged innocent, and was pulled out of the water. If he floated, he was held to be guilty. Early on, those found guilty by the ordeal were mutilated and banished from the realm. By the early thirteenth century, anyone convicted of a felony was hanged.[36]

Although the presenting jury did not, strictly speaking, decide the final question of guilt or innocence, it was more than simply a jury of accusation. The jury had many ways of preventing the accused from going to the ordeal. A jury of presentment could present a man as having been accused of a crime, but then tell the justice that he was "not suspected." In those circumstances, the individual would not go to trial, but would instead be released if he was able to find pledges for his good behavior.[37] The Assize of Clarendon had called for twelve men from each hundred and four men from each vill to come to make presentments. The practice developed in such a way that the jury of the twelve hundred jurors was the first to make their presentments. If they decided that a man they had named was not suspected, he would go free. If they decided that he was suspected, the question would then be put to the four men (possibly five, since each vill also sent its reeve) of each of the four vills closest to the scene of the crime. If, and only if, they also suspected him, he would proceed to the ordeal.[38] In this way, the jurors of the vill could effectively veto the presentment of the hundred jurors. Thus, by the early thirteenth century, a person accused by the jury of presentment would only go to the ordeal if both the jury of the hundred and the juries of the four neighboring vills, a total of thirty-two people, said they suspected the individual.[39] The jury of presentment could not convict a person on its own, but it could essentially acquit one.

Although presentment became an important institution of English criminal law in the decades after 1166, it was not the only, or even primary, way of bringing suspected felons into court in the late twelfth century. The appeal of felony was a method by which a private party could accuse another party of a felony. Guilt or innocence would ordinarily be settled by trial by battle between the accuser and the accused, but trial by ordeal was also available if one of the parties was unable to undertake trial by battle. The appeal of felony might end in a jury trial, however. A defendant who did not want to go to battle or ordeal could challenge the appeal by means of a writ *de odio et atia* (of hatred and spite). The writ called a jury together to decide a limited question: whether the defendant was "appealed out of hatred and spite or because he was guilty."[40] If the jury decided that the private accuser had brought the appeal out of hatred and spite, the defendant was set free. If it decided he was guilty, he still went to the ordeal or trial by battle.[41] The jury in a case of hatred and spite, like a presenting jury, could acquit the defendant, but could not convict him. Writs *de odio et atia* were fairly common. They cost money to obtain, but defendants lost little else in seeking one. The worst-case scenario was that they would go to the same ordeals or battles that they would have gone to without the writ, and there was always the possibility that the jury would find in their favor.[42]

Although the ordeal was the primary means of deciding guilt or innocence, juries were also occasionally used in place of the ordeal to decide the final question. A party who did not want to undergo the ordeal could purchase the right to a special inquest from the king. The king would then send a writ ordering an inquest into the defendant's case. These inquests were exceptions to the general rule and were generally only available to the wealthy, but they did establish a precedent for use of the jury as a mode of proof rather than an accusing body.[43]

Thus, the best historical evidence indicates that, by 1215, juries had become regular parts of the administration of justice, both civil and criminal, in England. They were used widely in land cases and were used to ferret out criminals. However, people in 1215 probably would not have thought, as later generations did, especially from the seventeenth century onwards, that the jury was a great bulwark of liberty against the crown. Juries certainly allowed the preferences of the local community to enter into the exercise of justice. Presenting juries could prevent suspects from going to the ordeal. But juries served not so much as protection against royal power, but as extensions of it. The jury of presentment was a method the crown used to keep tabs on the country with its limited resources by compelling members of the local community to work for the king.

What is more, jury service was far from popular. Jury service was considered an onerous task, one where people were forced to do the king's work, and was widely resented. Jurors often failed to appear on the appointed day and were fined for their non-appearance. In some cases, parties simply gave up because they were unable to get enough jurors to fill the jury.[44] The wealthy purchased exemption from jury service from the king, which forced lower gentry and free peasants to take on a larger share of the jury work in the county. Today's complaints about jury duty have a long history.

In 1215, when Magna Carta was drafted, juries were more apt to be seen as the means by which the king co-opted locals into the royal administration than as instruments of popular participation. It is no surprise that, in the years immediately following Magna Carta's issuance, no one, including those who had been involved in drafting the charter, thought that it contained a guarantee of trial by jury.

Magna Carta And The Jury

Chapter 39 of the 1215 version of Magna Carta is one of the most famous sections of the charter. It was included in all subsequent reissues of the charter, eventually becoming chapter 29 of the revised 1225 version, which was the version of Magna Carta that came to be regarded as England's first statute. It reads:

> No free man shall be taken or imprisoned or disseised [deprived of his land] or outlawed, or exiled, or in any way ruined, nor will we go against or send against him, except by the lawful judgment of his peers, or by the law of the land.[45]

At first blush, the words "judgment of his peers" appear to guarantee trial by jury. By the eighteenth century, they were certainly read that way. However, there are several problems with this interpretation. In order to read chapter 39/29 of the charter as *guaranteeing* trial by jury, it would have to read "except by the lawful judgment of his peers *and* by the law of the land." Instead, the text of the charter provides "or by the law of the land." The text as we have it guarantees that a free man will be tried in one of two ways, but it offers them as alternatives. The king

John Lilburne reading from Coke's *Institute* at his trial. Frontispiece from John Lilburne (1614?–1657). *The Tryal of Lieutenant Colonel John Lilburn. . . . the 24th, 25th, and 26th of October, 1649.* London: H. Hills, 1710. Law Library, Library of Congress

need not try the free man by judgment of his peers; he can opt to try him by the law of the land instead.

The "or" in chapter 39/29 has caused trouble for generations of lawyers and scholars who want to read Magna Carta as the origin of the jury right. They have gone to great lengths to get around it. F. W. Maitland, the father of English legal history, argued that the Latin word *vel* used in the passage could also mean "and."[46] While he produced evidence that *vel* could, at times, mean "and," that was a rare usage of the word. It is much more likely that the drafters meant judgment of peers and law of the land to be alternatives.

A guarantee of judgment of peers *or* the law of the land seems strange to us today. What would it mean to be tried by the lawful judgment of one's peers, but not in accord with the law of the land? This is only a problem because we tend to read the phrase "law of the land" (*lex terrae*) to mean something like trial according to the proper procedures and established substantive law, the law that is observed in this land. We read it as meaning something like what we mean when we say "the law of the United States" or "the law of New York." The similar phrase "law of the realm" is used elsewhere in the charter to mean something like the general law of England.[47] But "law of the land" also had a much more specific meaning in the early thirteenth century. It could refer to a person's oath. We saw earlier that the jurors had to be law-worthy (*legalis*) because they had to swear an oath, which in Latin was often called a *lex*. In fact, some contemporary texts used the phrase *lex terrae*, or "law of the land," to refer to an oath.[48] An oath was taken in many different types of procedures, including trial by battle and ordeal. But even if the word "*vel*" in chapter 29/39 means "and," it is still unlikely that the chapter was meant to guarantee trial by jury, because the phrase "judgment of his peers" probably does not refer to the jury at all. Medieval courts usually operated according to a logic of communal judgment. The king's court was the exception rather than the rule. England was a patchwork of different jurisdictions. Sheriffs presided over county courts, which were attended by the free landholders of the county. The hundred, a smaller division within the county, had its own court that met more frequently than the county court. Lords held courts to settle disputes between their tenants; honour courts for their more exalted tenants; and manor courts for the peasants who worked the land. Towns had their own courts, as well.[49]

We have a sense for how these courts operated from the literature of the time, both monastic chronicles and chivalric epics and romances. They describe these courts as institutions in which judgment was made by the community. Consider the following example, which shows the litigants' peers taking a role in judging a case. The cartulary of the priory of St. Peter at Bath describes a case that was heard in the bishop of Bath's court in 1121. While the bishop was sitting in his court, celebrating the feast of the apostles Peter and Paul, he received a writ from the king's son William ordering him to "justly seize Modbert of the land which Grenta of Stoke has held," land that was, at the time, being held by the priory of St. Peter.[50] The bishop said that he agreed "to do what I have been ordered by the son of my lord by this letter, if it is just. However, my friends and lords, who are solemnly gathered in this court on the occasion of the apostolic feast-day, I beg you to discuss which is the more just cause in this matter."[51] After the prior and Modbert produced witnesses and a charter, the bishop put it to "those amongst you whom we know to be neither advocates nor supporters of the parties" to "diligently study the case and decide by what final judgment it shall be solved."[52] The "older and more learned in the law" then left, consulted, and made a judgment.[53] This was a fairly common pattern in courts of the period. The parties to the case entered the bishop's court—not constituted specifically as a law court, but simply as the collected body of the bishop's vassals—and expected to be judged not by the bishop, but by his vassals, their peers. Evidence suggests that this type of trial by one's peers, by the people beneath the lord who made up the lord's court, was the standard form in most courts in England.[54] The barons were simply asking for that mode of trial to be extended to them in the king's court, that they not be judged by the king, but by their peers, their fellow barons.

Sifting through the historical evidence, it seems most likely that chapter 39/29 was only meant to require that the accused would be tried either by peers, on the one hand, or by ordeal or battle, on the other. It foreclosed the possibility that the accused could simply be declared guilty by an act of the king's will, without any trial at all, but it did not guarantee that the trial would be by jury. This responded to a specific grievance that the barons had against John.[55] John was accused of too often acting on his own to determine that someone merited punishment, rather than putting the matter to his court.[56] The drafters of Magna Carta wanted guarantees that they would only be deprived of their land or arrested by judgment rather than the whim of the King, but they do not seem to have been overly concerned with the judgment's exact form. Judgment could be had by peers, by ordeal, or by battle, any of the forms commonly used in England in the early thirteenth century. Magna Carta guaranteed a trial, but not a trial by jury.

The Fourth Lateran Council And The Criminal Jury

Magna Carta was not the only momentous event of 1215. In November of the same year, five months after Magna Carta was issued, Pope Innocent III (r. 1198-1216) opened a general council of the Western Church, called the

Fourth Lateran Council.[57] The council's ambitious agenda included substantial reform of the Western Church, and the council had an important impact, for good and ill, on subsequent European history. It was the first council to require Jews and Muslims to wear distinctive, identifying clothing, for instance.[58] It also called for substantial reforms to the administration of canon law, including the introduction of additional rights for accused parties.[59] It was the council's program of separating the sacred from the secular—of requiring priests to separate themselves from the secular life and forbidding them to marry and participate in certain types of occupations that it saw as too worldly—which proved to have significant implications for trial by jury in England.

Canon 18 placed certain restrictions on clerics, including a mandate that clerics were not to "bestow any blessing or consecration on a purgation by ordeal of boiling water or of cold water or of the red-hot iron . . ."[60] Canon 18 did not forbid judicial ordeals altogether; it simply said that clerics could not offer a blessing in them. But the blessing was crucial to the ceremony, and without it, the ordeal could not function. If God was to participate in the ordeal, the ordeal pit must be blessed by a priest, and the accused was often given the Eucharist before the ordeal, which required the participation of a priest as well.[61] The priest's participation was a critically important part of the agreed-upon method of resolving disputes, and without it the courts were at a loss.

A pressing problem that now faced the English royal courts was what should be done with people who were suspected of serious crimes if they could not be tried by ordeal. This issue did not affect the royal courts immediately, however. Just months after Magna Carta was issued in June of 1215, civil war broke out between John and the barons. By October of 1216, however, John had died (of natural causes) and his son, Henry III, at nine years of age, was crowned king. The war came to an end in September of 1217 and the kingdom settled into an uneasy peace. The king's courts had not operated regularly since the war began, but in November of 1218 the regency government prepared to send out the first eyres—groups of justices sent to the counties as travelling courts—since 1209.[62] It was only then that the courts were faced with the question of what to do about the trial of felons.

The eyre was already underway on January 26, 1219, when Peter des Roches, the young king's guardian, and Hubert de Burgh, his justiciar, sent a letter telling the eyre justices how to proceed in cases of "robbery, murder, arson, and similar things."[63] Des Roches and de Burgh wrote to the justices that "judgment by fire and water is forbidden by the Roman Church."[64] They were not sure what should replace it, however. Their instructions to the justices were to put off trying these suspects until they could come up with a solution. They ordered the justices to do different things with respect to different classes of criminals:

> those who are accused of the aforesaid greater crimes, and who are suspected of those things of which they are accused and in regard to whom, although they might abjure the realm, there is still suspicion that afterwards they might do ill, shall be held in our prison and safely guarded, so that they do not incur peril of life or limb by reason of our prison. Those who are accused of medium crimes touching which the judgment of fire and water would be suitable if it were not forbidden, and touching whom if they abjure our realm there would be no suspicion of evildoing afterwards, shall abjure our kingdom. Those who are charged with lesser crimes and in regard to whom there is no suspicion, shall find safe and secure pledges to keep our allegiance and peace and thus shall be loosed in our land.[65]

The most problematic of these categories, from the justices' perspective, were those "accused of the aforesaid greater crimes," who were to be kept in prison. Prison was not generally used as a punishment in twelfth- and thirteenth-century England, and the prisons were not designed for long-term incarceration. The justices didn't have any way to try these people, and keeping them locked up indefinitely did not seem practical. Casting about for alternatives, the justices made greater use of inquests *de odio et atia*, even in cases where the defendant had not asked for one.[66] The justices began to adapt these inquests to suit their current needs. Recall that an inquest *de odio et atia* traditionally could acquit, but not convict. The justices of 1218 sentenced some people based on a guilty verdict from a jury brought by writ of *de odio et atia*. They did not sentence them to hang, however, but instead to pay a fine.[67] The justices seemed to be wary of using the jury to sentence an accused felon to death, but they were willing to mete out a lesser punishment to felons on the basis of a jury verdict. These unasked-for juries presumably alleviated some of the strain on the prisons.

Two suspects were hanged on the weight of a jury verdict in 1218, but the verdict was declared to be illegal by the justices of the central courts at Westminster. Their heirs complained and the court agreed that the two men were "hanged wickedly and unjustly because . . . they could not be condemned through the verdict of the jurors."[68] The justices and the king's council re-asserted that the jury could only be used to ask intermediate questions, like whether an appeal was brought out of hatred and spite, not to determine guilt. This example offers more evidence that Magna Carta's "judgment of his peers" did not yet resemble the common law jury.

In the winter of 1220, the justices at Westminster went a step further towards using juries to convict. Some appeals were brought by people known as approvers, felons who had turned state's evidence. Felons who were caught might save their necks by confessing and agreeing to bring appeals of felony against others, generally the felons' accomplices.[69] The approver would then have to fight judicial duels against them. He would be kept at public expense while he brought the appeals, and if he survived the number of appeals and duels he had agreed upon with the king's officials—the *Bracton* treatise gives the sample number as five, so it is unlikely that he would—he would be granted his "life and members," but not much more.[70] The approver would be forced to abjure the realm for the rest of his life and would be mutilated—probably losing his nose or an ear—as a very tangible mark of his crime, to warn people who might come across him that he was a convicted felon.[71]

The party accused by an approver could respond that he need not answer "a confessed thief, one who ought to have no right to speak against a law-abiding man . . ."[72] He would bring a writ *de fidelitate* to prove that he was "a law-abiding man and within the assise of the lord king etc. and in frankpledge or has a lord who avows him."[73] He would make his proof to a jury. Just as in the procedure for the writ *de odio et atia*, the jury could acquit, but not convict. If the jury decided that the accused was a law-abiding man and need not answer, then he would be released. If it decided he was not a law-abiding man, he would still go to the duel to try to prove his innocence that way.

At the bench at Westminster in 1220, the justices were confronted with some problematic cases. In one of them, a woman who had confessed to theft, named Alice, had made a deal with the court to act as an approver. Technically she could not be an approver, because a woman was barred from fighting a judicial duel, but the court allowed her to make her accusations anyway.[74] All of those she accused would, therefore, be sent to the ordeal, since it was used as an alternative to judicial combat in appeals where that form of proof was unavailable. But the ordeal had been forbidden by the Lateran Council. The justices might have left the people appealed by Alice in prison while the king's council decided what to do with them; what they did instead was give them the option of a speedier trial. The court asked the defendants if they would empower the jury to decide both innocence and guilt. The roll of the court tells us that "they placed themselves upon the verdict *for good and ill* (*de bono et malo*)."[75] They probably shouldn't have. The entry tells us that all the jurors said that they were thieves, and laconically ends with the word *suspendantur* ("they were hanged").[76] This was not the most auspicious beginning for the criminal jury trial, at least not if we believe that the criminal jury's role is to defend the rights of the accused.

By 1220, the justices had clearly decided it was permissible to give accused persons, in cases brought both by appeal and by presentment, the option of putting themselves on the jury "for good and ill." In cases of presentment, the justices would simply allow the jury of presentment, the jury that had originally presented the accused as suspected of a felony, to sit as a trial jury. The procedure followed was very similar to that that had previously been followed for ordeals. Recall that the twelve hundred jurors and the jurors of the four nearest vills—which each sent four men and their reeve to the court—had to agree that the person was suspected in order to send the individual to the ordeal. When the courts started using juries to convict, they similarly required that the hundred and the four vills, a total of thirty-two people, agree that the suspect was guilty in order to convict.[77] The trial by jury for good or ill was initially optional; the suspected felon could choose to accept the jury or to go back to prison. But when an accused felon announced that "he does not wish to place himself upon the country" in 1221, the justices responded by forcing a jury upon him. They added twenty-four knights to the twelve hundred jurors, making a trial jury of thirty-six, which gave a verdict against him.[78]

Trial by jury had therefore been established as the ordinary way to try felons in the royal courts by 1221. There are two points that are important to notice about these early trial juries. First, trial by jury was not designed to protect the accused from the king and his judicial machinery by giving him trial by his neighbors. If anything, it represented a decrease in the procedural safeguards the accused received. By simply adopting the jury of presentment as the trial jury, the royal courts had taken a step out of the process. Under the pre-1215 system, if the juries of the hundred and the four nearest vills said they suspected the accused, he still had a chance to save his neck if he succeeded at the ordeal. The trial jury took the ordeal out of the process and left the accused at the mercy of his neighbors. Second, the justices of the royal courts were reluctant to use jurors to try accused felons. The large size of the early trial juries probably reflected a discomfort among the justices with leaving the final question of guilt or innocence in the hands of the defendant's neighbors instead of in the hands of God. There was thus no sense that the accused had a right to be tried by a jury of his peers. If anything, contemporaries thought that trial by jury was a troubling development.

Connecting Magna Carta With The Jury

Over time, people in England came to think of trial by jury as a protection against royal tyranny and, over time, they began to associate it with Magna Carta. In some ways, this was a natural connection to make. As early as the fourteenth century, the jury of presentment was coming to be thought of as part of the procedural guarantees of chapter 29 of Magna Carta. In a statute of 1351, parliament expanded upon the guarantee of chapter 29 by adding that "from henceforth none shall be taken by petition or suggestion made to our lord the King, or to his council, unless it be by indictment or presentment of good and lawful people of the same neighborhood where such deed be done, or by process made by writ original at the common law."[79] The authors of this statute read the jury of presentment into Magna Carta's guarantees, but they did not read it into the "judgment of his peers" language. Rather, they connected it to the charter's "law of the land" language.[80] The phrase, "law of the land," for which the original drafters had probably intended a narrow meaning, namely, trial by ordeal or battle, had by then taken on a broader meaning. In the statute of 1351, it meant the procedural forms followed in the king's courts. A statute of 1354 confirmed this reading of chapter 29. The statute amended the guarantee of chapter 29 to "no man, of whatever estate or condition he may be, shall be put out of his land or tenement, nor be taken or imprisoned, or disinherited, without being brought to answer by due process of law (*due process de lei*)."[81] This provision expanded the coverage of chapter 29 from any "free man" to any "man, of whatever estate or condition he may be," and, more importantly for our purposes, it specified that the term "law of the land" was a right to be tried by the proper procedure, which, as the earlier statute had specified, included the jury of presentment. This

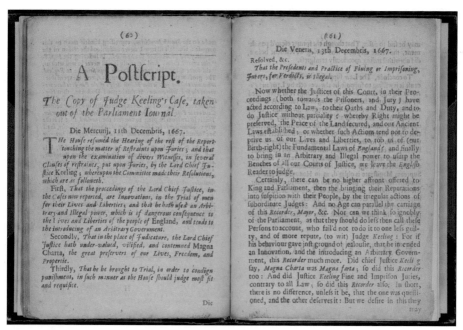

William Penn (1644–1718). *Peoples Antient and Just Liberties Asserted in the Tryal of William Penn and William Mead.* London, 1670. Law Library, Library of Congress

statute is the first known use of the phrase "due process of law," so important to the American constitutional tradition.

Magna Carta was important to the political battles of the thirteenth and, to a lesser extent, fourteenth centuries, but after that it receded from the political scene. It arose from its dormancy in the political battles of the seventeenth century, heralded by Chief Justice Sir Edward Coke, who fought a protracted battle against King James I over the proper relationship between the king and the law. In his *Institutes of the Lawes of England,* Coke read the words "or by the law of the land" in chapter 29 to be a guarantee that a person would not be taken or imprisoned except by "presentment of good and lawfull men."[82] Coke, like the authors of the fourteenth-century statutes, thus found the grand jury guaranteed in Magna Carta. Coke's arguments about the connection between Magna Carta and the jury were extended by William Penn, the Quaker leader and founder of Pennsylvania, who, during his trial for illegal assembly, selectively misread Coke's gloss on chapter 29's words "by lawful judgement" to guarantee trial by jury in criminal cases, as well. Coke thought that the provision applied only to the trial of peers by the House of Lords, but where Coke had "Lords," Penn substituted "jury."[83] Coke's "the Lords must heare no evidence, but in the presence, and hearing of the prisoner" becomes "The jury ought to hear no evidence, but in the hearing and presence of the prisoner" in Penn's writings.[84] Penn exported this view of Magna Carta to America. When Penn drew up the *Fundamental Laws of West New Jersey* in 1676, he included the following provision:

> That no Proprietor, freeholder or inhabitant of the said Province of West New Jersey, shall be deprived or condemned of life, limb, liberty, estate, property or any ways hurt in his or their privileges, freedoms or franchises, upon any account whatsoever, without a due tryal, and Judgment passed by twelve good and lawful men of his neighborhood first had.[85]

The language clearly draws upon chapter 29 of Magna Carta, but in place of the phrase "lawful judgment of his peers or by the law of the land," we have "due trial, and Judgment passed by twelve good and lawful men of his neighborhood," language that clearly contemplates a trial jury.[86] Other colonial acts would do the same.[87] It thus became a truism in America that Magna Carta guaranteed a right to trial by jury in criminal cases.

The grand jury and the criminal trial jury are enshrined in the United States Constitution. The fifth amendment's guarantee that "[n]o person shall be held to answer for a capital, or otherwise infamous crime, unless on a presentment or indictment of a Grand Jury" echoes language Coke used in the *Institutes* to gloss chapter 29.[88] It applies only to federal courts. The sixth amendment, which has been incorporated against the states, as well, guarantees trial by jury in criminal

410—OPINION

6   DUNCAN *v.* LOUISIANA.

The history of trial by jury in criminal cases has been frequently told.[15] It is sufficient for present purposes to say that by the time our Constitution was written, jury trial in criminal cases had been in existence in England for several centuries and carried impressive credentials traced by many to Magna Carta.[16] Its preservation and proper operation as a protection against arbitrary rule were among the major objectives of the revolutionary settlement which was expressed in the Declaration and Bill of Rights of 1689. In the 18th century Blackstone could write:

> "Our law has therefore wisely placed this strong and two-fold barrier, of a presentment and a trial by jury, between the liberties of the people and the perogative of the crown. It was necessary, for preserving the admirable balance of our constitution, to vest the executive power of the laws in the prince: and yet this power might be dangerous and destructive to that very constitution, if exerted without check or control, by justices of *oyer* and *terminer* occasionally named by the crown; who might then, as in France or Turkey, imprison, dispatch, or exile any man that was obnoxious to the government, by an instant declaration that such is their will and pleasure. But the founders of the English law have, with excellent forecast, contrived that . . . the truth of every accusation, whether preferred in the shape of indictment, information, or appeal, should afterwards be confirmed by the unanimous suffrage of twelve of his equals and neighbours, indifferently chosen and superior to all suspicion." [17]

[15] *E. g.,* W. Forsyth, History of Trial by Jury (1852); J. B. Thayer, A Preliminary Treatise on Evidence at the Common Law (1898); W. S. Holdsworth, History of English Law (3d ed. 1922).
[16] *E. g.,* 4 W. Blackstone, Commentaries on the Laws of England 349 (Cooley ed. 1899).
[17] *Id.,* at 349–350.

Historians no longer accept this pedigree. See, e.g., 1 F. Pollock & F. M. Maitland, The History of English Law Before the Time of Edward I at 173 & n. 3 (2d ed. 1909).

United States Supreme Court. Duncan v. Louisiana (1968). Printed document with hand-written notes. Byron R. White Papers, Manuscript Division, Library of Congress

cases. By the time the constitution was written, both of these guarantees were widely understood as having their origins in Magna Carta. More curious is the seventh amendment, which guarantees trial by jury in all civil cases "at common law, where the value at issue shall exceed twenty dollars." Civil juries had never been guaranteed in the English courts. In fact, the procedures associated with some of the common-law writs did not include a jury. The writ of debt is the primary example, but there were doubts as late as the late fourteenth century as to whether a jury was the proper procedure for a writ of trespass, as well.[89] Nevertheless, some members of the constitutional convention connected the civil jury to Magna Carta.[90] Others noticed that it was very difficult to base the right to a civil jury in the common-law tradition, and almost impossible to find its origin in Magna Carta.[91]

Conclusion

Magna Carta was not originally intended to guarantee trial by jury. It could not have been; juries were an unusual trial method at the time the charter was written. Far from thinking that trial by one's neighbors was an important safeguard against royal tyranny, contemporaries worried that a guilty verdict by a jury of the neighborhood might not be sufficient to send a man to the noose. That does not take anything away from Magna Carta's importance to the Anglo-American legal tradition, however. Magna Carta is significant today primarily because of the ways people have creatively reinterpreted and even misinterpreted the text over the centuries. Later generations, who saw the jury as a "valuable safeguard to liberty" and the "palladium of free government," read the jury into chapter 39/29 of Magna Carta, and from there the legend of Magna Carta and the jury entered our American constitutional tradition.[92]

THE

MERRYMAN

HABEAS CORPUS CASE,

BALTIMORE.

THE PROCEEDINGS IN FULL, AND

OPINION OF CHIEF JUSTICE TANEY.

THE UNITED STATES GOVERNMENT A MILITARY DESPOTISM.

JACKSON, MISS.: J. L. POWER.

1861.

HABEAS CORPUS AND MAGNA CARTA
Justin Wert

At the beginning of the twentieth century, Charles McIlwain observed that the new histories of Magna Carta were portraying the Charter as a *document of reaction* that could only fulfill its purported greatness "when men [were] no longer able to understand its real meaning."[1] Characteristic of these early-twentieth-century writers was Edward Jenks, who, in his 1904 article *The Myth of Magna Carta* came to the conclusion that real beneficiaries of the document—the *liber homo* of chapter 39—were not "the people"[2] we traditionally imagine, but rather an "aristocratic class . . . who can no more be ranked amongst the people, than the country gentleman of to-day."[3] Although Jenks' position is often criticized as extreme, it is nevertheless the case that virtually all of Magna Carta's modern commentators recognize vast historical inaccuracies in the Whiggish accounts of the Charter's development up until the late nineteenth century.[4] What these new revisionist histories suggested was that Magna Carta's greatest provisions—due process and trial by jury—only became great when, forgetting or ignoring the Charter's seemingly lackluster beginnings, generations subsequent to 1215 gave them new meaning.

But despite Magna Carta's admittedly feudal origins, we continue to regard the Charter as the foundational expression of modern constitutionalism. What this suggests, then, is that as we attempt to make sense of Magna Carta, we should not begin *at* Runnymede, but *after* it, accounting along the way for other political and legal developments that helped facilitate the Charter's transformation into its elevated position in the Western legal tradition. When we do, we quickly discover that the uses of Magna Carta's seemingly liberty-regarding provisions did not develop through time in one unilinear direction toward ever-increasing freedom. We also see that Magna Carta became linked to other

The Merryman Habeas Corpus Case, Baltimore, Jackson, Mississippi: J. L. Power, 1861. Rare Book and Special Collections Division, Library of Congress

developing procedural legal mechanisms—like habeas corpus—that tracked similarly uneven and oftentimes oppressive routes.

As I argue in this chapter, habeas corpus and Magna Carta remain rhetorical partners because political actors can repair to their idealized forms and use them strategically to enforce their own normative conceptions of constitutional governance.

The first section of this chapter traces the separate developments of Magna Carta and habeas corpus, discusses how the early uses of habeas corpus in England were very different from the use of the writ to protect individual liberty, and shows how and why Magna Carta and habeas corpus became linked during the seventeenth century in England through notions of due process. We see that their link was in no way preordained, and that legal elites had to rewrite the histories of both to link them together. The next section examines in detail the development of habeas corpus in the New World and particularly in the United States, touching briefly on the seventeenth and eighteenth centuries and then turning to the antebellum period, particularly with respect to slave law. We see the attendant troubles with the due process link in the application of habeas corpus during the antebellum period, which also reveals very different approaches to habeas corpus among states and between the states and the federal government. The chapter then discusses habeas corpus development in the post–Civil War period and then briefly turns to developments in the twentieth century. Like others before, legal elites had to rewrite the history of habeas corpus in the twentieth century as they expanded the writ's reach, a project that relied heavily upon similarly Whiggish histories of habeas corpus and Magna Carta during the seventeenth century. Finally, the chapter concludes by arguing that the shifting conceptions of due process that ultimately form the basis of Magna Carta and habeas corpus actually provide more room for more humane understandings of each, even if that means that less noble ones could sometimes gain the upper hand.

Habeas Corpus And Magna Carta: Linkages

One of the most effective tools used to enforce subsequent reinterpretations of the core of Magna Carta's procedural provisions after Runnymede was the simultaneous, but initially wholly separate, development of the writ of habeas corpus. This writ has been so intertwined with our understanding of Magna Carta that in both Coke's *Institutes* and Blackstone's *Commentaries*, it is portrayed in the same lofty terms as the Charter itself, as "the great and efficacious writ"[5] that serves to free those who may be "taken, or committed to prison *contra legem terrae*, against the Law of the land."[6] Reborn together in the early seventeenth century during the battles between the Common Law and Chancery courts of James I (r. 1603–1625), habeas corpus henceforth served as the preferred legal mechanism to enforce substantive readings of Magna Carta's *legem terrae*—now read as the *due process*—provision of chapter 39.[7] By the eighteenth century, Blackstone felt confident enough to assert that habeas corpus was now "another Magna Carta."[8]

But like the Great Charter that it came to enforce, the origins of habeas corpus suggest that the writ was not always deserving of its modern encomiums. The first recorded appearance of habeas corpus was, in fact, in 1199, predating Magna Carta by sixteen years.[9] Originally part of the *mesne* process of early legal adjudication, the writ was widely used to ensure the presence of parties in court.[10]

In the fifteenth century, a distant variant of modern habeas corpus appeared as the King's Chancery courts began to use habeas corpus, along with writs of certiorari, to remove cases from inferior courts into their own. Hardly concerned with the vindication of individual rights or issues of due process as we understand them today, this *cum causa* version of habeas corpus served to enforce the privilege of certain classes, such as "clergy, members of Parliament, ministers of the King, and officers of superior courts,"[11] to enjoy legal proceedings in more sympathetic jurisdictions. Moreover, some early commentators, like Coke, evidently mistook Magna Carta's chapter 36 for habeas corpus, which states that "[n]othing in future shall be given or taken for a writ of inquisition of life or limbs, but freely it shall be granted, and never denied."[12]

Permutations of habeas corpus developed throughout the sixteenth century that allowed the writ to be used in criminal matters to discharge prisoners if they were held unlawfully. And with the constitutional crises of the early seventeenth century, habeas corpus' prior use both as a tool in jurisdictional conflicts and as a developing legal challenge to unlawful imprisonment quickly set it against monarchical power.

In *Darnel's Case* (1627),[13] for example, Magna Carta and habeas corpus were partially reinvented, with habeas corpus now explicitly enforcing a more capacious reading of Magna Carta's *legem tarrae* (chapter 39).[14] Imprisoned by the Privy Council for failure to pay the king's tax through forced loans, Darnel petitioned the King's Bench for a writ of habeas corpus challenging the jurisdiction of the Council to hold him. The Crown's response to the writ, however, stated that Darnel was being held *per speciale mandatum Domini Regis*, and not as the result of indictment or other established common-law legal processes. Darnel argued that habeas corpus served to "return the cause of the imprisonment, that it may be examined in this court."[15] Although a return was made and a cause provided, substantively, there was "no cause at all expressed in it."[16] John Selden, one of Darnel's counsels, contended further that the king's return violated chapter 39's *per legem terrae* provision by imprisoning subjects without "presentment or by indictment."[17] He then went on to argue that if "*per special mandatum* be within the meaning of these words . . . then this act has done nothing."[18]

In response, Sir Robert Heath, who argued the Crown's position in the case, agreed that the "fundamental grounds of argument upon this case begins with Magna Carta,"[19] but he argued that the substantive meaning of the *legem terrae* provision certainly encompassed any command of the king. The king's cause, while not *expressed*, was simply not yet *ripe*, and the "judicature have ever rested satisfied therewith . . . if a man be committed by the commandment of the king, he is not to be delivered by a Habeas Corpus in this court, for we know not the cause of the commitment."[20] Although Darnel was ultimately successful, the very suggestion that habeas corpus was the natural guarantor of Magna Carta's *legem terrae* provision along with the increasingly popular assertion that the king's prerogative was no part of the *legem terrae* were salient developments.[21]

The next year, in 1628, Parliament passed the Petition of Right. In the Commons, a version of the Petition was put forward that specifically allowed habeas corpus to challenge detentions (especially by the Crown) that lacked a specific cause of commitment, thus attacking the *Darnel* decision directly. Leading the debate in Parliament was Sir Edward Coke, who, at the same time, was completing his *Institutes on the Law of England*. Coke's section on chapter 39—*Nisi per legem terrae*—not only read it as "without due process of law,"[22] but further asserted that due process simply meant the "Common Law."[23] Tellingly, he then asked, "What remedy hath a party grieved"[24] under due process to rectify false imprisonment? Coke's answer, in two chapters in this section, was "habeas corpus."[25]

With habeas corpus' role as the preferred enforcement mechanism for Magna Carta's *legem terrae* provision asserted by Coke, the writ received further imprimatur in the Habeas Corpus Act of 1679.[26] The 1679 Act, however, was not the palladium of liberties that some, like Blackstone, would later assert. Although the Act decreased time limitations in returns to the writ, allowed individual judges—not just full courts—to issue the writ during vacation, and sought to prohibit transfers of prisoners out of the realm to avoid the writ's reach, it also contained limitations to the writ that seem inimical to modern sensibilities. Significantly, although the Act was limited to criminal detentions, it excepted from its protections those people detained for "felony if ordered by justices of the peace"[27] and it did not allow the release of prisoners completely unless the writ challenged the timeliness of an indictment.[28] What the Act did suggest, though, was that the substantive content of the *legem terrae*, now enforced through habeas corpus, was primarily aimed at correcting the arbitrary nature of royal prerogative, and not providing a wider set of personal rights.

Habeas Corpus Act of 1679. London: John Bill, Henry Hills, and Thomas Newcomb, 1681. Law Library, Library of Congress

Habeas Corpus And Magna Carta In The New World

The fusion of Magna Carta's *legem terrae* and the writ of habeas corpus would, of course, make its way into the nascent American colonies, initially through Coke and then primarily through Blackstone, who, in his *Commentaries*, proclaimed that the Habeas Corpus Act of 1679 was "another *Magna Carta*."[29] Blackstone asserted that the "glory of the English law consists in clearly defining the times, the causes, and the extent when, wherefore, and to what degree, the imprisonment of the subject may be lawful."[30] As a "natural inherent right"[31] that is "established on the firmest basis by the provisions of *magna carta*,"[32] it is best supported and defended by "habeas corpus."[33] But even before Blackstone, and as early as the 1680s, Massachusetts, New York, and Pennsylvania attempted to guarantee the writ modeled on the provisions of the 1679 Act, but these measures were summarily annulled by the Privy Council. In the first few decades of the eighteenth century, royal governors in Virginia, North Carolina, and South Carolina provided for the writ through proclamation, not statute.[34]

But in *Federalist No. 84*,[35] Alexander Hamilton seemed to suggest that habeas corpus, now enumerated in the proposed Constitution, brought within its protection our most fundamental rights, and did so in a more effective manner than would a Bill of Rights, or even Magna Carta itself.[36] For Hamilton, the protection of fundamental rights was already secured more fully in the Constitution as it stood with no amendments than if specific rights were enumerated. Along with the prohibitions against *ex post facto* laws, bills of attainder, and grants of nobility, Hamilton proposed that the habeas corpus clause in Article 1 was the primary defense against arbitrary arrests and imprisonments, which in his words, were the "favorite and most formidable instruments of tyranny."[37] Mere parchment barriers, according to Hamilton, such as those that would eventually be enumerated in the first eight amendments, could never be as powerful in guaranteeing individual liberty as the simple protection of habeas corpus. Hamilton then went on to distinguish the rights guaranteed in the unamended Constitution from "bills of rights" more generally, which he considered to be simply "stipulations between kings and their subjects, abridgements of prerogative in favor of privilege, reservations of rights not surrendered to the prince. Such was MAGNA CHARTA, obtained by the barons, sword in hand, from king John."[38] Here, then, habeas corpus further assumed the burden of Magna Carta's *legem terrae* provision through a Whiggish fiction that allowed the Great Writ of Liberty to become a fundamental guarantor of due process in the Constitution.

To be sure, our modern notion of habeas corpus as a remedy that, in the words of Justice Oliver Wendell Holmes, can "cut through all forms and go . . . to the very tissue"[39] of unconstitutional detention, never crossed the minds of Selden, Coke, or Blackstone. Important limitations, modeled on the 1679 Act, would continue to constrain both habeas corpus' procedural reach and the set of substantive rights that the writ was now imagined to protect in the United States. Like Magna Carta before it, habeas corpus' power was only ever as large and far-reaching as contemporary notions of due process allowed.[40] Like the Privy Council's acceptance of the king's *speciale mandatum* as consistent with the *legem terrae*, habeas corpus would also reflect the limits of substantive rights and legitimate governmental processes.

Habeas Corpus In Antebellum America

In antebellum America, for example, habeas corpus was used to enforce substantive rights and limit governmental procedural abuses on both the state and national levels, but what exactly constituted due process was widely divergent. Moreover, procedural limitations to the writ all but prevented national courts from removing cases from state jurisdictions into their own.[41] These limitations in part spurred the development of habeas corpus, as this concept was used in some Southern states to vindicate asserted due process rights of slaveholders when their *property* was absconded or stolen.[42] Some Northern states, on the other hand, advanced a more capacious notion of due process and aggressively used habeas corpus to thwart the enforcement of the fugitive slave clause of the Constitution.[43]

Before the Civil War and Reconstruction, habeas corpus developed on two different tracks in the United States, one state and one federal. Section 14 of The Judiciary Act of 1789[44] stated that:

> All the before mentioned courts of the United States shall have the power to issue writs of *scire facias, habeas corpus,* and all other writs not specifically provided for by statute, which may be necessary for the exercise of their respective jurisdictions, and agreeable to the principles and usages of law. And either of the justices of the Supreme Court, as well as judges of the district courts, shall have the power to grant writs of *habeas corpus* for the purpose of an inquiry into the cause of commitment. – *Provided,* That writs of *habeas corpus* shall in no case extend to prisoners in gaol, unless where they are in custody, under or by colour of the authority of the United States, or are committed for trial before some court of the same, or are necessary to be brought into court to testify.

This effectively precluded federal habeas corpus review for state prisoners in the antebellum period.

On the state level, though, habeas corpus developed in protean ways, sometimes vindicating idealized due process rights, but sometimes serving the very opposite.[45] State variation in the use of habeas corpus to adjudicate slavery law tracked the sectional and geographic divisions before the Civil War. Northern states often employed habeas corpus on the state level to protect their free black populations from kidnappings even though they often acquiesced to Southern state demands to recover fugitive slaves.[46] This meant that there were sharp differences in the use and development of habeas corpus on the state level during the antebellum period. Some states, like Mississippi, explicitly provided statutory habeas corpus remedies for slaveholders to recover their slaves when they were stolen.[47] Mississippi's habeas corpus provisions provided for the use of the writ to deliver up a slave to inquire into cases of contested legal ownership. In part, the

Mississippi law provided that habeas corpus could issue to determine whether "any slave or slaves for life shall be taken or seduced out of the possession of the master, owner, overseers of such slaves, by force, stratagem or fraud."[48] In the 1824 case of *Scudder v. Seals*, for example, a habeas corpus petition was issued to bring before the Supreme Court of Mississippi the bodies of two slaves, Dicey and Daniel, to inquire into the legality of their current owner's title.[49] The court determined that Dicey and Daniel, who had been willed to their former owner's daughter, were effectively stolen from her. The habeas corpus proceeding then returned the slaves to the owner.

Issues of state sovereignty also cross-cut state habeas corpus in the south. In *Nations v. Alvis*, the Supreme Court of Mississippi refused to release a slave on habeas corpus to her original owner because the theft had occurred in Tennessee, not Mississippi, where the slave was held.[50] The court ruled that although the use of habeas corpus to recover stolen slaves was a "prompt and effectual remedy,"[51] the notion of state sovereignty "cannot, by any inherent authority, claim respect beyond the jurisdiction of the state which enacts them."[52] The use of habeas corpus to retrieve or recover property was limited to that inquiry only, not only in Mississippi, but in other Southern states as well. Legitimate questions concerning the actual freedom of African Americans sometimes arose in cases involving their disputed ownership, and most Southern states increasingly determined that jury trials, not habeas corpus proceedings, were the most appropriate legal mechanisms for decisions involving fundamental rights of property.[53] Because most states simply required a return to a habeas corpus writ that could show some legitimate justification for detention, though, the ubiquitous presumption in slave states that blackness implied servitude significantly limited the utility of the writ for more libertarian causes.

In Northern states, habeas corpus laws were enacted in the late eighteenth and early nineteenth centuries as part of Revolutionary-inspired slavery prohibitions and manumissions and also in reaction to fugitive slave problems, especially kidnapping. Here, too, there were important variations. Border states such as Pennsylvania were more likely to be conciliatory toward their slave-state neighbors with respect to early fugitive slave issues, while New England states such as Massachusetts explicitly linked habeas corpus to its kidnapping statutes as early as 1785.[54]

Even as some states were moving toward gradual abolition, states such as New Jersey routinely allowed habeas corpus to issue in order to resolve disputed claims of title to slaves. In *The State v. Anderson*, for example, the Supreme Court of New Jersey issued a writ of habeas corpus to inquire into the detention of a slave child named Silas.[55] Silas' mother, Betsy, was sold pursuant to her owner's will, which stated that she was to remain a slave for only fifteen years after his death. However, during her tenure as a slave for her new owner, she gave birth to a child. The owner then claimed the child as a slave for life, arguing that his property was damaged because she had given birth. The court ultimately ruled that the child was free, and Betsy was also to be free after her fifteen years of servitude.

In the same year, another case came to the Supreme Court of New Jersey that presented a similar probate question.[56] After the death of his master, a slave, Tom, was sold to a man named Bloomfield, along with the original owner's other slaves. Evidence was presented to the court that argued that Tom's owner had always wished him to be free at his death: at times he was heard to have stated that "they had sucked the same breasts, and that he should never serve another master."[57] The court then issued a writ of habeas corpus. Bloomfield's counsel argued that for a slave to be free, his master must do more than "mention it to a third party."[58] The court, relying again on the owner's complete power over his property, ruled that his verbal intention was enough, and Tom was discharged with his freedom. Just four years later, however, the same court ruled that a verbal intention to free a slave upon an owner's death was not enough for freedom. In the words of the court, the slaves in question "must go with the other property, and legally belong to the defendant."[59] Although the habeas corpus petition failed to free the slaves, the court nevertheless refused to hold those who filed the writ liable for court costs and damages to the defendant. The court justified its position by saying that "they would not in any case compel the prosecutors of these writs to pay costs; it was a laudable and humane thing in any man or set of men to bring up the claims of these unfortunate people before the court for consideration."[60]

On the state level in the antebellum period, then, while habeas corpus did have a due process component, it was often in no way concerned with freedom.

Nevertheless, there were two important antebellum congressional modifications in habeas corpus jurisdiction for federal courts. In 1833, Congress modified federal court habeas corpus jurisdiction to include habeas corpus petitions from those who might be detained by state authorities when enforcing federal law.[61] In 1842, Congress again expanded federal court habeas corpus authority for foreign nationals detained by state governments.[62] The 1833 Act was used to remove from state to federal courts cases in which federal marshals were arrested by state authorities for enforcing the fugitive slave provisions of the Compromise of 1850.[63] This unintended consequence—which was recognized as such by federal court judges at the time—nevertheless fueled significant backlash from states that were actively using their own newly improved state habeas corpus powers to thwart federal fugitive slave legislation and protect their free black populations from kidnappings. The Jacksonian regime's habeas corpus expansion might not have been needed after the passage of the Force Bill,[64] but the provision nevertheless remained law, buttressing both the enforcement of the Democratic Party's vision of constitutional governance with respect to the maintenance of slavery as well as state-level Republican backlash during the 1850s.[65] What is most interesting about the 1833 Act is that it was never used for its original purpose, which was to provide a legal mechanism for the removal of cases involving federal revenue officers who might be arrested by state authorities.[66]

The 1842 Act resulted from the McLeod Affair. On December 30, 1837, the American steamboat *Caroline* was destroyed by British troops as it lay moored in Schlosser, New York. Canadian insurgents, who had recently engaged British troops in Ontario, hoped that the *Caroline* would bring much-needed provisions to their resistance efforts. That day, however, British troops sacked the ship, burned it, and sent it over Niagara Falls, killing two people. The administration of U.S. President Martin Van Buren directed Secretary of State John Forsyth to protest the British actions. His protests were met with the response that the United States had failed to quell its citizens' involvement in British and Canadian affairs.[67]

Alexander McLeod, a Canadian, was subsequently arrested by New York authorities for his suspected involvement in the assault on the ship. Angered, the British government demanded that McLeod be released because he was acting on orders directly from the British Crown. His actions, according to the British government, were public, not private, and were simply the extension of a sovereign nation. Importantly, in Secretary Forsyth's reply, he not only disagreed with the characterization of McLeod's actions as public, which might have precluded his prosecution by the state of New York, but he also stated that the federal government did not have the power to reach into the criminal proceedings of the states.[68]

When John Tyler assumed the presidency, his secretary of state, Daniel Webster, reversed the United States' previous position on McLeod's actions but still maintained that the federal government did not have the ability to reach into the domain of state criminal law to free McLeod. Convinced that the government was powerless, but sympathetic to Britain's position, Webster even went so far as to enlist the help of Attorney General John Crittenden to aid in McLeod's defense in New York courts. With little subsequent fanfare, McLeod was held over for trial and then subsequently acquitted.[69]

In March 1842, just a few months after McLeod's acquittal, another participant in the raid on the *Caroline* was arrested. In order to avert another international incident, and well aware of similar situations in which foreign nationals were detained by state authorities, President Tyler proposed that Congress remedy this problem through appropriate habeas corpus legislation. As would be expected, the initial wording of the bill from the Senate Judiciary Committee, which provided for the removal of cases from state to federal courts via habeas corpus for "any act done . . . under the law of nations . . . or authority of any foreign State or sovereignty,"[70] met with spirited resistance, particularly from Democrats. Not only did these habeas corpus provisions potentially threaten the traditional criminal justice domain of state courts, but in the minds of some Southern members of Congress, they might inspire foreigners to incite slave revolts in states, only to have their cases removed to federal court and dismissed.[71] The final bill, which equally divided Whigs and Democrats, provided that federal habeas corpus authority would extend to

> all cases of any prisoner or prisoners in jail or confinement, where he, she, or they, being subjects or citizens of a foreign State, and domiciled therein, shall be committed or confined, or in custody, under or by authority of law, or process founded thereon, of the United States or any one of them; for or on account of any act done or omitted under any alleged right, title, authority, privilege, protection, or exemption, set up or claimed under the commission, or order, or sanction, of any foreign State or sovereignty, the validity and effect whereof depend upon the law of nations, or under color thereof.[72]

What is important to understand about the two antebellum changes to federal habeas corpus court jurisdiction is the overtly political origins of those changes and their federalism dimensions. Like previous English changes to habeas corpus, both the 1833 and 1842 acts were engineered by political regimes to meet critical challenges to their ability to govern. For Andrew Jackson, habeas corpus changes were necessary to enforce a core regime principle in the form of a centrist federalism that, while deferential to states' rights as a political proposition, was nevertheless unyielding on the basic enforcement powers of the national government. For the Tyler administration, as for others before it, the ability of the federal government to operate with legitimacy and authority on the international stage required habeas corpus changes to remove state cases against foreign nationals to federal courts.

These changes also directly implicated issues of federalism and states' rights, and criticisms of both changes in this regard were swift.[73] Both acts are often cited by contemporary critics in support of broad arguments about the inevitability of increased federal habeas corpus court supervision of state criminal trials. But there is nothing in the history of these two acts that suggests that they were initiated for reasons other than the enforcement and maintenance of core regime principles of Jacksonian Democrats in the early 1830s and Whigs in the early 1840s.

Moreover, the regime principles that were enforced through these changes to habeas corpus were never conceived as having anything remotely to do with the individual rights of the potential petitioners in the ways with which we are familiar today. The removal of state cases to federal habeas corpus courts for federal revenue officers or foreign nationals was a far cry from the use of habeas corpus to vindicate the rights of minority criminal defendants in Southern state courts during the height of Jim Crow. If anything, these changes were solicitous of majorities, not minorities.

The unintended use of the 1833 Act described above began soon after the passage and implementation of the Compromise of 1850, which in part strengthened fugitive slave laws. The essential parts of the Fugitive Slave Act in the Compromise of 1850 provided that the Act's provisions were to be carried out by commissioners appointed by United States circuit courts who would have authority to issue certificates of removal for fugitive slaves. If United States marshals refused to carry out their duties in reclaiming slaves, they were to be fined $1,000. Marshals were also to be held liable for the value of slaves in their custody. Slave owners had two options in reclaiming their property. In the first, the Act reaffirmed slave owners' common-law right of reception, which would allow them to seize physically their property anywhere, in any state, at any time, and in any way. After the seizure, they could then bring the slave to a United States commissioner, who would issue a certificate of removal. Alternatively, slave owners could first apply for a certificate of removal and then, with the aid of United States marshals, who could call forth a *posse commitatus*, physically recover their property. Hearings for certificates before the commissioners could not involve any testimony from slaves themselves. Just as important, the Act also prohibited any interference in the rendition of fugitive slaves "by any process issued by any court, judge, magistrate, or other person whomsoever."[74] Effectively gutting any meaningfully substantive review of a suspected fugitive's status through habeas corpus, a writ of habeas corpus could still theoretically issue, but a certificate of removal was all that was needed to answer the writ.[75]

Before signing the bill into law, President Millard Fillmore first requested that his attorney general, John Crittenden, advise him on the constitutionality of the bill with respect to its effect on habeas corpus, specifically the very real possibility of the Act's *de facto* suspension of the writ in its prohibitions against legal "molestations."[76] Crittenden's response was that the bill did not jeopardize habeas corpus "in any manner."[77] At issue, of course, was the larger problem of conflicting habeas corpus writs between states and the federal government, as well as the extent to which habeas corpus could be used (on either level) to inquire into the substantive issues associated with detention. The Compromise of 1850 seemed to preclude any use of the writ by states to frustrate the return of fugitive slaves. Moreover, suspecting that collisions between state and federal power were imminent immediately after the Compromise was signed into law, Supreme Court Justice Robert Grier and Circuit Court Judge John Kane personally requested that President Fillmore use federal troops in the enforcement of the law. Not wanting to foment Northern uneasiness concerning this issue, Fillmore agreed to provide troops only in emergencies. Nevertheless, the president remained committed "to bring[ing] the whole force of the government to sustain the law."[78]

These habeas corpus issues would come to implicate the 1833 Act in early 1853 in *Ex parte Jenkins* when four slave catchers were arrested for trespass in Pennsylvania during a violent seizure of a slave named Thomas.[79] The marshals then filed a habeas corpus writ in federal circuit court arguing that their detention was unconstitutional. Justice Grier and Circuit Court Judge Kane ruled that the 1833 Habeas Corpus Act allowed the writ to issue from federal to state courts, and the marshals were discharged. The unintended consequence of the 1833 Act's use in these types of cases did not escape either judge; in fact, their use of it suggests that they thought that the 1833 Act's application to these types of cases was only a natural application of the Act's general propositions and intent.[80] It was just this type of state interference with federal law that originally prompted Congress to provide federal habeas corpus relief for tariff officers should they be detained by South Carolina authorities during the nullification crisis. With respect to similar state-level interference with the fugitive slave provisions of the Compromise of 1850, Justice Grier proclaimed, "The extreme advocate of state rights would scarcely contend that in such cases the courts of the United States should be wholly unable to protect themselves or their officers."[81] Here again, habeas corpus became a central tool in the larger political process of sustaining and enforcing core constitutional principles during the antebellum period.

Of course, backlash against this coalition and its use of habeas corpus was already brewing. No case better exemplifies these tensions, especially with respect to the use of habeas corpus to serve competing jurisdictional and political regimes, than *Ableman v. Booth*.[82] Here, Chief Justice Roger Taney faced head-on the dual-track development of state and federal habeas corpus during the antebellum period as he was forced to resolve the question of whether an affirmative grant of a state habeas corpus writ by Wisconsin state courts should be obeyed by federal courts. The scenario was a familiar one: Sherman Booth, an abolitionist editor, was arrested by U.S. Marshall Stephen Ableman for helping a fugitive slave named Joshua Glover escape his jail cell and flee to Canada.[83]

For Taney, the practical problem with Wisconsin's position—particularly its use of habeas corpus—was that it effectively precluded any kind of national enforcement, prosecution, and judicial resolution of national criminal law. If states exercised this supposed authority to use habeas corpus to free those detained, indicted, and prosecuted within their states' territorial jurisdiction, they would quickly undermine any national legislative and judicial power. The result would be that "because State courts would not always agree . . . it would often happen, that an act which was admitted to be an offence, and justly punished, in one State, would be regarded as innocent, and indeed praiseworthy, in another."[84]

Taney's argument then moved to one of the strongest assertions of national power that the Court had as yet made. Without specific authority to issue habeas corpus for federal prisoners either from its own state constitution or from the national one, it was forever to be understood that "no State can authorize one of its judges or courts to exercise judicial power, by *habeas corpus* or otherwise, within the jurisdiction of another independent government."[85] Although both the state and national governments will inevitably exercise their jurisdictional powers within the same territorial limits, Taney forcefully asserted that these powers are derived from:

> separate and distinct sovereignties, acting separately and independently of each other, within their respective spheres. And the sphere of action appropriated to the United States is as far beyond the reach of the judicial processes issued by a State judge or State court, as if the line of division was traced by landmarks and monuments visible to the eye.[86]

Importantly, toward the end of the opinion, Taney nevertheless held that states were not prohibited from issuing the Great Writ for those held within their jurisdictions. What they could not do, however, was go beyond an answer to the writ when it was determined that a prisoner was held by authority of the United States. Thus there could not be any substantive inquiry into the constitutionality of the law by which a prisoner was held—this power was reserved to the Supreme Court alone.[87] As it had so often, then, habeas corpus—and the substantive rights it would protect, including Magna Carta's due process ideals—would yield to *procedural* adjustments to those substantive rights by political elites.

Civil War, Reconstruction, And The Gilded Age

Certainly, the Republican regime during the Civil War and Reconstruction would redefine some substantive fundamental rights, and, as would be expected, habeas corpus was similarly redefined, both in its procedural reach and in its substantive application, to enforce these rights. During this time, the substantive rights that habeas corpus sought to protect—due process and equal protection rights for newly freed slaves—were borne out, but only temporarily. The substantive and procedural changes to the writ by political regimes during the Civil War and Reconstruction ultimately led to decreased substantive protections by the end of the nineteenth century.[88]

The major habeas corpus developments in this period—Lincoln's suspension and Taney's response; Congress' legislation that retroactively gave an *imprimatur* to executive suspension; the Habeas Corpus Act of 1867 and its subsequent repeal; and the Supreme Court's own judicially created habeas corpus rules for review of state habeas corpus cases in the 1880— tracked a pattern of increased use of habeas corpus by federal courts for state prisoners initially predicated on new substantive rights. But the use of habeas corpus to enforce these new rights soon gave way to a decreased commitment for those particular rights and new commitments for a different set of substantive rights that habeas corpus did not reach, specifically substantive due process rights of property and contract during the Gilded Age.[89]

Significantly, after Reconstruction, some members of Congress felt that the provisions for the removal of state cases to federal courts were an insult to state courts. With decreased support throughout the country for aggressive national supervision of the kinds of fundamental due process rights that had been pushed for during the height of Reconstruction, Congress reinstated the Court's appellate power to hear habeas corpus cases under the 1867 Habeas Act,[90] and explicitly invited the Court to set its own rules for these cases. Not surprisingly, in the first case to come before them, *Ex parte Royall*,[91] the Court announced what would become to be known as the "exhaustion requirement,"[92] which required that habeas corpus petitioners first exhaust all state appellate avenues before even the lowest federal court could entertain the writ.[93]

Twentieth Century And Beyond

Beginning in the first half of the twentieth century, habeas corpus slowly developed into a legal remedy for almost any due process violation, coming as close as any time in its history to reflecting the idealized due process ideals in the seventeenth century rewriting of habeas corpus and Magna Carta. Covering a catalogue of fundamental rights wider than Magna Carta ever promised, the esteemed law professor Zechariah Chafee proclaimed that habeas corpus' substantive reach now included:

> the right to be accused by a grand jury, to be immune from double jeopardy, not to be deprived of liberty without due process of law, to a speedy

and public trial by a jury of the vicinage, to be informed of the nature of the accusation, to be confronted with the witnesses against him, to call his own witnesses and have his own lawyer.[94]

In *Fay v. Noia* (1963), which came at the apex of the Supreme Court's liberalization of habeas corpus during the 1960s, Justice Brennan said of modern encomiums for the writ:

> These are not extravagant expressions. Behind them may be discerned the unceasing contest between personal liberty and government oppression. It is no accident that habeas corpus has time and again played a central role in national crises, wherein the claims of order and of liberty clash most acutely, not only in England in the seventeenth century, but also America from our very beginnings, and today. Although in form the Great Writ is simply a mode of procedure, its history is inextricably intertwined with the growth of fundamental rights of personal liberty. For its function has been to provide a prompt and efficacious remedy for whatever society deems to be intolerable restraints.[95]

Ansel Adams (1902–1984). *Mess Line, Noon, Manzanar Relocation Center, California* [Japanese internment camp], 1943. Prints and Photographs Division, Library of Congress (LC-DIG-ppprs-00173)

NOTICE

Headquarters
Western Defense Command
and Fourth Army

Presidio of San Francisco, California
May 5, 1942

Civilian Exclusion Order No. 41

1. Pursuant to the provisions of Public Proclamations Nos. 1 and 2, this Headquarters, dated March 2, 1942, and March 16, 1942, respectively, it is hereby ordered that from and after 12 o'clock noon, P. W. T., of Monday, May 11, 1942, all persons of Japanese ancestry, both alien and non-alien, be excluded from that portion of Military Area No. 1 described as follows:

> All of that portion of the City and County of San Francisco, State of California, within that boundary beginning at the intersection of Presidio Avenue and Sutter Street; thence easterly on Sutter Street to Van Ness Avenue; thence southerly on Van Ness Avenue to O'Farrell Street; thence westerly on O'Farrell Street to St. Joseph's Avenue (Calvary Cemetery); thence northerly on St. Joseph's Avenue to Geary Street; thence westerly on Geary Street to Presidio Avenue; thence northerly on Presidio Avenue to the point of beginning.

2. A responsible member of each family, and each individual living alone, in the above described area will report between the hours of 8:00 A. M. and 5:00 P. M., Wednesday, May 6, 1942, or during the same hours on Thursday, May 7, 1942, to the Civil Control Station located at:

> 1530 Buchanan Street,
> San Francisco, California.

3. Any person subject to this order who fails to comply with any of its provisions or with the provisions of published instructions pertaining hereto or who is found in the above area after 12 o'clock noon, P. W. T., of Monday, May 11, 1942, will be liable to the criminal penalties provided by Public Law No. 503, 77th Congress, approved March 21, 1942, entitled "An Act to Provide a Penalty for Violation of Restrictions or Orders with Respect to Persons Entering, Remaining in, Leaving or Committing Any Act in Military Areas or Zones," and alien Japanese will be subject to immediate apprehension and internment.

4. All persons within the bounds of an established Assembly Center pursuant to instructions from this Headquarters are excepted from the provisions of this order while those persons are in such Assembly Center.

J. L. DeWITT
Lieutenant General, U. S. Army
Commanding

Headquarters Western Defense Command and Fourth Army. *Civilian Exclusion Order No. 41*. Presidio of San Francisco, California, May 5, 1942. Law Library, Library of Congress

175

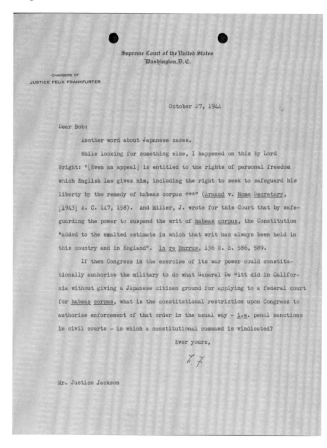

Felix Frankfurter (1882–1965) to Robert H. Jackson (1892–1954), October 27, 1944. Typed letter. Robert Jackson Papers, Manuscript Division, Library of Congress

Perpetuating the myth of habeas corpus' progressive development as much as anyone before him, Brennan then asserted that as early as the sixteenth century, habeas corpus simply "prefigured the union of the right to due process drawn from Magna Charta."[96] Brennan's encomiums to Magna Carta are replete within his habeas corpus opinions. In fact, *Fay v. Noia* was one-third of the "habeas trilogy"[97] cases that the Court handed down in 1963, effectively widening federal habeas corpus access for state prisoners more than at any other point before or since in American history.[98]

Conclusion

What, then, are we to make of the historically inaccurate accounts of Magna Carta and habeas corpus? One profitable way might be to treat Blackstone's assertion of habeas corpus as *another Magna Carta* not as an account of origins for either Magna Carta or habeas corpus, but rather as an account of their capacity to develop and change over time. Blackstone's attribution of habeas corpus' new role as successor

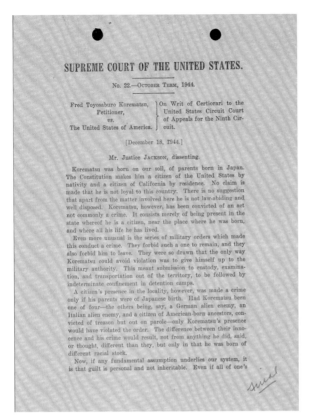

SUPREME COURT OF THE UNITED STATES.

No. 22.—OCTOBER TERM, 1944.

Fred Toyosaburo Korematsu, Petitioner, vs. The United States of America. } On Writ of Certiorari to the United States Circuit Court of Appeals for the Ninth Circuit.

[December 18, 1944.]

Mr. Justice JACKSON, dissenting.

Korematsu was born on our soil, of parents born in Japan. The Constitution makes him a citizen of the United States by nativity and a citizen of California by residence. No claim is made that he is not loyal to this country. There is no suggestion that apart from the matter involved here he is not law-abiding and well disposed. Korematsu, however, has been convicted of an act not commonly a crime. It consists merely of being present in the state whereof he is a citizen, near the place where he was born, and where all his life he has lived.

Even more unusual is the series of military orders which made this conduct a crime. They forbid such a one to remain, and they also forbid him to leave. They were so drawn that the only way Korematsu could avoid violation was to give himself up to the military authority. This meant submission to custody, examination, and transportation out of the territory, to be followed by indeterminate confinement in detention camps.

A citizen's presence in the locality, however, was made a crime only if his parents were of Japanese birth. Had Korematsu been one of four—the others being, say, a German alien enemy, an Italian alien enemy, and a citizen of American-born ancestors, convicted of treason but out on parole—only Korematsu's presence would have violated the order. The difference between their innocence and his crime would result, not from anything he did, said, or thought, different than they, but only in that he was born of different racial stock.

Now, if any fundamental assumption underlies our system, it is that guilt is personal and not inheritable. Even if all of one's

Dissenting opinion by Justice Robert Jackson in *Korematsu v. United States*. Supreme Court Decision, No. 22, December 18, 1944. Law Library, Library of Congress

to Magna Carta could easily be questioned and then summarily rejected as nothing more than what Alfred Kelly called "law office history," whereby lawyers pick and choose facts that construct a supposedly inevitable narrative purely in the service of their own position.[99] Certainly accounts of both Magna Carta and habeas corpus fall prey to this vice as the substantive rights of the barons that the Great Charter most likely sought to protect at the time—like the substantive "rights" of slave owners that habeas corpus was used to protect—are too often ignored or forgotten.

Another profitable way to understand the link between habeas corpus and Magna Carta would be to see habeas corpus as a repository for Magna Carta's due process ideals. Here, though, we have to pay more attention to the attendant *political* context of habeas corpus development. If due process is a murky and changing notion in Magna Carta, it is for habeas corpus too. Like Magna Carta, habeas corpus is simply not the counter-majoritarian check against executives or political majorities that we tend to assume. Because habeas corpus and the Whiggish ideals of Magna Carta are often tools of political regimes, they often serve powerful interests first. This is certainly true of habeas corpus *and* the revisionist histories of Magna Carta that relied so heavily on a critique founded on the feudal character of the Barons. We can understand their link better, then, if we understand both as procedural more than substantive rights. Their real power is in their procedural ability to change substantive rights. This means that both have the potential to enforce conceptions of rights that are consistent with our best ideals. But it also means that they have the potential to enforce our worst ideals, too. This was certainly the case in the slave law of antebellum America. Both habeas corpus and Magna Carta, then, are procedural repositories—markers if you will—for changing notions of what we mean by due process.

Nevertheless, the very fact that the substantive and procedural due process rights that Magna Carta and habeas corpus have protected through the centuries have varied considerably, even in negative directions, is proof enough of their liberty-yielding potential. In this sense, our acceptance of less than accurate

United States Supreme Court. *Boumediene v. Bush*, 553 U.S. 723 (2008). Washington, D.C.: Government Printing Office, 2012. Law Library, Library of Congress

histories is, at the very least, testament to our normative preference for more capacious notions of personal rights and liberties.

In McIlwain's 1914 article critiquing Whiggish accounts of Magna Carta, he came to the conclusion that while some modern rights, like trial by jury, were never implied in Magna Carta in the way that we imagine today,[100] "we may still hold, as our fathers did, that the law of the land is there."[101] Intentional or not, then, the wisdom of the Barons who managed to secure feudal rights at Runnymede was present in the framing of procedural rights like *legem terrae,* that were specific enough to protect their most immediate substantive concerns but, fortuitously, general enough to remind us that there is still work left to be done.

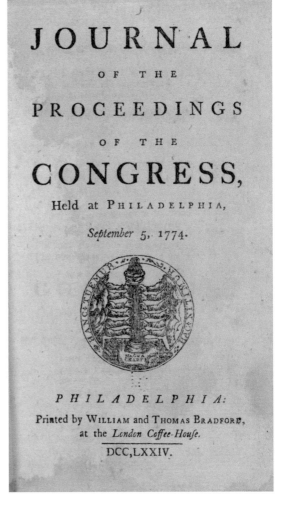

Journal of the Proceedings of the Congress, Held at Philadelphia, September 5, 1774. Philadelphia: William and Thomas Bradford, 1774. Rare Book and Special Collections Division, Library of Congress

JOURNAL

OF THE

PROCEEDINGS

OF THE

CONGRESS,

Held at PHILADELPHIA,

September 5, 1774.

PHILADELPHIA:

Printed by WILLIAM and THOMAS BRADFORD, at the *London Coffee-House.*

DCC,LXXIV.

EXECUTIVE POWER

England's Lord Chief Justice Edward Coke bars King James I from the "King's Court" making the court, by law, independent of the executive branch of government.

MAGNA CARTA AND THE JUDGES— WHY MAGNA CARTA MATTERS

The Right Honourable Lady Justice Arden D.B.E.[1]

In this study of Magna Carta, I wish to focus on the role of the judges, the vision which Magna Carta had for them, and how it is to be realised today—eight hundred years on. This is a topical subject because, since the last centenary of Magna Carta in 1915, the UK has had, all within the last half century, at least three statutes of great significance to the constitutional framework of the UK—the European Communities Act 1972, the Human Rights Act 1998, and the Constitutional Reform Act 2005. In addition, the UK has had two major high-level inquiries of particular interest and importance in relation to the judicial function, namely, the Commission on a UK Bill of Rights and the inquiry of the House of Lords Constitution Committee into the judicial appointments process. I do not propose to discuss the recommendations of these two inquiries. What I wish to examine is the context in which these inquiries arise. They are building on the foundations which Magna Carta laid.

Nearly eight hundred years ago, King John, acceding to the demands of the Barons, set the Great Seal of England on the Charter of Liberties we now call Magna Carta "in the meadow which is called Runnymede, between Windsor and Staines."

In the years which followed, Magna Carta was confirmed over thirty times by royal charter; it was directed to be read out twice yearly in the great cathedrals of the land; archbishops and bishops were directed to pronounce sentences of excommunication on those who by word, deed, or counsel went against the Charter; and Kings were expected to confirm Magna Carta at the start of their reign. This gives us some idea of Magna Carta's importance in mediaeval England. Not all of the provisions of the document signed by King John were reconfirmed, but most were, and indeed some of the clauses remain the law of the land.

A panel from the bronze doors of the U.S. Supreme Court, Washington, D.C. Courtesy of U.S. Supreme Court

In this study, I propose to examine an aspect of Magna Carta which, as far as I know, has not been examined before, at least not in the course of this series of Magna Carta lectures. I propose to examine the role which Magna Carta assigned to the judges, and ask whether the features of the judicial role envisaged by Magna Carta have changed and how they are being realised today.

To do this, I have to start by exploring the significance of Magna Carta from the point of view of the law and the administration of justice by the judges. I propose to concentrate on the following clauses:

> "(17)   Ordinary lawsuits shall not follow the royal court around, but shall be held in a fixed place.
>
> . . .
>
> (39)   No free man shall be seized or imprisoned, or stripped of his rights or possessions, or outlawed or exiled, or deprived of his standing in any other way, nor will we proceed with force against him, or send others to do so, except by the lawful judgment of his equals or by the law of the land.
>
> (40)   To no one will we sell, to no one deny or delay right or justice.
>
> . . .
>
> (45)   We will appoint as justices, constables, sheriffs, or other officials, only men that know the law of the realm and are minded to keep it well."

Clause 45 did not appear in later versions of Magna Carta after 1215, and clause 40 was renumbered as clause 29 in at least one later version, but nothing turns on these points for present purposes. Clauses 39 and 40 are still in force today by virtue of the Charter of 1225.

What Was The Significance Of These Four Provisions Of Magna Carta?

Magna Carta is a monumental affirmation of the rule of law. It proceeds on the all-important assumption that disputes are to be decided in accordance with the law. This was not a new idea but an important confirmation of it. As Lord Irvine LC put it, "[t]he primary importance of Magna Carta is that it is a beacon of the rule of law".[2] Laws LJ has described Magna Carta as a "proclamation of the rule of law".[3] The King was not above the law and he could not displace the due application of the law by his judges. Moreover, by providing for the judicial determination of disputes according to the law of the land, Magna Carta laid the foundations of what we know today as due process of law. It also gave judges what has been their traditional and vital role of acting as a bulwark for the individual

Henry de Bracton (d. 1268). On the limits of kingship in *De Legibus et Consueditudinibus Angliae* [On the Laws and Customs of England]. London: Richard Tottel, 1569. Law Library, Library of Congress

against arbitrary action by the state. The concept of due process is an element within the concept of the rule of law.

This is not the place for a detailed exposition of the concept of the rule of law, which may be found instead in Lord Bingham's remarkable book *The Rule of Law*.[4] In a speech which he gave on Magna Carta,[5] Lord Bingham summed up its achievements in these terms:

> "Conditioned as we are today by our own knowledge of political and constitutional development over the last nine centuries, it calls for the exercise of real historical imagination to appreciate the enormity, the grandeur of what was done at Runnymede. King John entered the meadow as a ruler acknowledging no secular superior, whose word was law. He left the meadow as a ruler who had acknowledged, in the most solemn manner imaginable, that there were some things even he could not do, at any rate

without breaking his promise. This, then, is the enduring legacy of Magna Carta: the lesson that no power is absolute; that all power, however elevated, is subject to constraint; that, as was to be said by Dr. Thomas Fuller some centuries later, 'Be you never so high, the law is above you'".

In addition, there is significance in the fact that clause 17 provided that the judges were to sit in a fixed place. This court became the Court of Common Pleas, as opposed to the Court of the King's Bench, which followed the King around the country, and as opposed to the Court of Chancery. The Court of Common Pleas existed down to the end of the nineteenth century. The fact was that, before Magna Carta, the King often took the decisions in disputes between his subjects as he went around the country, without involving his judges, or his judges made the decisions but applied the *lex regni*.

Putting the judges into a fixed place, away from the King, achieved two ends in particular. First, it laid the foundation for the doctrine of separation of powers. Judges were to be separate from the King, who made laws by royal decree. The doctrine of separation of powers has been much debated and developed in the eight centuries since Magna Carta. The separation was only gradual: At least until the end of the eighteenth century, judges could be members of Parliament as well as holding judicial office. Most recently, the doctrine was invoked as the principal reason for setting up the new Supreme Court of the United Kingdom pursuant to the Constitutional Reform Act 2005. The Supreme Court replaced the House of Lords, which had been the highest court in the land since 1399, although the concept of the Lords of Appeal in Ordinary only came about pursuant to the Appellate Jurisdiction Act 1876. Secondly, the separation of judges from the King's court made clear that judges were to operate independently of the King. This led to the development of the concept of judicial independence.

Clause 45 provides that the judges were to apply the law of the realm. What was the significance of that? It was the law of the realm as opposed to the law of the King, canon law, or local law. I have already explained that some judges were attached to the royal court. Other judges were people in the locality who were trusted by the local inhabitants to try disputes or to hear criminal cases. There were, of course, no professional judges. The judges were often priests and so they were very familiar with canon law, which was derived from Roman law.[6] The significance of requiring judges to apply the law of the realm was that they would have to apply the law that was built up by tradition and accepted by the population. So the law of the realm was the law of England, including the law applied by local custom in different areas of England. Significantly, the law of the realm was the law of the

Thomas Jefferson (1743–1826) to James Madison (1751–1836), March 15, 1789, regarding a bill of rights to curb executive and legislative branches. Manuscript letter. James Madison Papers, Manuscript Division, Library of Congress

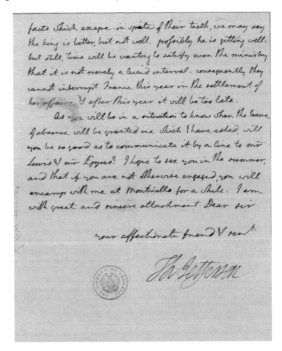

people or, as it was and is called: the common law. As it was put in a work known as *The Mirror of the Justices* published in about 1290, it is called common law "because it is given to all in common".[7] This emphasis on commonality suggests that the common law is a system of law in which all members of society are to have a share.

Moreover, Magna Carta, by requiring judges to apply the law of the realm, authorised the judges to apply the common law. This was an enormous shift of power away from the King and to the judges. In the fullness of time, the authority to apply the common law was taken to include the authority to develop the common law, but the judges had to exercise restraint. They adopted a theory known as the declaratory theory of the common law. They were loath to admit that they were developing the common law, and instead expressed themselves as simply declaring common law which had previously lain hidden. This theory continued for many hundreds of years: only comparatively recently has it been said that judges "do not believe in fairy tales anymore, so we must accept that for better or worse judges do make law".[8] It is, therefore, no longer denied that judges are developing the law, but this is always subject to Parliamentary sovereignty. The judges cannot develop the law so that it contradicts a statute; nor do they develop the law in an area that ought properly be left to Parliament, for example, because to lay down the law needs more than the judges can do by judicial decision in a particular case.

185

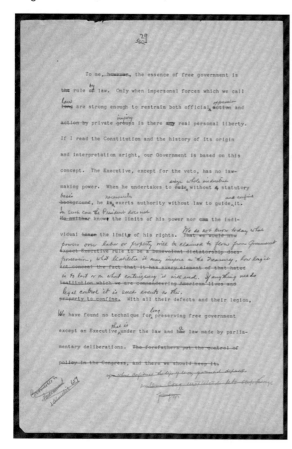

Draft opinion in the *Youngstown Sheet and Tube, Co. v. Sawyer,* May 22, 1952. Typescript with handwritten notes. Robert H. Jackson Papers, Manuscript Division, Library of Congress

Furthermore, by providing that any interference with an individual's liberty had to be authorised by the law of the land,[9] which was to be applied by the judges, Magna Carta expressly recognised something that it is today easy to take for granted but which is utterly fundamental, namely that every person should have the right not to have his liberty taken away other than in accordance with a decision of a court and due process of law. Clause 39 outlawed detention by order of the King or, in more modern terms, mere executive detention, not prescribed by law, for whatever reason.

And, by providing for the judicial determination of disputes, Magna Carta laid the foundations of certainty and consistency in the law and for the law to be administered in a public place, thus laying the foundations of open justice for all.

The provision in clause 40 that justice would not be sold or delayed was also a vitally important guarantee in all courts, even in the King's Bench and the Court of Chancery. However, in parenthesis, it should be noted that this clause was never applied to the sale of writs, which was an important source of revenue for many Kings. This is an opportunity which has not escaped elected governments in recent times as court fees have been substantially increased for the Treasury's benefit. However, court fees cannot be of such an amount as to bar a person from obtaining access to a court.[10]

As to the barons who caused King John to apply the Great Seal to Magna Carta, it is of course impossible to believe that they had any idea of the epic nature of the act on which they were engaged. They were, almost certainly, seeking to protect their own rights and interests against excessive royal power, and possibly even to put themselves above the law. It is now generally accepted that when clause 39 refers to the judgment of a person by his peers, it is in fact referring to the judgment of the barons by the barons, and not to trial by jury. But, once it became accepted, as it did, that it was not just the barons but every free person who was entitled to the protection of Magna Carta, the parallel with trial by jury was obvious. It is also to be noted that clause 40 was not the source of *habeas corpus*, which was a remedy developed by the judges.

Magna Carta was originally called the Great Charter, not because of its contents, but because it was executed contemporaneously with a shorter document called the Charter of the Forest. Its execution did not mean that all was sweetness and

Federal Supplement: Jones v. Clinton (869 F. Supp. 690 (E.D. Ark. 1994). St. Paul, Minnesota: West Publishing Company, 1995. Law Library, Library of Congress

light afterwards. Kings continued to err. In addition, the legal system did not meet all the high ideals which Magna Carta suggested that it should. Thus, for instance, the Tudors established the Court of Star Chamber,[11] which acted as an immediate agent of the King's prerogative.[12] The tyrannical proceedings of the Star Chamber under the Stuarts, especially Charles I, in political cases led to its abolition in 1641 by an Act of Parliament that referred to Magna Carta and stated that cases "ought to be tried and determined in the ordinary courts of justice, and by the ordinary course of law".[13] Trial methods in ordinary courts did not meet modern standards either, since trial by ordeal and trial by battle were for many years the order of the day. But, over time, the ideals of Magna Carta became embedded.

Of course, no mention is made of the relationship of the common law to statute law. That Great Council of the nation, known as Parliament, had not yet been convened.[14] When it was, it became accepted that the common law should be subject to the will of Parliament. The doctrine of Parliamentary sovereignty, as it is now known, is explored by Lord Bingham in a speech which he gave in King's College, London in October 2007.[15]

I pose the question: Why was Magna Carta so significant for the role of judges and the administration of justice in England? Quite simply, Magna Carta laid the foundations for some of the most fundamental concepts of our legal system. These concepts echo two major themes, which overlap. The first theme may be called the constitutional theme, and it involves:

1. The separation of powers;
2. The birth of the judiciary as a separate arm of the constitution of England;
3. The independence of the judiciary;
4. The incorruptibility of the judiciary; and
5. The development of the common law, based in theory on long tradition but in reality representing judge-made law.

There is a second, equally important, theme based on the role of the individual in relation to the state, involving:

1. The judiciary as the bulwark of individual liberty against arbitrary action by the state;
2. The rule of law;
3. Equality before the law;
4. Due process;
5. Open justice; and
6. Certainty and consistency in the law.

The second theme then is all about liberty and, it might be said, the first theme is the framework which allows the second theme to flourish. Liberty begins historically with liberty of the person in the sense of freedom from arbitrary arrest. It has been developed over the centuries to include other freedoms, such as freedom of expression and freedom of self-realisation. Most recently, it has been developed in terms of respect for one's home and private life.

Magna Carta thus gave us fundamental law. It is little wonder that we call this the Great Charter of our Liberties.

It is not within the scope of this study of Magna Carta to explore the ways in which the provisions of Magna Carta, which I have set above, have found their way into the written constitutions of many democracies around the world but I will give one example, where it finds particularly clear expression: the Fourteenth Amendment of the Constitution of the United States, which reads:

> "XIV. Section 1. . . . [N]or shall any State deprive any person of life, liberty, or property, without due process of law; nor deny to any person within its jurisdiction the equal protection of the laws."

Magna Carta also finds clear reflection in the International Convention on Civil and Political Rights,[16] the Universal Declaration of Human Rights,[17] and the European Convention on Human Rights.[18] Magna Carta belongs today, not only to England, but to the world.

NO TAXATION
WITHOUT REPRESENTATION

THE PATRIOTIC AMERICAN FARMER.
J-N D-K-NS—N Esqr. BARRISTER at LAW:
Who with Attic Eloquence and Roman Spirit hath Asserted,
The Liberties of the BRITISH Colonies in America.

Tis nobly done, to Stem Taxations Rage,
And raise, the thoughts of a degenrate Age,
For Happiness, and Joy, from Freedom Spring,
But Life in Bondage, is a worthless Thing.

Printed for & Sold by R. Bell. Bookseller

KING JOHN, MAGNA CARTA AND TAXATION

Jane Frecknall-Hughes

Introduction

During the reign of England's King John (1199–1216), many innovative or exorbitant financial measures were implemented which caused great resentment among those on whom they were imposed, especially the barons.[1]   Of the 63 clauses in the 1215 Magna Carta, over 50 reflect contemporary fiscal grievances in one way or another, signifying a deep discontent with the ways in which sums of money were exacted or goods/financial rights appropriated arbitrarily by the Crown. However, the fame and afterlife of Magna Carta rests chiefly on Clauses 39 and 40, promising respectively that no one shall be arrested, imprisoned, stripped of his rights/possessions, etc., except by lawful judgment of his peers or the law of the land; and that no one will be sold or refused or experience delay in receiving justice. As a result, the concept of Magna Carta "as some kind of proto-constitutional or human-rights type document has resonated through popular perception through the ages" (Frecknall-Hughes, 2012, p. 245).[2] As Breay (2002, p. 7) comments:

> Over time, its true origin and meaning have become obscured by myths and misunderstandings about its content and significance, as it has come to symbolise principles which played little part in its creation. . . . But it was the ways in which the charter was used after the death of King John, rather than the events of 1215, which guaranteed its status and longevity.

Magna Carta itself was not framed as a law, but took the form of a sealed letter, addressed by John to his barons, and owes much in its form to the coronation charters of previous kings (see Vincent, 2012, pp. 10–14), containing idealised promises made when a king was crowned, which is reflected in a desire to see things re-established as they were of old, for example, in the restoration of forest boundaries, in Clause 53, to how they were under Henry II and Richard I.

The Patriotic American Farmer J-n D-k-ns-n Esqr. Barrister at Law [John Dickinson]. Engraving, between 1870–1880. Prints and Photographs Division, Library of Congress (LC-DIG-ppmsca-37771)

The predominant concern of Magna Carta was to "redress the fiscal abuses which the barons believed John had perpetrated" (Frecknall-Hughes, 2012, p. 246). In other words, it was primarily the outcome of a tax rebellion,[3] a view also taken by Burg (2004, pp. 84–86). Breay (2002, p. 7) also suggests that the document addressed abuses of justice and feudal rights—and it is not difficult to see underlying fiscal issues here too. Holt (1992b, p. 176) comments that "the King's financial policy, in all its many aspects, was one of the main concerns of the Magna Carta", although this is not often the main consideration in discussions of the document. The wealth of financial records[4] available from John's reign supports the fact that Magna Carta was thus a (financial) peace treaty between John and the barons, twenty-five of whom agreed to act as 'suretors' to guarantee that the king would adhere to the agreement, with a further 38 standing ready to act in a like manner, if any of the 25 should fail (Norgate, 1902, pp. 235–236).

This chapter considers the various clauses of Magna Carta in light of what has been uncovered by historians about contemporaneous fiscal abuses during John's reign. However, it is first necessary to say something about John's need for money, and the nature of national revenues in the twelfth and thirteenth centuries.

John's Need For Revenues

John's reign was affected by many factors coming together which created a need for additional finance. One of the most commonly cited is the loss of Normandy in 1204[5] and its accompanying revenues at a period when wars with the French were endemic, such wars being fought in France to try to retain control of the Angevin[6] empire states. At the same time, the machinery of government needed more paid officials as it grew and became more complex (see Waugh, 1997, p. 58), a complexity that is evident in the mass of financial records that survive from the reign. John was also affected by what had happened in the reign of his brother and predecessor, Richard I ('The Lionheart'), who had built many castles, which needed maintenance (see Barratt, 1999, p. 86). Richard too had needed additional funds to support his leadership of the Third Crusade and for his ransom when captured by Duke Leopold of Austria on his return home. John inherited a greatly impoverished kingdom. Richard too had had recourse to increasing revenues by various means, but apart from one minor revolt in the 1190s, had not been subject to the degree of baronial dissatisfaction that arose in John's reign. One of the reasons for this may have been the moderating influence of Hubert Walter.

Walter was a significant figure in state finance during this period as he had served under Henry II and Richard I, being Richard's justiciar[7] (1193–1198) and later John's chancellor (1199–1205). He was also Archbishop of Canterbury. As John asked Walter to be his chancellor—a role he filled until his death—it is very probable that he relied on Walter's experience to develop the more successful of his innovative fiscal measures: with his experience under Henry and Richard, Walter was likely to know what would succeed and what would not. Walter's main biographers, Cheney (1967) and Young (1968), attest to his administrative skills and diplomatic talents, and there is no other likely candidate to whom to attribute such ideas. In the earlier years of John's reign there seems evidence of careful guidance, whereas after Walter's death in 1205, John's measures become increasingly extortionary as he lacked Walter's moderating influence. It is arguable that Walter's death was as significant as the loss of Normandy in terms of fiscal importance. Not all agree on John's need for funding, however. Barratt (1996, 2001), who has analysed the revenues received by John and Richard I respectively, suggests that the loss of Normandy did not have such an impact as has been suggested: John did have significant resources available to him after this time as he was mustering resources to attempt to recover lost territory.

In general, too, John's reign coincided with the gradual change-over from a domain-based state to a tax-based state, which occurred in Europe during the twelfth and thirteenth centuries. In a domain-based state, a ruler depends wholly on income derived from Crown lands and property, which are administered personally, to support him and his government. In a tax-based state, such income is supplemented or indeed, superseded, by income raised from taxes on non-Crown owned property (e.g., that of the Church) or activities (e.g., trade), and the state is seen more as an entity independent of its rule, especially in fiscal terms (Ormrod, 1999, p. 38; Swanson, 1999, p. 100). The transition reflects the fact that rulers' personal income became insufficient to finance their activities and ambitions, which were often military, hence they had to resort to state financial resources, the most important of which were raised from taxation. For understanding the context of John's reign, this is an important backdrop.

Twelfth- And Thirteenth-Century Revenues

Most writers (e.g., Mitchell, 1914) categorise revenues in the twelfth and thirteenth centuries as ordinary or extraordinary. Ordinary revenues were those that were levied every year through normal government processes in order to sustain a ruler and his activities. If such revenues were insufficient, then additional finance was sought by means of extraordinary revenue—'extraordinary' because it was not levied ordinarily and new measures or machinery had to be put in place to collect it. Mitchell (1914, p. 1) lists the ordinary revenues as follows:

- the county farm, a fixed sum paid by the sheriff for the privilege of farming the revenue of the royal desmesne and the fines of the local courts;

- amercements ('fines' in the modem sense of the word) imposed by the king's justices for violation of the law;

- the *firma burgi*, a lump sum paid by certain towns for the privilege of farming the town revenues (which worked in a similar manner to the county farm);

- the income from feudal incidents, reliefs, marriages, wardships, escheats,[8] etc.; and

- fines or oblations (offerings), payments to the king for such privileges as permission to marry a certain person, the custody of the lands of minors, the bringing of cases into the king's court, the delaying or expediting of a trial, and the grant and confirmation of charters (some of these overlapped with feudal incidents).

To the above should be added:

- income from the royal forest

Extraordinary income is (per Mitchell, p. 1 and p. 13):

- the aid on the knight's fee, called also scutage or shield money (see later for a detailed definition);

- carucage, levied on a unit of plough land called a carucate;

- tallage, levied on the towns and desmesne lands of the Crown;

- *auxilia* and *dona*, taken from Jewish or other money lenders, prelates, and religious houses; and

- taxes on movables.

To this list should be added:

- Church revenues which John received between the years 1208 and 1214, during the papal Interdict.

Most of the above measures had existed under Henry II and Richard I, or even before (appropriation of Church revenues being an obvious exception). Some of them are not easily categorised as taxes, such as farming the royal desmesne, which might seem more like rent collection. This perhaps raises a question about what are the defining characteristics of a tax, but for the purpose of this chapter, all revenue-raising measures are considered taxes or tax equivalents. The following sections consider the following sources of revenue—the county farm, incidental income (from amercements, feudal incidents, oblations, etc.), the royal forest, scutage, carucage, tallage, *auxilia* and *dona*, taxes on movables and Church revenues—to show the ways in which John attempted to increase income and also their effect on (especially) the barons who agreed to act as suretors. There were five main ways in which John tried to increase revenues: (i) by an 'add-on' to an already existing and accepted revenue source, as in the case of the county farm and scutage; (ii) by creating a new tax, such as carucage; (iii) by raising the rate of a tax, for example, as in the case of scutage; (iv) by levying a tax more frequently, as in the case of both scutage and tallage ((iii) and (iv) being felt to be extortion when carried too far); and (v) by opportunism, as in the case of appropriating the Church revenues. Magna Carta clauses make clear the deep resentment over John's methods when left unchecked.

Ordinary Income

The County Farm

The ordinary revenue from the county farm was a main source of English state revenue at this time (Barratt, 2001, p. 637). County sheriffs, on taking office, would agree to pay to the Crown a lump sum in respect of the royal demesne lands for which they were responsible. The sheriff was then responsible for collecting this sum, and anything collected over and above this was the sheriff's profit (Warren, 1987, p. 151). The system had considerable potential for extortion and abuse, which is reflected in Clause 25 of Magna Carta:[9]

> All counties, hundreds, wapentakes, and trithings[10] (except our demesne manors) shall remain at the old rents, and without any additional payment.

A wealth of back story underlies this clause. Henry I (John's grandfather, who reigned 1100–1135) had originally fixed the amount of the farms, which seemed to have remained stable, despite a civil war between the rival claimants to his throne, Stephen and Matilda. Owing to climate changes in the twelfth century, which favoured the cultivation of cereal crops, the county farm became very profitable for sheriffs, but because the lump sum payments were fixed, the Crown could not tap into these profits. Henry II (John's father, who reigned 1154–1189) had introduced a 'tap in' mechanism in the form of an increment, charged separately to the sheriffs in addition to the farms. He could, of course, have re-assessed the farms themselves but this might have been "too serious a breach of a customary assessment" (Harris, 1964, pp. 532–533).

The notion of an increment was clever, and in accordance with thinking elsewhere (see later, under scutage). The increment was separate from the farm, differently assessed and appeared to some extent to be negotiable. If the sheriff felt that the increment was too high, any dispute about payment could be confined to the increment: the farm lump sum would be unaffected. If the farm itself had been re-assessed and was disputed, it could have led to a refusal to pay the entire farm. However, the threat of a re-assessment as an exercise of royal power would always be present. In 1194, during the reign of Richard I, 'The Lionheart' (John's brother and immediate predecessor), Hubert Walter commissioned itinerant justices to examine the profitability of the royal demesne. In that same year Richard himself imposed extensive increments (Harris, 1964, p. 533), which remained in place when John acceded to the throne. John seems to have charged even higher increments, which resulted in the sheriffs attempting to recoup the increments by extortionary measures (Norgate, 1902, pp. 214–215).

In 1204, John seems to have begun an experiment aimed at increasing revenues from the shrievalties (sheriffdoms). Individuals known as *baillivi* ('custodians') replaced many existing sheriffs, who were dismissed. *Baillivi* (who still seem to have been referred to as sheriffs), were required to account for a variable sum, above the standard farm, known as a *proficuum* ('profit' or 'profits'), which meant that they accounted for income and expenditure on an item-by-item basis. It remains unclear how the *proficuum* was assessed and whether it was the same as an increment or imposed in addition to or instead of it. There are different opinions as to whether this system was a success or not. Warren (1987, p. 153; 1997, pp. 152–153) and Painter (1949, p. 120) consider that it was until 1208, when it foundered, but Harris (1964, p. 538ff), using Pipe Roll figures for 1209–1212, disagrees, finding that a number of counties went over to or returned to the custodial system in this period.

Although the picture of what was happening is not entirely clear, it does seem that there was an attempt to implement a new system, which may have operated alongside the older one, with the ultimate aim of superseding it. In some cases it clearly failed and was unpopular. Sometimes individuals offered sums of money so as not to have to implement it while others did not produce accounts. Harris (1964, p. 538) cites the instance of John Cornard, sheriff of Norfolk and Suffolk from 1205 to 1209 in this regard, and of William de Cahaignes of Sussex (p. 539), who had no profit so could not account for any: decline in profits was not unusual. Under this system, individuals might actually be owed money by the Crown, especially if they were responsible for the upkeep of castles that were in their bailiwick. The system required care in accounting and administration, which might explain the decline in income which occurred by 1214. By 1213, however, it seems that the system had reverted only to the county farm being collected, with both John's and Richard's increments being abandoned, as is reflected in the 1215 Magna Carta clause—although this was omitted from re-issues of the document. As the system was first implemented in 1204, it may be attributable to Hubert Walter as a means to obtain more income from sheriffs' profits, but then waned when he was not there to monitor or control it.

Amercements, Feudal Incidents, Oblations, etc.

Incidental income from amercements, feudal incidents, oblations, etc., would always arise, but owing to the nature of the events that gave rise to them, the amount of income they generated would be unpredictable: no one could predict, for example, when someone might commit an offence, want to get married, die, and so on. The Angevin kings used the justice system as a means of raising revenue (Ormrod, 1999, p. 23), and the extent to which it was abused is clear from a number of clauses in Magna Carta. Clauses 17, 18, 19, 24, 32, 34, 45, and 55 refer to the need for due process of law in various aspects—place, type of action, volume of business, use of appropriate officials, length and duration of punishment, etc. Clauses 20, 21, and 22 require that amercements for offences be proportionate to the offence, whether the offender be a free man, earl, baron, or clergyman. Warren (1987, p. 159) comments that amercements were so numerous that at one point the Exchequer had to stop recording them, so they were clearly a burden, especially if imposed disproportionately.

While amercements could be imposed, and were imposed, by the courts, subjects, especially the earls and barons, would often be able to purchase their way out of offences by buying the king's goodwill (*benevolentia*). If one of the king's tenants committed a misdemeanour by, for example, putting a fish-weir in a river without royal permission, although he might be amerced for the offence through the court system, John would often prefer the offender to buy his goodwill at an exorbitant rate. This meant that tenants would become indebted to the Crown, and John used this as a means of controlling them. Warren (1997, p. 182) gives the example of Roger de Cressi, who married an heiress without obtaining the necessary royal permission (see below). John seized the lands of both, and it cost Roger 1,200 marks[11] and 12 palfreys[12] to regain the king's goodwill and his lands.

As it was considered an honour to have the king act as judge in a case, subjects might also offer money to obtain this privilege, with some proffering "as much as £100" (Warren, 1997, p. 101), although the king would often accept much less, such as half a mark, to judge an ordinary case. Looking at this through a modern lens, it is difficult to interpret it as other than a kind of bribery in a corrupt system (see also Norgate, 1902, p. 215). John adjudicated in the dispute between William de Mowbray and William de Stuteville in the latter's claim to a barony. He accepted 2,000 marks from de Mowbray, but the court gave judgment in favour of de Stuteville. This might have been a fair outcome, with the money guaranteeing no more than John's presence as a judge, but given John's predilection for breaking his word, it may be unlikely. John did spend more time in England than his predecessors, however, and took great interest in the legal system, apparently detecting even minor transgressions. Warren

(1997, p. 182, citing Pipe Roll 12 John) notes that in 1210 Robert de Vaux was obliged to give five palfreys to the king "to keep quiet about the wife of Henry Pinel" and 750 marks for goodwill. It remains unclear, however, what this all meant.

Magna Carta also contains a considerable number of clauses relating to succession dues payable by heirs to gain their property on the death of a parent, the rights of heirs, the guardianship/wardship of underage heirs and their lands, a guardian's duties, marriage of heirs, rights (especially financial rights to dowries) of widows on the death of a husband, remarriage of widows, intestacy, the handling of lands falling vacant because of the lack of an heir or a felony (an escheat) (Clauses 2, 3, 4, 5, 6, 7, 8, 27, 37, 43). The fact that these issues dominate the early clauses of the document indicates their importance and the level of abuse that was rife. 'Feudal incident' is often used to refer to matters concerning inheritance or the devolution of property, but there is no hard and fast rule about the use of terminology, as income from fines and oblations was often linked to the same kind of events. The succession due (known as a relief) payable by an heir in order to inherit property was not fixed, and while £100 was reasonable under Henry I, John often asked for much more, with 600 marks frequently being required. In 1211 William Lacy paid 7,000 marks (being out of favour at the time) with William de Stuteville and William FitzAlan each paying 10,000 marks. As Warren (1997, p. 183) comments, "[t]he king had the whip hand". A widow would become a ward of the king, and have to pay between 100 and 300 marks for the right to her dowry, even if she was an heiress in her own right. Hugh Bardolf's widow was charged 2,000 marks (ibid.). McKechnie (1914, p. 212) comments that "John made a regular traffic in the sale of wards".

> Brief entries in John's Exchequer Rolls condense many a tragedy. In his first year, the widow of Ralph of Cornhill offered 200 marks, with three palfreys and two hawks, that she might not be espoused by Godfrey of Louvain, but remain free to marry whom she chose, and yet keep her lands. This was a case of desperate urgency, since Godfrey, for the love of the lady or of her lands, had offered 400 marks, if she could show no reason to the contrary. It is satisfactory to learn that the lady escaped.
>
> McKechnie, 1914, p. 213

John also asked 20,000 marks of Geoffrey de Mandeville as the price for Geoffrey to marry John's former wife, Isabelle of Gloucester[13] (see Warren, 1997, pp. 182–183).

Such exorbitant demands extended to paying for an heiress in marriage for a son, for wardship of minors' estates, for official posts, such as forest warden or castle constable, etc. Often sums asked would be more than individuals could pay at any one time, with the consequence that they became the king's debtors, frequently for many years. John encouraged this, as it meant he had financial power over his tenants, the more so as debtors had to pledge their estates formally to the Exchequer. If a debtor defaulted, then estates were forfeit—which happened to the earl of Leicester from 1207 to 1215. John also used debt as a tool to show favour or harass his enemies. He pardoned William Fortibus for the relief owed for the inheritance of his mother, Hawise, countess of Aumale, who had been John's mistress. Clauses 9, 26, and 27 of Magna Carta detail procedures appropriate for dealing with debtors who default, with the clear implication that debts had been subject to 'over-recovery', if not outright thievery,[14] which had manifestly occurred in other contexts. Clauses 28, 30, and 31 refer to goods being taken by royal officials without the consent of the owners while Clause 52 promises explicitly the return of "lands, castles, franchises [and] his right" to those dispossessed without proper legal judgment, with Clauses 56 and 57 making similar promises in respect of Welshmen and Clause 55 promising the return of amercements unjustly levied. Clause 50 promises to eliminate from office John's foreign retainers who had used their offices for such 'strong-arm' tactics, explicitly naming the relations of Gerard d'Athée, *viz.*, Engelard de Cigogné, Peter, Guy and Andrew de Chanceaux, Guy de Cigogné, Geoffrey de Martigny and his brothers, Philip Marc and his brothers and nephew Geoffrey, and "the whole brood of the same". While Magna Carta does not say exactly what these individuals had done, the evidence of various misdeeds can be found in other contemporary documents (see McKechnie, 1914, p. 445). Clause 51 also promises to remove from England the body of foreign mercenaries whom John also employed and who were very much resented.

As a consequence of getting into debt with the king, individuals often had recourse to Jewish money lenders, but this did not often help in the longer run. There was interest to pay, and if a money lender died, the Crown automatically became heir, so the debt could end up again in the king's hands. Clauses 10 and 11 of Magna Carta set out procedure to deal with debt on death. If a man dies indebted to Jewish money lenders, his heir will not pay interest while he is under age, nor will the Crown take anything but the principal sum if the debt falls into the Crown's hands. Likewise the widow of the deceased will have her dowry returned and not be responsible for the principal, which will only be repaid out of the estate residue after the needs of under-age heirs have been met.

Another means of controlling the barons was to demand family members as hostages as security for good conduct (see also later). In one noted case, this had appalling repercussions. The medieval chronicler Roger of Wendover suggests that John became hostile to William de Briouze and his family as a result of remarks made by William's wife, when royal messengers came to demand hostages of her husband in 1208, allegedly because William defaulted on money he had promised to pay for his lordship of Limerick. William's wife refused, and in doing so, commented on the fate of John's nephew, Arthur, the son of his brother Geoffrey, who had disappeared without trace, with John possibly having had him murdered.[15] Although William had flourished in the earlier years of John's reign, he died in 1211, exiled from his estates and from England as a consequence of John's ill will, possibly a result of him thinking de Briouze had become too powerful or because he was suspicious of him in some way. His wife and son were deliberately starved to death in one of John's prisons, despite an offer of 40,000 marks in ransom. Warren (1997, p. 185) notes that every chronicle of the period refers in some way to this story, which is indicative of its contemporary significance. Magna Carta refers outright to the return of hostages taken from barons' families in Clause 49—and this may have had further implications (see later). It also refers to hostages taken in terms of international politics (very common at the time). Clause 58 says that the son of Llywelyn and all Welsh hostages will be returned, and with regard to the return of the sisters and hostages of Alexander, king of Scotland, he will be treated in the same way as the English barons (Clause 59).

The Royal Forest

The royal forest comprised areas of land kept chiefly for the king to hunt and to provide him with other benefits, such as produce for the royal household and the king's table. Areas designated as royal forest (whether wooded or not) were subject to a separate forest law, which was extremely stringent and dealt with matters such as cutting timber and gathering firewood, making clearings (assarts), allowing pigs to forage for acorns (agisting), taking dogs into the forest, pasturing cattle, etc., which were variously permitted for a fee. Forest law rested on the arbitrary will of the king, not on common law, so some disapproved of it.[16] Forestry matters were dealt with by an itinerant court, a forest eyre, which dealt out punishments—frequently amercements—for breaches of forest law. There was a great deal of money made from the forest, either from fees for allowing certain activities or from amercements levied from breaches of the law: forest eyres brought in about £2,000 on average, though one in 1212 created debts of about £5,000 (see Warren, 1997, pp. 162–163). Following the civil war between Stephen and Matilda, there had been considerable uncertainty as to what comprised forest, although Henry II clarified the rules in a forest assize in about 1166. Three clauses in Magna Carta (44, 47, and 48) refer to the forest law, chief among which is a promise to disafforest the lands that had additionally been deemed forest in John's reign, as the area of forest had increased over time.

There are many stories about the harshness with which forest law was enforced. The office of forester was a rich one: Warren (1997, p. 163) reports that John's chief forester loaned the king 3,350 marks against future forest income.

Extraordinary Income

Scutage

Scutage was originally a feudal service due (*servitia debita*, literally 'services owed', also referred to as an aid on the knight's fee) to the king in return for the grant of land made to a tenant-in-chief (baron). In return for the right to occupy land and receive income and produce from it, tenants-in-chief had an obligation to create and provide a specified number of knights to go and fight for the king when he asked for them. The tenant-in-chief provided each knight with an amount of land from his own holding to maintain him (known as a fee, hence a knight was said to be 'enfeoffed'). However, it was common for scutage to be commuted to a sum of money by the time of Henry II, Richard I, and John, hence scutage was also known as 'shield money'. The growing cash economy of the twelfth century facilitated this, also the levying of scutage at different rates (e.g., two, three marks, etc., per fee). The idea was that this would provide the king with funds to hire mercenaries for his army.

By the reign of Henry II, it had become unclear how many knights had been en-feoffed. Henry carried out an inquest in 1166, whereby it became clear that there were fees in existence in excess of the *servitia debita*, as some tenants had enfeoffed more knights than specified, while others had enfeoffed fewer. Excess fees, however, would become a possible means of raising extra revenue, which may be reflected under John, with the prevalence of the fine. A fine is not a financial penalty in the modern sense (this is an amercement in medieval terms), but derives from the Latin word *finis*, which means basically 'end' and is used in the context of reaching a financial agreement. Hence, as well as paying scutage, tenants often paid a sum of money in fine,[17] though it is unclear whether such a payment was regarded as part of the scutage or a separate amount. What the fine actually represented is, in any given case, unclear, as it seems to have been calculated both as a single sum and a fixed amount per fee. Mitchell (1914, p. 27) suggests that the fine was calculated in two ways: a lump sum by virtue of which the tenant himself was exempt from service but was given the right to collect scutage from his sub-tenants; and a fine for his personal service, as he could be liable for this even though he paid scutage in respect of his knights. Mitchell (1914, p. 5) further suggests that these "sums were called fines *ne transfretent* or *pro passagio*". The term "*ne transfretent*" means literally "in order that they should not cross the sea". More precisely, the word '*fretum*' inherent in the verb *transfretare* means at root 'strait', so may refer to the Channel, rather than seas in general. Perhaps the fine was paid to avoid overseas service for tenant or knights, especially in France, although they might still be called upon to serve in England. Serving overseas was unwelcome: the northern barons in 1214 refused to undertake an expedition to Poitou on the grounds that service overseas was not due. "*Pro passagio*" literally means 'for the passage' or 'for the passing', which could refer to the same idea, but is more likely to refer to the tenant-in-chief being granted permission by the king to recoup his scutage and fine from his own sub-tenants and lesser vassals. As there were more fees in existence than the *servitia debita*, John always had in the background a threat of re-assessment and reform of the *servitia debita* to reflect the true situation in his reign, so this would ever hang over the tenants-in-chiefs' heads. However, it does appear that under John, scutage was being split into two different taxes, similar to the *proficuum* from county farms considered earlier. The concept of an additional levy over and above a base amount is so like the *proficuum* that it is hard to resist the conclusion that the same mind lies behind them, namely that of Hubert Walter.

It was likely to be less expensive to pay both scutage and fine than to provide the full military service that the king could demand. Although wars provided the opportunity for enrichment from booty, a knight going overseas on military service would require substantial support in terms of horses and arms, which he or his overlord would need to provide—and a campaign would be of unknown duration at the outset. The commutation of scutage to money, even with a fine to pay in addition, would mean that the financial outlay had specified limits (Harvey, 1970).

It would also appear that fines were not necessarily levied at the same rate for individuals, giving rise to the suggestion that this element was negotiable and could be varied to suit the payee's situation. Henry II, after the 1166 inquest, had attempted to extend scutage and collect it on all knights enfeoffed, but the tenants-in-chief had resisted and he only succeeded in obtaining a slight increase (Warren, 1987, p. 156, citing Keefe, 1983, p. 52). John—and Walter—may have succeeded overall where Henry had failed, as they refrained from tampering with what might be termed the 'base line'.

John did attempt to collect scutage more frequently and at higher rates than either his brother or father, as Tables 1 and 2 show.

Mitchell (1914, p. 9) remarks that John went against custom in levying scutage at the outset rather than the end of campaigns and that often "the character of the operations which followed would hardly justify their levy". He concluded a truce in 1199 straight after his arrival in France; in 1201 no fighting appears to

Table 1: Rates and Frequency of Scutage under John

Year	Rate	Reason (excuse?)
1199	2 marks	Campaign against Philip Augustus
1201	2 marks	War against the Lusignans
1202	2 marks	War against Philip Augustus
1203	2 marks	War against Philip Augustus
1204	20 shillings	War against Philip Augustus
1205	20 shillings	Invasion of Poitou and Gascony
1206	20 shillings	Invasion of France
1209	20 shillings	War against Scotland
1210	2 marks or 26 shillings and 8 pence	Expedition to Ireland
1211	3 marks or 40 shillings	Two expeditions against the Welsh
1214	3 marks or 40 shillings	Invasion of Poitou

Adapted from Frecknall-Hughes, 2012, p. 253

Table 2: Comparison of Scutage Levies–Henry II, Richard I, and John

King	Years Scutage Levied	Rates
Henry II (35-year reign)	1159	10 shillings
	1161	2 marks
	1162, 1165, 1186	1 mark
	1172, 1187	20 shillings
Richard I (10-year reign)	1189/90, 1195, 1198	20 shillings
John (16-year reign)	11 collections (per Table 1)	20 shillings–3 marks (or 40 shillings)

Adapted from Frecknall-Hughes, 2012, p. 254

have taken place (Norgate, 1902, p. 81)—and scutage was paid in part on John's departure and in part later, with some barons paying but being allowed to return home once they had reached Portsmouth (Mitchell, 1914, p. 35); and in 1209 John concluded a truce again without any fighting having taken place, having marched as far as Norham, apparently against the Scots. Scutage was apparently levied without the usual summons in 1202 and 1203, and in 1204 and 1205, an army was summoned but not despatched. Scutage seems to have been levied in

1205 after the army was dismissed. The barons were opposed to the expedition to Poitou and Gascony in 1205, and the northern barons in 1214 opposed fighting in Poitou, on the grounds that overseas service was not owed. Scutage was levied, but against much opposition.

The discontent arising as a result of John's apparent misuse of scutage appears reflected in Clause 12 of the *Magna Carta*, which says that no scutage shall be levied without the "common counsel of the kingdom". Clause 15 of the Charter also restricts the practice of taking aids by the barons. Clause 14 sets out the mechanics of how the "common counsel" was to be obtained—by a specified process of sending a summons to meet at a named place, with due notice (at least 40 days), to archbishops, abbots, earls, and greater barons. It is tempting to find in this "common counsel" "the modern doctrine that the Crown can impose no financial burden on the people without consent of Parliament" (McKechnie, 1914, p. 232), but this would be pressing the meaning of the clause too far. Only the king's tenants were to be notified, and for one identified purpose. Nonetheless, Clauses 12 and 14 do indicate clearly an instance of taxes requiring due process for their imposition and some degree of consent by those on whom they were being imposed.

Clause 16 of the Charter says that no one should perform more service in respect of a fee than is due from it. Mitchell (1914, pp. 23–24) cites some apparent instances of double exaction where both money and military service were rendered. For example, the abbot of Ramsey paid eight marks on his four fees, although his knights served with the king,[18] as also did the bishop of Winchester;[19] and the earl of Devon paid 30 marks in scutage while his knights were in the king's service.[20] Those who performed military service usually received a 'writ of quittance' (a document acknowledging that they should not pay money too), but these might be delayed where a tenant held lands in more than one county.[21]

Carucage

John levied carucage only, in 1200. As this was so long before the date of Magna Carta, it is thus not surprising that the Charter does not mention it. Given what we have seen thus far, had it still been in operation in 1215, it is likely that it would have merited a mention, as it was very unpopular. Carucage seems to have been based on an earlier tax implemented in 1198 by Hubert Walter to raise funds for war with France (Jurkowski et al., 1998, pp. xvii–xix). The tax was based on a unit of land called a carucate, which was 100 acres of plough land. Walter may have used a similar measure to raise tax for Richard's ransom in 1194 (Mitchell, 1914, p. 7). A carucate was the same as a hidage, which was the measure of land upon which a very old tax, namely Danegeld, was based, so carucage may have been an attempt to bring Danegeld up to date. Although this latter tax was originally levied to provide resources to fight the Danes (hence its name, though this was only conferred in the twelfth century), Henry I levied it frequently, but Henry II only twice. Its fall into desuetude seems to have been because geldable lands could not provide sufficient resources to fund continental wars and also because records of which were geldable lands had been lost in large part because of the civil war between Stephen and Matilda.

In 1200, John levied the tax to raise 20,000 marks, which he had promised to Philip Augustus as a relief for his lands in France. It met with considerable opposition, especially from the Cistercian monks, and was described by Abbot Ralph of Coggeshall as a "very heavy exaction which greatly impoverished the peoples of the land" (Carpenter, 1998, p. 1220). The tax aimed to assess all property regardless of how it was held or who held it, including the Church (Mitchell, 1951, p. 108). Although no records remain of how the tax was collected or administered, or how much money was raised, there was a complex procedure for assessing liability.

> A commission was appointed for each shire consisting of two nominees by the crown and two by the shire court. Each hundred was to nominate two knights before whom a delegation of the reeve and four men from each vill[22] testified. Landlords or their stewards could challenge or confirm the testimony of the villagers. When the knights of the hundred were satisfied they reported to the county commissioners, who, when they were satisfied had the details enrolled with copies for the sheriff, the hundred and estate stewards. . . . [E]state holders were responsible for the payments due from their lands in each vill; the money was to be tendered to the headman of the hundred and the two knights who had conducted the assessment; they paid it over to the sheriff who accounted for it at a special exchequer of receipt.
>
> Warren, 1987, p. 147

This complicated administrative machinery could easily have impeded actual collection. The tax was unpopular and unsuccessful—unusual for a measure attributable directly to Walter, and because it used long-established land-based elements associated with Danegeld with which people would have been familiar. Its use of plough land as a basis of assessment would have meant that most people would have been affected by it, as England was chiefly an agricultural society at the time. It attempted to be exact and wide-reaching and was, perhaps, ahead of its time. Mitchell (1951, p. 154) suggests that it may have been an attempt to establish an effective land tax, and did not succeed because the levies on personal property or movables (see later) were more lucrative and more easily administered as amounts due were less cumbersome to calculate.

Tallage

Tallage was an arbitrary, though customary, tax levied on the towns and desmesne land of the Crown. It was a way of increasing funds from the towns and lands directly under Crown control, and applied to unfree tenants. It was very similar to the 'aid' or *auxilium* (see below), which was levied from vassals and free tenants. Like an aid, tallage was only levied "when the king had urgent need of additional money, and although it could be imposed at the king's will, it could not be refused, the amount to be paid was not determined arbitrarily but was open to negotiation" (Warren, 1987, p. 154). Itinerant justices required each urban or manorial community to make the king a collective offer, which, if deemed acceptable, the community was allowed to portion out and collect. If amount was not acceptable or the money was not forthcoming in due course, the justices would implement *per capita* (i.e., individual) assessments, which sheriffs would collect, distraining debtors where necessary. John levied tallage more frequently than his predecessors—some nine times during his reign (1199–1200, 1201, 1203, 1204, 1205, 1206, 1210, 1211, and 1214) with scutage often being levied in the same years, preferring to use *per capita* assessments rather than collective offers. While the 1199–1200 tallage appears to have been a general levy (Mitchell, 1914, p. 31), not all areas or groups of subjects were necessarily assessed in any one levy. The 1201 tallage was collected in the bishopric of Lincoln and Yorkshire, with some sort of aid being collected only in the Channel Islands (Mitchell, 1914, p. 45). In 1203, it was collected in thirteen counties with an account of collections.

It is noticeable that in the period before 1204–05, tallage was levied three times, whereas it was levied six times subsequently. This is consistent with the suggestion that the years 1204–1205 marked a turning point in John's fiscal exactions, with the loss of Normandy and the death of Hubert Walter. The year 1204 saw a collection in fourteen counties, 1205 twenty-six counties, and 1206 thirty-two counties (Mitchell, 1914, pp. 61, 68, 76, 82), with a collection in 1210 from cities, towns, the king's manors, and lands in hand (Mitchell, 1914, p. 100). In 1210 also the Jews were tallaged for 66,000 marks, with one of the medieval chroniclers reporting (see Norgate, 1902, p. 137) that at the beginning of the year, the king ordered all Jews in England, men and women alike, to be arrested and tortured to compel them to give up their wealth.

It was reported that the king wrung ten thousand marks from one Jew at Bristol by causing seven of his teeth to be torn out, one every day for a week.

Norgate, 1902, p. 137

A final tallage was taken in 1214 (levied against manors and towns), to raise money to help pay the indemnity for the withdrawal of the papal Interdict (see later), originally set at 100,000 marks (Mitchell, 1914, p. 117). It was imposed by both a collective offer and a *per capita* assessment, and seems to have been successful. Tallage was not, however, used again as a tax until 1220, under John's son, Henry III.

Magna Carta makes no reference to tallage, which, given the thesis of this chapter, might seem rather surprising until one considers that the king was largely wringing money from his own possessions, which he was entitled to do—and from groups such as the Jews, whose status in England was very uncertain, given the persecution that had occurred during Richard's reign and the ongoing measures by Pope Innocent III in the 1200s. The barons would not be affected by tallage—though the accounts of how it was levied do add to the overall picture given by John's other exactions.

Auxilia And Dona

An 'aid' or *auxilium* was a tax given voluntarily, at least in theory, to help (hence 'aid') royal finances, and there were three occasions when it was usual for a 'gracious' (meaning 'reasonable') aid to be collected. These were for the ransom of the king, making his eldest son a knight and once marrying his eldest daughter (Ormrod, 1999, p. 27). Magna Carta, Clause 12, refers specifically to these reasons as permitting an aid to be taken, but also applied in that clause the same restrictions to *auxilia* as it did to scutage, so there is a clear implication that there were 'extraordinary' aids, raised when the king was in urgent need of funds. An aid was different from tallage (see above), which was a forced payment, but as McKechnie (1914, p. 234) comments: "[t]here were times when 'voluntary' aids . . . could not safely be withheld". Clauses 12 and 13, offering protection to the city of London and other cities, boroughs, towns, and ports and their "liberties and free customs" support this interpretation.

Dona, on the other hand, were gifts, often raised from religious houses or churchmen, although the use of terminology is inexact. The word 'aid', unhelpfully for the modern reader, was often used to refer to a tax in general (for example, scutage was commonly referred to as an 'aid on the knight's fee'), and a gift might be anything but a present to the king—though calling it such might have been useful in disguising the nature of the exaction. Some religious houses paid a contribution in 1199 which was variously referred to as a *donum, promissum,* or *tallagium,* while a levy in Dorset in 1203 was called *auxilia* (Mitchell, 1914, pp. 32, 61). It was not always clear what a payment meant, as sometimes it gave exemption from military service, but at others was in no way connected to this, as in the instance of the charge against 26 religious houses in 1204 (Mitchell, 1914, p. 105). The nature of the payment might depend on whether tenure of a religious house carried with it the obligation to provide military service or not (see Mitchell, 1914, p. 70 and p. 77, footnote 325). Mitchell (1914, p. 105) refers to "enormous sums" being taken from religious houses after the 1210 Irish campaign, though these comments derive from the medieval chroniclers rather than the Pipe Rolls. The fact of there being an Interdict meant that during these years John had no check on any activities against religious houses—and no chancellor or Archbishop sympathetic to the Church.

Taxes On Movables

John levied taxes on movable property in four years of his reign at a rate of one-fortieth in 1201 of the revenues of one year, one-seventh and one-fifth in 1203, one-fifteenth in 1204, and one-thirteenth in 1207. Taxes on movable property to raise state finance had not been used before the twelfth century and even then had not been implemented extensively, although the concept was familiar from the idea of the ecclesiastical tithe. The tax was applied to movable goods, which included gold, silver plate and ornaments, and animals but not to precious stones or clothes (Jurkowski et al., 1998. p. xiii). Two of the Church's taxes saw the concept applied at a national level, with a tax of approximately one-fortieth of annual income and of chattels being levied in 1166 for the relief of the Holy Land (Warren, 1987, p. 148) and again in 1188, for the Saladin Tithe, in response to the Pope's appeal to rescue Jerusalem from the Muslims. The king (Henry II) demanded from all laymen and clergy who had not taken the Cross (i.e., become Crusaders) one-tenth of their annual income and movable property (except arms, horses, dress, and precious stones). The assessment was at parish level and each man "swore to the value of his revenues and personal property" before a commission (Mitchell, 1914, p. 6). A similar tax was levied in 1193–1194 at the rate of one-quarter of revenues and movables to raise the ransom demanded by Duke Leopold for Richard. It seems likely that "lump sum payments were accepted in lieu of careful assessment" (Warren, 1987, p. 148) in order to raise money quickly. Obviously, these taxes are likely to have been dealt with by Hubert Walter. While such taxes were exceptional and appealed to a deep moral obligation, they were also undoubtedly innovative and levied at a national level, and John undoubtedly benefited from Walter's experiences, particularly in dealing with the ransom to free Richard.

The 1201 levy under John was raised (again) in response to a papal request for aid for the Holy Land. Churchmen paid by order of the Pope in respect of their spiritual and temporal holdings, with the money being collected by the bishop of each diocese. John also contributed one-fortieth of his desmesne revenues, escheats, wardships, and lands in hand and asked earls, barons, knights, and freemen to contribute to the same degree. Each man calculated his own liability without formal assessment, though the tax collectors drew up a roll containing contributors' names and the amount due, arranged by vills. The amount due from the royal desmesne was recorded on a separate roll, and anyone who refused to pay was reported by name to the king (Mitchell, 1914, p. 45). Although it is improbable that substantial sums were raised, the detailed accounting and collection machinery were new and provided a precedent for later similar levies in John's reign, for example, 'the fifteenth' as it became known, levied in 1204 on the property of merchants. The fifteenth was novel in being a type of customs duty levied at the ports. Six or more men from each port, one knight, and one clerk (called '*baillivi* of the fifteenth') were selected to collect and administer the tax, which involved drawing up a roll with the merchants' names and amounts due. They reported to three men appointed by the king (see Mitchell, 1914, p. 69). Although this tax is usually dated 1204, Warren (1997, p. 122) comments that there is evidence of it at least two years previously. Barratt (1996, p. 841), in his review of the amounts of revenue collected in John's reign, feels that this tax is insignificant and disregards it, as the evidence is sparse. However, Ormrod (1999, p. 32) considers it as the forerunner of the later customs duties which became part of the Crown's ordinary revenue. The tax was levied for about five years until there was a truce with Philip Augustus of France and free trade was again permitted. The fifteenth seems to have been implemented to control continental trade, especially with France, and to ensure that maritime power was in John's hands.[23] The restrictions on trade were very unpopular with merchants, such that a specific clause (Clause 41) was included in Magna Carta, affirming their freedom to come and go at will.[24]

A levy of one-seventh of the personal property of earls, barons, and clergy was made in 1203 (Mitchell, 1914, p. 54), although the underlying rationale for it remains unclear. The chroniclers report that it was levied because the barons had deserted John on his return to England in December 1203, but the tax was levied in the summer, so this rationale may not be valid. In the same year, there was a levy of a fifth part of one year's revenues taken in the Channel Islands in respect of the lands of bishops, abbots, clerks, knights, rear-vassals, and others in support of the knights and sergeants entrusted with the defence of the islands (Mitchell, 1914, pp. 62–63). Cheney (1967, p. 79) notes that the chronicler, Roger of Wendover, attributed an important role to Hubert Walter in exacting the tax from the clergy.

The largest levy on revenue and movables was the thirteenth (more exactly, actually 12 pence in the mark) taken in 1207, which seems to have been requested in the form of a 'gracious aid'. However, the reason for John requesting these funds remains unclear, as he appeared to have no immediate need of them. A possible reason was a future need to recover lands lost in France to Philip Augustus in France, which could have been a genuine reason or not. Although a council of barons was persuaded by John to agree to the levy, prelates in a first council had refused, although both laity and clergy (mostly) did later pay, with many clergy paying a lump sum in fine. The tax was collected in ways not unlike the 1188 levy, using the vill and a form of self-assessment, although teams of special justices were despatched to each county, some of which were numerous (fourteen reported for Lincolnshire). The levy seems to have garnered about £60,000 (Mitchell, 1914, pp. 84–92; Warren, 1987, pp. 148–149), and although a separate Exchequer of the Thirteenth was set up to collect the tax, no real details have survived.[25] There was a stringent penalty for refusal to comply: forfeiture of chattels and indefinite imprisonment. The Archbishop of York was forced into exile and his lands were seized as a consequence of his opposition to the tax (Mitchell, 1951, p. 8).

This tax of 1207 exhibited some important characteristics, in that it had a national flavour, moving away from feudal taxation; was (possibly) levied against an unspecified future need; was levied on property, not land; was paid by most classes of society, excepting some clergy; was collected nationally by special royal justices, using the vill and a form of self-assessment; and was legitimised in that one or more councils agreed to it. It also aimed at full, immediate collection, unlike other taxes: the county farm was payable in instalments, and scutage and tallage were paid over time, though technically due all at once.

> The county commissioners were to deliver the rolls of assessment to the sheriff every two weeks and the collection was to be made with all possible haste.
>
> Jurkowski et al., 1998, p. 105

Harriss (1975, p. 18) remarks on the writ levying the 1207 tax as using language "more national than feudal in tone", while Maddicott (1997, p. 24) explicitly sees it as "heavy national taxation" and as a measure, which combined with John's more frequent scutage levies to "extend . . . the social and fiscal range of royal government" and which was at the root of Clause 14 of the original Magna Carta. The amount raised was significant and was approved by councils, and the levy was referred to as an aid, the kind, perhaps, that the barons did not want to see raised without the "common consent" set out explicitly in Clause 14. John's deteriorating relationship with the barons in later years meant that he was unable to raise such a tax again. Arguably, the appropriation of Church revenues from 1208 (see below) filled any void.

Church Revenues

When Hubert Walter died in 1205, the see of Canterbury fell vacant. Pope Innocent III appointed Stephen Langton to the vacant see, but John refused to accept him, wishing to have appointed to the post his own candidate, John de Gray, his secretary and the Bishop of Norwich, who was well known in England (Langton was not). It would have been usual for the king's wishes to be respected, as de Gray was certainly an eligible candidate. Innocent III, however, favoured Langton, as he could be trusted to carry out a programme of religious reform which the Pope planned. As a consequence of John's refusal to accept Langton, England was put under a papal Interdict which lasted from 1208 to 1214. In an age when Catholicism was the predominant faith in Europe and the Pope's power immense, it is impossible to overestimate the importance of the Interdict. It meant that England was virtually excommunicated, and while baptism and confession of the dying were allowed, no other religious rites were permitted. Despite this, John quickly took advantage of the financial possibilities presented and almost immediately after the Interdict was imposed, he sent in officers to seize Church property (Harper-Bill, 1999, p. 306), making it known that the property could be regained for a price. Even so John retained some portion of the Church revenues (Warren, 1997, pp. 167–168). English kings often looked enviously on the Church's wealth, although Harper-Bill (1999, p. 303) remarks that "John was probably no more assertive or rapacious in his relationship with the Church before 1205, and even before 1208, than his royal predecessors". However, the fact of Hubert Walter occupying the role Archbishop of Canterbury as well as chancellor in the period before his death in 1205 is likely to have deflected John's attention away from the Church's wealth.

Most sources agree that as a result of the Interdict, John just became richer, though it is not possible to estimate how much the Church revenues brought him (Warren, 1997, p. 168)—and he did not cease levying other taxes. Profits from bishoprics taken in hand amounted to £9,275 in the year 1212 alone (Bartlett,

2000, p. 405). Church lands falling vacant because of the death of an abbot would come into John's hands—the lot of some 17 monasteries by 1213 (Warren, 1997, p. 173). Clause 46 of Magna Carta reflects some of the unease felt about this, stating that an abbey founded by barons under charter or of which they have had long tenure "shall have custody in a vacancy, as [it] ought to have".

Another scheme thought up to obtain further money from the clergy was the ransom of their womenfolk. Although priests were supposedly celibate, many had married or kept housekeepers who were more likely mistresses. Henry I had fined the clergy for disobeying Church rules, but at the same time sold them licences to carry on. John ordered all such womenfolk to be seized and held for ransom. Many of the clergy hastened to obtain their release (Warren, 1997, p. 168).

Although the Interdict was profitable for John, it could not be sustained forever. While the barons might have no objections—money was filling the king's coffers "without drawing a single penny from their own" (Norgate, 1902, p, 128)—many clergy also occupied government offices, and their dual role as Crown and Church officials was uncomfortable. Also, obedience to the Church was usual. In 1214, John conceded and accepted Stephen Langton, but it cost him 100,000 marks, 40,000 before the Interdict was lifted and 12,000 marks *per annum* thereafter. Some 13,000 of the 40,000 marks were pardoned (Warren, 1997, p. 210), but even then, John levied tallage to pay the rest. The freedom of the Church to elect its own officials is given a key place in Clause 1 of Magna Carta, and Stephen Langton is named in the Preamble (along with other clerics and noblemen) and in Clause 62 as one of those advising the king to grant the Charter. The final clause of the document (63) ends with a promise that the English Church shall be free.

The 25 Barons

Identifying The Barons

Clause 61 of Magna Carta refers to 25 barons acting as suretors to ensure that the king did not go back on his agreement to abide by the Charter.

> Namely, that the barons choose twenty five barons of the kingdom, whomsoever they will, who shall be bound with all their might, to observe and hold, and cause to be observed, the peace and liberties we have granted and confirmed to them by this our present Charter , so that if we, or our justiciar, or our bailiffs or any one of our offices, shall in anything be at fault toward anyone, or shall have broken any one of the articles of peace or of this security, and the offence shall be notified to four barons of the

aforesaid twenty five, the said four barons shall repair to us or our justiciar, if we are out of the realm, and laying the transgression before us, petition to have that transgression addressed without delay.[26]

The clause goes on to confer on the barons the power to redress a transgression, should the king not do so; enjoins anyone in the country to obey the barons in such a case; permits replacement of any one of the twenty-five who might die, be absent, or be incapacitated (the remainder of the twenty-five being allowed to replace him as they deem appropriate (McKechnie (1914, p. 469) refers to this as "co-optation"); and allows the barons to take a majority decision if all cannot be present. Per Norgate (1902, pp. 235–236), a further 38 barons stood ready to stand in for any of the twenty-five who might fail. Two other clauses (52 and 55) refer to the 25 having the power to give judgment in cases of dispute over restoration of "lands, castles, franchises [and] his right" to any dispossessed illegally (52) and remission of fines (55), the latter together with Stephen Langton, if he could be present. However, Clause 55 also acknowledges that some of the twenty-five themselves might be bringing suits to recover fines, so makes provision for them to be replaced by another for such an occasion. This provides some degree of evidence that the twenty-five might themselves have had financial grievances against the king. That they did so the following discussion makes clear.

It is difficult at this remove in time to appreciate the financial burden imposed on the barons by the enormous amounts of money they had to pay, but the magnitude of the sums mentioned cannot be under-emphasised: indeed, many of the sums mentioned previously still seem very large in this day and age. To provide a better context, it seems that a knight's wage when on active service (with some variation) was about eight pence, so the sums we have seen mentioned must have ranked as fortunes at the time (see Hollister, 1960). The barons, while wealthy, would hold their wealth predominantly in the form of lands and manors. If such assets did not generate sufficient income to pay the taxes demanded, then the assets themselves could be seized in lieu of payment. This meant that the king gained his taxes and at the same time deprived individuals of the wealth that conferred power, status, and prestige. As a means of control, it could go too far and have exactly the opposite effect from that desired.

Magna Carta itself does not name the twenty-five barons who were finally chosen, and there is no real information about how they were chosen. The information as to their identity comes from five sources, one discovered as late as 1968. Two lists are provided by the medieval chronicler Matthew Paris, a monk of St. Albans (writing about 1250) in his *Chronica Majora* and *Liber Additamentorum*, and a third

Table 3: List of Barons Chosen as Suretors to King John

1. Richard de Clare, Earl of Hertford

2. William de Fortibus/Forz, Earl of Aumâle/Albemarle

3. Geoffrey de Mandeville/Magnavil, Earl of Gloucester

4. Saer/Saire/Sayer de Quincey/Quinci, Earl of Winchester

5. Henry de Bohun, Earl of Hereford

6. Roger Bigod, Earl of Norfolk (and Suffolk)

7. Robert de Vere, Earl of Oxford

8. William Marshall the younger, heir to the Earl of Pembroke

9. Robert fitz Walter the elder, Dunmowe Castle, Essex

10. Gilbert de Clare, heir to the Earl of Hertford

11. Eustace de Vesci/Vescy, Alnwick, Northumberland

12. Hugh Bigod, heir to the Earl of Norfolk

13. William de Mowbray, Axholme Castle, Lincolnshire

14. William (de) Hardell, Mayor of London

15. William de Lanvalei/Lanvallei, Stanway Castle, Essex

16. Robert de Ros/Roos, Hamlake Castle, Yorkshire

17. John de Lacy/Laci/Lacie/Lasci, Halton Castle, Constable of Chester

18. Richard de Perci/Percy, feudal baron, Yorkshire

19. John fitz Robert, Warkworth Castle, Northumberland

20. William Malet/Mallet, Curry-Malet, Somerset

21. Geoffrey de Say/Saye, feudal baron, Sussex

22. Roger de Mumbezon/Montbegon, Horneby, Lancashire

23. William de Huntingfield, feudal baron, Suffolk

24. Richard de Munfichet/Muntfichet/ Montfichet, feudal baron, Essex

25. William d'Albini/d'Aubigney/ d'Aubigné Belvoir Castle, Leicestershire

Adapted from Frecknall-Hughes, 2010, p. 93

"in a late-thirteenth century collection of law tracts" (Harleian manuscript) (Holt, 1992a, p. 478).[27] Cheney (1968, p. 283) refers to a further St. Albans list.[28] The fifth list was discovered by Cheney in 1968 in Lambeth Palace library in a manuscript originating in Reading Abbey.[29] Although there are some slight differences between the different lists, there is overall a remarkable consistency between them.[30] The names of the twenty-five are given in Table 3.

It is suggested by Richardson (1944, p. 433) that Geoffrey de Mandeville, Saer de Quincy, Richard de Clare, and Robert de Vere form the sub-group of four barons referred to in Clause 61.

Cheney (1968, p. 291) remarks that the first eleven names are in the same order in the St. Albans, Harleian, and Lambeth lists, possibly indicating a common source, which may have been the Articles of the Barons, "a remarkable and chance survival from the negotiations of 1215" (Holt, 1992a, p. 245). Cheney further suggests (1968, p. 306) that:

> A comparison of the Charter [Magna Carta] with the Articles of the Barons suggests that when the Articles were drawn up the draftsmen were planning an orthodox charter of liberties; separate documents were envisaged to safeguard its observance. But in the event the only safeguard was included in the Charter in the . . . sanctions of clause 61. . . . But a comparison of the texts suggest that eleven of the chief magnates were designated as executors of the Charter before the remainder were picked.

Thus the names of the first eleven would be well known, but the remaining fourteen less so. Also, as the first eleven were great magnates, it is unsurprising that their names appear first. The names in the Lambeth list are also accompanied by a number of knights, though it is unknown what this actually means, as there is not necessarily any connection between the number and the number of knights the barons had enfeoffed.

Effects Of John's Exactions On The Barons

Powicke (1965, p. 207) notes that:

> [t]he personnel of the opposition to King John in 1215 requires much detailed investigation. Local connexions and the evidence given in the Fine Rolls and other records of personal grievances have never been thoroughly examined.

In terms of the twenty-five suretors, there is relatively little research that attempts to uncover how they were personally affected, and that is explored here (Round, 1904; Painter, 1949, Powicke, 1965, Holt, 1992a, 1992b). Painter (1949, p. 204) comments that:

> [g]eneral grievances produce general discontent, but they have to be extremely acute before they can in themselves cause a revolt against a reasonably strong government. A rebellion requires leaders, and they are more likely to have more personal reasons for their disaffection than any general dislike of the government's policy. The grievances of John's feudal vassals as a whole supplied excellent tinder, but the spark had to come from men with personal reasons for hating the king and his government.

The evidence is compelling for these reasons commonly being financial in origin. While not all the barons would necessarily have been affected by all the exactions,

215

it is clear that some bit particularly viciously. It is not surprising to find these twenty-five men in rebellion against the king and thus willing to act in the capacity of suretors. It seems as if they might have nothing more to lose in financial terms.

Incidental Income

In terms of incidental income (amercements, feudal incidents, oblations, etc.), there are some obvious instances of exactions, bound to cause great grievances, that can be traced to individual suretors. For example, Vincent (2005a) points to the fact of John de Lacy in September 1213 being "forced to offer a massive fine of 7,000 marks" payable over three years in order to obtain possession of his father's estates. He also had to surrender to the king his main castles of Pontefract in Yorkshire and Donington in Leicestershire, while still keeping them garrisoned. If he had rebelled, the surrendered property would have been confiscated. Moreover, when he did finally gain possession of Castle Donington in 1214, he was obliged to surrender his younger brother as a hostage for his good behaviour. Despite all this, he appears to have stayed loyal to the king as late as 1215, being then pardoned for the 4,200 marks of the 1213 fine that were still owed. Afterwards "he veered opportunistically between the rebel and royalist camps" (Vincent, 2005a). In January 1216, he sought to come to terms with the

The Repeal or the Funeral of Miss Ame-Stamp [1766]. Etching. Prints and Photographs Division, Library of Congress (LC-DIG-ppmsca.31157)

king, "perhaps in the light of the king's capture of Castle Donington" (*ibid.*), again surrendered his brother as hostage, and repudiated the terms of Magna Carta. He rebelled again before the king's death in October. While it is easy to see that John's behaviour could easily have been the root of de Lacy's rebellion, his loyalty does seem to have been uncertain when unrestrained by financial bonds—so attempts to ensure that loyalty might have seemed reasonable.

William Marshall the younger, son of William Marshall the elder, earl of Pembroke, was surrendered to the king in 1205 as a hostage by his father, when John doubted the latter's loyalty. He stayed as a hostage for some seven years, until 1212 (Walker, R.F., 2005). Finding the younger William Marshall in opposition to the king is not therefore unexpected. Richard de Montfichet "was sold in wardship to Roger de Lacy, constable of Chester, in return for a proffer of £1,000, which seems never to have been paid". He was aged about ten at the time and this was a result of his father dying. In 1210, the wardship was sold back to his mother for a fine of 1,100 marks (Vincent, 2005b).

In October 2014, John charged Robert de Vere 1,000 marks as a relief (including a wardship) for succeeding his brother as earl of Oxford. However, the earldom does not seem to have been conferred. DeAragon (2005) suggests that this relief was "high for a baronage of moderate extent such as de Vere's, but his primary grievance may have been John's withholding of the earldom", though the king did recognise him as earl by June 1215.

The dispute between the de Mowbray and de Stuteville families has been mentioned earlier. This was a long-standing matter concerning the claims of the de Stutevilles to the de Mowbray barony, which Henry II had settled in favour of the de Mowbrays. The claim was reopened in John's reign (on the grounds that the original agreement had not been confirmed by the Crown) when in April 1200, John issued a charter to William de Stuteville, promising him justice toward William de Mowbray (the suretor) "in a suit for the entire Mowbray barony" (Painter, 1949, p. 29). De Stuteville promised to pay 3,000 marks for this, with de Mowbray counter-offering 2,000 for just treatment. In the 1201 settlement (for de Stuteville), de Mowbray gave de Stuteville nine knights' fees, in addition to ten given to his father, and the manor of Brinklow worth £12 *per annum*. In 1207, de Mowbray still owed 1,940 marks, which John attempted to collect from the vassals of the de Mowbray barony. The de Mowbray family had had a previous royal judgment reversed on a claim they thought settled, so resentment against such treatment is easily comprehended.

Richard de Percy "was uncertain from one year to the next of the title to most of his estates" (Holt, 1992b, p. 21). He was confronted throughout his life by the counter-claims of his nephew, William, the son of his elder brother, as Richard was a younger brother who had inherited. The Percy lands were divided between them, and William was a minor, until at least 1212, in the custody of William Briwerre, one of the king's most influential advisers, whose daughter he eventually married (following Holt, 1992b, p. 21). The legal wrangles were not settled until 1234. It is interesting to note that Richard's claim to his lands and title mirrored John's claim to the throne, as his nephew Arthur would have had a defensible counter-claim (see earlier). The devolution of the de Mandeville lands between Geoffrey de Mandeville and Geoffrey de Say was also the subject of a similar suit. As mentioned earlier, Geoffrey de Mandeville was also obliged to pay 20,000 marks to John for the right to marry John's former wife, Isabelle of Gloucester. The reason for so high a price being demanded probably lies in some quarrel or other. The full truth is never likely to be known (Norgate, 1902, pp. 289–293; Round, 1904).

Roger de Montbegon was involved in a long-standing attempt to regain disseised[31] lands in Nottinghamshire, where he was opposed in local courts by the sheriff, Philip Marc, one of John's 'strong-arm' men, whose presence in office was so resented as to merit inclusion in Magna Carta, Clause 50. However, during the case he himself committed a number of transgressions, such as refusing to accept the decision of a local court. Holt (1992b, p. 6) gives the dates of much of this activity as 1217 and after, so it is possible that this has deeper origins, given that he appears as a suretor.

Scutage and Taxes on Movables

Taxes such as scutage and those on movable property would be likely to bite deeply into the revenues, cash, and other assets of the barons because much of their wealth was derived from land. Painter (1949, p. 19 and pp. 296–297) suggests some numbers for the baronies in England at this time—197 lay baronies with a further thirty-nine ecclesiastical baronies. He suggests that a reasonable-sized barony might comprise about thirty knights' fees, with some 75 percent of the knights' fees overall belonging to baronies having thirty or more fees. He further suggests that thirty-nine of the lay barons were in revolt before Magna Carta, with thirteen in open revolt in 1215, at the time of the Charter. These thirteen held "approximately 1,475 knights' fees against the 1,580 who were not in revolt" (*ibid.*). Painter admits that figures are inexact, but not all the barons were in open rebellion in 1215, which may do much to support his earlier contention (p. 204) that many of the grievances were personal.

Holt (1992b, p. 33), speaking of the northern barons, points out, however, that they were more than just feudal landlords.

They were great landlords and keen businessmen, active enclosers and improvers of their lands, owners of vast sheep flocks, benefactors and patrons of great monasteries, founders both of religious houses and of market and municipal privileges. Their interests even extended into commerce and industry. Robert de Ros exported wool and leather from the Humber and imported wine. Eustace de Vesci developed Alnmouth as a licensed port. . . . The Percys had forges at Spofforth.

Such activities would have been hit by the taxes on movables, sometimes levied in the same year as scutage. Supporting Painter's view, he also comments (*ibid.*):

> By and large they were the 'outs', excluded from the spoils of office, despite a family tradition of service to the Crown in many cases, despite the earlier administrative experience which some of them enjoyed, and despite the expectancy of office which their social position gave them. In addition many of them had personal wrongs, grievances and problems to set right.

In this respect he names, among others, William de Mowbray, Richard de Percy, Roger de Montbegon, Robert de Ros, and John de Lacy, whose names appear in the list of suretors.

Some of the grievances against scutage can be traced quite easily. For example, the Bigod family seems to have had a history of disputed inheritance, dating back to the reign of Henry II. Roger Bigod, second earl of Norfolk, had received Crown support in a bitter struggle with his half-brother over possession of the earldom and stayed loyal to John until nearly the end of his reign, when he joined the rebels. Church (2006) explicitly comments on possible financial reasons for this.

> Financial pressure may have been a reason. The scutage due on some 160 knights' fees, which the earl came to hold by the end of his life, was liable to be heavy, so much so that in 1211 Bigod struck a bargain with the king to pay 2000 marks (£1333 6s. 8d.) for respite during his lifetime from demands for arrears, and for being allowed to pay scutage on only 60 fees in future. He was pardoned 360 marks of the debt, but paid the substantial sum of 1340 marks in 1211 and 1212.

In consequence of joining the rebellion, Roger Bigod (supported by his son, Hugh) had his lands seized, not regaining them until 1217.

Other barons also had extensive fees. Robert fitz Walter, a leader of the baronial revolt, inherited lands in Dunmow, Essex, and Baynard's Castle, London, which comprised sixty-six knights' fees. An additional thirty-two were brought by his wife, Gunnora, daughter and heiress of Robert de Valognes. Some 110 fees were attached to the lands of William d'Albini, earl of Arundel (in Arundel itself), with seventy-six more at Castle Rising and Buckenham in Norfolk (Painter, 1949, p. 21). John de Lacy had large estates

> comprising more than 100 knights' fees together with the northern baronies of Pontefract, Clitheroe, Penwortham, Widnes, and Halton, held by descent in the female line from the lacy lords of Pontefract, and in the line of direct male descent as heir to the lands and office of the constables of Chester
>
> Vincent, 2005a

William Malet had fee obligations for 22 ½ knights at Curry Mallet in Somerset. At Christmas 1209, John appointed him as sheriff of Dorset and Somerset, when these two counties offered him a fine requesting that he replace William Brewer. Malet served until 1212, by which date

> he was in financial difficulties with the king, and by 1214 owed 2,000 marks, which remained unpaid in 1221, although he had made an agreement in 1214 to serve King John with ten knights and twenty soldiers in Poitou in exchange for cancellation of his debt.
>
> Turner, 2005

Similar issues affected Henry de Bohun, first earl of Hereford, who was involved in a dispute over his lands at Trowbridge, which were claimed by William Longspée, earl of Salisbury. John took the lands in hand, but allowed William's agents to levy scutage from the tenants, which appears to have been the catalyst which forced de Bohun to the side of the rebel barons. He had earlier (1204–1211) been involved in resolving his claim to "his mother's dower lands, the estates and twenty fees of the lordship of Ratho, Edinburghshire" (Walker, D., 2005).

Another surety baron, Richard de Montfichet inherited the barony of Stansted Montfichet, which, *per* Vincent (2005b), "comprised nearly fifty knights' fees" and a "claim to the custody of the royal forests in Essex, forfeited by his grandfather Gilbert de Montfichet (*d.* 1186/7), probably for his part in the rebellion of Henry, the Young King, in 1173". Richard managed to regain custody of the forfeited forests at Runnymede in 1215, with Vincent (2005b) suggesting that he join the rebel barons in the hope of such a recovery and because of his kinship with Robert fitz Walter and Richard, earl of Clare.

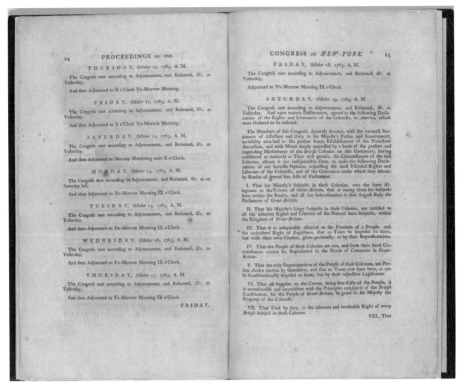

1765 Stamp Act Congress, New York in *Proceedings of the Congress at New-York*. Annapolis [Md.]: Jonas Green, 1766. Rare Book and Special Collections Division, Library of Congress

If all the scutage due on the fees outlined above were to be estimated, it would represent a huge sum, either in men-at-arms or ready cash. Although a formal summons was required, scutage could be demanded almost at will, which was also a cause of resentment, with Clause 14 thus including a requirement for due notice. The frequency with which John tried to collect scutage, combined with the taxes on movables (including on agricultural produce, animals, and trading activities), would have meant an intolerable burden. From the king's perspective, however, scutage presented a dilemma. While it provided the means to raise an army (either by the provision of knights or if commuted to money, to hire mercenaries), it also meant that the barons themselves could build up armies of loyal retainers. This can never have escaped the king's notice, although it rarely attracts specific attention. Barons often held tracts of land that were separated by great distances, which would make them more complicated to manage on a daily basis and would make raising personal armies more difficult. Perhaps allocating feudal lands that were many miles apart was a device to counter potential army-raising, although land-holdings might be changed if land was given as a dowry with a bride—hence another reason for the king to take an interest in matters of baronial marriage.

Family Connections

Powicke (1965, pp. 209–213) points out that there were strong family ties between the 25 suretors, specially commenting on the link by marriage between the de Vere, de Mandeville, de Say, and de Bohun families, and while this should not be pressed too closely, "the existence of close family ties does seem . . . to have been a significant factor in forming a definite group of people personally hostile to King John" (p. 212). A similar point is made by Strickland (2007).

> William d'Aubigny, for example, was the uncle of Robert de Ros, the lord of Wark-on-Tweed in Northumberland and Helmsley in Yorkshire, and also first cousin of Robert Fitzwalter, while John fitz Robert was John de Lacy's cousin. William de Lanvallei had married Fitzwalter's niece; William de Forz, count of Aumale in Normandy and a major landowner in Cumberland, Yorkshire, and Lincolnshire, was married to the daughter of Richard de Montfichet; both Hugh Bigod and Gilbert de Clare had married sisters of William Marshal the younger; and Henry de Bohun had married Geoffrey de Mandeville's sister. In turn, Geoffrey and his brother William were married to daughters of Robert Fitzwalter.

We do not often hear about medieval women in their own right, but they are the invisible thread linking families together, and as the quote from Strickland shows, the web of relationships, often forged by marriage, was tangled. Land given to women as a dowry or inherited by them often resulted in land-holdings being restructured.

Sometimes too, there were long-standing friendships, about which Strickland (2007) also remarks.

> In rare instances, close ties of friendship are known to have existed, for instance between William de Forz and Robert de Ros, or between Robert Fitzwalter and Saher de Quincy, who had served together in Normandy in 1203 as castellans of Vaudreuil and were brothers-in-arms, each bearing the other's blazon on his seal. Conversely, there can have been little love lost between Geoffrey de Mandeville and Geoffrey de Say, whose rival claims to the Mandeville lands had been exploited by John.

None of this needs point to any political groupings, but it clearly indicates that many of the twenty-five barons would know each other, and would be likely to

Pennsylvania Journal and Weekly Advertiser, October 24, 1765. Serial and Government Publications Division, Library of Congress

be aware of a great deal about each other's affairs. In terms of financial matters, Strickland makes this point more explicitly, thus providing additional grounding for the ideas expressed in this chapter.

> More tangibly, several of the northerners had been accustomed to stand surety for each other for the payment of fines or proffers to the king, suggesting a significant degree of solidarity

Conclusion

When all the taxes and financial exactions imposed by John are considered, in conjunction with the individual Magna Carta clauses and the effect on individual suretors, a consistent picture emerges of immense fiscal burdens, made worse after the loss of Normandy and the death of Hubert Walter, which removed the moderating and acceptably innovative influence on John's revenue-raising that was evident before his death. It is not surprising that John's increasing defiance of custom and extortionary practice in his fiscal impositions led to a resistance which culminated in the baronial rebellion and the demand for restraint on (especially) the king's financial powers as expressed in Magna Carta. It may be even more surprising that the full-scale revolt did not happen sooner, and it is, perhaps, the fact of Church revenues being collected during the period of the Interdict which prevented it happening earlier.

John's reign is important in tax history terms for other reasons, which have emerged in the above discussions. A need to derive revenues from assets and sources not under a ruler's direct control, as part of the transition from a desmesne-based to a tax-based state, to finance government machinery as well as military and other ambitions, coupled with a need for consent to taxation (to a degree at least), also emerges in respect of taxes on movables (especially the thirteenth) and scutage, which is manifest in Magna Carta clauses. There is also a movement towards taxation on a national, rather than an entirely feudal basis (again, the thirteenth of 1207 and carucage). A perceived need for regular income at a national level to put the state on a sound financial footing, as opposed to levying taxes for special purposes, is also, perhaps, implicit, in the 1207 tax and some of the later scutages—but this cannot be pressed too far. John is acknowledged by nearly all writers as a greedy king, with a fondness for wealth, so it may be impossible to divorce some of the outcomes of his reign from his personal characteristics.

Over fifty clauses of the sixty-three in the 1215 Magna Carta have been cited in this chapter as reflecting in one way or another the outcome of a massive financial struggle consequent on John's extortionary measures, linked to an overriding sense of the inequity and illegality of some of those measures. It is significant to note, however, that a large proportion of the key financial restrictions and other promises was removed in subsequent reissues—namely, Clauses 10, 11, 12, 14, 15, 25, 27, 42, 45, 48, 49, 50, 51, 52, 53, 55, 57, 58, 59, 62, 62, and 63 (see Bray, 2002, pp. 49–54; Vincent, 2012, p. 4). As Vincent (2012, p. 4) comments, despite the long "after-life" of certain clauses

> . . . the charter as a whole was already treated as an archaic relic as long ago as 1300, when it was for the last time granted a full reissue by a king of England, King John's grandson Edward I. By then, it had already become more a totemic monument to past struggles than something tailored to current political circumstance.

He notes, however, its revival as a "political manifesto, cited by Parliamentarians as a check upon the Stuart kings and their claims to 'absolute' power" (p. 4). For example, the 1628 *Petition of Right* defined the particular liberties of the king's subjects that he must not infringe, predominant among which is Parliament's right to levy taxation. Tax, it seems, was ever hovering in the background as something that should be subject to a force other than the arbitrary will of the monarch.

MAGNA CARTA AND CULTURE

KING JOHN AND MAGNA CARTA IN POPULAR CULTURE

Carolyn Harris

King John was not a good man,
And no good friends had he.
He stayed in every afternoon…
But no-one came to tea.
And, round about December,
The cards upon his shelf
Which wished him lots of Christmas cheer,
And fortune in the coming year,
Were never from his near and dear,
But only from himself.

A. A. Milne, "King John's Christmas" 1927.[1]

Most of the kings and queens of England best known for their villainy also have their defenders and received comparatively sympathetic portrayals in popular culture. King Henry VIII is best known for ordering the beheading of two of his six wives, but recent biographies emphasize his cultural patronage during the early years of his reign[2] and the 2007–2010 television series *The Tudors* depicted Henry composing music for his lute and engaging with philosophers, theologians, and artists in addition to his disastrous marriages.[3] The most famous example of a villainous king's rehabilitation is Richard III. William Shakespeare's play *Richard III* depicted him as a hunchbacked monster who ruthlessly eliminated his relatives, including his nephews, the Princes in the Tower, to seize the

Robin Hood Defies King John in Frederick Warde's Superb Production of Runnymede *by Wm. Greer Harrison*. Cincinnati and New York: Strobridge Lith. Co., ca. 1895. Prints and Photographs Division, Library of Congress (LC-DIG-pnp.var.0757)

throne.[4] Richard's villainy was accepted by much of the public until the publication of Josephine Tey's historical detective novel *The Daughter of Time*, in 1951, which suggested that Richard might have been the victim of Tudor propaganda.[5] Today, the Richard III Society, established in 1924, has thousands of members worldwide,[6] and the discovery of Richard III's remains in 2012 reignited the debate over whether he was monstrous or misunderstood.

King John is the exception to this trend toward comparatively sympathetic portrayals of monarchs with longstanding negative reputations. The vast majority of portrayals of John in popular culture depict him as a villain. The fictional John is not a ruthless villain like his grandson Edward I, as depicted by Patrick McGoohan in Mel Gibson's Academy Award–winning 1995 film, *Braveheart*,[7] but a snivelling, cowardly villain plagued by insecurities. The few attempts to create a more balanced portrait of John have not penetrated the popular consciousness. The accepted negative view of John affects the place of Magna Carta in popular culture. The Great Charter is often celebrated in isolation from the political circumstances of its creation or treated as a victory of the forces of "good" against an "evil" king. Fictional portrayals of John and his barons deliberating over the creation of Magna Carta, with equal weight given to the concerns of both sides, are extremely rare.

The earliest well-known fictional portrayal of John is Shakespeare's play *King John*, which dates from the late 1580s or early 1590s[8] and is based on George Peele's 1589 history play *The Troublesome Reign of King John*.[9] In the first three acts, Shakespeare portrays John challenging his nephew, Arthur, duke of Brittany, and King Philip II of France for control of his kingdom and being excommunicated by Pope Innocent III for refusing to accept Stephen Langton, author of Magna Carta, as Archbishop of Canterbury. In last two acts, Philip II's son invades England at the invitation of John's barons, and John reconciles with the papacy to fight the revolt. Chronologically, the signing of Magna Carta occurred between these two sets of events, but Shakespeare omits any mention of the Charter, let alone a dramatic confrontation between the king and his barons at Runnymede meadow. This omission is so disconcerting to modern audiences that it has been blamed for the steep drop in the play's popularity in the twentieth century. In 2011, Canadian journalist Barbara Kay wrote in the *National Post*, "Shakespeare's history play *King John* omitted the signing of the Magna Carta, of all things, rather like writing a play about George Washington and omitting the American Revolution."[10] The play reached peak popularity during the nineteenth century—the first film depiction of King John is an 1899 silent clip of John's death scene in Act V—but it is rarely performed today.[11]

Shakespeare, however, was writing for Elizabethan audiences, not a modern audience with a present-day view of Magna Carta's importance to the development of civil liberties. Shakespeare appears to have admired John's willingness to confront the papacy and held a negative perception of the barons because they seemed to threaten England's independence by inviting a French invasion. During Elizabeth I's reign, Magna Carta was a comparatively obscure document best known to legal scholars.[12] Without mention of the Great Charter in the play, the First Barons' Revolt appears to be a threat to English liberties rather than an attempt to safeguard them. For Elizabeth I's Protestant subjects, a strong monarch was necessary to defend England from external threats such as the papacy or continental Roman Catholic kingdoms such as France and Spain.

Despite Shakespeare's clear respect for a monarch willing to challenge papal supremacy, the play still makes clear that he also saw John as an unscrupulous villain. Medieval chroniclers blamed John personally for the disappearance of his nephew and rival for the throne, Arthur, duke of Brittany in 1204.[13] Although the historical Arthur was sixteen and had already led an army to assert his claim to the throne, Shakespeare depicted Arthur as an innocent child threatened by the machinations of his uncle and the king of France. In one of the play's most moving scenes, Arthur persuades his jailor, Hubert de Burgh, to disregard his uncle's order to put out his eyes with a hot poker.[14] When John is blamed for Arthur's disappearance, he begins a descent into paranoia, accusing his subjects of plotting against him.[15] By the end of the play, John is dead and order is restored to England through the ascension of his son, Henry III. Shakespeare may have admired certain aspects of John's reign and been dismissive of Magna Carta, but the depiction of his treatment of Arthur demonstrates that the dramatist still viewed the king as a villain.

The development of the Robin Hood legends further influenced the popular perception of John's villainy, especially in comparison to his elder brother and predecessor, King Richard I, "the Lion-Heart," who went down in history as a chivalric hero. During Elizabeth I's reign, the same period as Shakespeare's *King John*, the Robin Hood legends underwent a crucial transformation that brought the struggle between Richard and John into the popular consciousness. Before the sixteenth century, the Robin Hood legends contained few indications of the time period for the outlaw's exploits. Robin was simply an outlaw who was not beholden to any authority, represented as the May King in May Day festivities and a popular subject for amateur theatricals at the court of Henry VIII.[16] The vague historical setting became precise during Elizabeth I's reign. The wild outlaw became a nobleman loyal to Richard, opposing the tyranny of his king's brother, John.

In 1820, Sir Walter Scott's historical novel *Ivanhoe* added further details to the legends, presenting Robin as the Saxon landowner, Robin of Locksley.[17] Scott's interest in England's Anglo-Saxon heritage influenced his portrayal of both John and Magna Carta. His characterization of Robin contributed to the popular perception that Magna Carta represented a return to an older, Anglo-Saxon law code that had been abandoned after the Norman Conquest of 1066, while John acted as a "Norman" oppressor of the English. Scott's portrayal of John and Magna Carta followed the writings of seventeenth-century jurist Sir Edward Coke (1552–1634), who was responsible for the revival of Magna Carta from the comparative obscurity of Tudor times.

Coke placed Magna Carta in a continuum of English common law that predated the Norman Conquest of 1066 and viewed it as a key document within England's "ancient constitution."[18] This interpretation of Magna Carta spread around the world because Coke was also the author of legal textbooks and wrote at a time when English explorers and merchants were establishing colonies around the world. The *Institutes of the Laws of England*, Coke's four-volume work affirming the primacy of Magna Carta to English law, eventually became the standard legal text in the Thirteen Colonies, read by future signatories of the American Declaration of Independence, including John Adams, Thomas Jefferson, and James Madison.[19] The publication of *Ivanhoe* brought the villainous King John, the loyal Robin Hood, and the primacy of Magna Carta to a broad popular audience.

By the twentieth century, the legendary Robin was portrayed in film as part of national struggle against John's attempts to usurp his brother Richard's throne. In the 1938 film *The Adventures of Robin Hood*, starring Errol Flynn, a pompous bejewelled John (Claude Rains) announces that he intends to raise taxes, ostensibly to ransom King Richard from the Holy Roman Emperor, and make himself regent of England. The prince makes a petulant speech to his incredulous barons: "Confound it, what are you all gobbling at? Is it so strange that I decide to rule when my brother is a prisoner? Who is to say I shouldn't!"[20] Rains' portrayal of John as snivelling traitor set the tone for all subsequent portrayals of John in films about Robin Hood.

The characterization of the future John as a cowardly villain provided plenty of material for satire in comedic films. For many children, their first introduction to medieval England is the 1973 Walt Disney Productions animated film *Robin Hood*, where John, voiced by Peter Ustinov, is depicted as a lion without a mane, "a phoney King of England" who sucks his thumb and whines, "Mummy always liked Richard best!"[21] The 1993 satirical film directed by Mel Brooks, *Robin Hood: Men in Tights*, also presented John (Richard Lewis) as a comic villain with a facial mole that moves to a different place in every scene. At the end of the film, Richard (Patrick Stewart) returns from crusade and declares to a cheering crowd, "Brother, you have surrounded your given name with a foul stench. From this day forth, all the toilets in the kingdom shall be known as … Johns!"[22] John is the ostensible villain of both films, but he is never a threatening presence. Instead, Robin, Richard, and their allies laugh at him, and his transparent schemes to present himself as a legitimate ruler of England, and the audience laughs with them.

Since the Robin Hood films are usually set in the reign of Richard instead of John, they rarely include explicit references to Magna Carta. An exception is the 2010 film *Robin Hood*, starring Russell Crowe.[23] The film diverges from Scott's depiction of Robin as Robin of Locksley by presenting the title character as the son of a stonemason who assumes Locksley's identity after the nobleman is killed returning from the Third Crusade with Richard. In a series of flashbacks, Robin reveals that his true father, the stonemason, was beheaded because he supported a Charter that would guarantee rights for all Englishmen. In his new identity as Robin of Locksley, Robin unifies the barons and persuades John to sign the Charter. The fictional Charter is far more radical than the historical Magna Carta, which addressed the grievances of the barons rather than English society as a whole. Just as Shakespeare's *King John* reflected the concerns of Elizabethan audiences regarding papal interference in English affairs, the 2010 *Robin Hood* film reflects twenty-first-century perceptions of Magna Carta as a foundational document for Common Law throughout the English-speaking world. The film views John and Magna Carta through modern eyes. The legacy of a century of Robin Hood films denigrating John's character also has a subtle influence on the 2010 film. Oscar Isaac portrays John as a more serious figure than in previous Robin Hood films, but he is still reprimanded by his mother, Eleanor of Aquitaine, and jeopardizes his realm through the pursuit of pleasure, neglecting state business to spend mornings in bed with his second wife, Isabelle of Angouleme (Léa Seydoux).

The depiction of John as a cowardly villain in Robin Hood films had such a strong impact on the popular imagination that it influenced other on-screen depictions of the Plantagenet dynasty independent of the Robin Hood legends. In James Goldman's 1966 play *The Lion in Winter*,[24] which was adapted as an Academy Award–winning film starring Katharine Hepburn and Peter O'Toole in 1968[25] and for television in 2003,[26] John is a snivelling teenager who is despised by his mother and easily manipulated by his elder brothers and Philip II of France. Even John's father, who ostensibly favours him above his other sons, is dismissive of him. When

Princess Alais of France informs Henry II that "I can't be your mistress if I am married to your son," Henry replies, "Why can't you? Johnny wouldn't mind."[27] In addition to his character failings, John is also portrayed as physically repellent. Alais objects to the proposed marriage by remarking, "I do not like your Johnny … he has pimples and he smells of compost."[28] At sixteen, John already appears to be a completely unsuitable future king in character and appearance.

In the 1978 BBC miniseries *The Devil's Crown,* John (John Duttine) demonstrates insecurities regarding his mother's relationship with Richard that are reminiscent of the animated *Robin Hood* film from the same decade. After he rides to Eleanor's rescue at the 1202 Siege of Chateau Mirabeau, he asks her, "Am I as good as Richard?" In contrast to most other on-screen depictions of King John, *The Devil's Crown* covers his entire reign, culminating in Magna Carta.[29] The Great Charter appears as a reaction to years of villainous and perfidious actions by the king. Over the course of the miniseries, John orders the blinding and mutilation of his nephew Arthur (Simon Gipps-Kent) and then strangles Arthur with his bare hands. When Maud de Braose, the wife of a prominent baron refuses to hand over her son to the king as a hostage because of Arthur's fate, she is starved to death in a dungeon with her child. John appears to delight in the torment of his enemies, enjoying a meal within view of the starving Maud. Historically, the fate of the Braose family inspired the right to due process enshrined in Magna Carta, and the Great Charter appears after the deaths of Maud and her son in the miniseries. When King John finally engrosses Magna Carta with his seal, the wax cracks as soon as it dries, symbolizing his intention to abjure the Great Charter. The 2011 film *Ironclad* depicts the events that followed King John's rejection of Magna Carta, dramatizing the king (Paul Giamatti) waging war against his barons.[30] The besieged Rochester Castle is compared to Magna Carta in the epilogue as both "still stand today."

While portrayals of John in film focus on his villainy, historical novelists have attempted to present the king and his barons as more nuanced figures, responding to the unique political circumstances of early thirteenth-century England. In Elizabeth Chadwick's 2011 novel, *To Defy a King*, the story is told from the perspective of the discontented noble families who supported Magna Carta with only a few scenes from the king's viewpoint.[31] This approach demonstrates the goals of the barons and the divisions between them, revealing how controversial Magna Carta was at the time of its inception and removing the focus from the king.

One of the most nuanced portrayals of both King John and Magna Carta in historical fiction appears in *Here Be Dragons*, the 1985 novel by Sharon Kay Penman about Llewellyn the Great, Prince of Wales, and his marriage to John's illegitimate daughter, Joanna.[32] In a lengthy conversation about the nature of the Charter, the Welsh royal couple place the document in a broader historical context, discussing how John's extended presence in England as well as his dishonesty contributed to the discontent of the barons.

Llewellyn explains to his wife:

> Henry [II] and Richard both ruled with a heavy hand but they were gone from the kingdom for years at a time, occupied by events in Normandy, Anjou, Poitou. Those absences gave their English barons a needed respite, some breathing space. But for nigh on ten years, John has been anchored in England, riding the length and breadth of the realm, bringing his courts and his constables, collecting taxes, levying scutage, making enemies.[33]

Through the perspective of Llewellyn, Penman complicates the traditional fictional portrayal of Magna Carta as a charter between a villainous king and his wronged barons. Instead, the very presence of John in England, governing his kingdom rather than being an absentee monarch on the continent or on crusade prompted the barons to attempt to codify their traditional prerogatives. After Llewellyn's explanation, Joanna observes, "You're saying that the true significance of this charter is that it changes privileges into rights?"[34] Joanna and Llewellyn both agree that Magna Carta is a "novel concept" and that is a shame that war between the king and his barons was inevitable.[35]

Magna Carta does not always appear in popular culture in conjunction with King John. In Rudyard Kipling's 1922 poem "What Say the Reeds at Runnymede," the king is mentioned in passing, but the rights enshrined in the Charter take centre stage. Kipling sets the clauses of Magna Carta to verse, writing,

> "At Runnymede, at Runnymede,
> Your rights were won at Runnymede!
> No freeman shall be fined or bound,
> Or dispossessed of freehold ground,
> Except by lawful judgment found,
> And passed upon him by his peers.
> Forget not, after all these years,
> The Charter signed at Runnymede."[36]

While novels, plays and films focus on the King's failings and the barons' grievances, the removal of King John from the centre of the narrative allows Kipling to address his readers directly, reminding them of the lasting significance of the Charter's text.

The content of Magna Carta has also been showcased on commemorative postage stamps. A United Kingdom stamp from 1999 states five key ideas codified by the Charter, "Freedom," "Lawful Judgement," "Liberty," "Justice," and "Equal Rights."[37] An American postage stamp commemorating the 750th anniversary of the Great Charter in 1965 focused on the historical significance of a king accepting limits on his power imposed by his subjects, depicting the barons presenting Magna Carta at Runnymede.[38] Like Kipling's poem, the postage stamps show the lasting historical significance of the Great Charter.

POST ON BULLETIN BOARD

5-Cent MAGNA CARTA
COMMEMORATIVE POSTAGE STAMP

UNITED STATES POSTAGE 5¢

MAGNA CARTA 1215

AVAILABLE AT YOUR LOCAL POST OFFICE
JUNE 16, 1965

The 5-cent stamp marking the 750th anniversary of the great charter, the basis of English and American common law, will be first placed on sale at Jamestown, Virginia, on June 15, 1965.

The stamp, designed by Brook Temple of New York City, visually communicates the first successful challenge of the Divine right of kings. In the top panel, in black against a gold background, is a procession of barons, their banners flying defiantly. In the lower panel, black on purple, is the crown. The subordinate position of the crown indicates the triumph of the people in their quest for representation under the law.

The Magna Carta stamp will be printed on the Giori presses, issued in panes of 50, with an initial printing of 112,000,000. Due to the arrangement of the colors it will be necessary to run the sheets through the press twice, resulting in two plate numbers on each pane.

Collectors desiring first day cancellations may send addressed envelopes, together with remittance to cover the cost of the stamps to be affixed, to the Postmaster, Jamestown, Virginia 23081. Requests must be postmarked no later than June 15, 1965. Endorse envelope to Postmaster "First Day Covers Magna Carta Stamp."

U.S. GOVERNMENT PRINTING OFFICE : 1965 OF—766-770

Magna Carta U.S. Postage Stamps, first day covers and flyer, June 15, 1965. Courtesy of Nathan Dorn and Martha Hopkins

Today, Magna Carta continues to inform popular culture. In July 2013, rapper Jay-Z exhibited the cover art for his album *Magna Carta … Holy Grail* in Salisbury Cathedral, next to one of the surviving copies of the Great Charter.[39] Magna Carta has long inspired musical compositions, as demonstrated by John Philip Sousa's 1927 "Magna Carta March," but the recent Jay-Z album demonstrates the Charter's ability to transcend genres. The Dean of Salisbury, the Very Reverend June Osborne explained to the *Salisbury Journal*, "Jay Z, through his album, is creating a huge awareness of this historic document and its modern significance to a huge au-

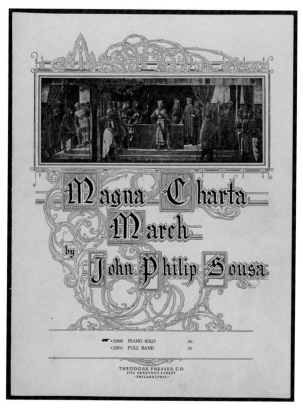

John Philip Sousa (1854–1932). *Magna Charta March*, 1927. Manuscript score and printed sheet music. Music Division, Library of Congress

dience in the run up to its 800th anniversary in 2015. We hope to welcome many of his fans here this summer to see the artwork in the Chapter House alongside our Magna Carta."[40] Nearly eight hundred years after King John affixed his seal to Magna Carta, the King and the Charter remain cultural landmarks as writers, artists, musicians, and filmmakers continue to be inspired by the universal themes of human rights and the nature of good governance.

Piccolo
Flutes
Oboes
E♭ Clarinet
B♭ Clarinets
Alto Clarinet
Bass Clarinet
Soprano
Alto
Tenor
Baritone
Saxophones
Bassoons
B♭ Cornets
Trumpets (2nd & 3rd B♭ Cornets)
Fluegelhorns
Horns (Altos.)
Baritones
Trombones
Basses (Tubas.)
Drums
Tympani Bells.
Nr. 36. Carl Fischer, New York.

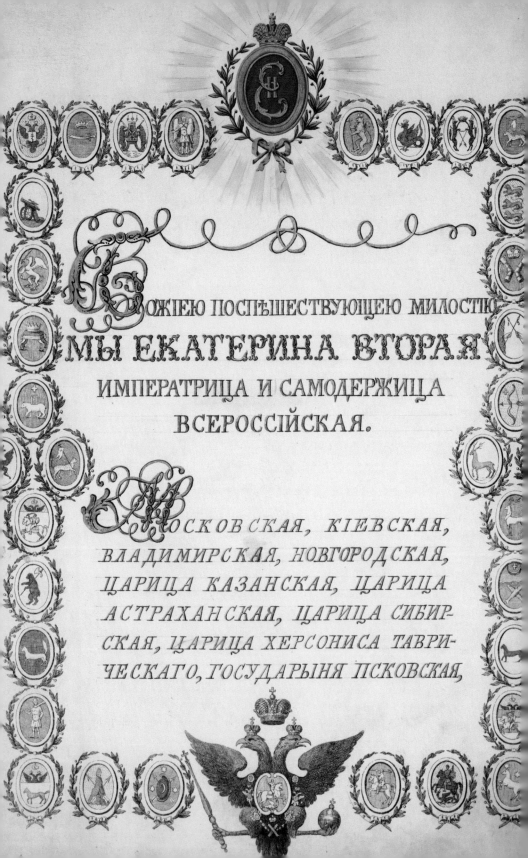

Божіею поспѣшествующею милостію

МЫ ЕКАТЕРИНА ВТОРАЯ

ИМПЕРАТРИЦА И САМОДЕРЖИЦА ВСЕРОССІЙСКАЯ.

МОСКОВСКАЯ, КІЕВСКАЯ, ВЛАДИМИРСКАЯ, НОВГОРОДСКАЯ, ЦАРИЦА КАЗАНСКАЯ, ЦАРИЦА АСТРАХАНСКАЯ, ЦАРИЦА СИБИРСКАЯ, ЦАРИЦА ХЕРСОНИСА ТАВРИЧЕСКАГО, ГОСУДАРЫНЯ ПСКОВСКАЯ,

MAGNA CHARTA
OR THE GREAT CHARTER OF KING JOHN
GRANTED AT RUNNYMEDE, JUNE 15, A.D. 1215,
IN THE SEVENTEENTH YEAR OF HIS REIGN.

John, by the grace of God King of England, Lord of Ireland, Duke of Normandy, and Aquitaine, and Count of Anjou, to his Archbishops, Bishops, Abbots, Earls, Barons, Justiciaries, Foresters, Sheriffs, Governors, Officers, and to all Bailiffs, and his lieges, greeting. Know ye, that we, in the presence of God, and for the salvation of our soul, and the souls of our ancestors and heirs, and unto the honour of God and the advancement of Holy Church, and amendment of our Realm, by advice of our venerable Fathers, Stephen, Archbishop of Canterbury, Primate of all England and Cardinal of the Holy Roman Church, Henry, Archbishop of Dublin, William of London, Peter of Winchester, Jocelin of Bath and Glastonbury, Hugh of Lincoln, Walter of Worcester, William of Coventry, Benedict of Rochester, Bishops; of Master Pandulph, Sub–Deacon and Familiar of our Lord the Pope, Brother Aymeric, Master of the Knights–Templars in England; and of the Noble Persons, William Marescall, Earl of Pembroke, William, Earl of Salisbury, William, Earl of Warren, William, Earl of Arundel, Alan de Galloway, Constable of Scotland, Warin Fitz Gerald, Peter Fitz Herbert, and Hubert de Burgh, Seneschal of Poitou, Hugh de Neville, Matthew Fitz Herbert, Thomas Basset, Alan Basset, Philip of Albiney, Robert de Roppell, John Mareschal, John Fitz Hugh, and others our liegeman have, in the first place, granted to God, and by this our present charter confirmed, for us and our heirs for ever:

1. That the church of England shall be free, and have her whole rights, and her liberties inviolable; and we will have them so observed, that it may appear thence, that the freedom of elections, which is reckoned chief and indispensable to the English church, and which we granted and confirmed by our charter, and obtained the confirmation of the same from our Lord the Pope Innocent III., before the discord between us and our barons, was granted of mere free will; which charter we shall observe, and we do will it to be faithfully observed by our heirs for ever.

2. We also have granted to all the freemen of our kingdom, for us and for our heirs for ever, all the underwritten liberties, to be had and holden by them and their heirs, of us and our heirs for ever: If any of our earls, or barons, or others, who hold of us in chief by military

Zhalovannaia Gramota Dvorianstvu. St. Petersburg, 1785. Law Library, Library of Congress

service, shall die, and at the time of his death his heir shall be of full age, and owe a relief, he shall have his inheritance by the ancient relief; that is to say, the heir or heirs of an earl, for a whole earldom, by a hundred pounds; the heir or heirs of a baron, for a whole barony, by a hundred pounds; the heir or heirs of a knight, for a whole knight's fee, by a hundred shillings at most; and whoever oweth less shall give less, according to the ancient custom of fees.

3. But if the heir of any such shall be under age, and shall be in ward when he comes of age, he shall have his inheritance without relief and without fine.

4. The keeper of the land of such an heir being under age, shall take of the land of the heir none but reasonable issues, reasonable customs, and reasonable services, and that without destruction and waste of his men and his goods; and if we commit the custody of any such lands to the sheriff, or any other who is answerable to us for the issues of the land, and he shall make destruction and waste of the lands which he hath in custody, we will take of him amends, and the land shall be committed to two lawful and discreet men of that fee, who shall answer for the issues to us, or to him to whom we assign them; and if we sell or give to any one the custody of any such lands, and he therein make destruction or waste, he shall lose the same custody, which shall be committed to two lawful and discreet men of that fee, who shall in like manner answer to us as aforesaid.

5. But the keeper, so long as he shall have the custody of the land, shall keep up the houses, parks, warrens, ponds, mills, and other things pertaining to the land, out of the issues of the same land; and shall deliver to the heir when he comes of full age, his whole land, stocked with ploughs and carriages, according as the time of wainage shall require, and the issues of the land can reasonably bear.

6. Heirs shall be married without disparagement, and so that before matri- mony shall be contracted those who are near in blood to the heir shall have notice.

7. A widow, after the death of her husband, shall forthwith and without difficulty have her marriage and inheritance; nor shall she give anything for her dower, or her marriage, or her inheritance, which her husband and she held at the day of his death; and she may remain in the mansion house of her husband forty days after his death, within which time her dower shall be assigned.

8. No widow shall be distrained to marry herself, so long as she has a mind to live without a husband; but yet she shall give security that she will not marry without our assent, if she holds of us; or without the consent of the lord of whom she holds, if she hold of another.

9. Neither we nor our bailiffs shall seize any land or rent for any debt, so long as the chattels of the debtor are sufficient to pay the debt; nor shall the sureties of the debtor be distrained so long as the principal debtor has sufficient to pay the debt; and if the principal debtor shall fail in the payment of the debt, not having where-withal to pay it, then the sureties shall answer the debt; and if they will they shall have the lands and rents of the debtor, until they shall be satisfied for the debt which they paid for him, unless the principal debtor can show himself acquitted thereof against the said sureties.

10. If any one have borrowed anything of the Jews, more or less, and die before the

debt be satisfied, there shall be no interest paid for that debt, so long as the heir is under age, of whomsoever he may hold; and if the debt fall into our hands we will only take the chattel mentioned in the deed.

11. And if any one shall die indebted to the Jews, his wife shall have her dower and pay nothing of that debt; and if the deceased left children under age, they shall have necessaries provided for them, according to the tenement of the deceased; and out of the residue the debt shall be paid, saving however, the service due to the lords; and in like manner shall it be done touching debts due to others than the Jews.

12. No scutage or aid shall be imposed in our kingdom, unless by the general council of our kingdom; except for ransoming our person, making our eldest son a knight, and once for marrying our eldest daughter; and for these there shall be paid a reasonable aid. In like manner it shall be concerning the aid of the City of London.

13. And the City of London shall have all its ancient liberties and free customs, as well by land as by water: furthermore we will and grant, that all other cities and boroughs, and towns and ports, shall have all their liberties and free customs.

14. And for holding the general council of the kingdom concerning the assessment of aids except in the three cases aforesaid, and for the assessing of scutages, we will cause to be summoned the archbishops, bishops, abbots, earls, and greater barons of the realm, singly by our letters. And furthermore we shall cause to be summoned generally by our sheriffs and bailiffs, all others who hold of us in chief, for a certain day, that is to say, forty days before their meeting at least, and to a certain place; and in all letters of such summons we will declare the cause of such summons. And summons being thus made, the business of the day shall proceed on the day appointed, according to the advice of such as shall be present, although all that were summoned come not.

15. We will not for the future grant to any one that he may take aid of his own free tenants, unless to ransom his body, and to make his eldest son a knight, and once to marry his eldest daughter; and for this there shall be only paid a reasonable aid.

16. No man shall be distrained to perform more service for a knight's fee, or other free tenement, than is due from thence.

17. Common pleas shall not follow our court, but shall be holden in some place certain.

18. Assizes of novel disseisin, and of mort d'ancestor, and of darrien presentment, shall not be taken but in their proper counties, and after this manner: We, or, if we should be out of the realm, our chief justiciary, shall send two justiciaries through every county four times a year, who, with four knights, chosen out of every shire by the people, shall hold the said assizes, in the county, on the day, and at the place appointed.

19. And if any matters cannot be determined on the day appointed for holding the assizes in each county, so many of the knights and freeholders as have been at the assizes aforesaid, shall stay to decide them, as is necessary, according as there is more or less business.

20. A freeman shall not be amerced for a small fault but after the manner of the fault; and for a great crime according to the heinousness of it, saving to him his contenement; and after the same manner a merchant, saving to him his merchandise. And a villein shall be amerced after the same manner, saving to him his wainage, if he shall fall under our mercy; and none of the aforesaid amerciaments shall be assessed but by oath of honest men in the neighborhood.

21. Earls and barons shall not be amerced, but by their peers, and after the degree of the offence.

22. No ecclesiastical person shall be amerced for his lay tenement, but according to the proportion of the others aforesaid, and not according to the value of his ecclesiastical benefice.

23. Neither a town nor any tenant shall be distrained to make bridges or banks, unless that anciently and of right they are bound to do it.

24. No sheriff, constable, coroner, or other our bailiffs, shall hold pleas of the Crown.

25. All counties, hundreds, wapentakes, and tythings, shall stand at the old rents, without any increase, except in our demesne manors.

26. If any one holding of us a lay-fee die, and the sheriff, or our bailiffs, show our letters patent, of summons for debt which the dead man did owe to us, it shall be lawful for the sheriff or our bailiff to attach and inroll the chattels of the dead, found upon his lay-fee, to the value of the debt, by the view of lawful men, so as nothing be removed until our whole clear debt be paid; and the rest shall be left to the executors to fulfill the testament of the dead, and if there be nothing due from him to us, all the chattels shall go to the use of the dead, saving to his wife and children their reasonable shares.

27. If any freeman shall die intestate, his chattels shall be distributed by the hands of his nearest relations and friends, by view of the church; saving to every one his debts which the deceased owed to him.

28. No constable or bailiff of ours shall take corn or other chattels of any man, unless he presently give him money for it, or hath respite of payment by the good-will of the seller.

29. No constable shall distrain any knight to give money for castle guard, if he himself will do it in his person, or by another able man in case he cannot do it through any reasonable cause. And if we lead him, or send him in an army, he shall be free from such guard for the time he shall be in the army by our command.

30. No sheriff or bailiff of ours, or any other, shall take horses or carts of any freeman for carriage, but by the good-will of the said freeman.

31. Neither shall we nor our bailiffs take any man's timber for our castles or other uses, unless by the consent of the owner of the timber.

32. We will retain the lands of those convicted of felony only one year and a day, and then they shall be delivered to the lord of the fee.

33. All weirs for the time to come shall be put down in the rivers of Thames and Medway,

and throughout all England, except upon the seacoast.

34. The writ which is called Praecipe, for the future, shall not be made out to any one, of any tenement, whereby a freeman may lose his court.

35. There shall be one measure of wine and one of ale through our whole realm; and one measure of corn, that is to say, the London quarter; and one breadth of dyed cloth, and russets, and haberjeets, that is to say, two ells within the lists; and it shall be of weights as it is of measures.

36. Nothing from henceforth shall be given or taken for a writ of inquisition of life or limb, but it shall be granted freely, and not denied.

37. If any do hold of us by fee-farm, or by socage, or by burgage, and he hold also lands of any other by knight's service, we will not have the custody of the heir or land, which is holden of another man's fee by reason of that fee- farm, socage, or burgage; neither will we have the custody of such fee-farm, socage, or burgage, except knight's service was due to us out of the same fee- farm. We will not have the custody of an heir, nor of any land which he holds of another by knight's service, by reason of any petty serjeanty that holds of us, by the service of paying a knife, an arrow, or the like.

38. No bailiff from henceforth shall put any man to his law upon his own bare saying, without credible witnesses to prove it.

39. No freeman shall be taken or imprisoned, or disseised, or outlawed, or banished, or any ways destroyed, nor will we pass upon him, nor will we send upon him, unless by the lawful judgment of his peers, or by the law of the land.

40. To none will we sell, to none will we deny, or delay, right or justice.

41. All merchants shall have safe and secure conduct, to go out of, and to come into England, and to stay there, and to pass as well by land as by water, for buying and selling by the ancient and allowed customs without any evil tolls; except in time of war, or when they are of any nation at war with us. And if there be found any such in our land, in the beginning of the war, they shall be attached, without damage to their bodies or goods, until it be known unto us or our chief justiciary, how our merchants be treated in the nation at war with us; and if ours be safe there, the others shall be safe in our dominions.

42. It shall be lawful for the time to come, for any one to go out of our kingdom, and return safely and securely, by land or by water, saving his allegiance to us; unless in time of war, by some short space, for the common benefit of the realm, except prisoners and outlaws, according to the law of the land, and people in war with us, and merchants who shall be in such condition as is above mentioned.

43. If any man hold of any escheat, as of the honour of Wallingford, Nottingham, Boulogne, Lancaster, or of other escheats which be in our hands, and are baronies and die, his heir shall give no other relief, and perform no other service to us, than he would to the baron, if it were in the baron's hands; we will hold it after the same manner as the

baron held it.

44. Those men who dwelt without the forest, from henceforth shall not come before our justiciaries of the forest, upon common summons, unless such as are impleaded, or are pledges for any that are attached for something concerning the forest.

45. We will not make any justices, constables, sheriffs, or bailiffs, but of such as know the law of the realm and mean duly to observe it.

46. All barons who have founded abbeys, and have the kings of England's charters of advowson, or the ancient tenure thereof, shall have the keeping of them, when vacant, as they ought to have.

47. All forests that have been made forests in our time, shall forthwith be disforested; and the same shall be done with the water banks that have been fenced in by us in our time.

48. All evil customs concerning forests, warrants, foresters and warreners, sheriffs and their officers, rivers and their keepers shall forthwith be inquired into in each county, by twelve sworn knights of the same shire, chosen by creditable persons of the same county; and within forty days after the said inquest, be utterly abolished, so as never to be restored: so as we are first acquainted therewith, or our justiciary, if we should not be in England.

49. We will immediately give up all hostages and writings delivered unto us by our English subjects, as securities for their keeping the peace, and yielding us faithful service.

50. We will entirely remove from our bailiwicks the relations of Gerard de Atheyes, so that for the future they shall have no bailiwick in England; we will also remove Engelard de Cygony, Andrew, Peters, and Gyon, from the Chan- cery; Gyon de Cygony, Geoffrey de Martyn and his brothers; Philip Mark, and his brothers, and his nephew, Geoffrey, and their whole retinue.

51. As soon as peace is restored, we will send out of the kingdom all foreign soldiers, cross-bowmen, and stipendiaries, who are come with horses and arms to the prejudice of our people.

52. If any one has been dispossessed or deprived by us, without the legal judgment of his peers, of his lands, castles, liberties, or right, we will forthwith restore them to him; and if any dispute arise upon this head, let the matter be decided by the five-and-twenty barons hereafter mentioned, for the preservation of the peace. As for all those things of which any person has, without the legal judgment of his peers, been dispossessed or deprived, either by King Henry our father, or our brother King Richard, and which we have in our hands, or are possessed by others, and we are bound to warrant and make good, we shall have a respite till the term usually allowed the crusaders; excepting those things about which there is a plea depending, or whereof an inquest hath been made, by our order, before we undertook the crusade, but when we return from our pilgrimage, or if perchance we tarry at home and do not make our pilgrimage, we will immediately cause full justice to be administered therein.

53. The same respite we shall have (and in the same manner about adminis- tering justice, disafforesting the forests, or letting them continue) for disaffor- esting the forests, which Henry our father, and our brother Richard have afforested; and for the keeping of the lands which are in another's fee, in the same manner as we have hitherto enjoyed those wardships, by reason of a fee held of us by knight's service; and for the abbeys founded in any other fee than our own, in which the lord of the fee says he has a right; and when we return from our pilgrimage, or if we tarry at home, and do not make our pilgrimage, we will immediately do full justice to all the complainants in this behalf.

54. No man shall be taken or imprisoned upon the appeal of a woman, for the death of any other than her husband.

55. All unjust and illegal fines made by us, and all amerciaments imposed unjustly and contrary to the law of the land, shall be entirely given up, or else be left to the decision of the five-and-twenty barons hereafter mentioned for the preservation of the peace, or of the major part of them, together with the aforesaid Stephen, archbishop of Canterbury, if he can be present, and others whom he shall think fit to take along with him; and if he cannot be present, the business shall notwithstanding go on without him; but so that if one or more of the aforesaid five-and-twenty barons be plaintiffs in the same cause, they shall be set aside as to what concerns this particular affair, and others be chosen in their room, out of the said five-and-twenty, and sworn by the rest to decide the matter.

56. If we have disseised or dispossessed the Welsh, of any lands, liberties, or other things, without the legal judgment of their peers, either in England or in Wales, they shall be immediately restored to them; and if any dispute arise upon this head, the matter shall be determined in the marche by the judgment of their peers; for tenements in England according to the law of England, for tenements in Wales according to the law of Wales, for tenements of the marche according to the law of the marche; the same shall the Welsh do to us and our subjects.

57. As for all those things of which a Welshman hath, without the legal judgment of his peers, been disseised or deprived of by King Henry our father, or our brother King Richard, and which we either have in our hands, or others are possessed of, and we are obliged to warrant it, we shall have a respite till the time generally allowed the crusaders; excepting those things about which a suit is depending, or whereof an inquest has been made by our order, before we undertook the crusade; but when we return, or if we stay at home without performing our pilgrimage, we will immediately do them full justice, according to the laws of the Welsh and of the parts before mentioned.

58. We will without delay dismiss the son of Llewellin, and all the Welsh hostages, and release them from the engagements they have entered into with us for the preservation of the peace.

59. We will treat with Alexander, King of Scots, concerning the restoring his sisters and hostages, and his right and liberties, in the same form and manner as we shall do to the rest of our barons of England; unless by the charters which we have from his father, William,

late King of Scots, it ought to be otherwise; but this shall be left to the determination of his peers in our court.

60. All the aforesaid customs and liberties, which we have granted to be holden in our kingdom, as much as it belongs to us, towards our people of our kingdom, as well clergy as laity shall observe, as far as they are concerned, towards their tenants.

61. And whereas, for the honour of God and the amendment of our kingdom, and for the better quieting the discord that has arisen between us and our barons, we have granted all these things aforesaid; willing to render them firm and lasting, we do give and grant our subjects the underwritten security, namely, that the barons may choose five-and-twenty barons of the kingdom, whom they think convenient; who shall take care, with all their might, to hold and observe, and cause to be observed, the peace and liberties we have granted them, and by this our present charter confirmed; so that if we, our justiciary, our bailiffs, or any of our officers, shall in any circumstance fail in the performance of them towards any person, or shall break through any of these articles of peace and security, and the offence be notified to the four barons chosen out of the five-and-twenty before mentioned, the said four barons shall repair to us, or our justiciary, if we are out of the realm, and laying open the grievance, shall petition to have it redressed without delay; and if it be not redressed by us, or if we should chance to be out of the realm, if it should not be redressed by our justiciary, within forty days, reckoning from the time it has been notified to us, or to our justiciary, (if we should be out of the realm,) the four barons aforesaid shall lay the cause before the rest of the five-and-twenty barons; and the said five-and-twenty barons, together with the community of the whole kingdom, shall distrain and distress us in all possible ways, by seizing our castles, lands, possessions, and in any other manner they can, till the grievance is redressed according to their pleasure; saving harmless our own person, and the persons of our queen and children; and when it is redressed, they shall obey us as before. And any person whatsoever in the kingdom, may swear that he will obey the orders of the five-and-twenty barons aforesaid, in the execution of the premises, and will distress us, jointly with them, to the utmost of his power; and we give public and free liberty to any one that shall please to swear to this, and never will hinder any person from taking the same oath.

62. As for all those of our subjects who will not, of their own accord, swear to join the five-and-twenty barons in distraining and distressing us, we will issue orders to make them take the same oath as aforesaid. And if any one of the five-and-twenty barons dies, or goes out of the kingdom, or is hindered any other way from carrying the things aforesaid into execution, the rest of the said five-and-twenty barons may choose another in his room, at their discretion, who shall be sworn in like manner as the rest. In all things that are committed to the execution of these five-and-twenty barons, if, when they are all assembled together, they should happen to disagree about any matter, and some of them, when summoned, will not, or cannot, come, whatever is agreed upon, or enjoined by the major part of those that are present, shall be reputed as firm and valid as if all the five-and-twenty had given their consent; and the aforesaid five-and-twenty shall swear, that all the premises

they shall faithfully observe, and cause with all their power to be observed. And we will not, by ourselves, or by any other, procure anything whereby any of these concessions and liberties may be revoked or lessened; and if any such thing be obtained, let it be null and void; neither shall we ever make use of it, either by ourselves or any other. And all the ill will, indignations, and rancours that have arisen between us and our subjects, of the clergy and laity, from the first breaking out of the dissensions between us, we do fully remit and forgive: moreover all trespasses occasioned by the said dissensions, from Easter in the fifteenth year of our reign, till the restoration of peace and tranquility, we hereby entirely remit to all, both clergy and laity, and as far as in us lies do fully forgive. We have, moreover, caused to be made for them the letters patent testimonial of Stephen, lord archbishop of Canterbury, Henry, lord archbishop of Dublin, and the bishops aforesaid, as also of master Pandulph, for the security and concessions aforesaid.

63.   Wherefore we will and firmly enjoin, that the Church of England be free, and that all the men in our kingdom have and hold all the aforesaid liberties, rights, and concessions, truly and peaceably, freely and quietly, fully and wholly to themselves and their heirs, of us and our heirs, in all things and places, for ever, as is aforesaid. It is also sworn, as well on our part as on the part of the barons, that all the things aforesaid shall be observed bona fide and without evil subtilty. Given under our hand, in the presence of the witnesses above named, and many others, in the meadow called Runnymede, between Windsor and Staines, the 15th day of June, in the 17th year of our reign.

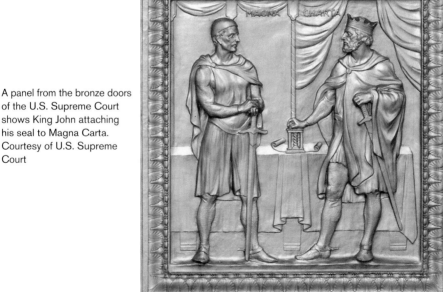

A panel from the bronze doors of the U.S. Supreme Court shows King John attaching his seal to Magna Carta. Courtesy of U.S. Supreme Court

Endnotes

Magna Carta and the Rule of Law

Justice Sandra Day O'Connor

This article originally appeared in *The Majesty of the Law: Reflections of a Supreme Court Justice* and is reproduced here with the author's permission.

1. Winston S. Churchill, *The Birth of Britain* 257 (1956).

2. A Confirmation of the Great Charter, and the Charter of the Forest, Statutes Made at London the Tenth Day of October, Anno 25 Edw. I. and Anno Dom. 1297, in The Statutes at Large from Magna Charta to the End of the Eleventh Parliament of Great Britain, Anno. 1761, at 274 (1762) (all spellings have been Americanized).

3. 1 John Winthrop, The History of New England from 1630 to 1649, at 160 (1825).

4. John Adams, "A Defence of the Constitutions of Government of the United States of America Against the Attack of M. Turgot, in His Letter to Dr. Price, Dated the Twenty-Second Day of March, 1778," in *The Works of John Adams* 404 (1851).

5. U.S. Const., Art. I, § 7.

6. U.S. Const., Amdt. 1.

7. U.S. Const., Amdt. 6.

8. U.S. Const., Art. III, § 1.

9. J.C. Holt, *Magna Carta* 461 (2d ed. 1992) (as translated from the original Latin text).

10. U.S. Const., Amdt. 5.

11. *Solem v. Helm,* 463 U.S. 277, 284–285 (1983).

12. *Duncan v. Louisiana,* 391 U.S. 145, 151 (1968).

13. *Smith v. Bennett,* 365 U.S. 708, 712 (1961).

14. Holt, *supra* note 9, at 461 (1992).

Magna Carta in America, From the World's Fair to World War

Susan Reyburn

1. "The Lincoln Magna Carta Washington Ceremony." *The Times.* January 12, 1946.

2. Mearns, David C., and Clapp, Verner. *Magna Carta–The Lincoln Cathedral Copy Exhibited in the Library of Congress.* Washington, D.C.: Government Printing Office, 1941, p. 15. See also A. F. Kendrick, *The Cathedral Church of Lincoln.* London: G. Bell and Sons, 1902, pp. 59, 65, and 141 at http://gwydir.demon.co.uk/PG/BellsLincoln/BellsLincoln.htm.

3. Botfield, Beriah. *Notes on the Cathedral Libraries of England.* London : [W. Pickering], 1849, p. 268 and at http://archive.org/details/cu31924029534413. See also

The Archaeology Journal, "Contents of the Muniment Room of Lincoln Cathedral," Rev. Prebendary Wickenden, 1881, p. 311.

4. Aside from the Lincoln Cathedral copy, which is regarded as the best preserved and easiest to read, two others are in the British Library (once part of the British Museum) and the fourth is at Salisbury Cathedral.

5. Mearns, David C., and Clapp, Verner, p. 15. See also *The Archaeology Journal*, "Contents of the Muniment Room of Lincoln Cathedral," Rev. Prebendary Wickenden, 1881, p. 312.

6. "In Its Bullet-Proof Frame: Magna Carta Once More at Lincoln." *Illustrated London News*. February 2, 1946.

7. "Moving Magna Carta to New York—A Bullet Proof Case," *The Times*, April 10, 1939.

8. Bisset, James. *Commodore: War, Peace and Big Ships*. New York: Criterion, 1962, p. 437.

9. *Guide to the British Pavilion, United Kingdom Section*. London: H. M. Stationery's Office, 1940, p. 82.

10. "Magna Carta at World's Fair—Lincoln to Lend Copy to U.S.," *The Sunday Times*, January 22, 1939, p. 18. See also the *Annual Report of the American Scenic and Historic Preservation Society*. No. 26, 1921, p. 184.

11. Letter, Sol Bloom to Archibald MacLeish, October 9, 1939. Library of Congress Central Files, Container 787. Manuscript Division, Library of Congress.

12. Letter, Archibald MacLeish to Franklin D. Roosevelt, November 2, 1939. Library of Congress Central Files, Container 787. Manuscript Division, Library of Congress.

13. Letter, President Franklin D. Roosevelt to Archibald MacLeish, November 4, 1939. Library of Congress Central Files, Container 787. Manuscript Division, Library of Congress.

14. The Declaration of Independence and the U.S. Constitution were transferred to the National Archives in 1952.

15. "Magna Carta's First Headline in 700 Years!" *Chicago Tribune*, November 29, 1939.

16. "Congress Library Gets Magna Carta," *New York Times*, November, 29, 1939.

17. "Lothian, at Fair, Denounces Duce," *New York Times*, June 13, 1939.

18. Remarks, "Deposit of Magna Carta," Archibald MacLeish. Washington, D.C., November 28, 1939. Library of Congress Central Files, Container 787. Manuscript Division, Library of Congress, and at http://www.loc.gov/item/mff000141/.

19. Jefferson's books remain the nucleus of the Library of Congress. In 1980, the building where Magna Carta was exhibited was renamed for him.

20. Remarks, "Deposit of Magna Carta," Archibald MacLeish. Washington, D.C., November 28, 1939. Library of Congress Central Files, Container 787. Manuscript Division, Library of Congress, and at http://www.loc.gov/item/mff000141/.

21. MacLeish recognized that there was scholarly debate over the charter's meaning for medieval commoners and their descendants. "I am aware of course that the precise historical significance of Magna Carta is in dispute among the doctors," he said in his speech. But he believed that even if the document was intended by its creators "to safeguard the vested rights of a few land-owners and deer-killers in thirteenth-century England," its limitation of absolute power was the idea that mattered.

22. "Magna Carta's First Headline in 700 Years!" *Chicago Tribune*, November 29, 1939.

23. Ibid.

24. *Magna Carta—The Lincoln Cathedral Copy Exhibited in the Library of Congress—* Some Notes Prepared by David C. Mearns & Verner Clapp, Washington, D.C., 1939, 1941.

25. "The British Pavilion," *Hartford Courant*, February 19, 1940.

26. Letter, Archibald MacLeish to Lord Lothian, April 16, 1940. Library of Congress Central Files, Container 787. Manuscript Division, Library of Congress.

27. *Guide to the British Pavilion, United Kingdom Section.* London: H. M. Stationery's Office, 1940, p. 70 (errata notice pasted in).

28. "Lothian, at Fair, Denounces Duce," *New York Times*, June 13, 1939.

29. "New York Fair Bomb Kills Two," *Los Angeles Times*, July 5, 1940. "Bomb from British Pavilion Kills 2, Hurts 5 at N.Y. Fair," *Washington Post*, July 5, 1940, and "Police Die in Blast," *New York Times*, July 5, 1940.

30. "Mysterious Box at World's Fair," *New York Times*, July 8, 1940.

31. Letter, Archibald MacLeish to Lord Lothian, September 6, 1940. Library of Congress Central Files, Container 787. Manuscript Division, Library of Congress.

32. Letter, Lord Lothian to Archibald MacLeish, September 18, 1940. Library of Congress Central Files, Container 787. Manuscript Division, Library of Congress.

33. Letter, Archibald MacLeish to Sam Barlow, October 29, 1940. Library of Congress Central Files, Container 787. Manuscript Division, Library of Congress.

34. Ibid.

35. Letter, Archibald MacLeish to Sam Barlow, December 6, 1940. Library of Congress Central Files, Container 788. Manuscript Division, Library of Congress.

36. Rose, William Ganson. *Cleveland: The Making of a City.* Kent State University Press, 1990, p. 995.

37. Letter, Archibald MacLeish to Phillip Cohen, December 5, 1940. Library of Congress Central Files, Container 787. Manuscript Division, Library of Congress.

38. Roosevelt, Franklin D. "Third Inaugural Address," January 20, 1941.

39. Letter, Verner Clapp to Archibald MacLeish, January 18, 1941. Library of Congress Central Files, Container 787. Manuscript Division, Library of Congress.

40. Memorandum, Office of the Superintendent of the Library Buildings to Mr. Bond, March 6, 1941. Library of Congress Central Files, Container 787. Manuscript Division, Library of Congress. Related information on exhibit case in the LC Central Files, Exhibitions, 25-1.

41. "The War and the National Muniments," Robert Penn Warren, *Quarterly Journal of Current Acquisitions*, Vol. 2, No. 1 (Nov. 1944), p. 65.

42. Archibald MacLeish notes, telephone conversation with Lord Halifax, December 26, 1941. Library of Congress Central Files, Container 787. Manuscript Division, Library of Congress.

43. Only the Declaration of Independence had a short respite from its hiding place at Fort Knox. It returned to Washington, D.C., in April 1943 and was displayed for a week at

the Jefferson Memorial as part of the dedication ceremonies for the new monument. Because space was so limited at Fort Knox, the Library of Congress evacuated more than 4,700 boxes (equivalent to more than eight miles of shelved items) containing rare books, manuscripts, and maps (including L'Enfant's plan of Washington, D.C., some of George Washington's papers, and Thomas Jefferson's first inaugural address) to universities in Pennsylvania and inland Virginia.

44. Letter, Archibald MacLeish to Henry Morgenthau, December 30, 1941. National Archives, Secret Service Records at http://preview.archives.gov/education/research/exhibit/images/macleish-letter-print.pdf.

45. Letter, Archibald MacLeish to Lord Halifax, January 2, 1942. Library of Congress Central Files, Container 788. Manuscript Division, Library of Congress.

46. Letter, Archibald MacLeish to Dean R. A. Mitchell, January 2, 1942. Library of Congress Central Files, Container 788. Manuscript Division, Library of Congress.

47. Letter, Dean R. A. Mitchell to Archibald MacLeish, February 21, 1942. Library of Congress Central Files, Container 788. Manuscript Division, Library of Congress.

48. Warren, p. 66.

49. Message, Henry Morgenthau to Archibald MacLeish, October 5, 1944. Library of Congress Central Files, Container 788. Manuscript Division, Library of Congress.

50. Press release, Office of Information, Library of Congress. "Exhibition Halls of the Library of Congress Open Two and Half Hours Earlier on Sunday," October 1944. Library of Congress Central Files, Container 787. Manuscript Division, Library of Congress.

51. Letter, Sol Bloom to Archibald MacLeish, September 29, 1944. Library of Congress Central Files, Container 787. Manuscript Division, Library of Congress.

52. A versatile and resourceful man, Bloom at the age of twenty-three oversaw construction of the Midway Plaisance and managed its attractions for the 1893 Columbian World's Exposition in Chicago.

53. Letter, Sol Bloom to Archibald MacLeish, October 2, 1944. Library of Congress Central Files, Container 787. Manuscript Division, Library of Congress.

54. Note, Archibald MacLeish to David C. Mearns, September 29, 1944. Library of Congress Central Files, Container 787. Manuscript Division, Library of Congress.

55. Memorandum, Mortimer Taube to Archibald MacLeish, October 3, 1944. Library of Congress Central Files, Container 787. Manuscript Division, Library of Congress.

56. Mearns used examples drawn from the Reports from the Commissioners Appointed by His Majesty to Execute the Measures Recommended by a Select Committee of the House of Commons Respecting the Public Records of the Kingdom, &c., 1800–1819.

57. Memorandum, David C. Mearns to Archibald MacLeish, October 4, 1944. Library of Congress Central Files, Container 787. Manuscript Division, Library of Congress.

58. Letter, Archibald MacLeish to Sol Bloom, October 6, 1944. Library of Congress Central Files, Container 787. Manuscript Division, Library of Congress.

59. The Oxford English Dictionary notes that the term is usually used without the definite article. Congressman Bloom would likely be pleased to know that when the Library of Congress staged an exhibit, *Magna Carta: Muse and Mentor*, in 2014–15, featuring

the Lincoln Magna Carta, it did *not* use the definite article when referring to the charter by name. The exhibit marked the charter's 800th anniversary and the 75th anniversary of its first visit to the Library.

60. Letter, Nevile Butler to Archibald MacLeish, August 10, 1945. Library of Congress Central Files, Container 788. Manuscript Division, Library of Congress. Private letter to MacLeish, who was no longer Librarian of Congress.

61. Letter, Luther Evans to the Secretary of State, July 10, 1945. Library of Congress Central Files, Container 788. Manuscript Division, Library of Congress.

62. "The Lincoln Magna Carta—Washington Ceremony," *The Times*, January 12, 1946.

63. Remarks, Dean R. A. Mitchell, January 11, 1946. Library of Congress Central Files, Container 787. Manuscript Division, Library of Congress.

64. Acme Photo. "Moving Day," January 11, 1946. Library of Congress Central Files, Container 788. Manuscript Division, Library of Congress.

65. Bisset, p. 438.

66. Ibid, p. 439.

Bisset, a much beloved and respected naval officer, served in World Wars I and II, and spent most of 1945–46 transporting 750,000 servicemen home, including American soldiers. As a young sailor, he was serving aboard the *Carpathia* when it rescued more than 700 survivors of the *Titanic* sinking in 1912.

67. Letter, John Balfour to Luther Evans, May 13, 1946. Library of Congress Central Files, Container 788. Manuscript Division, Library of Congress.

68. The Lacock Abbey Magna Carta is one of only four original copies from 1225 known to exist.

69. Letter, Luther Evans to Nevile Butler, stamped September 28, 1945. Library of Congress Central Files, Container 788. Manuscript Division, Library of Congress.

70. Parliamentary Debate, fifth series, vol. 141, cols. 117–121.

71. Ibid.

72. Parliamentary Debate, fifth series, vol. 141, cols.1466–1474.

73. "Magna Carta Put on Display Beside Original Constitution," *Washington Post*, December 16, 1946, and "Lacock Abbey Magna Carta," *The Times*, December 16, 1946.

74. *Notes on the Lacock Abbey Magna Carta of 1225*, Arthur Jeffries Collins, U.S. Government Printing Office, Washington, D.C., 1947.

75. Letter, Arthur Jefferies Collins to Luther Evans, January 6, 1949. Library of Congress Central Files, Container 788. Manuscript Division, Library of Congress.

76. Mearns and Clapp, from the Foreword.

William Marshal, Earl of Pembroke (ca. 1146–1219)

The Right Honourable The Lord Igor Judge

1. Generally I have relied on the chapter devoted to William Marshal in *Magna Carta—Uncovered*, co-authored with Anthony Arlidge QC (shortly to be published in London, 2014) for which the main sources were D Crouch, *William Marshal, Court, Career and Chivalry in the Angevin Empire 1147–1219* (London, 1990); S Painter, *William Marshal, Knight Errant, Baron and Regent of England* (Baltimore, MD 1933); D

Carpenter, *The Struggle for Mastery for Britain 1066–1284* (London, 2004); and J C Holt *Magna Carta* (Cambridge, 2001). Selden Society, *English Law Suits from William 1 to Richard 1, Vol. 2* (London, 1991), 620, 621.

2. Edward Fosse, The Judges of England 1066–1870 (London, 1870).

3. D Crouch, William Marshal, Court, Career and Chivalry in the Angevin Empire 1147–1219 (London, 1990).

4. D Crouch, *Ibid.*

5. D Jones, The Plantagenets, The Kings Who Made England (London, 2012), 220.

6. J R Maddicott, The Origins of the English Parliament 924–1327 (Oxford, 2010), 148.

Magna Carta's Enactment

William C. Koch, Jr.

1. This essay has been modified from its original version. For the original, see William C. Koch, Jr. *Reopening Tennessee's Open Courts Clause: A Historical Reconsideration of Article I, Section 17 of the Tennessee Constitution*, 27 U. Mem. L. Rev. 333 (Winter 1997).

2. A.E. Dick Howard, The Road from Runnymede, Magna Carta and Constitutionalism in America 7, 220 (1968).

3. William S. McKechnie, Magna Carta, A Commentary on the Great Charter of King John 49 (2d ed. 1914).

4. MCKECHNIE, *supra* note 2, at 22.

5. William F. Swindler, Magna Carta, Legend and Legacy 79 (1965).

6. MCKECHNIE, *supra* note 2, at 107, 109.

7. HOWARD, *supra* note 1, at 7.

8. MCKECHNIE, *supra* note 2, at 196; SWINDLER, *supra* note 4, at 87.

9. 1 WILLIAM BLACKSTONE, COMMENTARIES *127–28; 1 EDWARD COKE, THE SECOND PART OF THE INSTITUTES OF THE LAWS OF ENGLAND, A Proeme to the Second Part of the Institutes (London, E. & R. Brooke 1797).

10. MCKECHNIE, *supra* note 2, at 122.

11. MCKECHNIE, *supra* note 2, at 108.

12. HOWARD, *supra* note 1, at 385; MCKECHNIE, *supra* note 2, at 170.

13. This is the most common interpretation of the Latin text, which reads as follows: "NULLUS liber homo capiatur vel imprisonetur, aut disseisiatur, aut utlagetur, aut exuletur, aut aliquo modo destruatur, nec super eum ibimus, nec super eum mittemus, nisi per legale judicium parium suorum vel per legem terre." MCKECHNIE, *supra* note 2, at 375.

14. The Latin text of this chapter reads as follows: "NULLI vendemus, nulli negabimus, aut differemus, rectum aut justiciam." MCKECHNIE, *supra* note 2, at 395.

15. 1 William Blackstone, Commentaries *424; 1 Edward Coke, The Second Part of the Institutes of the Laws of England, A Proeme to the Second Part of the Institutes 50 (London, E. & R. Brooke 1797); 2 James Kent, Commentaries on American Law *12–13.

16. MCKECHNIE, *supra* note 2, at 395.

17. MCKECHNIE, *supra* note 2, at 4.

18. SWINDLER, *supra* note 4, at 21.

19. Four Norman kings ruled England from 1066 until 1154. William I ruled from 1066 to 1087; William II from 1087 to 1100; Henry I from 1100 to 1135; and Stephen from 1135 to 1154.

20. MCKECHNIE, *supra* note 2, at 5.

21. MCKECHNIE, *supra* note 2, at 77.

22. MCKECHNIE, *supra* note 2, at 77–79.

23. SWINDLER, *supra* note 4, at 26.

24. MCKECHNIE, *supra* note 2, at 80.

25. Henry of Anjou ruled from 1154 to 1189. The eight Plantagenet or Angevin monarchs ruled England from 1154 to 1399.

26. MCKECHNIE, *supra* note 2, at 87.

27. MCKECHNIE, *supra* note 2, at 87–88; SWINDLER, *supra* note 4, at 34.

28. MCKECHNIE, *supra* note 2, at 89, 395–96.

29. King John ruled England from 1199 to 1216.

30. MCKECHNIE, *supra* note 2, at 91.

31. SWINDLER, *supra* note 4, at 34.

32. MCKECHNIE, *supra* note 2, at 376–77.

33. MCKECHNIE, *supra* note 2, at 378, 383

34. MCKECHNIE, *supra* note 2 at 72, 396–97; SWINDLER, *supra* note 4, at 98.

35. HOWARD, *supra* note 1, at 7; MCKECHNIE, *supra* note 2, at 87.

36. MCKECHNIE, *supra* note 2, at 381–83.

37. MCKECHNIE, *supra* note 2, at 376–77.

38. MCKECHNIE, *supra* note 2, at 378, 386.

39. MCKECHNIE, *supra* note 2, at 379–80.

40. MCKECHNIE, *supra* note 2, at 385.

41. MCKECHNIE, *supra* note 2 at 396.

42. MCKECHNIE, *supra* note 2, at 139.

43. HOWARD, *supra* note 1, at 8; MCKECHNIE, *supra* note 2, at 45–46; SWINDLER, *supra* note 4, at 100–01.

44. SWINDLER, *supra* note 4, at 101–02.

45. MCKECHNIE, *supra* note 2, at 139; SWINDLER, *supra* note 4, at 104.

46. HOWARD, *supra* note 1, at 8; SWINDLER, *supra* note 4, at 104.

47. HOWARD, *supra* note 1, at 8; SWINDLER, *supra* note 4, at 105.

48. MCKECHNIE, *supra* note 2, at 139.

49. SWINDLER, *supra* note 4, at 105.

50. MCKECHNIE, *supra* note 2, at 142.

51. MCKECHNIE, *supra* note 2, at 141–42.

52. MCKECHNIE, *supra* note 2, at 142–43.

53. SWINDLER, *supra* note 4, at 105.

54. MCKECHNIE, *supra* note 2, at 145–46; SWINDLER, *supra* note 4, at 107.

55. MCKECHNIE, *supra* note 2, at 146. For a more detailed discussion of the contents of the Charter of the Forest, see SWINDLER, *supra* note 4, at 112–16.

56. SWINDLER, *supra* note 4, at 107. Professor McKechnie's work on Magna Carta provides a detailed discussion of the differences between the tentative reissue of the Charter in 1216 and the Charter of Liberties of 1217. *See* MCKECHNIE, *supra* note 2, at 146–51.

57. MCKECHNIE, *supra* note 2, at 151–52.

58. MCKECHNIE, *supra* note 2, at 152–53.

59. MCKECHNIE, *supra* note 2, at 154; SWINDLER, *supra* note 4, at 112.

60. MCKECHNIE, *supra* note 2, at 120; SWINDLER, *supra* note 4, at 241.

61. MCKECHNIE, *supra* note 2, at 155. The language of Magna Carta became stereotyped after 1225. Later Plantagenet and Lancastrian monarchs confirmed Magna Carta in the language of the 1225 Charter. Changes in the law were included in supplementary documents. MCKECHNIE, *supra* note 2, at 158–59.

62. SWINDLER, *supra* note 4, at 112.

63. SWINDLER, *supra* note 4, at 98.

64. SWINDLER, *supra* note 4, at 316–17. The Latin text of Chapter 29 is

    NULLUS liber homo capiatur, vel imprisonetur, aut disseisietur de libero tenemento suo, vel libertatibus, vel liberis consuetudinibus suis, aut utlagetur, aut exuletur, aut aliquo modo destruatur, nec super eum ibimus, nec super eum mittemus, nisi per legale judicium parium suorum, vel per legem terrae. Nulli vendemus, nulli negabimus, aut differemus justitiam, vel rectum.

    1 COKE, *supra* note 14, at *45.

65. MCKECHNIE, *supra* note 2, at 123–24; SWINDLER, *supra* note 4, at 226.

66. HOWARD, *supra* note 1, at 2, 370.

67. 1 Bernard Schwartz, The Bill of Rights, A Documentary History 7 (1971).

68. EDWARD DUMBAULD, THE BILL OF RIGHTS AND WHAT IT MEANS TODAY 90 (1957); HOWARD, *supra* note 1, at 298–99; Christopher Wolfe, *The Original Meaning of the Due Process Clause, in* THE BILL OF RIGHTS: ORIGINAL MEANING AND CURRENT UNDERSTANDING, 213, 220 (Eugene W. Hickok, Jr. ed., 1991).

69. McKechnie, *supra* note 2, at 398; Ray Stringham, Magna Carta, Fountainhead of Freedom 56 (1966).

Magna Carta and Religion, for the Honor of God and the Reform of Our Realm

Robin Griffith-Jones

1. On 7 June 2014 the Temple Church held an international conference, *Magna Carta, Religion and the Rule of Law*. The papers, with additional chapters, are published under the same title, edited by Professor Mark Hill QC and myself, by Cambridge

University Press, 2015. In the following pages I draw with gratitude on several of the important chapters in this volume.

2. This is emphasized by Rabbi Lord Sacks, 'The Great Covenant of Liberties: Biblical Principles and Magna Carta', in *Magna Carta, Religion and the Rule of Law* (above, n. 1)

3. English Churches ('les yglises d'Engleterre') in the Norman-French version republished by J C Holt, 'A vernacular-French Text of Magna Carta, 1215', (1974) 89 *EHR* 346-64. N Vincent, 'Stephen Langton, Archbishop of Canterbury', in *Étienne Langton: prédicateur, bibliste, theologien*, eds L-J Bataillon, N Beriou, G Dahan and R Quinto (Turnhout, 2010), pp 51–123, lists some of the precedents for the grant of such liberty.

4. R H Helmholz, *The Oxford History of the Laws of England*, vol 1 (Oxford, 2004), p 116.

5. Edward Grim, eye-witness of the murder, in M Staunton (ed), *The Lives of Thomas Becket* (Manchester, 2001), p 201.

6. J C Holt, *Magna Carta*, 2nd ed. (Cambridge 1992), pp 418–28.

7. Ibid., pp 429–40.

8. Richard Helmholz, The Oxford History of the Laws of England, I, 2004, 55–6.

9. C R Cheney and W H Semple, *Select Letters of Innocent III* (London, 1953), p 155.

10. J C Holt, *Magna Carta*, p 219, discusses the terms of the oath and its significance.

11. Roger of Wendover in *Chron Maj* II. 552–4. Roger's account is defended (against, for example, Holt) by J H Baldwin, above n. 000. Roger relays the story, *ut fama refert*; he is either party to an invention, and suspects or knows as much; or the meeting was (as it must have been) as private as it was dangerous.

12. *Chron Maj* II.552-1.2

13. Select Letters of Innocent III, 196.

14. John Baldwin, 'Master Stephen Langton, future Archbishop of Canterbury: This Paris Schools and Magna Carta', (2008) 123 *EHR*, 811–46. He extends this argument to embrace the biblical conception of due process, J H Baldwin, 'Due Process in Magna Carta: Its Sources in English Law, Canon Law and Stephen Langton', in *Magna Carta, Religion and the Rule of Law* (above, n. 1).

15. Translations are from the Vulgate.

16. Vincent, 'Stephen Langton', pp. 74–5.

17. Langton's episcopal *familia* included the canonists William of Bardnay and Adam of Tilney. Eustace, Bishop of Ely and papal judge delegate, was said to have been active in the negotiations leading to Runnymede. R H Helmholz, 'Magna Carta and the ius commune', (1999) 66 *University of Chicago Law Review* 297–371, at 361.

18. For a challenge to Helmholz's argument, J Hudson, 'Magna Carta, the ius commune and English Common Law', in *Magna Carta and the England of King John*, ed. J S Loengard (Woodbridge, 2010), pp 99–119.

19. Helmholz, 'Magna Carta and the ius commune', and now 'Magna Carta and the Law of Nations' in *Magna Carta, Religion and the Rule of Law* (above, n.1). The *Liber Augustalis* also, less predictably, punished the preparers of love potions.

20. H J Berman, *Law and Revolution* (Cambridge, Mass, 1983), p 294.

21. D Carpenter has challenged Baldwin's appraisal of Archbishop Langton's role,

principles, character, and role, 'Archbishop Langton and Magna Carta: His Contribution, His Doubts and His Hypocrisy', (2011) 126 *EHR* 1041–65.

22. B Tierney, Religion, *Law and the Growth of Constitutional Thought* (Cambridge, 1982), pp. 12–13. 'The Papal Revolution' is the favoured term of H Berman in his classic *Law and Revolution: The Formation of the Western Legal Tradition* (Harvard, 1983).

23. *Chron Maj* II, pp 454–6.

24. L Siedentop, *Inventing the Individual* (London, 2014).

25. I Judge, 'Magna Carta', in *Magna Carta, Religion and the Rule of Law* (above. n.1).

26. J Stevenson (ed), *Chronica de Mailros* (Edinburgh, 1835), pp 117–9. I am grateful to Professor David Carpenter for bringing these verses to my attention.

27. A E Sullivan, *The Church shall be free* (Charlottsville, 1965 [in *Magna Carta Essays*, ed. A E Dick Howard]), p 5.

28. http://www.bbc.com/news/uk-19739066, 27 September 2012 (accessed 31 May 2014).

29. https://www.gov.uk/government/news/british-values-article-by-david-cameron (accessed 11 July 2014).

30. 'I believe we should be more confident about our status as a Christian country, more ambitious about expanding the role of faith-based organisations, and, frankly, more evangelical about a faith that compels us to get out there and make a difference to people's lives,' *Church Times*, 17 April 2014, http://www.churchtimes.co.uk/articles/2014/17-april/comment/opinion/my-faith-in-the-church-of-england (accessed 21 August 2014). In response: 'David Cameron fosters division by calling Britain a Christian Society', *Daily Telegraph*, 20 April 2014 http://www.telegraph.co.uk/comment/letters/10777417/David-Cameron-fosters-division-by-calling-Britain-a-Christian-country.html (accessed 31 May 2014)..

31. http://www.telegraph.co.uk/news/religion/10789740/Rowan-Williams-I-didnt-really-want-to-be-Archbishop.htm (accessed 21 August 2014). Lord Williams was using 'quite' in the English sense to qualify—and not in the American sense to strengthen—his claim.

32. B Hale, 'Freedom of Religion and Belief', Annual Human Rights Lecture for the Law Society of Ireland, 13 June 2014; T Etherton, 'Religion, the rule of law and discrimination', (2014) 16 Ecc LJ 265–282.

33. *Taylor's Case* (1676) 1 Vent 293, 86 ER 189; T Etherton, 'Religion, the Rule of Law and Discrimination', (2014) 16 *Ecc LJ* (2014) 265–282.

34. Accessible at http://www.publications.parliament.uk/pa/ld201415/ldhansrd/text/140718-0001.htm (accessed 2 August 2014).

35. They are eloquently expounded by Martha Nussbaum in (eg) *The Therapy of Desire* (Princeton, 1994). Baroness Mary Warnock wrote forthrightly about the influence (which she believed to be ill-informed and harmful) actively exercised by religious bodies on recent debates in the UK about the start and end of life, M Warnock and E Macdonald *Easeful Death: Is There a Case for Assisted Dying?* (Oxford, 2008)

36. We have at the Temple Church given much thought to Islam and English law, ever since Rowan Williams, as Archbishop of Canterbury, delivered for us his lecture on sharia law. See R Griffith-Jones (ed), *Islam and English Law* (Cambridge, 2013).

37. J Billaud, 'Ethics and Affects in British Sharia Councils: "A Simple Way of Getting to Paradise"', in *Islam and Public Controversy in Europe*, ed N Gole (Farnham, 2014), pp 159–75.

38. *Refah Partisi (Welfare Party) and Others v. Turkey* (No 2) (2003) 37 EHRR 1 (GC); *Lautsi v Italy* (2012) 54 EHRR 3 (GC). These points are made by W Hallaq, 'Quranic Magna Carta: On the Origins of the Rule of Law in Pre-Modern Islam', and A Gomaa, 'Justice in Islamic Legislation' in *Magna Carta, Religion and the Rule of Law* (above, n.1).

39. J Dyson, 'Strengthened by the Rule of Law: The Message of Magna Carta for Religions Today', in *Magna Carta, Religion and the Rule of Law* (above, n.1).

40. Diasporic traditions may find such accommodation easier to conceive. It is a principle in Judaism and Islam that the laws of the host-state are to be observed: in Judaism, since the exile to Babylon; in Islam, as part of the law of contract. We may be seeing, in a growing Muslim population in the West, an increasingly reluctant complaisance in the face of this subaltern position.

41. J Winthrop, *History of New England* (1630–49), in H D Hazeltine, 'The Influence of Magna Carta on American Constitutional Development, (1917) 17 *Columbia Law Review* 1 (10).

42. J C Holt, *The Northerners* (Cambridge, 1991), 2.

43. F M Powicke and C R Cheney, *Councils and Synods with Other Documents Relating to the English Church*, 2 vols (Oxford, 1964), vol 2, part I, p 138.

44. Powicke and Cheney, *Councils and Synods*, vol 2, part 1, pp 474–9; and now D Carpenter, 'Magna Carta 1253: the ambitions of the Church and the divisions within the realm', (2013) 86 *Historical Research* 180 and 'More light on Henry III's confirmation of Magna Carta in 1253', (2013) 86 *Historical Research* 192.

45. See Magna Carta, Religion and the Rule of Law (above, n. 1), passim.

The Legal Force and Effect of Magna Carta

Sir John Baker

1. In this paper the numbering of the 1225 charter is followed, since the 1215 charter never had any legal consequences.

2. The bull *Etsi karissimus*, dated 24 August 1215, survives in the British Library and is printed in C. Bémont, *Chartes des Libertés Anglaises* (Paris, 1892), pp. 41–44.

3. Readings were lectures, always given on statutes. For the previously unpublished readings referred to in this paper see J. Baker ed., *Selected Readings and Commentaries on Magna Carta 1400–1604* (132 Selden Soc., forthcoming in 2015).

4. For the previously unpublished readings on chapter 1 see M. McGlynn ed., *The Rights and Liberties of the English Church: Readings from the pre-Reformation Inns of Court* (129 Selden Soc., forthcoming in 2014 or 2015).

5. E.g., *Rotuli Parliamentorum* [1783] (hereafter Rot. Parl.), i. 286; ii. 7; iii. 15. There is now an Internet edition, Parliament Rolls of Medieval England, but it is not as complete as the old edition.

6. Rot. Parl. iii. 100, no. 13.

7. W. Lambarde, *Eirenarcha* (1581), p. 436. This was also Selden's view: G. J. Toomer, *John Selden: A Life in Scholarship* (Oxford, 2009), i. 185. Selden's original opinion was that *lex terrae* meant wager of law, as a natural complement to the jury trial of *judicium parium*, though he later changed his mind and held that it meant English as opposed to Roman law. For Coke's more orthodox view see 2 Co. Inst. 55.

8. Such a claim seems to have been accepted in *R. v. Sir Hugh FitzHenry* (1293/4) Y.B. 30 & 31 Edw. I (Rolls Series), pp. 529–32 (misdated). Although Magna Carta was not mentioned, 'non debeo judicari nisi per meos pares' seems to allude to c. 29. As to peers of the realm cf. below, n. 12.

9. No precedents could be found when the notion was firmly rejected (as to an esquire) in *R. v. Thomas* (1554) Dyer 99. The doubt there had arisen from the phrase 'gentz de lour condition' in the Statute of Treasons 1350.

10. *Prohibitions del Roy* (1607) 12 Co. Rep. 63.

11. As to criminal cases, cf. *Gilbert Basset's Case* (1234) in *Bracton's Notebook*, ii. 664–7; discussed by F. M. Powicke in *Magna Carta Commemoration Essays* (1917), pp. 105–7.

12. In civil cases peers were entitled to claim a jury containing at least some knights: *Oxford History of the Laws of England*, vi. 354. This rule, revived in the sixteenth century, does not seem to have been related to c. 29 but to earlier requirements of substantial juries in important cases: see *Anon.* (1323) Mich. 17 Edw. II, Fitz. Abr., *Attaint*, pl. 69; *Helygan v. Bishop of Exeter* (1340) Y.B. Trin. 13 Edw. III (Rolls Series), p. 283, pl. 1, at p. 291; Fitz. Abr., *Challenge*, pl. 115; CP 40/319, m. 303.

13. In about 1330 the archbishop of York complained to the Council that the king's bailiff had seized the franchises of the port of Hull without judgment or due process, contrary to Magna Carta: Public Record Office, SC 8/11/515. Cf. *Countess of Pembroke v. Holand* (1328) SC 8/11/510, where the countess asked the Council that no writ should issue to oust her from a castle without her being summoned by due process according to the law of the realm.

14. 42 Edw. III, c. 1. This was in response to a Commons' petition: Rot. Parl. ii. 295, no. 10. For other assertions that Magna Carta might defeat other legislation, see C. H. McIlwain, 'Magna Carta and Common Law' in *Magna Carta Commemoration Essays*, ed. H. E. Malden (1917), at pp. 173–6.

15. 2 Co. Inst., proemium; ibid. 55 (referring to the abolition of the writ de *odio et atia* in 1285). It is necessary to bear in mind the distinction between alterations *contra jus* and those merely *praeter jus*: *Bracton on the Laws and Customs of England*, ed. G. E. Woodbine and S. E. Thorne, ii. 289.

16. M. Lobban, A History of the Philosophy of Law in the Common Law World, 1600–1900 (Dordrecht, 2007), p. 46.

17. *R. v. Allen and Tooley* (1614) 2 Buls. 186 at 191, *per* Coke C.J. This was not supported by his example of *odio et atia* (above, n. 15), since the statute of 1285 had (in a saving clause) expressly referred to Magna Carta.

18. *Ex parte Andrewes* (1650) 5 State Tr. 1. These proceedings were regarded after 1660 as those of an illegal regime; but the principle remained in place with respect to legitimate acts of Parliament.

19. *Ex parte Streater* (1653) ibid. 365 at col. 372, 386.

20. Rot. Parl. iii. 116, no. 88.

21. The writ of right initiated a suit in a seigniorial court, and the *justicies* initiated a suit before the sheriff in the county court.

22. 14 Edw. III, stat. 1, c. 14.

23. *Anon.* (1311) Y.B. Mich. 5 Edw. II (63 Selden Soc.), p. 6, pl. 4.

24. In 1377 the citizens of London complained to Parliament that protections were being issued contrary to Magna Carta, and they achieved a modest legislative reform: Rot. Parl. iii. 28, no. 133; 1 Ric. II, c. 28. The later 'prerogative' form of protection, without cause shown, was ruled to be invalid in 1587: 109 Selden Soc. lxxxiii–lxxxv.

25. The only remedy lay in Parliament, or in the king's grace. In *Grey v. Mautravers* (c. 1330) SC 8/48/2400, a petitioner asked the king to order the judges to proceed in such a case, lest he be disinherited contrary to Magna Carta; for this case see also *The Eyre of Northamptonshire 1329–30*, ed. D. W. Sutherland (97 Selden Soc., 1981), pp. 470–1. A later example of improper use is *Melton's Case* (1535) in Baker, *Collected Papers*, iii. 1392–4.

26. *Brownlow v. Michell and Cox* (1615) 1 Rolle Rep. 206; Moo. 842. The case was settled, but the arguments against the writ were fully reported.

27. *Bracton*, ii. 110; iii. 43. This was made explicit in the 1215 charter (clause 61), but the elaborate and somewhat hostile enforcement procedure was dropped in 1225.

28. *The Mirror of Justices*, ed. W. J. Whitaker (7 Selden Soc., 1893), pp. 175–182.

29. 36 Edw. III, stat. 1, c. 13. In 1378 the Commons prayed that lands should not be granted out by patent without an inquest or evidence given in a court of record, so that an owner should not be deprived of them without answer, contrary to Magna Carta: Rot. Parl. iii. 46, no. 66. The petition was granted.

30. J. Baker, *Collected Papers in English Legal History* (Cambridge, 2013), ii. 962. This was in origin an equitable counterpart of the petition of right.

31. *Eyre of London 1321* (86 Selden Soc.), p. 296.

32. *Abbot of Glastonbury's Case* (1411) Y.B. Hil. 12 Hen. IV, fo. 12, pl. 3, at fo. 13, *per* Hankford J.

33. *Knotting's Case* (1407) Y.B. Mich. 9 Hen. IV, fo. 4, pl. 17; 51 Selden Soc. 5, *per* Gascoine C. J., but denied by Hankford J.; cf. Mich. 4 Edw. IV, fo. 25, pl. 3; Mich. 7 Edw. IV, fo. 16, pl. 11.

34. Y. B. Trin. 1 Edw. V, fo. 8, pl. 13, where there is the first explicit statement that the king can do no wrong.

35. *Anon.* (1437/38) 16 Hen. VI, Fitz. Abr., *Monstrans de faits*, pl. 182. Cf. *Tresham's Case* (temp. Edw. IV), remembered in Y.B. Mich. 1 Hen. VII, fo. 4, pl. 5, *per* Hussey C. J. (translation: 'the king cannot arrest a man on suspicion of treason or felony, as his other lieges may, because if he does wrong the party cannot have an action').

36. 94 Selden Soc., intro., p. 72; *OHLE*, vi. 192–3.

37. G. R. Elton, *Studies in Tudor and Stuart Politics and Government* (Cambridge, 1974–83), i. 88–9, citing Public Record Office, KB 8/4/51, 9/453/69 (here translated); J. P. Cooper, 'Henry VII's Last Years Reconsidered' (1959) 2 Historical Jnl 103 at p. 117.

38. *Serjeant Browne's Case* (1532) Spelman's reports, 93 Selden Soc. 183 at p. 184 (there misdated).

39. *Anderson v. Warde* (1554) Dyer 104.

40. *Marshall's Case* (1572) Harvard Law School MS 1192, fo. 25.

41. *Att.-Gen. v. Carpenters' Company of London* (1582) Cambridge University Library, MS Hh. 2. 9, ff. 253–254v.

42. Memorandum on Magna Carta, c. 29 (translated), to be printed for the first time in *Selected Readings and Commentaries on Magna Carta.*

43. 2 Co. Inst. 55.

44. 2 Co. Inst. 56. The two cases he cites are not reports but Latin records, in which no reasons are given.

45. E.g., *Withers's Case* (1610) British Library, MS Hargrave 278, ff 392v–394v; MS Add. 48486, fo. 423.

46. *Bagg's Case* (1615) 11 Co. Rep. 68; 1 Rolle Rep. 65, 224. This is generally regarded as the beginning of *mandamus*, but in 1584 Peryam J. said he had seen a record in Henry VIII's time where a citizen of London was disfranchised, 'and thereupon they directed their writ to the mayor etc. to restore him to his franchise [and] assessed a fine of an hundred marks upon every of them that were parties to the disfranchisement': Cro. Eliz. 33.

47. British Library, MS Harley 4841, fo. 3 (spelling modernised).

48. Ibid. ff. 3v, 51 (translated).

49. Above, p. **, n. 40. The case actually concerned a different point about access to justice rather than the extent of the justice available.

A Lexicographic Look at Magna Carta

Bryan A. Garner

1. H. W. Fowler, A Dictionary of Modern English Usage 338 (1926).

2. H. W. Fowler, *A Dictionary of Modern English Usage* 348 (Sir Ernest Gowers ed., 2d ed. 1965).

3. W. A. Jowitt, *Dictionary of English Law* 1123–24 (1959).

4. Robert W. Burchfield, *The New Fowler's Modern English Usage* 475 ("3d ed." 1996). Burchfield may well have gotten his misinformation from Sidney Greenbaum & Janet Whitcut, *Longman Guide to English Usage* 430 (1988) ("*Charta* is on the whole the preferred American spelling. *Carta* is the British one.").

5. Robert Allen, Pocket Fowler's Modern English Usage 411 (2d ed. 2008).

6. Eric Partridge, Usage and Abusage: A Guide to Good English 185 (1942).

7. Eric Partridge, Usage and Abusage: A Guide to Good English 178 (rev. ed. 1965).

8. Bergen Evans & Cornelia Evans, *A Dictionary of Contemporary English Usage* 286 (1957) ("Partridge declares to British users that for *Magna Charta* should be substituted either the Latin *Magna Carta* or the English *The Great Charter*, since 'Charta is neither Latin nor English.' And indeed it is not . . . ."); Roy H. Copperud, *American Usage and Style: The Consensus* 235 (1980) (same).

9. 2 Funk & Wagnalls New Practical Standard Dictionary of the English Language 803 (1949); Funk & Wagnalls New College Standard Dictionary 717 (1956) (same); 2 Funk & Wagnalls Standard Dictionary of the English Language 766 (int'l ed., 1978) (same).

10. The Random House Dictionary of the English Language 1156 (2d ed. 1987). Cf. The Random House College Dictionary 804 (rev. ed. 1988) (listing Magna Charta first).

11. The Oxford American Dictionary 398 (1980).

12. The New Oxford American Dictionary 1027 (2001).

13. *The Associated Press Stylebook and Libel Manual* 126 (Christopher W. French ed., rev. ed. 1987).

14. United Press International Stylebook 168 (1995).

15. *See, e.g.,* A. E. Dick Howard, "Magna Carta," in 3 *Encyclopedia of the American Constitution* 1195, 1196 (Leonard W. Levy et al. eds., 1986); *The Columbia Encyclopedia* 1658 (5th ed. 1993).

16. *See, e.g.,* 3 *Dictionary of American History* 324 (James Truslow Adams ed., 1940) (an encyclopedia [despite its title] relying heavily on McKechnie).

17. See, e.g., Black's Law Dictionary 1095 (10th ed. 2014).

18. See, e.g., James Stormonth, A Dictionary of the English Language 580 (1885); 6 Century Dictionary and Cyclopedia 3573 (rev. ed. 1911); George Philip Krapp, A Comprehensive Guide to Good English 374 (1927); Frank H. Vizetelly, A Desk-Book of Twenty-Five Thousand Words Frequently Mispronounced 571 (4th ed. 1929); Webster's New International Dictionary of the English Language 1479 (2d ed. 1934); James A. Ballentine, Law Dictionary with Pronunciations 781 (2d ed. 1948); Daniel Jones, An English Pronouncing Dictionary 266 (4th ed. 1937); Norman Lewis, Dictionary of Modern Pronunciation 180 (1963).

19. W. H. P. Phyfe, Ten Thousand Words Often Mispronounced 306 (1906).

20. Charles Harrington Elster, *The Big Book of Beastly Mispronunciations* 101 (2d ed. 2006); Bergen Evans, *Comfortable Words* 98–99 (1962).

21. Elster, *Big Book* at 428–30.

22. See Kenneth G. Wilson, The Columbia Guide to Standard American English 278 (1993).

23. See, e.g., Webster's Third New International Dictionary 1359 (1961); The World Dictionary of Foreign Expressions 235 (Laurie Haight ed., 1999).

24. Ray Stringham, Magna Carta: Fountainhead of Freedom vii (1966).

25. Butterworth's Australian Legal Dictionary 714 (1997).

26. Edward Coke, *The First Part of the Institutes of the Laws of England* § 103, at 80b–81a (1628; Francis Hargrave & Charles Butler eds., 14th ed. 1791).

27. John Harris, *Lexicon Technicum: Or, an Universal English Dictionary of Arts and Sciences* s.v. (1704). In two of these rationales Harris was anticipated by John Cowell: "The reason why it was tearmed *Magna charta*, was either for that it conteined the summe of all the writen lawes in England, or else that there was another Charter of the Forest, established with it, which in quantitie was the lesser of the two." Cowell, *The Interpreter* s.v. (1607).

28. Giles Jacob, *A New Law-Dictionary* s.v. (1729).

29. Id.

30. 17 *Encyclopaedia Britannica* 314 (11th ed. 1911).

31. Max Radin, *The Myth of Magna Carta*, 60 Harv. L. Rev. 1060, 1063 (1947).

32. Thomas Potts, A Compendious Law Dictionary 98 (1803).

33. Mostly in Latin and other Romance-language sources, such as 2 *Enciclopedia Legale* 67 (Francesco Foramiti ed., 1864) (Italian).

34. Samuel Roberts, *Digest of Select British Statutes* 1 (2d ed. 1847).

35. F. W. Maitland, The Constitutional History of England 160 (1931).

36. Giles Jacob, *A New Law-Dictionary* s.v. (1729).

37. 2 Fleta, *Commentarius Juris Anglicani* 93 (2d ed. 1685). *See also* 8 *Encyclopaedia Americana* 197 (Francis Lieber ed., 1836) (main-entry name); 3 *Universal Dictionary of the English Language* 3000 (Robert Hunter ed., 1897).

38. Edward Coke, *The First Part of the Institutes of the Laws of England* § 103, at 80b–81a (1628; Francis Hargrave & Charles Butler eds., 14th ed. 1791).

39. Id.

40. Id.

41. Henerico Spelmano, *Glossarium Archiaologicum* 374 (1687).

42. See., e.g., F. W. Maitland, The Constitutional History of England 160 (1931).

43. *See, e.g.,* Bryan A. Garner, *Garner's Dictionary of Legal Usage* 556 (3d ed. 2011) ("*Magna Carta* does not take the definite article."); Margery Fee & Janice McAlpine, *Guide to Canadian English Usage* 366–67 (2d ed. 2007) ("*Magna Carta* does not take the definite article *the* when it refers to the historical document."); Allan M. Siegal & William G. Connolly, *The New York Times Manual of Style and Usage* 196 (1999) ("*Magna Carta* (not *the* Magna Carta)"); Tim Austin, *The Times Guide to English Style and Usage* 87 (1998) ("*Magna Carta* (not *the* Magna Carta)").

44. Merriam-Webster's Concise Dictionary of English Usage 486 (2002).

45. Bryan A. Garner, *Garner's Modern American Usage* 521 (3d ed. 2009).

46. Geoffrey Robertson, "Human Rights: Legal Concepts," in 2 *Oxford International Encyclopedia of Peace* 355, 357 (Nigel J. Young ed., 2010).

47. 2 Noah Webster, An American Dictionary of the English Language s.v. (1828).

48. 6 *The New English Dictionary* 28 [pagination for *M*] (1908) (*New English* being the initial name of the *Oxford English Dictionary*).

49. Ben Jonson, *New Inn*, act I, sc. i (1630).

50. Louis Filler, A Dictionary of American Social Reform 475 (1963).

51. Thomas Potts, A Compendious Law Dictionary 98 (1803).

52. 2 Noah Webster, *An American Dictionary of the English Language* s.v. (1828) ("MAGNA CHARTA, *n.* [L. great charter.] 1. The great charter, so called, obtained by the English barons from king John, A.D. 1215. This name is also given to the charter granted in the ninth year of Henry III. and confirmed by Edward I.").

53. So called by William Sharp McKechnie, *Magna Carta* 155 (1914).

54. 2 Alexander M. Burrill, *A Law Dictionary and Glossary* 169 (2d ed. 1860). *Cf.* William Sharp McKechnie, *Magna Carta* 155 (1914) ("The third reissue . . . marked the final form assumed by Magna Carta; the identical words were then used which afterwards

became stereotyped and were confirmed, time after time, without further modification. It is this charter of 1225 which (in virtue of the confirmation of Edward I.) still remains on the statute book.").

55. *See Selected Letters of Pope Innocent III* 216 (Christopher R. Cheney & W. H. Semple eds., 1953).

56. Francis Stoughton Sullivan, An Historical Treatise on the Feudal Law, and the Constitution and Laws of England, with a Commentary on Magna Charta 373 (1772).

57. G. R. Hughes, *The Student Law Dictionary* 202 (1936).

58. 2 Alexander M. Burrill, A Law Dictionary and Glossary 169 (2d ed. 1860); Walter A. Shumaker & George Foster Longsdorf, The Cyclopedic Dictionary of Law 570 (1901); 2 Century Dictionary and Encyclopedic Lexicon of the English Language 933 (William Dwight Whitney ed., 1911); 17 Encyclopaedia Britannica 314 (11th ed. 1911); W. A. Jowitt Dictionary of English Law 1123–24 (1959).

59. 3 *Imperial Dictionary of the English Language* 97 (John Ogilvie & Charles Annandale eds., ca. 1886); 3 *Universal Dictionary of the English Language* 3000 (Robert Hunter & Charles Morris eds., 1897).

60. 9 Oxford English Dictionary 190 (2d ed. 1989).

61. J. C. Holt, *Magna Carta* 248 (2d ed. 1992).

62. 2 Funk & Wagnalls New Standard Dictionary of the English Language 1489 (Isaak K. Funk ed., 1943).

63. J. C. Holt, *Magna Carta* 255 (2d ed. 1992).

64. *Id.* at 255–59.

65. The Columbia Encyclopedia 1658–59 (5th ed. 1993).

66. *See* William Sharpe McKechnie, *Magna Carta: A Commentary on the Great Charter of King John* 493 (2d ed. 1914) (reproducing writ issued in 1215) ("Teste meipso apud Runimed. xxiij. die Junii anno regni nostri xvij."); *id.* at 494 (same) ("Teste me ipso apud Runimede, xix. die Junii, anno regni nostri xvij.").

67. William Camden, *Britannia, sive Florentissimorum Regnorum Angliae, Scotiae, Hiberniae et Insularum Adjacentium* 302 (1607) ("Subluit hic pratum quod dixit Renimed Anglus").

68. William Prynne, *The Soveraigne Power of Parliaments and Kingdomes* 10 (2d ed. 1643) ("who appointed the King a day to come and conferre with them in a Meade between Stanes and Windsor, called Running-meade"); *id.* at 17 ("upon the confirmation of the Great Charter and of the Forest by King John, it was agreed and enacted in that Parliamentary assembly at Running-mead").

69. William Atwood, *Jus Anglorum ab Anitquo* 13 (1681) ("The *Liberi Homines* were Tenants in Capite, or at least their Retinue and Tenants in Military Service, which were with them at Runnemede.")

70. Richard Baker, *A Chronicle of the Kings of England* 71 (1684) ("in a Meadow between Windsor and Stanes, called Running Mead, [King John] freely consented to confirm their former Liberties").

71. John Aubrey, *The Natural History and Antiquities of the County of Surrey* 166 (1718) ("On the Backside of Egbam, Northwards, lies *Rumney-Mead*, towards the Thames in which Meadow was sealed Magna Charta").

72. Francis Peck, et al. *Academia Tertia Anglicana; Or, the Antiquarian Annals of Stanford in Lincoln, Rutland, and Northampton Shires* 19 (1727) ("On the 15, of June, when the king met the rebellious barons at Runnimede").

73. 8 *The Scourge, A Satire* 16 (1765) ("To name the day, no English laws impede, when Magna Carta sprung from Runnymede"); *see also* J. Bew, *The Ambulator: Or, the Stranger's Companion in a Tour Round London* 36 (1782) ("Opposite is Runnymede, in which Magna Charta was signed.").

74. Adam Anderson, *An Historical and Chronological Déduction of the Origin of Commerce* 591 (1787) ("on King Henry the Third's signing of the old Magna Charta, near five hundred years before, at *Runny Mead"*).

75. 2 Charles Watkins, *A Treatise on Copyholds* 12 (1799) ("we are told that the celebrated place in this kingdom where the articles of Magna Charta were signed by King John was denominated Runemed.")

76. 2 Alexander M. Burrill, *A Law Dictionary and Glossary* 169 (2d ed. 1860) ("Runningmede or Runemede"); *see also* W.A. Jowitt, *Dictionary of English Law* 1123–24 (1959).

77. Id.

78. Walter A. Shumaker & George Foster Longsdorf, *The Cyclopedic Dictionary of Law* 570 (1901).

79. *See, e.g.,* Thomas Blount, *Glossographia: Or a Dictionary* s.v. (2d ed. 1661). *See also* Thamar E. Dufwa, *The Viking Laws and the Magna Carta* 39–77 (1963) (attributing 63 clauses to Magna Carta).

80. *See* Max Radin, *The Myth of Magna Carta*, 60 Harv. L. Rev. 1060, 1072 (1947) (counting 61 and 38). *See also* Samuel E. Thorne, "What Magna Carta Was," in *The Great Charter: Four Essays on Magna Carta and the History of Our Liberty* 3, 3 (1965) (stating that the 1215 charter had 61 clauses—although the appendix to the book [pp. 111–49] reproduces 63).

81. Burt Franklin, Magna Carta: A Commentary on the Great Charter of King John 139 (1914).

82. *See, e.g., The Oxford Companion to Chaucer* 303–04 (Douglas Gray ed., 2003) (skipping from *magic* to *Mahoun*). Other Chaucerian sources are similarly vacant with respect to Magna Carta. *See also* Max Radin, *The Myth of Magna Carta*, 60 Harv. L. Rev. 1060, 1082 (1947) ("If Chaucer never mentions Magna Carta, it is scarcely strange.").

83. *A New Variorum Edition of Shakespeare: The Life and Death of King John* 351 n.2 (Horace Howard Furness ed., 1919). *See also* 4 *Narrative and Dramatic Sources of Shakespeare* 21 (Geoffrey Bullough ed., 1962) ("Shakespeare . . . avoided introducing the barons' political resentment at John's inroads on their ancient privileges which in fact led to Magna Carta and its aftermath. For him their revolt must spring from virtuous disgust at John's maltreatment of Arthur [Duke of Bretagne, and nephew of King John] . . .").

84. Id.

85. See generally George W. Keeton, Shakespeare's Legal and Political Background (1967); Paul S. Clarkson & Clyde T. Warren, The Law of Property in Shakespeare and the Elizabethan Drama (1942); George W. Keeton, Shakespeare and His Legal Problems (1930); Cushman K. Davis, The Law in Shakespeare (1883).

86. *See* Anne Pallister, *Magna Carta: The Heritage of Liberty* 2 (1971) (stating that "in the fifteenth and sixteenth centuries the Charter declined in importance").

87. *See* O. Hood Phillips, *Shakespeare and the Lawyers* 52 (1972) ("Sir Frederick Pollock thought that the omission of Magna Carta (which was not yet a popular rallying cry anyway) was probably a deliberate touch of dramatic fitness; for John was becoming an English champion against foreign encroachment, and it would have spoilt that effect to bring in his constitutional differences with the barons.") (citing Frederick Pollock, *Outside the Law* 99 (1927)).

88. *See, e.g.,* James D. Teller, "The Law and Lawyers of Shakespeare," 4 *N.Y. State B. Ass'n Rep.* 162–70 (1881).

89. J. A. R. Marriott, *English History in Shakespeare* 35–36 (1918).

90. 3 Samuel Johnson, *A Dictionary of the English Language* s.v. (H. J. Todd ed., 1818).

91. *See The Letters of Samuel Johnson*, 5 vols. (Bruce Redford ed., 1982–1984).

92. Anne Pallister, Magna Carta: The Heritage of Liberty 2 (1971).

93. See 30 Oxford Dictionary of National Biography 308–10 (2004).

94. *See id.* at 310–23.

95. Sir Robert Megarry, *A Second Miscellany-at-Law* 196–97 (1973).

96. *Id.* at 198.

97. Charles Pigott, *A Political Dictionary* 85 (1796).

98. J. J. S. Wharton, *Law Lexicon, or Dictionary of Jurisprudence* 459–50 (2d Am. ed. 1860).

99. Jeremy Bentham, "A Protest Against Law-Taxes" (1793), in 2 *The Works of Jeremy Bentham* 573, 580 (John Bowring ed., 1843).

100. Granville Sharp, A Declaration of the People's Natural Right to a Share in the Legislatures 202–03 (1774).

101. *See* Antonin Scalia & Bryan A. Garner, *Reading Law: The Interpretation of Legal Texts* 278–80 (2012) (discussing ancient and modern sources supporting the proposition that "the legislature cannot derogate from its own authority or the authority of its successors").

102. J. C. Holt, *Magna Carta* 1 (2d ed. 1992). *See also* Anne Pallister, "The Charter Repealed," in *Magna Carta: The Heritage of Liberty* 89–107 (1971) (ch. 7).

103. *See* 4 *Lloyd's Encyclopaedic Dictionary* 676 (1895) ("Just before the weary Commons adjourned, they . . . passed a bill repealing a number of obsolete statutes, among which was *Magna Charta*. It was obvious that the spirit of the Great Charter had long since been embodied in a number of Acts of Parliament and legal decisions ranging between the time of King John and that of Queen Victoria." [*Daily Telegraph*, 8 Aug. 1874].).

104. Id.

105. Noah Webster, A Dictionary for Primary Schools 174 (1833).

106. Thomas Tayler, *The Law Glossary* 309 (4th ed. 1856).

107. The Pocket Oxford Dictionary of Current English 533 (8th ed. 1996).

108. Thomas Sheridan, A Complete Dictionary of the English Language s.v. (2d ed. 1789).

109. *See, e.g.*, 2 W.A. Jowitt & Clifford Walsh, *Jowitt's Dictionary of English Law* 1127–31 (John Burke ed., 2d ed. 1977) (2,000+ words). *Cf.* 2 W.A. Jowitt & Clifford Walsh, *Jowitt's Dictionary of English Law* 1127–31 (Daniel Greenberg ed., 3d ed. 2010) (a mere 247 words).

110. William S. Anderson, Ballentine's Law Dictionary with Pronunciations 762 (3d ed. 1969).

111. Erwin Griswold, Introduction, The Great Charter: Four Essays on Magna Carta and the History of Our Liberty vii, ix (1965).

112. A. E. Dick Howard, The Road from Runnymede: Magna Carta and Constitutionalism in America 299 (1968).

113. *See* Max Radin, *The Myth of Magna Carta*, 60 Harv. L. Rev. 1060, 1061 (1947) ("The *pares* [equals] of Chapter 39 are the great men, *magnates, primores, les grauntz*, that is, the prelates, earls, barons, and other great feudatories, who had defeated John.").

114. Anne Pallister, *Magna Carta: The Heritage of Liberty* iii (1971). *See also* Paul Gordon Lauren, "History of Human Rights," in 2 *Encyclopedia of Human Rights* 394, 396 (David P. Forsythe ed., 2009) ("By placing limits on . . . royal power, [Magna Carta] laid the basis for constitutionalism, or limited government, and established the foundation for certain individual rights.").

115. Philip B. Kurland, "Magna Carta and Constitutionalism in the United States," in *The Great Charter: Four Essays on Magna Carta and the History of Our Liberty* 48, 49 (1965).

116. Giles Jacob, *A New Law-Dictionary* s.v. (1729).

Magna Carta's American Journey

A. E. Dick Howard

* White Burkett Miller Professor of Law and Public Affairs, University of Virginia. I am grateful to Connor Crews and Daniel Stefany for their assistance and insights in the preparation of this article.

1. See Elizabeth Mancke, "Chartered Enterprises and the Evolution of the British Atlantic World," in *The Creation of the British Atlantic World*, eds. Elizabeth Mancke and Carole Shammas (Baltimore: The Johns Hopkins University Press, 2005), pp. 237–62; Ken MacMillan, "Bound by Our Regal Office: Empire, Sovereignty, and the American Colonies in the Seventeenth Century," in *British North America in the Seventeenth and Eighteenth Centuries*, ed. Stephen Foster (Oxford: Oxford University Press, 2013), pp. 67–102.

2. Francis Newton Thorpe, ed., *Federal and State Constitutions, Colonial Charters, and Other Organic Laws* (Washington, DC: Government Printing Office, 1909), Vol. VII, p. 3786.

3. Ibid.,Vol. VII, p. 3788.

4. Ibid.,Vol. III, pp. 1856–57 (Massachusetts Bay, 1629); Vol. III, p. 1681 (Maryland, 1632); Vol. III, p. 1635 (Maine, 1639); Vol. III, p. 533 (Connecticut, 1662); Vol. V, p. 2747 (Carolina, 1663); Vol. VI, p. 3220 (Rhode Island, 1663); Vol. V, p. 2765 (Carolina, 1663); Vol. VI, p. 3,220 (Rhode Island, 1663); Vol. V, p. 2,765 (Carolina, 1665); Vol. III, 1880–81 (Massachusetts Bay, 1691); Vol. II, p. 773 (Georgia, 1732). See also Ken MacMillan, "The Crown and the Atlantic Charters," in *The Atlantic Imperial Constitution: Center and Periphery in the Atlantic World* (New York: Palgrave Macmillan, 2011), pp. 11–29.

5. See Thomas G. Barnes, "Law and Liberty (and Order) in Early Massachusetts," in *The English Legal System: Carryover to the Colonies* (Los Angeles: William Andrews Clark Memorial Library, 1975), pp. 61–89.

6. Nathaniel B. Shurtleff, ed., Records of the Governor and Company of the Massachusetts Bay in New England (Boston, 1853), Vol. I, pp. 174–75.

7. Donald S. Lutz, ed., "The Massachusetts Body of Liberties," in *Colonial Origins of the American Constitution: A Documentary History* (Indianapolis, IN: Liberty Fund, 1998), p. 71. See Magna Carta (1215), Chapter 39. For the text of Magna Carta, see A. E. Dick Howard, *Magna Carta: Text and Commentary* rev. ed. (Charlottesville: University of Virginia Press, 1998).

8. *Commonwealth v. Alger*, 61 Mass. 53, 71 (1851).

9. Lutz, "The Massachusetts Body of Liberties," in *Colonial Origins of the American Constitution*, p. 71.

10. Prince Society, *The Hutchinson Papers* (Albany, 1865), Vol. I, pp. 216–17. John Philip Reid has called the petitioners' demands "perhaps the purest expression of rule-of-law to be found in Anglo-American history." John Phillip Reid, "Law's Hedge," in *Rule of Law: The Jurisprudence of Liberty in the Seventeenth and Eighteenth Centuries* (DeKalb: Northern Illinois University Press, 2004), pp. 33-51, 50.

11. Thomas Hutchinson, *The History of the Colony of Massachusetts-Bay* (London, 1760), Vol. I, p. 146.

12. Prince Society, *The Hutchinson Papers*, Vol. I, p. 227.

13. Richard B. Morris, Studies in the History of American Law: With Special Reference to the Seventeenth and Eighteenth Centuries (New York: Columbia University Press, 1930), p. 14.

14. Shurtleff, *Records of Massachusetts Bay*, Vol. II, p. 212.

15. George L. Haskins, *Law and Authority in Early Massachusetts* (New York: MacMillan, 1960), p. 120; Lutz, "The Laws and Liberties of Massachusetts," in *Colonial Origins of the American Constitution*, pp. 99, 124.

16. Magna Carta, Chapter 40.

17. 6 Howell's State Trials 951, 953 (1670). This source reprints Penn's account contained in *The People's Ancient and Just Liberties*.

18. Maurice Ashley, *Magna Carta in the Seventeenth Century* (Charlottesville: University Press of Virginia, 1965), p. 48.

19. 6 Howell's State Trials 986–87 (1670). Penn cited 42 Edw. III c. 1.

20. See William Blackstone, *Commentaries on the Laws of England* (Oxford, 1765), Vol. I, p. 91.

21. Thorpe, Constitutions, Colonial Charters, and Other Organic Laws, Vol. V, p. 2,548.

22. "Petition to Charles II," in Jean R. Soderlund, ed., *William Penn and the Founding of Pennsylvania, 1680–1684: A Documentary History* (Philadelphia: University of Pennsylvania Press, 1983), pp. 22–23.

23. "The Frame of Government and Laws Agreed Upon in England," in Soderlund, *William Penn and the Founding of Pennsylvania*, p. 129.

24. The Excellent Priviledge of Liberty and Property Being a Reprint and Fac-simile of the First American Edition of Magna Charta (Philadelphia, 1897), pp. 6–7. For context,

see Craig Yirush, Settlers, Liberty, and Empire: The Roots of Early American Political Theory, 1675–1775 (Cambridge: Cambridge University Press, 2011), pp. 29–31; Winthrop S. Hudson, "William Penn's English Liberties: Tract for Several Times," William and Mary Quarterly 26, no. 4 (October 1969): pp. 578–85.

25. John Blair Linn, ed., Charter to William Penn and Laws of the Province of Pennsylvania, Passed Between the Years 1682 and 1700 (Harrisburg, PA, 1879), p. 127.

26. James T. Mitchell and Henry Flanders, eds., Statutes at Large of Pennsylvania from 1682 to 1801 (Harrisburg, PA, 1896-1915), Vol. II, pp. 464–65.

27. See Jack P. Greene, Peripheries and Center: Constitutional Development in the Extended Polities of the British Empire and the United States, 1607–1788 (Athens: University of Georgia Press 1986), pp. 13–17.

28. Mitchell and Flanders, Statutes at Large of Pennsylvania, Vol. III, p. 468.

29. See M. H. Smith, The Writs of Assistance Case (Berkeley: University of California Press, 1978).

30. L. Kinvin Wroth and Hiller B. Zobel, eds., Legal Papers of John Adams (Cambridge, MA: Harvard University Press, 1965), Vol. II, pp. 140–42.

31. Ibid., Vol. II, pp. 127–28.

32. Charles Francis Adams, ed., Works of John Adams (Boston, 1850–56), Vol. X, p. 248.

33. Dr. Bonham's Case, 77 Eng. Rep. 644 (1610).

34. Blackstone, Commentaries, Vol. I, p. 91.

35. On Otis' arguments and political thought, see James R. Ferguson, "Reason in Madness: The Political Thought of James Otis," William and Mary Quarterly 36, no. 2 (April 1979): pp. 194–214.

36. Bernard Bailyn, ed., Pamphlets of the American Revolution, 1750–1776 (Cambridge, MA: Harvard University Press, 1965), Vol. I, pp. 476–77.

37. See Allen S. Johnson, "The Passage of the Sugar Act," William and Mary Quarterly 16, no. 4 (October 1959): pp. 507–14.

38. For the text of the Revenue Act of 1764, see 4 Geo. III, c. 15 in Danby Pickering, ed., The Statutes at Large: From the Magna Charta, to the End of the Eleventh Parliament of Great Britain (London, 1764), Vol. XXVI, pp. 33–52. For colonial reaction to the Act, see Francis D. Cogliano, Revolutionary America, 1763–1815: A Political History (London: Routledge, 2000), pp. 27–31. See also Edmund S. Morgan and Helen M. Morgan, The Stamp Act Crisis: Prologue to Revolution (Chapel Hill: University of North Carolina Press, 1953), pp. 21–39.

39. For the text of the Stamp Act, see 5 Geo. III, c. 12 in The Statutes at Large from the Fifth Year of the Reign of King George the Third to the Tenth Year of the Reign of King George the Third, Inclusive (London, 1771), Vol. X, p. 18. See also John Bullion, A Great and Necessary Measure: George Grenville and the Genesis of the Stamp Act, 1763–1765 (Columbia: University of Missouri Press, 1982).

40. For colonial reaction to the Stamp Act, see Cogliano, Revolutionary America, 1763–1815, pp. 31–38.

41. John Pendleton Kennedy, ed., Journals of the House of Burgesses of Virginia, 1761–1765 (Richmond, VA, 1907), p. 360.

42. Edmund S. Morgan, *Prologue to Revolution: Sources and Documents on the Stamp Act Crisis, 1764–1766* (Chapel Hill: University of North Carolina Press, 1959), p. 56.

43. Ibid., p. 52.

44. See Pauline Meier, From Resistance to Revolution: Colonial Radicals and the Development of American Opposition to Britain, 1765–1776 (New York: Knopf, 1972).

45. John Dickinson, An Essay on the Constitutional Power of Great Britain over the Colonies in America (Philadelphia, 1774), p. 62.

46. Morgan, Prologue to Revolution: Sources and Documents, pp. 62–65.

47. Kate Mason Rowland, *Life of George Mason, 1725–1792* (New York: G. P. Putnam's Sons, 1892), Vol. I, p. 150.

48. John Adams to Hezekiah Niles, 13 February 1818, in *Works of John Adams*, Adams, Vol. X, p. 282.

49. David Ramsay, *History of the American Revolution* (Philadelphia, 1789), Vol. II, pp. 319–20.

50. H. Trevor Colbourn, The Lamp of Experience: Whig History and the Intellectual Origins of the American Revolution (Chapel Hill: University of North Carolina Press, 1965), pp. 145–47.

51. Adrienne Koch and William Peden, eds., *The Selected Writings of John and John Quincy Adams* (New York: Knopf, 1946), pp. 23, 20. See also David McCullough, *John Adams* (New York: Simon & Schuster, 2001), pp. 59–61.

52. The Parliamentary History of England from the Earliest Period to the Year 1803 (London, 1813), Vol. XVII, pp. 1178–79, 1167–68, 1185.

53. See Peter D. G. Thomas, Tea Party to Independence: The Third Phase of the American Revolution, 1773–1776 (Oxford: Clarendon, 1991), pp. 26–87.

54. Peter Force, ed. *American Archives*, 4th Ser. (Washington, DC, 1837), Vol. I, p. 350.

55. Ibid., Vol. I, pp. 350–51.

56. Ibid., Vol. I, p. 667.

57. See David Ammerman, *In the Common Cause: American Response to the Coercive Acts of 1774* (Charlottesville: University Press of Virginia, 1977).

58. Worthington Chauncey Ford, ed., *Journals of the Continental Congress, 1774–1789* (Washington, DC, 1904–06), Vol. I, pp. 63–68.

59. Ibid., Vol. I, pp. 68–73.

60. Ramsay, History of the American Revolution, Vol. I, p. 136.

61. Paul Leicester Ford, ed., *Writings of John Dickinson* (Philadelphia, 1895), Vol. I, p. 262.

62. L. H. Butterfield, ed., *Diary and Autobiography of John Adams* (Cambridge, MA: Harvard University Press, 1961), Vol. II, pp. 128–29.

63. Ibid., Vol. II, p. 129.

64. Ibid.

65. Ibid., Vol. II, p. 131, note.

66. Alexander Hamilton, A Full Vindication of the Measures of the Congress (New York, 1774), p. 5.

67. For a discussion of the work of the Williamsburg convention, see A. E. Dick Howard, *Commentaries on the Constitution of Virginia* (Charlottesville: University of Virginia Press, 1974), Vol. I, pp. 6–8.

68. George Mason, To the Committee of Merchants in London, 6 June 1766, in Rowland, *Life of George Mason, 1725–1729*, Vol. I, p. 387.

69. Ibid., pp. 427–30. George Washington was closely associated with the Fairfax Resolves. Mason carried the resolutions to Mount Vernon the evening before the meeting at which they were adopted and at which Washington presided. Douglas Southall Freeman, *George Washington, A Biography* (New York: Scribner, 1948–57), pp. 111, 362. It is interesting that Washington, like so many other leaders, resisted British policies on the grounds of both natural rights and the British Constitution. Those policies, he said, were "not only repugnant to natural right, but subversive of the law and constitution of Great Britain itself." Ibid., Vol. III, p. 371.

70. Virginia Constitution, Article I, Section 1. The 1776 Declaration appears today as Article I of the Constitution of Virginia. Citations in this discussion are to the present Constitution.

71. Virginia Constitution, Article I, Section 2.

72. Ibid., Article I, Section 3.

73. Allan Nevins, The American States During and After the American Revolution, 1775–1789 (New York: The MacMillan Company, 1924), p. 146.

74. Virginia Constitution, Article I, Section 6.

75. Ibid., Article I, Section 7.

76. Ibid., Article I, Section 13.

77. Ibid., Article I, Section 8.

78. Ibid., Article I, Section 11.

79. Ibid., Article I, Section 9.

80. William Peden, ed., *Notes on the State of Virginia* (Chapel Hill: University of North Carolina Press, 1955), p. 118.

81. See Howard, Commentaries on the Constitution of Virginia, Vol. II, pp. 691–95.

82. Robert J. Taylor, ed., Massachusetts, Colony to Commonwealth: Documents on the Formation of Its Constitution, 1775–1780 (Chapel Hill: University of North Carolina Press, 1961), pp. 98–99.

83. Ronald M. Peters, *The Massachusetts Constitution of 1780: A Social Compact* (Amherst: University of Massachusetts Press, 1978), pp. 13–14, 21.

84. Andrew C. McLaughlin, "American History and American Democracy," *The American Historical Review* 20, no. 2 (1915): pp. 255, 264–65.

85. Massachusetts Constitution, Preamble.

86. Ibid.

87. Massachusetts Constitution, Part 1, Article I.

88. Ibid., Part 1, Article II.

89. Article II's language clearly implies, however, that there is no freedom of being unworshipful.

90. Massachusetts Constitution, Part 1, Article III.

91. Act for Establishing Religious Freedom, January 16, 1786 (current at Va. Code Ann. § 57-1); See, e.g., Everson v. Bd. of Ed. of Ewing Twp., 330 U.S. 1 (1947). In 1971, the language of Jefferson's statute was added to the Constitution of Virginia, Article I, Section 16.

92. Massachusetts Constitution, Part 1, Article X.

93. Ibid., Part 1, Article XII.

94. Ibid., Part 1, Article XI.

95. See Massachusetts Constitution, Part 1, Articles XIX–XXIII, XVI.

96. Thomas Jefferson, John Adams, and John Jay were notable absentees, all being abroad on the nation's business.

97. *Records of the Federal Convention of 1787*, ed. Max Farrand (New Haven: Yale University Press, 1911), Vol. I, p. 398.

98. Ibid., pp. 398–99.

99. Ibid., p. 50.

100. Oliver Ellsworth, "Letters of 'A Landholder,'" in Neil H. Cogan, ed., *The Complete Bill of Rights: The Drafts, Debates, Sources, and Origins* (New York: Oxford University Press, 1997), p. 700. Ellsworth's letters were printed in the *Connecticut Courant* and the *American Mercury* between November 1787 and March 1788.

101. "Address to the People of the State of New York on the Subject of the Proposed Federal Constitution," in Jonathan Elliot, ed., *Debates in the Several State Conventions on the Adoption of the Federal Constitution*, 2nd ed. (Washington, DC, 1846), Vol. II, p. 435.

102. Pauline Maier, *Ratification: The People Debate the Constitution, 1787–1788* (New York: Simon & Schuster, 2010), pp. 156–207.

103. Ibid., pp. 255–319.

104. Ibid., pp. 294–98, 306-09, 447–51.

105. See Robert Rutland, *The Birth of the Bill of Rights, 1776–1791* (Chapel Hill: University of North Carolina Press, 1955); Richard Lebunski, *James Madison and the Struggle for the Bill of Rights* (Oxford: Oxford University Press, 2006).

106. James Bryce, *The American Commonwealth* 3rd ed. (New York: Macmillan, 1899), pp. 25–26.

107. A. E. Dick Howard, "A Traveler from an Antique Land: The Modern Renaissance of Comparative Constitutionalism," *Virginia Journal of International Law* 50, no. 1 (Fall 2009): pp. 21–31.

American State Constitutions and the Three Faces of Magna Carta

G. Alan Tarr

1. Philip B. Kurland, "Magna Carta and Constitutionalism in the United States: The Noble Lie," *The Great Charter: Four Essays on Magna Carta and the History of Our Liberty* (Erwin N. Griswold ed. 1965) 49.

2. The ban on taxation without consent derives from clauses 12 and 14, and the law-of-the-land requirement is found in clause 39 of the Great Charter.

3. John Phillip Reid, Rule of Law: The Jurisprudence of Liberty in the Seventeenth and Eighteenth Centuries (2004) 14.

4. Geoffrey Hindley, A Brief History of the Magna Carta (2008) 289.

5. The most comprehensive treatment of the influence of Magna Carta, to which this study is indebted, is A. E. Dick Howard, *The Road from Runnymede: Magna Carta and American Constitutionalism* (1968).

6. Similar provisions were included in the founding charters of Massachusetts (1629), Maryland (1632), Connecticut (1662), Rhode Island (1663), and Georgia (1732).

7. Donald S. S. Lutz, The Origins of American Constitutionalism (1988) 60.

8. The quotations, which are representative, are from William Henry Drayton's letter to the Continental Congress, quoted in Howard, supra note 4, at 181.

9. Ralph V. Turner, *Magna Carta Through the Ages* (2003) 214.

10. G. Alan Tarr, Understanding State Constitutions (1998) 63.

11. Hamilton et al., *The Federalist Papers* (Charles Kesler ed. 1999) 275.

12. In fact, some of the opposition to Massachusetts' draft constitution of 1777 was based on its failure to incorporate guarantees found in Magna Carta. See Howard, note 5, at 209.

13. For law-of-the-land provisions, see Virginia Declaration of Rights, Sec. 8; Pennsylvania Declaration of Rights, Art. IX; North Carolina Declaration of Rights, Art. XI; Connecticut Declaration of Rights, Sec. 2; New York Constitution, Art. XIII; Vermont Declaration of Rights, Art. X; South Carolina Constitution, Art. XLI; Massachusetts Declaration of Rights, Art. XII; and New Hampshire Bill of Rights, Art. XV. For bans on excessive fines, see Virginia Declaration of Rights, Sec. 9; Pennsylvania Constitution, Sec. 29; Maryland Declaration of Rights, Art. XXII; North Carolina Declaration of Rights, Art. X; Georgia Constitution, Art. LIX; Massachusetts Declaration of Rights, Art. XXVI; New Hampshire Bill of Rights, Art. XXXIII; and New York Bill of Rights of 1787, Section 8.

14. Maryland, Art. XVII; North Carolina, Art. XIII; Delaware Declaration of Rights, section 12; and New Hampshire Declaration of Rights of 1784, Art. XIV.

15. Howard, supra note 5, at 369.

16. New York Constitution of 1777, Art. XXXV. For a similar provision, see New Jersey Constitution of 1776, Art. XXXII. More generally, see William E. Nelson, *Americanization of the Common Law: The Impact of Legal Change on Massachusetts Society, 1760–1830* (1975).

17. Lutz, supra note 7, at 63.

18. Thomas Paine, *Common Sense* (1776), at http://www.ushistory.org/paine/commonsense/sense4.htm.

Due Process–Open Court Provisions / Protection of Rights / Redress for Injuries

William C. Koch, Jr.

1. This essay has been modified from its original version. For the original, see William C. Koch, Jr. *Reopening Tennessee's Open Courts Clause: A Historical Reconsideration of Article I, Section 17 of the Tennessee Constitution*, 27 U. Mem. L. Rev. 333 (Winter 1997).

2.   *Neely v. State*, 63 Tenn. 174, 185 (1874).

3.   *Metropolitan Gov't v. Tennessee State Bd. of Equalization*, 817 S.W.2d 953, 955 (Tenn. 1991); *LaFever v. Ware*, 211 Tenn. 393, 400, 365 S.W.2d 44, 47 (1963); *State ex rel. Witcher v. Bilbrey*, 878 S.W.2d 567, 573 (Tenn. Ct. App. 1994). In order to fulfill this role, state courts should, where possible, decide cases on state constitutional grounds. Thus, in cases involving state and federal constitutional claims, state courts should analyze the state constitutional claim before reaching the federal constitutional claim. *Massachusetts v. Upton*, 466 U.S. 727, 735–36 (1984) (Stevens, J., concurring); *State v. Chapman*, 632 A.2d 674, 679 n.8 (Conn. 1993); *State v. Ball*, 471 A.2d 347, 350 (N.H. 1983); *Sterling v. Cupp*, 625 P.2d 123, 126 (Or. 1981); *West v. Thompson Newspapers*, 872 P.2d 999, 1006 (Wash. 1994); *State v. Badger*, 450 A.2d 336, 347 (Vt. 1982); *State v. Johnson*, 909 P.2d 293, 301 (Wash. 1996).

4.   Peter R. Teachout, Against the Stream: An Introduction to the Vermont Law Symposium on the Revolution in State Constitutional Law, 13 VT. L. REV. 13, 19 (1980).

5.   Paul W. Kahn, Interpretation and Authority in State Constitutionalism, 106 HARV. L. REV. 1147, 1163 (1993).

6.   Kahn, *supra*, note 4 at 1147–48.

7.   *Stratton Claimants v. Morris Claimants*, 89 Tenn. 497, 512–13, 15 S.W. 87, 90 (1891).

8.   *Barnes v. City of Dayton*, 216 Tenn. 400, 407, 392 S.W.2d 813, 816 (1965).

9.   *Prescott v. Duncan*, 126 Tenn. 106, 128–29, 148 S.W. 229, 234 (1912); *Pope v. Phifer*, 50 Tenn. (3 Heisk.) 682, 686 (1871).

10.   *Illustration Design Group, Inc. v. McCanless*, 224 Tenn. 284, 292, 454 S.W.2d 115, 118 (1970); *Williams v. Carr*, 218 Tenn. 564, 572, 404 S.W.2d 522, 526 (1966); *Cummings v. Beeler*, 189 Tenn. 151, 175–76, 223 S.W.2d 913, 923 (1949); The Judges' Cases, 102 Tenn. 509, 520, 53 S.W. 134, 136 (1899); *Ridley v. Sherbrook*, 43 Tenn. (3 Cold.) 569, 574 (1866); Kahn, *supra* note 4, at 814 (constitutions are the result of the direct acts of the people themselves).

11.   *Perry v. Lawrence County Election Comm'n*, 219 Tenn. 548, 551, 411 S.W.2d 538, 548, cert. denied, 389 U.S. 821 (1967); *Williams v. Taxing Dist.*, 84 Tenn. 531, 535 (1886); *Luehrman v. Taxing Dist.*, 70 Tenn. 425, 438–39 (1879).

12.   Stratton Claimants v. Morris Claimants, 89 at 513, 15 S.W. at 90.

13.   Kahn, *supra* note 4, at 1166.

14.   *Cumberland Capital Corp. v. Patty*, 556 S.W.2d 516, 519-30 (Tenn. 1977); *Parker-Harris Co. v. Tate*, 135 Tenn. 509, 513, 188 S.W. 54, 55 (1916) (quoting the observation of the Court of Civil Appeals that "[a]nalogy is still the great light, and history is a luminary of almost equal force"); *Aymette v. State*, 21 Tenn. (2 Hum.) 154, 156 (1840); *Vanzant v. Waddel*, 10 Tenn. (2 Yer.) 259, 270 (1829).

15.   *Screws v. United States*, 325 U.S. 91, 120 (1945) (Rutledge, J., concurring).

16.   OLIVER W. HOLMES, THE COMMON LAW 37 (Boston, Little, Brown & Co. 1881) ("The history of what the law has been is necessary to the knowledge of what the law is.")

17.   2 James Kent, Commentaries on American Law *7.

18.   William J. Brennan, Jr., *The Bill of Rights and the States, reprinted in* THE GREAT RIGHTS 67–68 (Edmund Cahn ed., 1963); ROBERT A. RUTLAND, THE BIRTH OF

THE BILL OF RIGHTS 1776–1791, at 76–78, 98–99 (reprint Northeastern U. Press 1991).

19. Willi P. Adams, The First American Constitutions 63 (1980).

20. ADAMS, *supra* note 18, at 72–73; RUTLAND, *supra* note 17, at 39. New Hampshire adopted a provisional constitution in January 1776 but did not adopt a permanent constitution until 1784. ADAMS, *supra* note 18, at 68–70.

21. New Jersey adopted its constitution on July 2, 1776, followed by Delaware on September 21, 1776, Pennsylvania on September 28, 1776, Maryland on November 8, 1776, and North Carolina on December 18, 1776. ADAMS, *supra* note 18, at 73–82.

22. Georgia adopted its constitution on February 5, 1777, and New York adopted its constitution on April 20, 1777. ADAMS, *supra* note 18, at 82–86.

23. South Carolina adopted its constitution on March 19, 1778; Massachusetts adopted its constitution on June 16, 1780; and New Hampshire adopted its constitution on June 2, 1784. Connecticut and Rhode Island continued to rely on their colonial charters until October 5, 1818, and November 5, 1842, respectively. ADAMS, *supra* note 18, at 66–67, 70, 72, 86. *See also* RUTLAND, *supra* note 17, at 41–42.

24. RUTLAND, *supra* note 17, at 13, 74.

25. *See* Edward Dumbauld, The Bill of Rights and What It Means Today 3 (1957); A.E. Dick Howard, The Road From Runnymede, Magna Carta and Constitutionalism in America 206 (1968).

26. Del. Declaration of Rights and Fundamental Rules of 1776, § 12, *reprinted in* 2 William F. Swindler, Sources and Documents of United States Constitutions at 198 (1973).

27. Md. Declaration of Rights of 1776, art. XVII, *reprinted in* 4 Swindler, *supra* note 25, at 373 (1975) *and in* 3 Francis N. Thorpe, The Federal and State Constitutions, Colonial Charters, and Other Organic Laws of the States, Territories, and Colonies 1688 (1909). Mass. Const. part I, art. XI, *reprinted in* 5 Swindler, *supra* note 25, at 94 (1975) *and in* 3 Thorpe, *supra*, at 1891. N.H. Const. of 1784, part I, art. XIV, *reprinted in* 6 Swindler, *supra* note 25, at 346 (1976) *and in* 4 Thorpe, *supra*, at 2455.

28. PA. CONST. of 1776, Plan or Frame of Government § 26, *reprinted in* 8 SWINDLER, *supra* note 25, at 283 (1979) *and in* 5 THORPE, *supra* note 26, at 3088.

29. N.C. DECLARATION OF RIGHTS of 1776, art. XIII, *reprinted in* 7 SWINDLER, *supra* note 25, at 403 (1978) *and in* 5 THORPE, *supra* note 26, at 2788.

30. VT. CONST. of 1786, ch. I, art. IV, *reprinted in* 9 SWINDLER, *supra* note 25, at 498 (1979) *and in* 6 THORPE, *supra* note 26, at 3752.

31. KY. CONST. of 1792, art. XII, § 13, *reprinted in* 4 SWINDLER, *supra* note 25, at 150 (1975) *and in* 3 THORPE, *supra* note 26, at 1275. Pennsylvania adopted an amended constitution in 1790 containing an expanded open courts provision stating:

> That all courts shall be open, and every man, for an injury done him in his lands, goods, person, or reputation, shall have remedy by the due course of law, and right and justice administered without sale, denial, or delay. Suits may be brought against the commonwealth in such manner, and in such courts, and in such cases as the legislature may by law direct.

PA. CONST. of 1790, art. IX, § 11, *reprinted in* 8 SWINDLER, *supra* note 25, at 293 (1979) *and in* 5 THORPE, *supra* note 26, at 3101. This provision later became the model for the open courts provision in Tennessee's Constitution of 1796.

32. DEL. CONST. of 1792, art. I, § 9, *reprinted in* 2 SWINDLER, *supra* note 25, at 206 (1973) *and in* 1 THORPE, *supra* note 26, at 569.

33. In its present form, TENN. CONST. art. I, § 17 states:

> That all courts shall be open; and every man, for an injury done him in his lands, goods, person, or reputation, shall have remedy by due course of law, and right and justice administered without sale, denial, or delay. Suits may be brought against the State in such manner and in such courts as the Legislature may by law direct.

34. TENN. CONST. art. I, § 17 also empowers the General Assembly to permit suits against the State, but it does not guarantee citizens the right to sue the state. This particular clause is not self-executing, and thus no one may sue the State without specific legislative authorization. *General Oil Co. v. Crain*, 117 Tenn. 82, 89, 95 S.W. 824, 826 (1906), *aff'd*, 209 U.S. 211 (1908); *North British & Mercantile Co. v. Craig*, 106 Tenn. 621, 629, 62 S.W. 155, 157 (1901); *Williams v. Register of West Tenn.*, 3 Tenn. (1 Cooke) 213, 217–18 (1812).

35. *Harrison, Pepper & Co. v. Willis*, 54 Tenn. (7 Heisk.) 35, 36 (1871); *Wilson v. State*, 50 Tenn. (3 Heisk.) 232, 235 (1871); *Fisher's Negroes v. Dabbs*, 14 Tenn. (6 Yer.) 119, 137 (1834); *Townsend v. Townsend*, 7 Tenn. (1 Peck) 1, 14 (1821).

36. *Bank v. Cooper*, 10 Tenn. (2 Yer.) 599, 612 (1831) (Peck, J.).

37. *Girdner v. Stephens*, 48 Tenn. (1 Heisk.) 280, 283 (1870); *Bank v. Cooper*, 10 Tenn. at 623 (Kennedy, J.); *Bristoe v. Evans*, 2 Tenn. (2 Overt.) 341, 346 (1815).

38. *Townsend v. Townsend*, 7 Tenn. (1 Peck) 1, 14–15 (1821).

39. Peter Fisher's will directed that his slaves be emancipated on his death. His executor refused to petition for their emancipation until the General Assembly enacted a statute in 1829 requiring executors to honor a testator's directions with regard to emancipation of slaves. Thereafter, two of the slaves filed suit under the 1829 statute. In 1831, the General Assembly enacted another statute providing that the 1829 statute was not intended to apply to wills executed prior to its enactment. *Fisher's Negroes v. Dabbs*, 14 Tenn. (6 Yer.) 119, 120–23 (1834).

40. Tennessee's judges continue to take a similar oath today. Part of the oath prescribed by TENN. CODE ANN. § 17-1-104 (1994) requires judges to commit themselves "to administer justice without respect of persons, and impartially to discharge all the duties incumbent on a judge or chancellor."

41. Fisher's Negroes v. Dabbs, 14 Tenn. at 137–38.

42. ALA. CONST. art. I, § 13; ARIZ. CONST. art. 18, § 6; ARK. CONST. art. 2, § 13; COLO. CONST. art. II, § 6; CONN. CONST. art. 1, § 10; DEL. CONST. art. I, § 9; FLA. CONST. art. 1, § 21; IDAHO CONST. art. I, § 18; ILL. CONST. art. 1, § 12; IND. Const. art. 1, § 12; KAN. CONST. Bill of Rights § 18; KY. CONST. Bill of Rights § 14; LA. CONST. art. 1, § 22; ME. CONST. art. 1, § 19; MD. CONST. Declaration of Rights art. 19; MASS. CONST. pt. 1, art. 11; MINN. CONST. art. I, § 8; MISS. CONST. art. 3, § 24; MO. CONST. art. I, § 14; MONT. CONST. art. II, § 16; NEB. CONST. art. I, § 13; N.H. CONST. pt. 1, art. 14; in N.C. CONST. art. I, § 18; N.D. CONST. art. I, § 9; OHIO CONST. art. I, § 16; OKLA. CONST. art. 2, § 6; OR. CONST. art. I, § 10; PA. CONST. art. 1, § 11; R.I. CONST. art. I, § 5; S.C. CONST. art. I, § 9; S.D. CONST. art. VI, § 20; TENN. CONST. art. I, § 17; TEX. CONST. art. 1, § 13; UTAH CONST. art. I, § 11; VT. CONST. ch. I, art. 4; W. VA. CONST. art. 3, § 17; WIS. CONST. art. I, § 9; WYO. CONST. art. 1, § 8.

43. DEL. DECLARATION OF RIGHTS AND FUNDAMENTAL RULES of 1776, § 12, adopted on September 21, 1776, provided:

> That every Freeman for an Injury done him in his Goods, Lands, or Person, by another Person, ought to have Remedy by the Course of Law of the Land and ought to have Justice and Right for Injury done him freely without Sale, fully without Denial, and speedily without Delay, according to the Law of the Land.

See 2 SWINDLER, *supra* note 25, at 198 (1973).

44. The PENNSYLVANIA CONSTITUTION OF 1776, PLAN OR FRAME OF GOVERNMENT, § 26 became effective on September 28, 1776, and provided, in part: "All courts shall be open, and justice shall be impartially administered without corruption or unnecessary delay." *See* 8 SWINDLER, *supra* note 25, at 283; 5 THORPE, *supra* note 26, at 3088.

45. ARIZ. CONST., art. 18, § 6 provides: "The right of action to recover for damages for injuries shall never be abrogated, and the amount recovered shall not be subject to any statutory limitation."

46. Like most historians, the legal commentators agree that Lord Coke's interpretation of Chapter 29 of Magna Carta shaped the American colonists' understanding of the right of Englishmen to seek judicial remedies. JENNIFER FRIERSON, STATE CONSTITUTIONAL LAW: LITIGATING INDIVIDUAL RIGHTS, CLAIMS AND DEFENSES ¶ 6.02 (1994); John H. Bauman, *Remedies Provisions in State Constitutions and the Proper Role of State Courts*, 26 WAKE FOREST L. REV. 237, 242 (1991); Note, in *Constitutional Guarantees of a Certain Remedy,* 49 IOWA L. REV. 1203 (1964); Comment, *Section 13: Constitutional Armor for the Common Law*, 35 ALA. L. REV. 128 (1984).

47. FRAME OF GOVERNMENT OF PENNSYLVANIA, Laws Agreed Upon in England V (1683). See 8 SWINDLER, *supra* note 25, at 259 (1979); 5 THORPE, *supra* note 26, at 3060.

48. Only ARIZ. CONST. art. 18, § 6 and ILL. CONST. art. 1, § 12 do not contain some version of this phrase. Ten provisions are almost exact copies of Lord Coke's explanation of the meaning of Chapter 29 of 1225 version of Magna Carta. *See* ARK. CONST. art. 2, 13; IND. CONST. art. I, § 12; ME. CONST. art. 1, § 19; MD. CONST. Declaration of Rights art. 19; MASS. CONST. pt. 1, art. 11; MINN. CONST. art. I, § 8; N.H. CONST. pt. 1, art. 14; R.I. CONST. art. I, § 5; VT. CONST. ch. I, art. 4; WIS. CONST. art. I, § 9.

49. Nineteen provisions, borrowing from Lord Coke, guarantee a remedy by "due course of law." *See* CONN. CONST. art. 1, § 10; DEL. CONST. art. I, § 9; IND. CONST. art. 1, § 12; KAN. CONST. Bill of Rights § 18; KY. CONST. Bill of Rights § 14; LA. CONST. art. 1, § 22; ME. CONST. art. 1, § 19; MD. CONST. Declaration of Rights art. 19; MISS. CONST. art. 3, § 24; NEB. CONST. art. I, § 13; N.C. CONST., art. I, § 18; OHIO CONST. art. I, § 16; OR. CONST. art. I, § 10; PA. CONST. art. 1, § 11; S.D. CONST. art. VI, § 20; TENN. CONST. art. I, § 17; TEX. CONST. art. 1, § 13; UTAH CONST. art. I, § 11; W. VA. CONST. art. 3, § 17. Six provisions, in the words of the Massachusetts Constitution of 1780, guarantee a "certain remedy." *See* ARK. CONST. art. 2, § 13; MINN. CONST. art. I, § 8; N.H. CONST. pt. 1, art. 14; OKLA. CONST. 2, § 6; R.I. CONST. art. I, § 5; VT. CONST. ch. I, art. 4. Five provisions require a "speedy remedy." *See* COLO. CONST. art. II, § 6; IDAHO CONST. art. I, § 18; MONT. CONST. art. II. § 16; OKLA. CONST. art. 2, § 6; S.C. CONST. I, § 9. Two provisions guarantee a remedy by "due process of law." *See* ALA. CONST. art. I, §

13; N.D. CONST. I, § 9. Finally, one provision simply guarantees a "remedy." *See* ILL. CONST. art. 1, § 12.

50.   ALA. CONST. art, I, § 13; COLO. CONST. art. II, § 6; CONN. CONST. art. I, § 10; DEL. CONST. art. I, § 9; FLA. CONST. art. 1, § 21; IDAHO CONST. art. 1, § 18; IND. CONST. art. 1, § 12; Ky. Const. Bill of Rights § 14; LA. CONST. Bill of Rights art. 11; MISS. CONST. art. 3, § 24; MO. CONST. art. I, § 14; MONT. CONST. art. II, § 16; NEB. CONST. art. I, § 13; N.C. CONST. art. I, § 18; N.D. CONST. art. I, § 9; OHIO CONST. art. I, § 16; OKLA. CONST. art. 2, § 6; PA. CONST. art. I, § 11; TENN. CONST. art. I, § 17; TEX. CONST. 1, § 13; UTAH CONST. art. I, 11; W. VA. CONST. art. 3, § 17; WYO. CONST. art. 1, § 8.

51.   OR. CONST. art. I, § 10. Oregon's only constitution was adopted in 1857. *See* 5 THORPE, *supra* note 26, at 2999.

52.   S.C. CONST. art. I, § 9. South Carolina's first four constitutions did not contain an open courts provision. It first appeared in S.C. Const. of 1868, art. I, § 15. *See* 6 THORPE, *supra* note 26, at 3282. This original version required the courts to be "public."

53.   PA. CONST. of 1790, art. IX, § 11. *See* 8 SWINDLER, *supra* note 25, at 293 (1979); 5 THORPE, *supra* note 26, at 3101. The five state constitutions specifically authorizing their legislatures to waive sovereign immunity include: N.D. CONST. art. I, § 9; OHIO CONST. art. I, § 16; PA. CONST. art. I, § 11; TENN. CONST. art. I, § 17; WYO. CONST. art. 1, § 8.

54.   *See, e.g., Lucas v. Bishop*, 273 S.W.2d 397, 399 (Ark. 1954); *Kirkpatrick v. Parker*, 187 So. 620, 624 (Fla. 1939); *Sullivan v. Midlothian Park Dist.*, 281 N.E.2d 659, 662 (Ill. 1972) (the provision is an "expression of philosophy," not a mandate to provide a remedy in a particular form); *Harrell v. Total Health Care, Inc.*, 781 S.W.2d 58, 62 (Mo. 1989); *Pullen v. Novak*, 99 N.W.2d 16, 21 (Neb. 1959); *Anderson v. Hodge Boats & Motors*, Inc., 814 S.W.2d 894, 896 (Tex. Civ. App. 1991); *Brown v. Wightman*, 151 P. 366, 366–67 (Utah 1915); *Shields v. Gerhart*, 658 A.2d 924, 928 (Vt. 1995). *But see, Harrington v. City of Portland*, 708 F. Supp. 1561, 1565 (D. Or. 1988) (construing OR. CONST. art. I, § 10 as creating and recognizing new rights).

55.   *See, e.g., Jackson v. Mannesmann Demag Corp.*, 435 So. 2d 725, 727 (Ala. 1983); *Lazarus Dep't Store v. Sutherlin*, 544 N.E.2d 513, 529 (Ind. Ct. App. 1989); *State v. Wagner*, 752 P.2d 1136, 1155–56 (Or. 1988); *Le Croy v. Hanlon*, 713 S.W.2d 335, 340–41 (Tex. 1986); *DeBry v. Noble*, 889 P.2d 428, 435 (Utah 1995); Hans A. Linde, *Without Due Process: Unconstitutional Laws in Oregon*, 49 Or. L. Rev. 125, 138–40 (1970). *But see, Potomac Elec. Co. v. Smith*, 558 A.2d 768, 787 (Md. Ct. Spec. App. 1989) (the open courts provision is the same as the due process clause).

Magna Carta and the Right To Trial By Jury

Thomas J. McSweeney

1.   The authors would like to thank Valerie Hans for her very helpful editorial contributions and Evan Steiner for his research assistance on this article.

2.   "In Magna Carta it is more than once insisted on as the principal bulwark of our liberties, but especially by chap. 29 that no freeman shall be hurt in either his person or property *"nisi per legale judicium parium suorum vel per legem terrae."* William Blackstone, *Commentaries on the Laws of England* (Oxford: Clarendon Press, 1765–69), 3: 350.

3. *U.S. v. Booker*, 543 U.S. 220, 239 (2005).

4. For example, the crowd-sourced Wikipedia entry on trial by jury observes that it "became an explicit right in one of the most influential clauses of Magna Carta."http://en.wikipedia.org/wiki/Jury_trial (accessed Aug. 8, 2014).

5. Charles W. Dunn and Edward T. Byrnes, *Middle English Literature* (New York: Routledge, 1990), 38.

6. John Hudson, *The Formation of the English Common Law* (Harlow, Essex, UK: Addison Wesley Longman, 1996), 139.

7. W. L. Warren, *Henry II* (Berkeley: University of California Press, 1973), 333.

8. Lords held their own manor and honor courts, for instance, and once Henry instituted his new procedures by writ and jury in the 1160s, much of their business began to shift to the king's court. Warren, *Henry II*, 317–8. Hudson, *Formation*, 145. For the contrary view, that Henry was merely trying to make lords' courts work as they were supposed to, see S. F. C. Milsom, *The Legal Framework of English Feudalism* (Cambridge: Cambridge University Press, 1976). For a compromise position, that Henry and his councilors were trying to strike a compromise between the royal power they wanted and the demands of Henry's barons, see Joseph Biancalana, "For Want of Justice: Legal Reforms of Henry II," *Columbia Law Review* 88, no. 3 (1988).

9. Paul R. Hyams, *Rancor and Reconciliation in Medieval England* (Ithaca, N.Y.: Cornell University Press, 2003), 156–8.

10. David Douglas and G. W. Greenaway, eds., *English Historical Documents, Volume 2: 1042–1189* (London: Eyre & Spottiswoode, 1953), 718–22.

11. Audrey Douglas has argued that the understanding of what exactly the assize was meant to protect changed over time. Originally the assize was only meant to protect land held as free alms (the land used to endow a parish church). According to Douglas, land held *as* free alms was later confused with land held *in* free alms (land that was gifted to an ecclesiastical body, such as a parish church or monastery, where the only services retained by the donor were spiritual ones, i.e., saying prayers for the donor's soul). Audrey W. Douglas, "Tenure in Elemosina: Origins and Establishment in Twelfth-Century England," *American Journal of Legal History* 24, no. 2 (1980): 127–9.

12. There were Church courts at almost every level of Church administration, and they had an expansive jurisdiction. Any dispute over marriage formation (i.e., whether a marriage was legitimate) was solely within the jurisdiction of the Church courts, for instance. By the thirteenth century, they would establish jurisdiction over the probate of wills of personal property (but not of land). The courts of the Church administered a very sophisticated system of law, known as canon law, which was as much the law in England as common law was.

13. Douglas and Greenaway, *English Historical Documents, Volume 2: 1042–1189*, 720–1.

14. Elsa de Haas and G. D. G. Hall, eds., *Early Registers of Writs* (London: Bernard Quaritch, 1970).

15. Ibid., 8. This is an example from a register of writs, essentially a formbook, from around 1210. Emphasis added.

16. For surveys of the literature on the origins of the English jury, *see* Ralph Turner, "The Origins of the Medieval English Jury: Frankish, English, or Scandinavian," *Journal of British Studies* 7 (1968). Mike Macnair, "Vicinage and the Antecedents of the Jury," *Law and History Review* 17, no. 3 (1999) and the following debate.

17. Turner, "Medieval English Jury," 35. They were even common in Muslim Sicily and North Africa. John A. Makdisi, "The Islamic Origins of the Common Law," *North Carolina Law Review* 77 (1998–99) 1687–96.

18. The chronicler Henry of Huntingdon said that William the Conqueror "sent his justices through every shire, that is to say, every province of England, and caused an inquiry to be made by sworn inquest . . ."Douglas and Greenaway, *English Historical Documents, Volume 2: 1042–1189*, 853.

19. For an overview of the criminal jury and the extent to which it was self-informing, see Daniel Klerman, "Was the Jury Ever Self Informing?," in *Judicial Tribunals in England and Europe, 1200–1700*, ed. Maureen Mulholland and Brian Pullan (Manchester: Manchester University Press), 58–80.

20. Juries of matrons were called, at times, to determine whether a woman was pregnant. The earliest reference to a jury of matrons dates to 1220. James Oldham, *Trial by Jury: The Seventh Amendment and Anglo-American Special Juries* (New York: New York University Press, 2006), 80–82; H. G. Richardson and G. O. Sayles, *Select Cases of Procedure without Writ under Henry III* (London: Selden Society, 1941), cliii. For examples of writs ordering that a jury of matrons be called, see Samuel E. Thorne, ed. *Bracton on the Laws and Customs of England*, 4 vols. (Cambridge, MA: Belknap Press, 1968–77), 2: 201–3.

21. It is not clear in the twelfth century whether unfree persons were initially barred from the king's courts entirely, or whether they were only barred from using the king's courts against their own lords. Royal justices seem to have held conflicting views on the matter. Paul Hyams, *King, Lords, and Peasants in Medieval England: The Common Law of Villeinage in the Twelfth and Thirteenth Centuries* (Oxford: Clarendon Press, 1980), 90–2, 99–102.

22. Hudson, *Formation*, 202.

23. R. C. Van Caenegem, *Royal Writs in England from the Conquest to Glanvill* (London: Selden Society, 1959), 52–3.

24. Hudson, *Formation*, 192–8.

25. Ibid., 198–201.

26. Ibid., 201–4.

27. The terms criminal and civil are of Roman origin and were not yet used in the royal courts.

28. Douglas and Greenaway, *English Historical Documents, Volume 2: 1042–1189*, 408.

29. Ibid.

30. Ibid., 411 (Assize of Northampton, 1176).

31. Douglas and Greenaway, *English Historical Documents, Volume 2: 1042–1189*, 411.

32. For an example of an ordeal liturgy, see Felix Liebermann, *Die Gesetze Der Angelsachsen*, vol. 1 (Niemeyer, Max, 1903), 491–3.

33. Ibid., 493. Translation by author.

34. R. C. Van Caenegem, *The Birth of the English Common Law*, 2nd ed.(Cambridge: Cambridge University Press, 1988), 64.

35. Liebermann, *Gesetze*, 1, 492.Translation by author.

36. Thomas Andrew Green, *Verdict According to Conscience: Perspectives on the English Criminal Trial Jury, 1200–1800* (1985), 10.

37. Roger D. Groot, "The Early-Thirteenth-Century Criminal Jury," in *Twelve Good Men and True: The Criminal Trial Jury in England, 1200–1800*, ed. J.S. Cockburn and Thomas A. Green (Princeton: Princeton University Press, 1988), 6.

38. Roger D. Groot, "The Jury of Presentment before 1215," *American Journal of Legal History* 26 (1982): 14–5.

39. We do not actually know how the hundred jury and the vills voted. There was one other way in which a person could go to the ordeal without the suspicion of the vills: if the hundred jurors presented additional evidence of the suspect's guilt. Groot, "The Early-Thirteenth-Century Criminal Jury," 6-7.

40. de Haas and Hall, *Early Registers*, 66.

41. Groot, "The Early-Thirteenth-Century Criminal Jury," 8.

42. Ibid.

43. Green, *Verdict According to Conscience*, 12–3.

44. David J. Seipp, "Jurors, Evidences, and the Tempest of 1499," in *"The Dearest Birth Right of the People of England": The Jury in the History of the Common Law*, ed. John W. Cairns and Grant McLeod (Oxford: Hart Publishing, 2002), 78.

45. J. C. Holt, *Magna Carta*, 2nd ed. (Cambridge: Cambridge University Press, 1992), 461–2. The 1225 version contains only minor changes. Some detail is added (a free man is not to be disseised of "any free tenement, or liberties, or free customs.") and chapter 40–the famous "To no one will we sell, to no one deny or delay right or justice"–is combined with this chapter. The substance, and particularly the part of about judgment of peers, remains the same. Ibid., 507–8.

46. Maitland did not believe that judgment of peers referred to trial by jury. He thought that the trial must also conform to the law of the land, however. He was seconded in this by William Sharp McKechnie. William Sharp McKechnie, *Magna Carta: A Commentary on the Great Charter of King John*, 2nd ed. (New York: Burt Franklin, 1914), 381–2.

47. Chapter 45 of the 1215 Magna Carta specifies that the king will not "make justices, constables, sheriffs or bailiffs who do not know the law of the realm [*legem regni*]." Holt, *Magna Carta*, 462–3.

48. The Glanvill treatise, a text on the workings of the royal courts written in the late 1180s, twice uses the phrase *lex terrae* to refer to a person's oath. G. D. G. Hall, ed. *The Treatise on the Laws and Customs of the Realm of England Commonly Called Glanvill* (Oxford: Clarendon Press, 1965), 36 (II, c. 19), 58 (V, c. 5); McKechnie, *Magna Carta*, 379.;

49. Warren, *Henry II*, 317–9.

50. R.C. Van Caenegem, *English Lawsuits from William I to Richard I*, vol. 1 (London: Selden Society, 1990), 192.

51. Ibid.

52. Ibid., 192-3.

53. Even that judgment was not a final judgment. The assembled vassals would generally make a medial judgment, deciding what kind of proof the parties would have to make

to prove their cases. In this case, the barons decided that Modbert could prove his case if he could present "two free and lawful witnesses from the familiars of the church . . . or by a signed and credible chirograph [charter] . . ." Ibid., 193.

54. Paul Hyams, "Henry II and Ganelon," *Syracuse Scholar* 4 (1983): 23–35. For a fictional example written at the court of Henry II involving King Arthur, one of his knights, and a fairy queen, see Marie de France's *Lanval*, where the hero, Lanval, is judged by Arthur's other knights and vassals. Marie de France, *The Lais of Marie De France*, trans. Robert Hanning and Joan Ferrante (Grand Rapids, Michigan: Baker Books, 1978), 105–25.

55. Holt, *Magna Carta*, 89–92.

56. Ibid., 82–3.

57. Jane Sayers, *Innocent IIi: Leader of Europe, 1198–1216* (London: Longman, 1994), 96; Thomas J. McSweeney, "Magna Carta, Civil Law, and Canon Law," in *Magna Carta and the Rule of Law*, ed. Daniel Barstow Magraw, Andrea Martinez, and Roy E. Brownell (Chicago: American Bar Association, 2014), 281–3, 304–9.

58. Harry Rothwell, ed. *English Historical Documents Volume III, 1189–1327*(London: Eyre & Spottiswoode, 1975), 672 (Canon 68).

59. Ibid., 663–4 (Canon 47).

60. Ibid., 654 (Canon 18).

61. Liebermann, *Gesetze*, 1, 491–3.

62. David Crook, *Records of the General Eyre* (London: Her Majesty's Stationary Office, 1982), 70–1.

63. *Patent Rolls of the Reign of Henry III Preserved in the Public Record Office*, vol. 1, 1216–25 (London: His Majesty's Stationery Office, 1901), 186.Translation by author.

64. Ibid. Much of this translation is derived from Doris M. Stenton, *Rolls of the Justices in Eyre for Yorkshire in 3 Henry III (1218–1219)*(London: Selden Society, 1937), xl.

65. Stenton, *Rolls of the Justices in Eyre for Yorkshire*, xl.

66. Groot, "The Early-Thirteenth-Century Criminal Jury," 12–3.

67. Ibid., 13.

68. *Curia Regis Rolls of the Reign of Henry III*. vol. 8, 3–4 Henry III (London: His Majesty's Stationary Office, 1938), 81.

69. Thorne, *Bracton*, 2: 429; Emilie Amt and S.D. Church, eds., *Dialogus De Scaccario, and Constitutio Domus Regis: The Dialogue of the Exchequer, and the Establishment of the Royal Household* (Oxford: Clarendon Press, 2007), 133.

70. Thorne, *Bracton*, 2: 430; Amt and Church, *Dialogue of the Exchequer*, 133.

71. *Dialogue of the Exchequer*, 133.

72. Thorne, *Bracton*, 433.

73. Ibid.

74. Groot, "The Early-Thirteenth-Century Criminal Jury," 17–8.

75. *Curia Regis Rolls*, 8: 274.

76. Ibid.

77. "The Early-Thirteenth-Century Criminal Jury," 27. We do not, however, know how the hundred and the four vills voted, or whether verdicts were required to be unanimous.

78. Ibid.

79. Danby Pickering, *Statutes at Large*, vol. 2, 15 Edw. III to 13 Hen. IV (Cambridge 1762), 53 (25 Edw. III 4).

80. Ibid.

81. Ibid., 97 (28 Edw. III 3).

82. Sir Edward Coke, *The Selected Writings of Sir Edward Coke*, vol. 2 (Indianapolis: Liberty Fund, 2003), 858 (Institutes, II: 50).

83. T.B. Howell, ed. *A Complete Collection of State Trials and Proceedings for High Treason and Other Crimes and Misdemeanors*, vol. 6, 1661–78 (London: 1810), 982.

84. Coke, *Writings of Sir Edward Coke*, 2, 856 (Institutes II:49); Howell, *State Trials*, 982; A.E. Dick Howard, *The Road from Runnymede: Magna Carta and Constitutionalism in America* (Charlottesville: University of Virginia Press, 1968), 80.

85. Francis Newton Thorpe, *The Federal and State Constitutions, Colonial Charters, and Other Organic Laws of the States, Territories, and Colonies Now or Heretofore Forming the United States of America*, vol. 5 (Washington: Government Printing Office, 1909), 2549. Howard, *Road from Runnymede*, 85.

86. Howard, *Road from Runnymede*, 85–6.

87. Ibid., 92.

88. Coke, *Writings of Sir Edward Coke*, 2, 858 (Institutes II: 50).

89. J. H. Baker, *An Introduction to English Legal History*, 4th ed.(London: Butterworths LexisNexis, 2002), 63.

90. Howard, *Road from Runnymede*, 222.

91. Ibid., 222, 28.

92. *The Federalist* no. 83 (Alexander Hamilton).

Habeas Corpus and Magna Carta

Justin Wert

Reprinted with permission from Magna Carta and the Rule of Law © 2014 by the American Bar Association. All rights reserved.

1. C. H. McIlwain, *Due Process of Law in Magna Carta*, 14 COLUM. L. REV. 27, 46 (1914).

2. Edward Jenks, *The Myth of Magna Carta*, 4 INDEP. REV. 260, 269 (1904).

3. Max Radin, *The Myth of Magna Carta*, 60 HARV. L. REV. 1060, (1947).

4. Id.; see also John Phillip Reid, 4 The Jurisprudence of Liberty: The Ancient Constitution in the Legal Historiography of the Seventeenth and Eighteenth Centuries, in THE ROOTS OF LIBERTY: MAGNA CARTA, ANCIENT CONSTITUTION, AND THE ANGLO-AMERICAN TRADITION OF THE RULE OF LAW (Ellis Sandoz ed., 1993); see also PAUL HALLIDAY, HABEAS CORPUS: FROM ENGLAND TO EMPIRE (2010); see also HERBERT BUTTERFIELD, THE WHIG INTERPRETATION OF HISTORY (1931) (putting forward the notion of "Whig" history).

5. Edward Coke, The Second Part of the Institutes of the Laws of England 55 (1797); 4 William Blackstone & St. George Tucker, Blackstone's Commentaries: With Notes of Reference to the Constitution and Laws of the Federal Government of the United States and of the Commonwealth of Virginia 290 (William Young Birch and Abraham Small 1803).

6. BLACKSTONE, *supra* note 5, at 131.

7. *See* William Duker, A Constitutional History of Habeas Corpus, 44–45 (1980); Halliday, *supra* note 4, at 15–16.

8. BLACKSTONE, *supra* note 5, at 131.

9. Daniel Meador, Habeas Corpus and Magna Carta: Dualism of Power and Liberty 8 (1966).

10. *Id.* at 9.

11. MEADOR, *supra* note 9, at 11.

12. Magna Carta 1215 ch. 36, in William Sharp McKechnie, *MAGNA CARTA: A COMMENTARY ON THE GREAT CHARTER OF KING JOHN, WITH AN HISTORICAL INTRODUCTION* 359 (2nd ed. 1914).

13. Darnel's Case (The Five Knights case), 3 How. St. Tr. 1 (K.B. 1627).

14. *See* HALLIDAY, *supra* 4, at 137–39.

15. William Cobbett, et al., A Complete Collection of State Trials & Proceedings for High Treason and Other Crimes and Misdemeanors 6–7 (London, 1809), available at https://archive.org/details/acompletecollec03cobbgoog.

16. *Id.* at 30.

17. *Id.* at 15.

18. Id.

19. *Id.* at 38.

20. *Id.* at 57.

21. MEADOR, *supra* note 9, at 13–15.

22. COKE, *supra* note 5, at 50.

23. Id.

24. *Id.* at 54.

25. MEADOR, *supra* note 9, at 16–17; *see also* HALLIDAY, *supra* note 4, at 137–39.

26. On the legislative history of the 1679 Habeas Corpus Act *see* Helen Nutting, *The Most Wholesome Law–The Habeas Corpus Act of 1679*, 65 AM. HIST. REV. 527 (1960) (discusses the legislative history of the 1679 Habeas Corpus Act).

27. Nutting, *supra* note 26, at 541.

28. Halliday, 242.

29. Blackstone, *supra* note 5, at 135; *see also* James R. Stoner, Common Law and Liberal Theory: Coke, Hobbes and the Origins of American Constitutionalism 21 (1992).

30. BLACKSTONE, *supra* note 5, at 135.

31. Id.

32. Id.

33. Id.

34. Dallin H. Oaks, *Habeas Corpus in the States—1776–1865*, 32 U. CHI. L. REV. 243, 251 (1965).

35. THE FEDERALIST No. 84 (Alexander Hamilton) (Bantam Dell ed., 2003).

36. "The privilege of the writ of habeas corpus shall not be suspended, unless when in cases of rebellion or invasion the public safety may require it." (Alexander Hamilton commenting on Article I, §9, Clause 2 of the United States Constitution). *Id.*at 523.

37. *Id.* at 522.

38. *Id.* at 523.

39. *Frank v. Mangum*, 237 U.S. 309, 346 (1915).

40. Justin Wert, Habeas Corpus in America: The Politics of Individual Rights 199 (2011).

41. For example, Section 14 of the Judiciary Act of 1789 did not provide for the hearing of State habeas corpus case by federal courts. 1 Stat. 73 (1789).

42. *See* cases discussed in WERT, *supra* note 40, at ch. 2.

43. Id.

44. Judiciary Act of 1789 1 Stat. 73 (1789).

45. WERT, *supra* note 40, at ch. 2.

46. Id.

47. Id.

48. 1 Miss. Comp. Stat. § 11; Oaks, *supra* note 34, at 243, 278; *see also* WERT, *supra* note 40, at 52 (for a more detailed list of antebellum slave law cases in the states).

49. *Scudder v. Seals*, 1 Miss. 154 **(**1824); *see also, Hardy v. Smith*, 11 Miss. 316 (1844) (where a similar course of events plays out).

50. *Nations v. Alvis*, 13 Miss. 338, 345 (1845).

51. *Id.* at 345

52. *Id.* at 345.

53. *See, e.g., Thornton v. Demoss*, 13 Miss. 609 (1846); *Weddington v. Sam Sloan* (of color), 54 Ky. 147 (1854); *Ruddle's Ex'or v. Ben*, 37 Va. 467 (1839).

54. *See* MORRIS, at 11.

55. *State v. Anderson*, 1 N.J.L. 41, 43 (1790).

56. State v. Adm'rs of Prall, 1 N.J.L. 4 (1790).

57. *Id.*

58. Id.

59. State v. Frees, 1 N.J.L. 299, 300 (1794).

60. *Id.*

61. Force Bill, 4 Stat. 632 (1833).

62. 5 Stat. 539 (1842).

63. CONG. GLOBE, 31st Cong., 1st Sess. 1502–1837 (1850)

64. Force Bill, *supra* note 61.

65. WERT, *supra* note 40, at 46–48.

66. *Id.* at 63.

67. David J. Bederman, Cautionary Tale of Alexander Mcleod: Superior Orders and the American Writ of Habeas Corpus, 41 EMORY L. J. 515, 517 (1992).

68. *Id.* at 518.

69. *Id,* at 526.

70. *Id.* at 527.

71. *Id.* at 528.

72. Act of 29 August 1842, 5 Stat. 539.

73. *See, e.g.,* Justice Brennan's opinion in *Fay v. Noia,* 372 U.S. 391, 401 at n.9 (1963).

74. Fugitive Slave Act, 9 Stat. 462 § 6 (1850)

75. Stanley W Campbell, The Slave Catchers: Enforcement of the Fugitive Slave Law 1850–1860, at 24–25 (2011).

76. *Id.* at n. 77.

77. *Id.* at 96–97.

78. *Id.* at 98.

79. *Ex parte Jenkins,* 13 F. Cas. 445 (1853).

80. Judge Kane argued "the phraseology of the [1833] statute is unequivocal in its import, and entirely consonant with its apparent object. It applies in broad and general terms to all officers of the United States, by whatever law or authority confined." *See id.* at 445, 451.

81. *Id.* at 448. Other antebellum cases in which the 1833 Act was used to discharge federal officers involved in fugitive slave renditions include *Ex parte Robinson,* 30 F. Cas. 965 (1856) and *Ex parte Sifford,* 22 F. Cas. 105 (1857).

82. *Ableman v. Booth,* 62 U.S. 506 (1859).

83. For a detailed account of the case *see* H. Robert Baker, The Rescue of Joshua Glover: A Fugitive Slave, the Constitution, and the Coming of the Civil War (2006).

84. *Id.* at 515.

85. *Ableman,* 62 U.S. at 515–516.

86. BAKER, *supra* note 83, at 515.

87. *Id.* at 522.

88. WERT, *supra* note 40, at 116.

89. *Id.* at ch. 3.

90. *Id.* at 111–113.

91. *Ex parte Royall,* 117 U.S. 241 (1886).

92. *Id.* at _. See *Duker,* 181

93. *Ex parte Royall*, 117 U.S. at 251.

94. Zechariah Chafee Jr., *The Most Important Human Right in the Constitution*, 32 B.U. L. REV. 143, 144 (1952).

95. *Fay*, 372 U.S. at 400–401.

96. *Id.* at 402.

97. *Id.* at 404, 426.

98. *See* the trilogy cases *Fay v. Noia*, 372 U.S. 391 (1963); *Sanders v. United States*, 373 U.S. 1 (1963); and *Townsend v. Sain*, 372 U.S. 293 (1963).

99. Alfred Kelly, *Clio and the Court: An Illicit Love Affair*, 1965 SUP. CT. REV. 119, 122 (1965).

100. For a discussion of this, please see Chapter 12.

101. McIlwain, *supra* note 1, at 51.

Magna Carta and the Judges–Why Magna Carta Matters

The Right Honourable Lady Justice Arden D.B.E.

1. M.A., LL.M (Cantab), LL.M (Harvard). Member of the Court of Appeal of England and Wales, former Chair of the Law Commission of England and Wales, ad hoc Judge of the European Court of Human Rights, Head of International Judicial Relations for England and Wales and member of the Permanent Court of Arbitration. A longer version of this article was first published under the title Magna Carta and the Judges: Realising the Vision. It was first published in (2012) 10 The Judicial Review 419, a publication of the Judicial Commission of New South Wales, Australia. The article will be republished by Oxford University Press in Arden, Shaping Tomorrow's Law, vol. 2 in 2015.

2. The Spirit of Magna Carta continues to resonate in Modern Law (2003) 119 LQR 227.

3. R (on the application of Bancoult) v. Secretary of State for Foreign and Commonwealth Affairs [2001] QB 1067 at [36].

4. Allen Lane Publishers, 2010.

5. Tom Bingham, Lives of the Law, Selected essays and speeches 2000–2010, Oxford 2013, published in a collection of Lord Bingham's essays by Oxford University Press.

6. Roman law and canon law may also have had an influence on the drafting of Magna Carta: see R.M. Helmholz, Magna Carta and the ius commune (1999) 66 University of Chicago Law Review 297.

7. Book I (Of Sins Against the Holy Peace), Chapter 1 (Of the Generation of Holy Law).

8. Lord Reid, The Judge as Lawmaker, (1972) 12 Jnl Soc Public Teachers of Law 22.

9. The only exception in clause 39 was for "the lawful judgment of his equals", which is considered below.

10. R (on the application of Witham v. Lord Chancellor [1998] QB 575.

11. Established by the Act of 1487 (3 Henry VII. C.I.), the Act of Pro Camera Stellata.

12. Sir William Holdsworth, A History of English Law (7 Ed., 1956), Sweet & Maxwell, Vol. 1 at p. 495.

13. 16 Charles I. C. Ss 4 and 5.

14. This occurred later in the thirteenth century, particularly with the convening by Simon de Montfort of Parliaments in 1264 and 1265: see generally, K Mackenzie, The English Parliament (Pelican, 1950).

15. Lord Bingham of Cornhill, The Rule of Law and the Sovereignty of Parliament, King's College, London, 31 October 2007, available at: http://www.kcl.ac.uk/news/news_details.php?news_id=672&year=2007

16. See, for example, article 9(1), which provides: "Everyone has the right to liberty and security of person. No one shall be subjected to arbitrary arrest or detention. No one shall be deprived of his liberty except on such grounds and in accordance with such procedure as are established by law."

17. See, for example, article 9, which provides: "No one shall be subjected to arbitrary arrest, detention or exile."

18. See, for example, article 5(1), which provides: "Everyone has the right to liberty and security of person. No one shall be deprived of his liberty save in the following cases and in accordance with a procedure prescribed by law: (a) the lawful detention of a person after conviction by a competent court . . ."

King John, Magna Carta and Taxation

Jane Frecknall-Hughes

1. The term 'baron' is used to denote an individual who was a tenant-in-chief of the king, that is, someone who held lands that had been granted by the Crown, for example, as a reward for services rendered. Such a person did not own the lands outright (although there was an expectation that a son would be able to inherit) as absolute ownership remained vested with the Crown, but could receive income generated by the lands and could himself grant smaller holdings of land to sub-tenants. The grant and sub-grant of lands carried with it the requirement of military service or labour—the essence of feudalism, though historians now debate how useful this is as a term to describe medieval society.

2. See also Turner, 2003.

3. This view of Magna Carta is explored and developed in the following papers, on which this chapter draws substantially, viz., Frecknall-Hughes, J. (2012), Re-examining King John and Magna Carta: Reflections on reasons, methodology and methods, in Musson, A. and Stebbings, C. (eds.), *Making Legal History: Approaches and Methodology*, pp. 244–263, Cambridge: Cambridge University Press; Frecknall-Hughes, J. (2010), Fiscal grievances underpinning the Magna Carta: Some first thoughts, in Tiley, J. (ed.), *Studies in the History of Tax Law IV*, pp. 89–106, Oxford and Portland, Oregon: Hart Publishing; Frecknall-Hughes, J. and Oats, L.M. (2007), King John's tax innovations—extortion, resistance and the establishment of the principle of taxation by consent, *Accounting Historians Journal*, 34(2): 75–107; Frecknall-Hughes, J. and Oats, L.M. (2004), John Lackland: A fiscal re-evaluation, in Tiley, J. (ed.), *Studies in the History of Tax Law*, pp. 201–226, Oxford and Portland, Oregon: Hart Publishing.

4. Such records include Pipe Rolls (basically audit documents), Rolls of Letters Patent, Rolls of Letters Close, Rolls of Charters, and the Rolls of the King's Household (*Curia Regis*), all aimed at keeping track of different material, for example, debts to the crown (Warren, 1997, pp. 125–135]. The term 'rolls' derives from the fact that records were

written on pieces of vellum, joined together and rolled up. For a discussion of the emergence of these and other written records, see Clanchy (1979).

5. See Powicke (1960) for the history of the loss of Normandy. Normandy was the base from which assimilation of other, large areas of (what is now modern) France took place to form the empire of the Angevin kings. Its loss would have had great symbolism. For a map, see Vincent (2012, p. 23).

6. 'Angevin' is used to describe the line of kings in direct line of descent from Geoffrey Plantagenet, Count of Anjou, and his wife, Matilda, the daughter of Henry I. Thus, Henry II, Richard I, John, and sometimes John's son, Henry III, are often referred to as Angevins. However, they are also often seen as the first in the Plantagenet line of kings and there is no hard and fast rule about terminology. Henry III is sometimes referred to as Plantagenet, sometimes as Angevin, although it would be unusual to find any king after Henry III being referred to as Angevin.

7. The justiciar was the chief minister of justice to the Norman and early Angevin kings, with power subordinate only to that of the king.

8. An escheat was land that had reverted to a superior lord because a tenant had died without heirs or had committed a felony. If an individual had lands originally granted by the king, then the lands would revert to the Crown.

9. The translation of Magna Carta used here is that of McKechnie (1914). The document itself does not have numbered clauses, but is a continuous stream of text.

10. These are all forms of land division.

11. One mark (*m*) was worth approximately two-thirds of one English pound sterling, which was in turn worth 20 shillings (*s*). A pound contained 240 pence (*d*) and one shilling thus contained 12 pence/pennies. These 'old' pounds and pence remained the basic English currency until 1971, when decimal currency was introduced. Marks and pounds co-existed in medieval times.

12. A palfrey is one of several different kinds of horses that existed in the twelfth and thirteenth centuries: plough-horses, for agriculture; and for other purposes, pack- or sumpter-horses, rounceys, palfreys, hunters, chasers, destriers, etc. The palfrey was the main type of horse ridden by the nobility and officials and was an expensive animal.

13. John's marriage to his first wife was eventually annulled in 1199 on the grounds of consanguinity, after a period of uncertainty in which dispensations were granted and then reversed. John and Isabelle were both great-grandchildren of Henry I (they were half second cousins), which relationship fell within the bounds of prohibited blood relationships at the time. John retained Isabelle's lands on the annulment.

14. This is, perhaps, also implicit in Clause 35 referring to standardisation of weights and measures.

15. Much credence was given to this rumour. Arthur was a possible heir to Richard, instead of John, as Geoffrey was older than John and would probably have become king had not he predeceased John. Geoffrey died in 1186 when Henry II was still alive, and Richard at one point designated Arthur as his heir (Gillingham, 1999, p. 136 and p. 227). All in all, John's accession to the English throne would have been regarded as unlikely at the time of his birth, as he was the eighth (and last) child and fourth son of Henry II and his wife, Eleanor of Aquitaine. While all his brothers predeceased him and only Geoffrey produced offspring, all John's sisters married and had children. A claim via the distaff line was not unheard of (Henry II inherited via his mother), nor was illegitimacy a bar (*viz.*, William 1, 'The Conqueror')—and Henry II had some twelve illegitimate children (Weir, 2002, p. 65).

16. For example, the author of the *Dialogus de Scacarrio* (*Dialogue about the Treasury*) attributed to Henry II's treasurer, Richard FitzNeal.

17. The view of Maitland (Pollock and Maitland, 1898, pp. 269–270, cited by Chew, 1922, 1923) that the scutage and fine were the same thing, that is, payments inflicted as punishment for disobeying a call to arms, is not now accepted. It is confusing, though, that 'fine' appears used in relation to negotiations over scutage as well as referring to any additional amount.

18. Pipe Roll, 1 and 7, John, Cambridgeshire and Huntingdonshire.

19. Pipe Roll, 2, John, Hampshire, m. 7 d.

20. Pipe Roll, 1, John, Devon, m. 14 d; 2, John, Devon.

21. Clause 29 of Magna Carta also contains a reference to the double exaction of service in guarding castles, also regarded as a form of military obligation. If a knight was willing to undertake this in person, or provided a substitute, then he should not have to pay money in lieu–and he was to be exempt if on other military service.

22. A vill was the smallest acknowledged measure of a community. It consisted of a number of households and their respective land. The word 'village' derives from it.

23. John is usually credited with the concept of a royal navy and taxes from tin mines in Devon and Cornwall may have been specifically dedicated to developing and maintaining the royal fleet (Warren, 1997, pp. 124–125).

24. McKechnie (1914, p. 343) comments that Clause 33, promising the removal of fish-weirs on all English rivers, also refers to an underlying grievance about trade. Fish-weirs created obstacles for boats, which, given the parlous state of roads at the time, were widely used for transport of trade goods. The presence of weirs meant that rivers were not freely navigable and so restricted trade.

25. The Pipe Roll of the main Exchequer for Michaelmas 1207 contains some references (see Jurkowski et al., 1998, p. 8).

26. The translation here of the original Latin is slightly adapted from that of McKechnie (1914, pp. 466–457).

27. British Museum, Harleian MS 476, fol. 64, which Holt (1992a, p. 478) refers to as the "best of the three". He also notes (*ibid.*) that these three lists "have been known since Blackstone's day" (referring to *Law Tracts* II, xxxii).

28. British Museum, Cotton MS Vitell, A.xx.

29. Lambeth Palace Library, MS 371, fol. 56ᵛ.

30. Spellings of names differ as orthodoxy in spelling was not established until after the advent of the printing press. For a more detailed discussion of the lists, see Frecknall-Hughes, 2010, p. 92.

31. 'Disseisin' referred to the process whereby a person was unrightfully deprived of real property.

King John and Magna Carta in Popular Culture

Carolyn Harris

1. A. A. Milne, "King John's Christmas" in *Now We Are Six*, (London: Methuen, 1927, 1989 edition), p 2.

2. See David Starkey, *Henry: Virtuous Prince*, (London: HarperPress, 2008) and Robert Hutchison, *Young Henry: The Rise of Henry VIII,* (London: Orion Publishing Group, 2011).

3. *The Tudors*, Dir. Michael Hirst, Showtime, 2007–2010.

4. William Shakespeare, *Richard III,* (London, Valentine Sims, 1597).

5. Josephine Tey, *Daughter of Time*, (London: Peter Davies, 1951).

6. "The Richard III society" FAQs http://www.richardiii.net/7_faqs.php.

7. *Braveheart*, dir. Mel Gibson, 1995.

8. A R. Braunmuller, *The Life and Death of King John* (Oxford: Oxford University Press, 2008), p. 2.

9. Ibid, p. 14.

10. Barbara Kay, "King's Speech a Boffo Movie, Pity About the Facts," *National Post,* January 28, 2011.

11. The exception to this trend is the Stratford festival in Stratford, Ontario, Canada, which has performed *King John* regularly since 1960.

12. Ralph V. Turner, "The Meaning of Magna Carta since 1215" in *History Today*, Volume: 53 Issue: 9 200.3.

13. See M. Dominca Legge, William the Marshall and Arthur of Brittany, Volume 55, Issue 131, pages 18–24, May 1982.

14. Shakespeare, *King John,* Act IV, Scene 1.

15. Shakespeare, *King John*, Act IV, Scene 2.

16. Amy License, "Robin Hood: Henry VIII's hero in green tights" in *New Statesman*, June 5, 2014.

17. Sir Walter Scott, *Ivanhoe* (London: A. Constable, 1820).

18. See Sir Edward Coke, The Second Part of the Institutes of the Laws of England: Containing the Exposition of Many Ancient and Other Statutes (London: E&R Brooke, 1797 edition).

19. See "Magna Carta and Its American Legacy," National Archives and Records Administration, http://www.archives.gov/exhibits/featured_documents/magna_carta/legacy.html.

20. *The Adventures of Robin Hood*, dir. Michael Kurtiz and William Keighley, 1938.

21. *Robin Hood*, dir. Wolfgang Reitherman, 1973.

22. Robin Hood: Men in Tights, dir. Mel Brooks, 1993.

23. *Robin Hood*, dir. Ridley Scott, 2010.

24. James Goldman, *The Lion in Winter: A Comedy in Two Acts* (New York: Samuel French Inc., 1966).

25. *The Lion in Winter,* dir. Anthony Harvey, 1968.

26. *The Lion in Winter*, dir. Andrei Konchalovsky, 2003.

27. Goldman, p. 7.

28. Goldman, p. 7.

29. *The Devil's Crown*, dir. Alan Cooke, Jane Howell, and Ronald Wilson, 1978.

30. *Ironclad*, dir. Jonathan English, 2011.

31. Elizabeth Chadwick, *To Defy a King* (London: Sphere, 2011).

32. Sharon Kay Penman, *Here Be Dragons* (New York: Ballantine Books, 1985).

33. Ibid, p. 457.

34. Ibid, p. 457.

35. Ibid, p. 458.

36. Rudyard Kipling, "What Say the Reeds at Runnymede," 1922, http://www.britannia.com/history/docs/kipling.html

37. Magna Carta, *The British Postal Museum and Archive*, http://postalheritage.org.uk/page/icons-magnacarta.

38. "Stamp Marks Magna Carta Anniversary," *The Palm Beach Post*, March 20, 1965.

39. "Jay-Z Installs Magna Carta Cover Art in Salisbury Cathedral," *The Telegraph*, July 3, 2013, http://www.telegraph.co.uk/culture/music/music-news/10158034/Jay-Z-installs-Magna-Carta-album-cover-art-in-Salisbury-Cathedral.html.

40. "Jay-Z Installs Magna Carta Album Cover Art in Salisbury Cathedral," *Salisbury Journal*, July 3, 2013 http://www.salisburyjournal.co.uk/news/10523942.Jay_Z_launches_album_artwork_at_Salisbury_Cathedral/.

References from Frecknall-Hughes' "King John, Magna Carta and Taxation" (p. 191)

Primary Sources

British Museum, Harleian MS 746.

British Museum, Cotton MS Vitell, A.xx.

Dialogus de Scacarrio of Richard FitzNeal, ed. Johnson, C., London, 1950.

Lambeth Palace Library, MS 371.

Matthaei Parisiensis Monachi Sancti Albani, Chronica Majora, ed. Luard, H.L., Vol. 2, Rolls Series, 57, 1872–1873, London, Longman & Co./Oxford, Parker & Co./Cambridge, Macmillan & Co./Edinburgh, A. & C. Black/Dublin, A. Thom).

Matthew Paris, *Liber Additamentorum*, British Museum, Cotton MS Nero D I.

Pipe Rolls: The Great Rolls of the Pipe, 1–14 John, ed. with introductions by Stenton, D.M., Kirkus, H.M., Slade, C.F. and Barnes, P.M., London: Pipe Roll Society, 1933–1935.

3 Car. 1 c. 1 (*Petition of Right*, 1628).

Secondary Sources

Barratt, N. (1996), The revenue of King John, *English Historical Review*, 111(443): 835–855.

Barratt, N. (1999), The revenues of John and Philip Augustus revisited, in Church, S.D. (ed.), *King John: New Interpretations*, pp. 75–99, Woodbridge: The Boydell Press.

Barratt, N. (2001), The English revenue of Richard I, *English Historical Review*, 116 (467): 635–656.

Bartlett, R. (2000), *England Under the Norman and Angevin Kings 1075–1225*, Oxford: Clarendon Press.

Breay, C. (2002), *Magna Carta: Manuscripts and Myths*, London: British Library.

Burg, D.F. (2004), *A World History of Tax Rebellions. An Encyclopedia of Tax Rebels, Revolts, and Riots from Antiquity to the Present*, London: Routledge.

Carpenter, D.A. (1998), Abbot Ralph of Coggeshall's account of the last years of King Richard and the first years of King John, *English Historical Review*, 113(454): 1210–1230.

Cheney, C.R. (1968), The twenty-five barons of *Magna Carta*, *Bulletin of the John Rylands Library*, 50: 280–307.

Cheney, C.R. (1967), *Hubert Walter*, London: Thomas Nelson & Sons Limited.

Chew, H. (1922), Scutage under Edward 1, *English Historical Review*, 30(118): 321–326.

Chew, H. (1923), Scutage in the fourteenth century, *English Historical Review*, 38(149): 19–41.

Church, S.D. (2006), Bigod, Roger (II), second earl of Norfolk (*c.* 1143–1221), *Oxford Dictionary of National Biography*, September 2004, online edn, May 2006.

Available at: URL http://www/oxforddnb.com/viewarticle/2379

[Accessed 20 March 2008]

Clanchy, M.T. (1979), *From Memory to Written Record, England 1066–1307*, London: Edward Arnold.

DeAragon, R. (2005), Vere, Robert de, third earl of Oxford (*d.* 1221), *Oxford Dictionary of National Biography*, September 2004, online edn, October 2005.

Available at: URL http://www/oxforddnb.com/viewarticle/28217

[Accessed 20 March 2008]

Frecknall-Hughes, J. (2012), Re-examining King John and *Magna Carta*: Reflections on reasons, methodology and methods, in Musson, A. and Stebbings, C. (eds.), *Making Legal History: Approaches and Methodology*, pp. 244–263, Cambridge: Cambridge University Press.

Frecknall-Hughes, J. (2010), Fiscal grievances underpinning the *Magna Carta*: Some first thoughts, in Tiley, J. (ed.), *Studies in the History of Tax Law IV*, pp. 89–106, Oxford and Portland, Oregon: Hart Publishing.

Frecknall-Hughes, J. and Oats, L.M. (2007), King John's tax innovations—extortion, resistance and the establishment of the principle of taxation by consent, *Accounting Historians Journal*, 34(2): 75–107

Frecknall-Hughes, J. and Oats, L.M. (2004), John Lackland: A fiscal re-evaluation, in Tiley, J. (ed.), *Studies in the History of Tax Law*, pp. 201–226, Oxford and Portland, Oregon: Hart Publishing.

Gillingham, J. (1999), *Richard I*, New Haven: Yale University Press.

Harper-Bill, C. (1999), John and the Church of Rome, in Church, S.D. (ed.), *King John: New Interpretations*, pp. 289–315, Woodbridge: The Boydell Press.

Harris, B.E. (1964), King John and the sheriffs' farms, *English Historical Review*, 79 (312): 532–542.

Harriss, G.L. (1975), *King, Parliament and Public Finance in Medieval England to 1369*, Oxford: Clarendon Press.

Harvey, S. (1970), The knight and the knight's fee in England, *Past and Present*, 49: 3–43.

Hollister, C.W. (1960), The significance of scutage rates in eleventh- and twelfth-century England, *English Historical Review*, 75(297): 577–588.

Holt, J.C. (1992a), *Magna Carta*, 2nd edn, Cambridge: Cambridge University Press.

Holt, J.C. (1992b), *The Northerners: A Study in the Reign of King John*, Oxford: Clarendon Press.

Jurkowski, M., Smith, C.L. and Crook, D. (1998), *Lay Taxes in England and Wales 1188–1688*, London: PRO Publications.

Maddicott, J.R. (1997), 'An infinite multitude of nobles': Quality, quantity and politics in the pre-reform parliaments of Henry III, in Prestwich, M., Britnell, R. and Frame, R. (eds.), *Thirteenth Century England, Vol. VII*, pp. 17–46, Woodbridge: The Boydell Press.

McKechnie, W.S. (1914), *Magna Carta. A Commentary on the Great Charter of King John*, 2nd edn, Glasgow: James Maclehose and Sons.

Mitchell, S.K. (1914), *Studies in Taxation Under John and Henry III*, New Haven: Yale University Press.

Mitchell, S.K. (1951), *Taxation in Medieval England*, New Haven: Yale University Press.

Norgate, K. (1902), *John Lackland*, London: Macmillan and Co.

Ormrod, W.M. (1999), England in the Middle Ages, in Bonney, R. (ed.), *The Rise of the Fiscal State in Europe c. 1200–1815*, pp. 19–52, Oxford: Oxford University Press.

Painter, S. (1949), *The Reign of King John*, Baltimore: Johns Hopkins Press.

Powicke, F.M. (1965), *Stephen Langton, Being the Ford Lectures Delivered in the University of Oxford in Hilary Term 1927*, London: Merlin Press Ltd.

Powicke, M. (1960), *The Loss of Normandy 1189–1204. Studies in the History of the Angevin Empire*, Manchester: Manchester University Press.

Richardson, H.G. (1944), The morrow of the Great Charter, *Bulletin of the John Rylands University Library*, 28: 422–443.

Round, J.H. (1904), King John and Robert Fitzwalter, *English Historical Review*, 19(76): 707–711.

Strickland, M. (2007), Enforcers of *Magna Carta* (act. 1215-1216), *Oxford Dictionary of National Biography*, online edn., Oxford University Press, October 2005, online edn, May 2007.

Available at: URL http://www/oxforddnb.com/view/theme/93691

[Accessed 20 March 2008]

Swanson, R.N. (1999), *The Twelfth Century Renaissance*, Manchester: Manchester University Press.

Turner, R.V. (2005), Malet, William (*c.* 1175-1215), *Oxford Dictionary of National Biography*, September 2004, online edn, October 2005.

Available at: URL http://www/oxforddnb.com/viewarticle/17881

[Accessed 20 March 2008]

Turner, R.V. (2003), *Magna Carta*, Harlow: Pearson.

Vincent, N. (2012), *Magna Carta. A Very Short Introduction*, Oxford, Oxford University Press.

Vincent, N. (2005a), Lacy, John de, third earl of Lincoln (*c.* 1192–1240), *Oxford Dictionary of National Biography*, Oxford University Press, September 2004, online edn, October 2005.

Available at: URL http://www/oxforddnb.com/article/15855

[Accessed 20 March 2008]

Vincent, N. (2005b), Monfichet, Richard de *(b.* after 1190, *d.* 1267), *Oxford Dictionary of National Biography*, Oxford University Press, September 2004, online edn, October 2005.

Available at: URL http://www/oxforddnb.com/article/19044

[Accessed 20 March 2008]

Walker, D. (2005), Bohun, Henry de, first earl of Hereford (1176–1220), *Oxford Dictionary of National Biography*, Oxford University Press, September 2004, online edn, October 2005.

Available at: URL http://www/oxforddnb.com/article/2773

[Accessed 20 March 2008]

Walker, R.F. (2005), Marshal, William (II), fifth earl of Pembroke (*c.* 1190–1231), *Oxford Dictionary of National Biography*, Oxford University Press, September 2004, online edn, October 2005.

Available at: URL http://www/oxforddnb.com/article/18127

[Accessed 20 March 2008]

Warren, W.L. (1997), *King John*, New Haven: Yale University Press.

Warren, W.L. (1987), *The Governance of Norman and Angevin England 1086–1272*, London: Edward Arnold.

Waugh, S.L. (1997), The third century of English feudalism, in Prestwich, M., Britnell, R. and Frame, R. (eds.), *Thirteenth Century England, Volume VII*, pp. 47–59, Woodbridge: The Boydell Press.

Weir, A. (2002), *Britain's Royal Families—The Complete Genealogy*, London: Pimlico.

Young, C.R. (1968), *Hubert Walter, Lord of Canterbury and Lord of England*, Durham: Duke University Press.

Index

Magna Carta